S0-BDO-198

Organizational Behavior Today

Leigh L. Thompson

Kellogg School of Management
Northwestern University

PEARSON

Prentice
Hall

Upper Saddle River, NJ 07458

Library of Congress Cataloging-in-Publication Data

Thompson, Leigh L.
   Organizational behavior today / Leigh L. Thompson.
     p. cm.
   Includes bibliographical references and index.
   ISBN-13: 978-0-13-185811-4 (pbk.)
   ISBN-10: 0-13-185811-4 (pbk.)
   1. Organizational behavior. I. Title.
   HD58.7.T4788 2007
   302.3'5—dc22

                 2007026534

Editor in Chief: David Parker
Senior Acquisitions Editor: Michael Ablassmeir
Product Development Manager: Ashley Santora
Project Manager, Editorial: Keri Molinari
Marketing Manager: Anne Howard
Associate Managing Editor: Renata Butera
Permissions Project Manager: Charles Morris
Senior Operations Supervisor: Arnold Vila
Art Director: Steven Frim
Interior Design: Jodi Notowitz
Cover Design: Steven Frim

Cover Illustration/Photo: Edward Hopper,
   American, 1882–1967, *Nighthawks,* 1942,
   Oil on canvas, 84.1 × 152.4 cm, Friends of
   American Art Collection, 1942.51, The Art
   Institute of Chicago. Photography © The Art
   Institute of Chicago.
Composition: Integra Software Services
Full-Service Project Management: Thistle Hill
   Publishing Services, LLC
Printer/Binder: C. J. Krehbiel
Typeface: 10/12 Times

Credits and acknowledgments borrowed from other sources and reproduced, with permission, in this textbook appear on the appropriate page within the text.

Copyright © 2008 by Pearson Education, Inc., Upper Saddle River, New Jersey, 07458.
Pearson Prentice Hall. All rights reserved. Printed in the United States of America. This publication is protected by Copyright and permission should be obtained from the publisher prior to any prohibited reproduction, storage in a retrieval system, or transmission in any form or by any means, electronic, mechanical, photocopying, recording, or likewise. For information regarding permission(s), write to: Rights and Permissions Department.

Pearson Prentice Hall™ is a trademark of Pearson Education, Inc.
Pearson® is a registered trademark of Pearson plc
Prentice Hall® is a registered trademark of Pearson Education, Inc.

Pearson Education LTD.
Pearson Education Singapore, Pte. Ltd
Pearson Education, Canada, Ltd
Pearson Education–Japan

Pearson Education Australia PTY, Limited
Pearson Education North Asia Ltd
Pearson Educación de Mexico, S.A. de C.V.
Pearson Education Malaysia, Pte. Ltd.

10 9 8 7 6 5 4 3 2 1
ISBN-13: 978-0-13-185811-4
ISBN-10:   0-13-185811-4

Brief Contents

Contents

Preface

You are a member of an organization. Being an effective organizational citizen and leader is the most important professional undertaking you can challenge yourself with. You can either learn it via pure experience (i.e., on the job) or prepare yourself as much as you can right now so that you make smart choices for yourself and your organization. Three core themes pervade nearly every sentence in the book:

Immediacy: This book is about you right now (not about you two to ten years from now, or famous people or hypothetical people). Your journey starts right now. Consequently, you should start using the tools described in this book (and on the corresponding Web site) for your organizational pursuits, including job interviews, work with other students, club memberships, and so on. This book is not about you in the future; it is about you right now.

Self-knowledge and self-development: The difference between good managers and great managers is that great managers are constantly on a self-improvement course. As such, you can best serve yourself and your organization by finding out as much as you can about yourself and people in general, and constantly thinking, "What can I do to improve myself?" Most students (and managers) are hungry for opportunities to evaluate themselves; this book and its supporting materials allow for a great deal of self-exploration. The accompanying Web site for this book allows you to examine your management knowledge and values.

Actionable theory: Theory without specific behavioral recommendations is not useful to most people; moreover, practical advice that has no empirical backing is not wise, either. The prescriptive advice in this book is all research-based.

Organizational Behavior Today is substantially shorter than many traditional OB books. It has 15 chapters. The last chapter encourages students to think about themselves from several different vantage points and focuses on topics such as emotional intelligence and creativity as it relates to work.

In **Chapter 1,** we define OB as the study of how people are influenced by organizations and, in turn, how people affect their organizations. We identify three content areas of OB: our thoughts or cognitions, our affect (or emotion, which also includes motivation), and our behavior. We introduce four levels of analysis for studying OB that recur throughout this book: the individual level, the interpersonal (one-on-one) level, the team (or small group or department) level, and finally, the most general level, that of the entire organization. A person's behavior in organizations is partly a function of the person and partly determined by the situation, such as norms and policies. We introduce five skills that people should develop: technical skills, decision-making (or judgment) skills, interpersonal skills, ethical and moral skills, and self-knowledge skills. We outline several tensions that represent dilemmas for most organizational actors: the pursuit of self versus organizational interest; focusing on the work to be done (task) or the people; putting work or family first; exploration or exploitation; promotion versus prevention; and dilettantism versus narrow focus. Finally, we consider several different methodologies—field studies, laboratory studies, classroom studies, case studies, meta-analysis, surveys and polls, and business pundits—for the advancement of OB research.

In **Chapter 2,** we emphasize how understanding ourselves and others is the most important aspect of organizational behavior. We judge people constantly and attempt to predict who will bring value to our organizations. However, prediction is a highly complex task. The more information we have about someone, the better we can predict his or her future behavior. Additionally, the more similar the assessment technique is to the actual work of the organization, the better is our predictive ability. We focus on measuring general intelligence, multiple intelligences, and emotional intelligence. Then we turn our focus to measuring personality according to the Big Five researchers, measuring the personality of the organization (organizational culture), and understanding the bias of misjudging others.

In **Chapter 3,** we make the point that ethical issues and challenges pervade every layer of the organization. It is not a question of whether you will face an ethical issue (you will); it is a question of how you will respond to that situation. Awareness of the most common ethical breaches is worth a pound of cure. Ethics is not simply "being a good person." Unethical organizational behavior is insidious, and there is no one moment when people conspire to commit wrongdoing. In fact, most people do not even perceive a situation as an ethical challenge: therefore, part of ethics education is raising awareness. We discuss cognitive mechanisms that lead to unethical behavior (rationalization, norms of self-interest, pluralistic ignorance, desensitization) and social-situational mechanisms (socialization tactics, conformity pressure, resource shortages, and stress). We outline perspective models for dealing with ethical issues.

Chapter 4 discusses several types of levels of communication. We point to the most common failures of communication. Moreover, we discuss how communication competencies and challenges change when different modalities are employed (e.g., face-to-face versus telephone versus e-mail). Most people don't consciously think about their communication style or effectiveness. Communication is a skill and people may learn how to improve their ability to effectively send and interpret messages. Each level (individual, interpersonal, team, and organizational), has its own communication challenges and required competencies. Because it is estimated that up to 60 percent of meaning is communicated nonverbally, we also focus on nonverbal communication.

In **Chapter 5,** we examine power as a personal characteristic of people that may stem from any of three motives: achievement, affiliation, or control; and we look at power in terms of benevolent and malevolent desires. We discuss several influence tactics, and we then turn the tables and examine the conditions under which powerful people and influential organizational actors are most likely to gain influence. It is the use of power that is at the heart of politics in organizations. Most people recoil from political organizational environments. However, it is naïve to believe that power is not a part of all organizations. The savvy organizational actor understands how to analyze power in herself and others, and how to use different types of power and influence effectively and responsibly.

The importance of relationships in organizations is the topic of **Chapter 6.** Many people think that relationship building comes naturally. People who fail to think about, understand, and improve their business relationships are doing a disservice to themselves, their team, and their organizations. To not be conscious of the choices we are making in relationships—whether they be voice, loyalty, neglect, or exit—is to not be aware of the most important aspect of organizational life. People in relationships are not so much self-interested, as they are interested in fairness. We discuss how the motive for equity is so strong that people feel compelled to restore it. We discuss how one-on-one relationships compose a person's social network in an organization. Most people are part of tightly organized, highly redundant clique networks; fewer people are boundary spanners.

In **Chapter 7,** we use the levels of analysis approach to analyze decision making at the intrapersonal, interpersonal, group, and organizational levels. At the intrapersonal level, we distinguish wants from shoulds, and approach-approach, approach-avoidance, and avoidance-avoidance decisions. At the interpersonal level of analysis, we analyze the classic prisoner's dilemma and conclude that the rational pursuit of self-interest leads to mutually unsatisfying outcomes. We then move up a level of analysis to group decision making and consider social dilemmas. We distinguish social dilemmas from prisoner's dilemmas. Finally, we analyze organizational-level decision making and discuss the Carnegie model and the garbage can model of decision making. We also describe the multiattribute decision-making model (MAUT). Throughout the chapter, we distinguish prescriptive models of decision making from descriptive models. The last part of the chapter considers the most common types of decision biases and methods for minimizing or eliminating bias.

Chapter 8 deals with conflict as a natural part of organizational life and an unavoidable aspect of human interaction. As pervasive as conflict is, however, most people have never had formal conflict resolution training. For this reason, many people are conflict avoidant. We discuss the three main types of conflict: relationship, process, and task conflict. We suggest that awareness of conflict is a first step in the effective management of conflict. We introduce negotiation as a skill that is necessary any time one person cannot achieve his or her objectives without the cooperation of another party. We build our discussion of negotiation around three key skills: distributive skills, which focus on allocating resources; integrative skills, which focus on creating value; and building trust between negotiators. We then consider third party intervention as an option for disputants who are unable to reach agreement on their own. We distinguish mediation from arbitration, in terms of process versus outcome control.

In **Chapter 9,** we review four major types of teams, distinguished in terms of their authority vis-à-vis the organization: manager-led teams, self-managing teams, self-directing teams, and self-governing teams. We also consider the three major types of work that teams do: tactical, problem-solving, and creative. We delve into group decision making and group brainstorming and conclude that groups are superior to individuals when it comes to group decision making, but (under most circumstances) inferior to individuals when it comes to idea generation. We put the team in the organizational context by analyzing team boundaries and consider how newcomers are not only socialized by their team, but influence their team as well.

Chapter 10 distinguishes leadership from management. Whereas management encompasses a variety of functions and behaviors, leadership is a relationship. We raise the thorny issue of whether leadership can be taught and use that discussion to identify four classes of leadership theories: trait theories, behavioral-style theories, situational theories, and contingency theories. The least support exists for trait theories, which indirectly suggests that leadership can be taught. Leadership is very difficult to study as laboratory investigations do not allow the act of leadership to be meaningfully contextualized, and field studies are often post-hoc in nature and do not allow causal inference.

In **Chapter 11,** we review attitude and behavior change at each of the four levels that have guided this book: the individual level, the interpersonal (one-on-one) level, the team level, and the level of the organization. We begin our analysis of organizational change by focusing on the developmental stages of organizations. In particular, we focus on Greiner's five phases of organizational growth and the particular crises that confront organizations at each stage of development. We distinguish evolutionary change from revolutionary change. We review theoretical models of organizational change, including Lewin's unfreezing-change-refreezing model, sociotechnical systems theory, Total Quality Management, reengineering, and restructuring. We then focus on prescriptive models of change, including Kotter's eight steps, Rao's PRESS model, and Beer and Nohria's Theory E versus Theory O change.

In **Chapter 12,** we distinguish two major branches of justice theory: distributive justice, which focuses on the allocation of outcomes, both good and bad, and procedural justice, which focuses on the methods and procedures that authorities and organizations use to enact justice. Fairness and justice are top of mind for most people in any relationship. And, when it comes to their jobs, nothing stirs up more emotion, ignites or extinguishes motivation as much as does the feeling of being treated fairly or not. We discuss the ultimate type of distributive justice in organizations: pay. And we note that in addition to base pay, there are a variety of compensation-incentive systems, such as incentive-based pay, profit-sharing, gain-sharing, and recognition, although none of these systems are perfect. We introduce equity theory as the leading theory of how people react when they perceive an injustice, and we note that contrary to popular thought, people do not want to blindly take advantage whenever and wherever they can. Instead, people want rewards to be distributed equitably. We also discuss evaluation systems, such as peer-feedback and 360-degree evaluations.

Diversity is multidimensional. It would be impossible (and undesirable) to diversify on every conceivable dimension. In **Chapter 13,** we use Gardenswartz and Rowe's four-dimensional model of diversity, which moves from a microfocus on personality diversity, to internal diversity, to external diversity, to, finally, organizational diversity. We identify the major barriers to diversity, which are primarily biased mind-sets, such as stereotyping, in-group favoritism, and organizational privilege systems. We discuss several ways to create and sustain diversity, including affirmative action, valuing diversity, and managing diversity. We focus on gender diversity in the workplace and note the pay gap between men and women. We document the glass ceiling and the double standards that often impede women's advancement in the organization. Finally, we raise the issue of cultural diversity and outline three key cultural differences that may help employees better understand cultural values and behaviors: individualism-collectivism; egalitarianism-hierarchy; and direct-indirect communication.

Chapter 14 introduces the place-time model of social interaction and examines how the incidence of non-face-to-face communication has increased rapidly in the business world. We focus on virtual teams and distinguish them from traditional teams. We discuss how information technology affects organizational behavior. Some positive effects include the equalization of group members' participation, greater task focus, less conformity, and lowered inhibitions. The distinct disadvantages include greater misunderstanding, lower rapport, increased risk of decision-making, and less focus (i.e., more multitasking). Finally, we discuss two sets of solutions or best practices when it comes to virtual team-work. One set of solutions is structural, and involves investment in technology or human resources. The other type of solution is process oriented and more psychological in nature, such as revisiting collective assumptions.

Chapter 15 considers the personal side of organizational behavior and raises questions such as, "Is it important to be happy at work?" and "How can I continue to motivate myself for several decades of work?" Experiencing psychological "flow" involves a precise combination of a person's skills and the challenge that is presented. There are four options for approaching organizational life: complaining, opting out, controlling, and engaging. As the current quality of your life is the best predictor of the future quality of your life, we focus on various models of the self-sustaining person, happiness as a skill, the link between physical health and mental health, and inspiration. The last part of the chapter considers executive coaching and managerial education for investing in one's skills and talents.

THE PERSON AND
THE ORGANIZATION

Before reading this chapter, complete the Organizational Identity exercise in the self-discovery section. There are three parts to it. Part 1 asks you to list the most "memorable" organizations you have been a part of, including: education, employment, sports teams, social or community groups, and so on. Part 2 asks you to indicate (with as much precision as possible) the organizations you would like to be a part of in the future. Be as specific and realistic as possible. Finally, Part 3 asks you questions about your organizational experiences, such as: Which was the single most effective organization you have ever been a part of, and why? Which organization provided you with the most significant challenge of your life?

Organizational Life

The organizations you have been a part of define who you are. Part of your identity is rooted in those organizations. Your organizational experiences have shaped you, and in turn, you have shaped those organizations. As a next step in understanding your organizational identity, go back to each organization you have listed in the exercise and indicate: (1) What is the key thing you learned or gained by being a member of that particular organization? (2) What do you think you brought to or gave to that organization? Then, meet with one other person to exchange and explain your unique organizational identities. Ask questions, explore similarities and differences.

This book is based on the belief that understanding organizations and our place in those organizations is the most important enterprise that we can possibly undertake. As the Organizational Identity exercise reveals, you don't need to be a seasoned corporate executive to have extensive experience in organizations. The younger you are, the more time you have ahead of you to spend in organizations and, therefore, the more you have to gain by investing in an understanding of organizations. As a case in point, consider the following facts:

You will give your job more time than any other aspect of your waking life. For people born after 1960, retirement age is 67. If most people earn their college degrees at 22 years of age, work for a few years, and then perhaps take 2 years for additional education, that means most people will work for about 40 years in an organization. Moreover, most of today's workers believe that they will be working during "retirement years."[1] In short, most people are opting to prolong their working lives. The United States has one of the highest labor force participation rates for people age 65 and over in the developed world. Which organization listed in your Organizational Identity exercise have you been a part of longest? Is it the most "rewarding" one? Which organization do you see yourself most invested in for the next 20 years? What do you hope to learn from that organizational experience? What are you going to offer to that organization? If you could build an organization of your own, modeled on one of your past experiences, which one would it be, and why?

You will be part of several organizations during your life. Organizational monogamy is a thing of the past. One poll revealed that 38 percent of managers, supervisors, and team leaders planned to change jobs within a year.[2] The average Gen Y person demands more flexibility and will hold 8 jobs before the age of 32.[3] The readers of this book will do the organizational equivalent of marrying, divorcing, and remarrying several times throughout their lifetime. Most of these career changes are ones that people engage in opportunistically, in their evolution as organizational members. However, be careful about job-hopping too frequently, because it could raise questions about how focused you are (see Exhibit 1.1 on changing jobs).

Think about your own organizational experiences. Focus on where you ended one organizational affiliation (e.g., graduation, change in job, a move, etc.) and began a new one. Looking back, what was the most difficult aspect of the transition? If you could give advice to someone making a similar transition, what advice would you offer?

Your choice of occupation, your job title, and the remuneration it affords you will affect your quality of life, your health care, ability to retire, and retirement age. Consider the retirement savings of a person who begins working full-time at age 26 at a starting salary of $40,000, versus a person who begins working at age 26 at a starting salary of $35,000. The difference seems small until you calculate the compounded effects of what each person's salary would be at the ripe age of 40, after, say, each person had received 5 percent annual salary increases and had worked continually. According to the Rule of 72 (divide 72 by the average growth rate), with an average growth rate of 5 percent per year, it will take approximately 14 years to double your salary. Therefore, by age 40, there will be a $10,000 salary gap between the starting salaries, not including benefits. Also, with the 5 percent growth rate, if you calculate the retirement benefits attached to those starting salaries, the higher starting salary will receive 6 percent more annually in Social Security benefits by the age of 50.[4] Another way of looking at it is to ask when you should retire? A 46-year-old who earns $190,000 a year could make the equivalent of over $800,000 in retirement savings from 401K and brokerage accounts by working until 65 rather than 60.[5]

EXHIBIT 1.1   Why a Job Hopper Needs Sure Footing

Many people consider leaving their (miserable) job for something better. But how many times can you change jobs before your résumé signals that you jump around too much? According to Wendy Wallbridge, president of On Your Mark Corporate Coaching and Consulting, "If you have a good story line about how your moves are part of an overall plan for developing your skills and competencies, it does not matter [how often you change jobs]." However, any job stint less than 12 months looks suspicious. It signals that you don't have sufficient attention span, or worse yet, you can't make a commitment. The best reason to leave one job for another is not money but, rather, the opportunity to develop new skills. But leaving your company is not necessary to do this; great opportunities may lie in a different department or office in your own company. Thus, one trick is to jump internally via networking, rather than rely on the bureaucracies of human resources. Also, just because you stay in one job at one company for years does not mean you are not learning—you can morph your job to take on new roles and responsibilities. According to this executive coach, "The number one skill to develop in this day and age is career self-reliance."

Source: Dahle, C. (2004, May 16). Why a job hopper needs sure footing. *New York Times,* Section 3, p. 11.

Despite these examples about salary, one point that we are going to make repeatedly in this book is that people don't work just for money. We work for fulfillment; we work to make a difference; and we work to help others. Most people want to be happily employed. For this reason, it is particularly worrisome that almost half of all American workers are unhappy with their jobs.[6] (See Exhibit 1.2 for a humorous description of one worker's insistence on the "right" to be happy at work.)

Look at the future you created in your Organizational Identity exercise. For each of the organizations you list yourself as involved in for the future, indicate the key reward or benefit you expect to get from this organization (i.e., money, fame, status, personal challenge, fulfilling relationships, etc.). Are the rewards you seek in the future similar to those that you have worked for in the past? Can you see a central theme or set of personal values?

There is good reason to expect the most from your organization and yourself. It is through organizations (and groups) that we have our greatest impact on the world. Management thinker and pundit Douglas Smith argues that, "Organizations are not just places where people have jobs. They are our neighborhoods, our communities. They are where we join with other people to make a difference for ourselves and others. If we think of them only as the places where we have jobs, we not only lose the opportunity for meaning,

EXHIBIT 1.2   The Right to Be Happy at Work

"I'm dysfunctional. I have a serious disorder," writes David Whitemyer, correspondent for *The Boston Globe.* "I call [my disorder] CSES, which is short for Career Satisfaction Entitlement Syndrome. Simply defined, CSES is a mutation of the widely held social tenet that each of us deserves to be happy, all of the time, in our work. It is a belief that someone other than yourself, or some force out of your control, is responsible for providing job happiness. When things are a bit slow at work, I get an itching for a challenge. When I've had a cruddy day, I feel like it's time for a change. Over the last 10 years, I've worked for five different companies. I left each one, of my own accord, regardless of the fact that each was providing me with good money, health insurance, and some periodic novelty. I wanted more, and I wanted it constantly, so I moved on. CSES is clearly a product of our short-attention-span culture. Every day has to be fulfilling. Work itself has become an extreme sport. If our job is to be satisfying, then it must give us an adrenaline rush. If not, then there must be something wrong. I also have to understand that happiness is an extreme. It comes and goes. Like job satisfaction, it is noticeable only by its absence. I'm learning to enjoy plain old work contentment."

Source: Whitemyer, D. (2002, July 7). View from the cube: Many American employees feel they're entitled to "fun" at work. *Boston Globe,* p. G11. Reprinted by permission of *Boston Globe* via Copyright Clearance Center.

but we endanger the planet."[7] For this reason, students of organizational behavior (OB) realize that people exercise their values through organizations.

Our involvement with organizations dramatically affects the quality of our lives for years to come. Those who enter the world of work and organizations with knowledge of how they work and function will be in the best position to bring value to those organizations and to themselves.

Defining Organizational Behavior

Human beings have been members of organizations since the dawn of time. However, the scientific study of organizational behavior is relatively young. The study of **organizational behavior,** also referred to as OB, is the study of how the thoughts, feelings, and behaviors of individuals and groups in organizations are influenced by the actual, implied, or imagined presence of others. As a case in point, consider the United States' decision in 2003 to invade Iraq. The thoughts of the U.S. military and political decision makers were indeed influenced by the belief that Iraq possessed (and was hiding) weapons of mass destruction. Subsequent investigations later revealed that the weapons of mass destruction did not actually exist, but at the time the decision was made to invade, the decision makers believed that they did exist. The point is: Sometimes our behavior is affected by our *beliefs* about other organizations.

People shape organizations and organizations influence people. For example, at the dawn of the computer age, Bill Gates and Steve Jobs were both young college students who were considered somewhat "nerdy" or "geeky." Bill Gates (Harvard) and Steve Jobs (Berkeley) both created organizations that were strongly influenced by their own "geeky" personalities. This is an example of how people can influence organizations. Similarly, think about how people are also influenced by the culture of the organizations they are a part of. We have all known people who seem to change once they join a particular sorority or fraternity. Which organizational experience changed you the most? Why?

Content Areas of OB

The content areas of OB cover three main features of interest: *thoughts* (also known as cognition), *affect* (also known as feelings or emotions), and *behavior* (or action). If you think about it, nearly any question anyone could ask about organizational life could fall into the domain of thoughts, feelings, and behaviors. For example, a *Business Week* article[8] might analyze how Frank Baldino Jr., CEO of Cephalon, Inc., skillfully markets new ideas into hit products (thoughts). A *New York Times* article[9] might look at how the fire department uses gentler, softer images to expand and diversify its recruitment (affect). And an *Inc. Magazine* article[10] might focus on disruptive office practices, such as interrupting and getting trapped in others' conversations (behavior).

The topical chapters in this book center around these key content areas: judgment and decision making (cognition), featured in Chapter 7; negotiation (behavior), featured in Chapter 8; understanding people (cognition), featured in Chapter 2; and relationships (which often involve emotions), featured in Chapter 6.

Level of Analysis

To build a science of OB, we must move beyond casual, everyday observation to sophisticated analysis. OB is a science; as such, the pursuit of that science requires that thoughts, feelings, and behaviors be observed, measured, quantified, and analyzed. With so many variables to think about, where should we begin? There are four key levels of analysis that OB researchers focus on. Think of levels of analysis like a camera that the OB researcher can use to look at things in a typical organization (see Exhibit 1.3). As a case in point, consider the organizational activities following the Hurricane Katrina disaster of 2005.

At a very detailed level, the OB researcher can set the camera lens on telephoto focus and observe the behavior, cognition, and affect of a single person (individual level of analysis). Consider, for example, Mr. John Ebanks. Mr. Ebanks was one of the last people to evacuate the New Orleans area. He refused to leave his house and waved off the rescuers

EXHIBIT 1.3   Levels of Analysis in OB

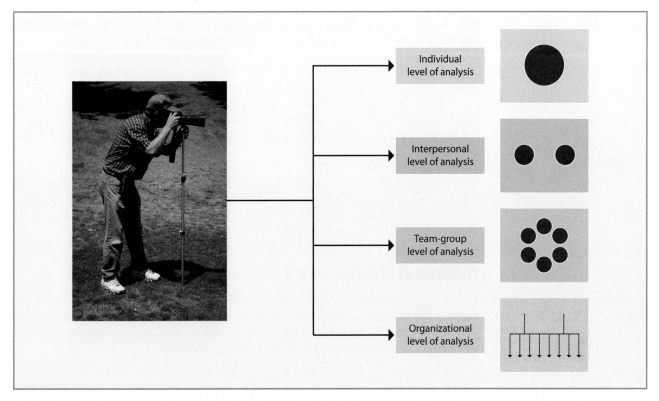

from his porch stocked with food, insect repellent, and other supplies. "You've got to protect your property, that's the main thing," he said. "This is all I've got. I'm pretty damn old to start over."[11] The OB researcher can widen the viewfinder and perhaps watch how this person interacts with her boss or a co-worker (interpersonal level of analysis). The interpersonal level of analysis focuses on the one-on-one relationship. In the Hurricane Katrina disaster, many people lost a child or spouse. Some very fortunate people were able to locate their missing child or spouse. For example, LaToya Adamore found her daughter after more than two weeks. Mother and daughter reunited in Dallas after volunteers found the 3-year-old near Galveston, Texas.[12] The relationship we have with our child or spouse is the most intense interpersonal relationship we can experience.

The OB researcher might further widen the viewfinder so that the entire team or business unit is visible and interesting group dynamics begin to be seen, such as how close together people stand, their eye contact during team meetings, and so on. In the Hurricane Katrina disaster, a key focus of news attention was on the gangs that looted stores and held others at gunpoint, even in the New Orleans Superdome.[13] Several news commentators as well as disaster survivors were perplexed at how victims of the same natural disaster could turn against each other during a time of hardship, rather than using each other as sources of strength and support. However, equally astounding displays of human generosity at the group level occurred as Houstonians offered disaster survivors a place in their homes.[14]

Finally, the widest possible view is that involving the organization itself. The OB researcher takes an aerial view of the organization and looks at the organization as a whole. Immediately following the Hurricane Katrina disaster, one key issue was the lack of organizational disaster relief. Many harsh questions were raised about the lack of government response to the disaster. In other words, many people criticized the Bush administration for failing to act swiftly.

Let's summarize the four levels of analysis that will thread through this book:

The **individual level** focuses on how the individual organizational member thinks, feels, and acts. The individual level encompasses decision making that we will read about in Chapter 7.

The **interpersonal level** focuses on how people in organizations relate on a one-on-one level to others. This involves communication ability, trust, and the ability to form and sustain relationships. The interpersonal level includes mentoring, coaching, communicating, and one-on-one negotiations such as those discussed in Chapter 8.

The **team level** is the fundamental building block of an organization. We focus on how teams set goals, resolve conflict, and achieve results. The team level obviously includes group dynamics, which are examined in Chapter 9.

Finally, the **organizational level** represents the broadest level of looking at the organization. Organizational culture and organizational norms permeate every layer of the organization. Organizational-level phenomena cannot be easily reduced to the behaviors of a given person or even a given team. We will discuss organizational change in Chapter 11.

In many cases, like the Hurricane Katrina disaster, different levels of analysis may be used to analyze the same situation. This does not mean that one level of analysis is wrong, and the other correct. Rather, it means that a given problem may be explored from different vantage points.

Guiding Principles of OB

The key question that nearly every manager will ask himself or herself at any point during a typical day is, "Why do people behave the way they do?" In a parallel fashion, scientists who study organizational behavior ask this very same question. In a nutshell, the answer to this question can be approached with the following equation:

$$\text{Behavior} = f \, \text{Person} + \text{Situation}$$

That is, a person's behavior is determined in some part by the person's own traits, abilities, and temperament and in some part by the demands and pressures of the particular situation. For example, consider the incredible seven hours that Ashley Smith spent being held hostage by escaped gunman Brian Nichols on March 12, 2005.[15] Unbelievably, Smith was able to convince Nichols to turn himself in to the police. Investigative reports of the incident focused on how Smith's depth of character, calm behavior, and ability to build empathy on the fateful night led to her being able to successfully stop Nichols's shooting spree. Thus, several analysts focused on unique aspects of this woman's personality as the key to her being let go unharmed and saving others from being killed. There were certainly situational factors as well, such as the fact that Nichols was tired and hungry after running all day and happened to have similar religious beliefs as Smith. In nearly any situation, our behavior is the result of our own personality plus certain things in the situation.

Another implication of the "person," as we have described it, is that characteristics of people are relatively stable across time and situation, can often be measured or assessed, and are difficult to change. In contrast, features of the "situation," as we have described them, are less stable, but are relatively easier to change or manipulate. For example, if a manager has trouble running effective team meetings because one person is too talkative (a "person" characteristic), it is much more difficult to change the person than it is to change the situation (such as enforcing a hand-raising rule or hiring a meeting facilitator).

Skills

This book is skill-focused in terms of preparing people for organizational challenges and opportunities. A key question concerns the skills that people will be judged on and, in turn, the skills they can use to assess the competencies of other people. It may seem unimaginable now, but you will eventually hire someone to work for you or with you. Choosing the right people is paramount for organizational success. As you might imagine, there is

EXHIBIT 1.4

Key Organizational Skills

- Technical and job-related skills
- Decision-making and judgment skills
- Interpersonal skills, such as conflict management and ability to motivate others
- Ethical and moral skills
- Self-appraisal skills, such as knowing your own limits

considerable debate on the skills thought to be essential for organizational work. We outline five broad types of skills (see Exhibit 1.4).

Technical Skills

Technical skills or job-related skills refer to depth and breadth of subject matter. For example, if a person needs to prepare financial reports, it is essential that she possess key accounting concepts. Similarly, if you are challenged to develop and deploy a change initiative, it is essential that you be able to draw upon a theory of change. Thus, technical skills simply refer to the variety of knowledge areas in business. The chapters of this book provide depth of knowledge in terms of job-related OB skills, such as negotiation (Chapter 8), change management (Chapter 11), and decision making (Chapter 7).

One of the most often cited criticisms of organizational behavior is that "it is all common sense" and that anything someone should know he or she can simply learn on the job. Moreover, many people eschew theory and disdain models, concepts, and charts unless they provide immediate practical "do this" knowledge. We could not disagree more. According to Kurt Lewin, "there is nothing as practical as a good theory."[16] What Lewin correctly recognized was that a practical tip is like giving a person a fish; a theory is more like teaching a person how to fish. This book and your courses in management and organizational behavior provide you with tools. The ideas you develop about people and organizations will have a profound impact on your behavior for decades to come.

The other reason why having a good theory is essential for managerial success is related to how your brain works. The typical person's short-term memory holds about seven, plus or minus two, pieces of information.[17] Stated another way, the average person only remembers about seven digits when given a string of random numbers. However, the person who has a theory will remember much more information because that person is *chunking* information, rather than approaching it in a piecemeal fashion. In other words, we overcome the 7 +/− 2 limits by grouping small bits of information into larger units or chunks. A chunk might be a word, phrase, sentence, or entire chapter (depending on one's expertise). For most Americans, the acronym FBI is one chunk, not three, and the date 1492 is one chunk; but the number 9214 is four chunks. If you have training or expertise in an area, then your capacity for forming chunks is much greater. Thus, this is why it is important for students to really understand material—not just memorize a series of disconnected facts. (As an exercise, visit the book's Website and read two articles from the *See it in the Real World* section. Read one article and then put it away and attempt to tell the story to a friend. Before reading the next article, make an outline of key questions to ask before you read the article and then read it. Then, tell the story to a friend. Usually, readers remember much more of the article that they mentally outlined than the one that they did not).

Moreover, the person who possesses a theory will focus on the right information, rather than superficial information, when interpreting a management situation. Consider students enrolled in a college physics course.[18] They were given a number of physics problems, such as "How soon will a train reach a destination that is 45 miles away, if the train is traveling 90 miles an hour?" The students were not asked to solve the problems, but rather to simply categorize the problems into groups. The novices—who did not have a theory of physics—classified the problems into superficial categories, such as "problems about trains," "problems about pulleys," and so on. In contrast, the experts—the students who held theories about physics—categorized the problems into more meaningful groupings, such as Newton's first law of physics. The message? People who develop theories about organizational behavior will approach problems in a much more sophisticated fashion and not fall victim to superficial detail.

Decision-Making and Judgment Skills

Technical expertise and depth of knowledge in the relevant subject areas of management are essential, but not enough for leadership in organizations. People also need **decision-making and judgment skills.** Think again about the United States' invasion of Iraq in 2003. Whether you agree or disagree with the decision to invade, it is important to recognize the invasion as the result of a decision-making process, in which a body of people who had high-level authority considered the courses of action available to the United States and the likely consequences from pursuing those courses of action. In other words, the ability to identify and evaluate different courses of actions for problems and challenges is a key aspect of decision making. Decision making is the heart of leadership, as well as change management and organizational strategy. What is the toughest decision you ever made in an organization? What did you learn about decision making that might help you in your future?

Interpersonal Skills

Interpersonal skills refer to the large body of skills utilized when interacting with other people. Some call these sets of skills "people skills"; others refer to them as "emotional intelligence." Interpersonal skills are essential and, indeed, thought to be the key measure that determines whether someone advances in an organization.[19] When did you display interpersonal skills in the organizations you listed? Can you remember a person in one of your organizations who demonstrated excellent interpersonal skills? What did this person do or say?

Interpersonal skills are difficult to assess and measure. In short, it is easy to see how someone might assess a person's technical competence in the area of accounting or information systems, and it might even be possible to examine judgment and decision-making skills, such as via game theory. But interpersonal skills are not easily measured via a paper and pencil test, although they are vital for the success of organizations.

Ethical and Moral Skills

It is highly controversial to list **ethics and morals** as skills per se because many people believe that they cannot be taught; but rather they reflect a person's character. We disagree. We think that developing ethical skills should have a place in management education. The purpose is not so much to agree on what set of ethical principles is right or wrong, but rather, for people to develop a personal awareness of their own ethical principles and morals—in short, to formalize what they might be only latently aware of. Consider the prisoner abuse scandal at Abu Ghraib in 2004. As uncovered by legal scholars M. Gregg Bloche and Jonathan Marks, who conducted an inquiry published by *The New England Journal of Medicine,* not only were some military doctors at Abu Ghraib enlisted to help inflict distress on the prisoners, but also the scarcity of basic medical care was at times so severe that it created another kind of torture. There was also medical disarray at the prison: amputations performed by non-doctors; chest tubes recycled from the dead to the living; a medic ordered, by one account, to cover up a homicide. A medic was allegedly ordered to take part in a ruse to make an inmate who died during questioning look as if he was alive when he was taken out of the prison.[20]

After reading the story about Abu Ghraib, what ethical and moral skills do you believe were lacking in that situation? If you were to be selected to take part in a change management process, what ethical training would you recommend to make sure another situation did not develop?

Self-Knowledge Skills

The question here is not how much you know (technical skills), but how well do you know your own limits? Such is the focus of **learning skills:** the ability to objectively reflect upon one's strengths, weaknesses, and areas of improvement—the ability to not only accept critical feedback but to consistently seek it out. A person who is willing to admit that a situation is outside of his or her domain of expertise and to bring in an expert demonstrates self-knowledge. Learning skills also refer to the different learning styles that people might have and the ability to appropriately adjust or tune to that.

Key Tensions and Challenges for People in Organizations

What is so vexing about organizational behavior? What are the key issues and tensions that will challenge you throughout your career? Before reading further, look at your Organizational Identity exercise. What are the most rewarding organizational experiences you've had? What are your most frustrating organizational experiences? Next, we outline six challenges that occur and reoccur for people throughout their tenure in an organization. They often take time to reveal themselves to the organizational actor and they may masquerade as other problems. Moreover, they often occur at different levels of analysis—intrapersonal, interpersonal, group, or organizational. The person who can correctly identify the key tension at hand is in a much better position to adequately respond to the challenge. We are not going to give answers; rather, we are going to highlight the tensions and challenge you to outline your own answers.

Self versus Organizational Interest

Most people will find themselves at the crossroads between furthering their own interests or that of the larger organization countless times during their career. Consider the choice that football star Pat Tillman made in May 2002. Tillman enjoyed a multimillion-dollar professional salary as a member of the Cardinals football team. However, he decided to put his country's interests ahead of his own and quit the team to join the U.S. army. Tillman's heroic efforts to provide cover for his fellow soldiers as they escaped from a canyon led to his tragic death via friendly fire in Afghanistan on April 22, 2004.[21] The implications of self versus organizational interest are serious and profound. Most people who have experienced success in their organizations realize that it is far better to give than to receive. This remains true for people who are fortunate to have great teammates and subordinates working alongside or under them. For example, smart bosses don't try to hide the talents of their best team members; they encourage them to realize their potential, even if it means that they leave. "Good bosses recognize talent and guard it fiercely, trying to eliminate turnover. Gifted bosses are willing to shove the best employees along, thereby encouraging employee turnover and gaining loyalty in return."[22]

Task versus People Focus

Organizations exist to be profitable and to be productive. Yet, organizational behavior is not just about getting the work done; it is about interacting with people. Consider the situation that occurred at Charles Schwab Corporation in 2003.[23] Charles Schwab prided itself on treating employees as family, not just as ends to profit maximization. However, by December of 2003, four rounds of layoffs swept through the company. Vice President Rene Kim had to lay off her most beloved colleague and friend at Charles Schwab, Joe Eleccion. She called him via cell phone, asked him if he was driving, and suggested that he pull off the road. Fighting back tears, she told him he was one of those chosen to go. This example places concern about people in direct contrast with concern about bottom-line corporate profitability. Most of us will be in such a situation in our own organization at some point in time. Think about your Organizational Identity chart. Have you ever worked with someone or for someone whom you liked but whose work was not adequate? Similarly, have you ever admired someone's ability to get work done, but not liked them as a person?

Work versus Family

In the opening of this chapter, we stated that people spend more waking hours on the job than they do with their family. Yet, few people regret not spending more time at work; they regret not spending more time with their family. To top things off, most of the work that organizational actors do is not piecemeal work, and most managers do not "clock out" at the end of a day. There is always more work to be done. How should people balance their investment in the organization and investment in their family? First, integrating work and family life is a collaborative effort on the part of the employee and the organization. Second, despite the negative media images of the dual-career couple struggling to make it to work and to the PTA meeting, research indicates that they are functioning at a high level. For example, Haddock and colleagues investigated 47 dual-career couples with children.[24] They structured their lives around 10 major strategies: valuing family, striving for partnership, deriving meaning from work, maintaining work boundaries, focusing and producing at work, taking pride in dual earning, prioritizing family fun, living simply, making decisions proactively, and valuing time. The trade-offs are real, however: interrupting a career for a child has serious impacts on earnings and mobility. Fortunately, organizational men and women are becoming more creative when it comes to work and family. For example, some couples team up to share a single job; some take turns as to who is working when (e.g., mom at home until kids are all school age; then dad stays home while mom goes back to her career, or vice versa); and of course, some work at home, where "there is no commuting."[25] "No back-stabbing. No office politics. No glass ceiling. No need to waste gas. No waiting in line at the post office."[26] *Business Week* recently touted the rise of the "mompreneurs"—superstar women who make both lives work (see Exhibit 1.5 for Pfeffer's views on work-life balance).

EXHIBIT 1.5

All Work and No Play Does Not Pay

Jeffrey Pfeffer noticed a striking difference in the vacation policies and work hours put in by Americans and Europeans. At Airbus, French managers get 5 weeks of vacation each year in addition to 4 weeks of vacation in July and August. Airbus' junior engineers get 9 weeks of vacation each year and no one works on weekends. Ever. (Airbus recently surpassed its larger U.S. competitor, Boeing, in commercial aircraft sales.) Long hours not only do not lead to productivity; they actually may be at the root of serious health and safety problems.

Source: Pfeffer, J. (2004, August). All work, no play. It doesn't pay. *Business 2.0.*, p. 50.

Exploration versus Exploitation

Jim March noted that companies cycle through periods of exploration in which they experiment with new methods, make mistakes, discover new processes, and often discover new solutions.[27] Companies often cycle into periods of exploitation in which a given company will commit to a given process with the goal of perfecting it and attempting to make it more effective. March refers to this as exploitation.

The same process can occur at an individual level. Take, for example, a student in college, who has not yet selected a major course of study (or a steady dating partner!). The student has enrolled in several different types of classes with the goal of finding out what she likes and what she is particularly good at. This illustrates the process of exploration. This same student, later in college, may commit to a major with the goal of writing a senior thesis on a given subject and may do extensive research with the goal of participating in a competitive thesis competition. To enter the competition, the student must follow very specific guidelines and rules to be best in class. This typifies the process of exploitation.

The point is that this student is not going to remain in a state of exploitation for the rest of her life. She will eventually join a company; probably engage in a period of exploration to determine where she best fits and to find ideal mentors, then perhaps cycle into a period of exploitation to demonstrate depth of knowledge in a particular area. At the same time, her company may be cycling though a similar process.

Promotion versus Prevention

At any given time, we may attempt to promote the occurrence of desired goals and states of affairs (e.g., winning an award) or we may focus our energy on preventing the occurrence of undesirable states of affairs (e.g., avoiding a break-up or bad grade). People who are **promotion focused** are concerned with their aspirations and accomplishments; people who are **prevention focused** are concerned with safety and responsibilities.[28] Regulatory focus theory argues that people in a promotion focus are sensitive to the presence and absence of positive outcomes and desire accomplishments, whereas people in a prevention focus are sensitive to the absence or presence of negative outcomes and desire security.[29] In a decision-making context, promotion-focused people engage in more risky decision making; prevention-focused people engage in more conservative decision making. Moreover, promotion versus prevention focus affects people's emotional responses to goal attainment. People with a promotion focus are more cheerful when they achieve their goals.[30] According to Higgins, promotion or prevention focus is a chronic way that people approach the world. However, it is possible to shift a person's regulatory focus (at least temporarily). For example, people who are told to focus on their goals are more likely to adopt a promotion focus. Think about your Organizational Identity chart. When were you in a promotion focus? What were your goals? When were you in a prevention focus? What were you trying to avoid?

Depth of Knowledge versus Breadth of Knowledge

One question that any student asks is whether it is better to be a subject expert in a narrow area or a more well-rounded student. At the extreme, consider a student who takes courses in one area and satisfies her breadth requirements by taking the minimal amount of courses in other areas versus a student who takes a broad variety of courses in several disciplines. The advice regarding knowledge depth versus breadth is mixed. The age-old adage "A jack of all trades and a master of none" suggests that people are best served by specializing. However, dilettantes—people who dabble in several fields and areas of studies—may have an advantage over specialists.[31] In particular, dilettantes are more diversified in terms of their personal assets. In this sense, they are better protected from occupations that become dead-ends. Moreover, dilettantes may be more enthusiastic about what they do.

Postscript

We have reviewed six challenges or tensions that will re-emerge throughout your organizational life. With tensions like these, it is no wonder there are executive education programs that promise rejuvenation. It is also no wonder that books like *The Corporate Athlete* are written to help one run long-distance races in the organizational world. Think about the future you created on your Organizational Identity chart. What do you think will keep you energized to continue to perform well for all the organizations you are a part of?

Building a Body of OB Science

How does the science of OB progress? If people are the key focus, how do we study them and their organizations? How can we establish best practices? How can we identify cause-and-effect relationships?

First, let us dispel a few myths: OB is not all common sense. The problem is that most everything looks obvious in hindsight; but only the expert is able to do accurate forecasting. To show this, Weinberg and Nord created pairs of statements that they believed most managers and students would say are true, if they only saw one of the statements.[32] (See Exhibit 1.6 for both statement lists). When students were given *either* statement, over 20 percent of the students regarded that statement to be true; and for five of the statements, over 40 percent of students regarded both as true—when logically, because the statements are polar opposites, that is impossible. Moreover, most students expressed a high level of confidence or certainty about their responses.

Second, OB is highly interdisciplinary. Think about the classes that you are currently enrolled in. What have you learned in another class that might help people in organizations? Because people are the subject matter of OB, this means that OB relies on and leverages insights from sociology, psychology, economics, communications, operations research, and computer and information science in its knowledge base. Think about the classes or courses you have liked the most in your life. How have you used the knowledge gained in those courses in the organizations listed on your timeline? In this book, you'll be exposed to research findings from several different disciplines relevant to OB.

Another question concerns how we might measure the impact that OB has. There are three ways of assessing impact. One method is a scientific measurement referred to as **citation counts.** On any given day, hundreds of journal articles are published about OB. The sad fact is that many of these articles will never be read by anyone nor cited by other researchers. However, some of these scientific articles will move the field and even receive a Nobel Prize! Thus, one way of measuring impact is to do a citation count of an author or a study. Pfeffer analyzed the extent to which OB research represented cumulative knowledge.[33] He referred to the tendency for scientific studies in a field to build on one another as **paradigm development.** He argued that paradigm development, as operationalized by technical certainty and consensus, has numerous positive consequences for the organization and the operation of the field. Pfeffer argued that, as a field of study, OB is not well positioned to make scientific progress.

It is one thing for scholars to cite another; it is quite another thing for businesses to use the knowledge generated by OB researchers. Thus, a second measure concerns whether ideas and research published in scholarly journals are being used and leveraged by businesses. One measure of this might be whether a given business book makes it to the top of the *New York Times* best-seller list. Some business books, such as *Who Moved My Cheese, Good to Great,* and *Execution,* have been on the best-seller charts for several years.

A final measure is the extent to which business and management theory and scholarship is valued outside the field. For example, if another area, such as social science or mathematics, leverages an idea from management, that is a testament to the impact of the idea.

Methods of OB

We've made reference to the scientific enterprise of OB. But what kinds of studies or investigations count toward intellectual capital? There are seven primary research methodologies

EXHIBIT 1.6   OB Knowledge

1. A supervisor is well advised to treat, as much as possible, all members of his/her group exactly the same way.	1. A supervisor is well advised to *adjust his/her behavior according to the unique characteristics of the members of his/her group.*
2. Generally speaking, individual motivation is greatest if the person has set goals for himself/herself which are difficult to achieve.	2. Generally speaking, individual motivation is greatest if the person has set goals for himself/herself which are *easy* to achieve.
3. A major reason why organizations are not so productive as they could be these days is that managers are too concerned with managing the work group rather than the individual.	3. A major reason why organizations are not so productive as they could be these days is that managers are too concerned with managing the *individual rather than the work group.*
4. Supervisors who sometime prior to becoming a supervisor have performed the job of the people they are currently supervising are apt to be more effective supervisors than those who have never performed that particular job.	4. Supervisors who sometime prior to becoming a supervisor have performed the job of the people they are currently supervising are apt to be *less* effective supervisors than those who have never performed that particular job.
5. On almost every matter relevant to the work, managers are well advised to be completely honest and open with their *subordinates.*	5. *There are very few matters in the workplace* where managers are well advised to be completely honest and open with their *subordinates.*
6. On almost every matter relevant to the work, managers are well advised to be completely honest and open with their *superiors.*	6. *There are very few matters in the workplace* where managers are well advised to be completely honest and open with their *superiors.*
7. One's need for power is a better predictor of managerial advancement than one's motivation to do the work well.	7. *One's motivation to do the work* is a better predictor of managerial advancement than *one's need for power.*
8. When people fail at something, they try harder the next time.	8. When people fail at something they *quit trying.*
9. Performing well as a manager depends most on how much education you have.	9. Performing well as a manager depends most on how much *experience* you have.
10. The most effective leaders are those who give more emphasis to getting the work done than they do to relating to people.	10. The most effective leaders are those who give more emphasis to *relating to people than they do to getting the work done.*
11. It is very important for a leader to "stick to his/her guns."	11. It is *not* very important for a leader to "stick to his/her guns."
12. Pay is the most important factor in determining how hard people work.	12. *The nature of the task people are doing* is the most important factor in determining how hard people work.
13. Pay is the most important factor in determining how satisfied people are at work.	13. *The nature of the task* is the most important factor in determining how satisfied people are at work.

Source: Weinberg, R., & Nord, W. (1982). Coping with "it's all common sense." *Exchange: The Organizational Behavior Teaching Journal,* 7(2), 29–33. Reprinted by permission of Organizational Behavior Teaching Society.

that permeate OB. There are advantages and disadvantages of each. (See Exhibit 1.7 for the advantages and disadvantages.) Imagine that you have been asked by your organization to examine whether positive feedback (e.g., compliments and praise) increases employee motivation. As we learn about each of the research methods of OB, we'll use this question as an example.

FIELD STUDIES **Field studies** are research investigations conducted within actual organizations. To examine the question of whether praise increases motivation in a field study, it would be necessary to gain access to an organization in which there is a sufficient number of people to study. Suppose that 30 district managers were grouped randomly into two conditions: Half would be instructed to give their subordinates praise and compliments on a daily basis (for a week or so); the other half would not be told to treat their subordinates any differently than usual. Next suppose that the sales performance of the

EXHIBIT 1.7   **Advantages and Disadvantages of OB Research Methods**

Research Method	Example	Advantage	Disadvantage
Field study	O'Reilly, C. A., & Chatman, J. A. (1994). Working smarter and harder: A longitudinal study of managerial success. *Administrative Science Quarterly,* 39, 603–627.	• Realism & relevance	• Less generalizability because only based on one company • Unless there is intervention (treatment via random assignment to conditions), no causal inference, only correlation
Laboratory study	Staw, B. (1976). "Knee-deep in the Big Muddy: A study of escalating commitment to a chosen course of action." *Organizational Behavior and Human Performance,* 16, 27–44.	• Causal inference	• Limited applicability • Studies often de-contextualized
Classroom study	Thompson, L., Gentner, D., & Loewenstein, J. (2000). Analogical training more powerful than individual case training. *Organizational Behavior and Human Decision Processes,* 82, 60–75.	• Convenience • Motivated participants	• Limited topical areas
Case study	Kuhle, B., Knox, K., & Ross, W. H. (1992). The Hormel strike at Austin Minnesota. *International Journal of Conflict Management,* 3, 45–68.	• Depth of focus • Surface validity	• No control group
Meta-analysis	De Dreu, C. K. W., & Weingart, L. R. (2003). Task versus relationship conflict, team performance, and team member satisfaction: A meta-analysis. *Journal of Applied Psychology,* 88, 741–749.	• Based on several studies (large N)	• Difficult to identify limiting conditions
Surveys/polls	Gallup Poll; Buckingham, M., & Coffman, C. (1999). *First break all the rules.* New York: Simon & Schuster.	• Large sample size • Results often reach larger audience (if published in popular press business book)	• Results are correlational, not causal • Often based on self-report, rather than direct observation
Business pundits	Buffett, W., & Reynolds, S. (1998). *Thoughts of chairman Buffett: Thirty years of unconventional wisdom from the sage of Omaha.* New York: Harper Business.	• Speak language that most can relate to • Reach large audience • Timely (if national awareness)	• No control group • Post hoc, nonscientific theorizing • Sampling on dependent variable

subordinates was measured for a period of one month. If praise did indeed increase motivation, we might expect to see that those who received compliments and praise had greater sales volume.

In one well-known research investigation, Rafaeli and Sutton studied the strategies of bill collectors in their actual jobs by listening to how bill collectors contact debtors.[34]

Chatman and O'Reilly studied motivation and success in MBA students and found a positive relationship between motivation and ability and career success.[35]

Thus far, the field methodology would seem to be very advantageous. The key disadvantage is that the results of field studies are not easily generalizable beyond the company studied. Another disadvantage is that field studies are often correlational (rather than causal) and it is not possible to infer cause-and-effect relationship unless the researcher is able to randomly assign organizational actors to different treatments. Stated another way, we can never be certain that the behaviors and best practices observed in a given company are in fact the causally efficacious determinants of a particular positive (or negative) result. For example, suppose that instead of assigning some bosses to give praise and others to withhold praise, you just measured whether bosses who happened to praise their employees had greater sales volume. The problem: There could be something other than praise itself that might increase sales volume. For example, it may not be praise that increases sales volume; it might be the fact that these bosses also provided special mentoring, or education, or some other type of support.

Field studies currently account for less than 15 percent of OB research, and at the height of their popularity were still dwarfed by lab studies.[36] (See Exhibit 1.8.)

LABORATORY STUDIES Laboratory investigations provide elegant and powerful solutions to the terminal problem of the field study. **Laboratory studies** are conducted within universities and research institutions and allow the researcher to create special treatments and to run simulations that are simply not possible in the field. To return to our praise and motivation example, a laboratory study might involve randomly assigning research participants to receive praise from an authority figure in a simulated organizational environment. Some would not receive praise. Motivation might be measured by examining how long research participants persisted in a difficult task, such as solving anagrams. The advantage of laboratory studies is that the researcher can accurately infer a causal relationship. Currently over 40 percent of OB research is laboratory studies.[37]

CLASSROOM STUDIES **Classroom studies** are increasingly common in OB; they offer many of the advantages of the lab (i.e., random assignment to conditions), but they take place within a classroom.[38] In a classroom investigation of praise and motivation, some students (randomly determined) might be given special praise (via written notes on a simulated project); other students receive feedback, but no specific praise per se. (It would

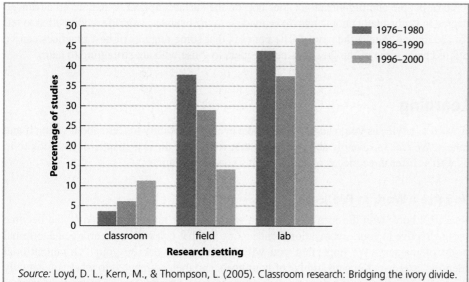

EXHIBIT 1.8

Distribution of OB Studies by Research Setting

Source: Loyd, D. L., Kern, M., & Thompson, L. (2005). Classroom research: Bridging the ivory divide. In *Academy of Management Learning & Education, 4*(1), 8–21, p. 13. Reprinted by permission of Academy of Management via Copyright Clearance Center.

be important that the grades and the assessed performance of students not differ.) Motivation might be measured by examining how long students spent writing a critique of a case in the class, or participating in a group exercise.

CASE STUDIES **Case studies** are essentially summaries of actual business situations. They are primarily used for teaching in the OB classroom, but they are published in OB journals and, therefore, are part of the body of research. They are similar to field investigations except that they are often post-hoc, meaning that they are conducted following an organizational event. To return to our example of examining how praise affects motivation, a case study might involve an intensive examination of a single leader (known for giving praise).

META-ANALYSIS As you might guess, there is usually more than one investigation on any given topic in OB. Perhaps somewhat disconcertingly, studies may produce contradictory findings. For example, De Dreu and Weingart noticed that some investigations reported that task conflict was associated with increased team productivity, whereas other investigations reported the opposite finding.[39] In such a situation, the proper course of action is to combine the studies in a systematic fashion that is sensitive to sample size. Some answers to the puzzles of contradictory findings can be found by conducting a meta-analysis. In a meta-analysis, a researcher obtains data from several original studies and then combines them into one big data set. In this way, a **meta-analysis** puts all the knowledge together to measure the size of an effect or to solve an enigma. One of the key steps in conducting a meta-analysis is to do a thorough literature review. As an exercise, visit your library's online journal search system. Choose psychological info or, more generally, social science and type in the key words: *praise and job motivation*. Make a note of how many citations appear. Attempt to narrow your search by typing in *positive feedback and job motivation* and see how many citations appear.

SURVEYS AND POLLS Sometimes, business problems are particularly pressing or particularly timely, and a poll of several thousand people can be run. For example, consider the book *First Break All the Rules*.[40] The authors surveyed over eighty thousand managers. As an exercise, visit the University of Michigan's survey site, www.isr.umich.edu/src/projects.html. Find out if there is an existing database on praise and motivation.

BUSINESS PUNDITS Another type of research that is increasingly common in OB is the story told by a business pundit, for example, Warren Buffett or Jack Welch. Because the topic of people and organizations does not, on the surface, appear to require an advanced degree to study, many people who have made it in the business world feel compelled to tell (or are invited to tell) their story. The belief is that some nuggets of best practices can be offered from some of the great business leaders to those who are struggling to learn.

Learning

A word of advice as you read this book: Take every opportunity to learn about yourself and others. We feel so strongly about learning that we devote the last chapter of the book to it, as well as offer three pieces of advice in this very first chapter.

You Are a Work in Progress

Read this book with the idea that you can work on your management skills and become more effective in your organizational endeavors, but that you will never arrive at a terminal point of mastery. We hope that you will continue to work on your "Organizational Identity" exercise. Keep an archive of your goals and then compare it to what you actually do. Each one of us is a work in progress; we will never "arrive" at a final state of perfection. This means that you will encounter novel-appearing organizational situations each year of your life. It also means you will continue to make mistakes. In many of those instances, you will have a working model of how to optimally deal with that situation. In some instances, what you believed would work will not work. This is not a failure on your part. In fact, it is an opportunity to learn and continually improve your skills.

In keeping with the idea that you are a work in progress, we urge you to do three things systematically as you make your way through this book and your coursework. First, test your understanding of the concepts after you read each chapter. The chapters of the book build on one another systematically, and you will want to know early on if you are lacking some key concepts. This will also make each chapter of the book more interesting to read. Second, actively try to apply at least one concept from each chapter to a real situation. Specifically, as you watch the news or read articles in the paper, try to apply at least one concept you have read or discussed that week. To help you do this, we have included some business stories from the popular press in the accompanying Website. However, there is no substitute for actively applying the concepts yourself. Third, and finally, explore at least one of the "self-assessment" tools that accompany each chapter. If you connect a concept to some aspect of yourself, it will be better ingrained in your long-term memory.

Engage in Double-Loop versus Single-Loop Learning

Chris Argyris suggests that people can diagnose their incompetence and increase their effectiveness if they engage in double-loop learning.[41] Unfortunately, says Argyris, most people practice single-loop learning. **Single-loop learning** occurs when errors are corrected without questioning or examining our basis assumptions. **Double-loop learning** occurs when errors are corrected by changing the governing values and then the actions. To illustrate the difference between single- and double-loop learning, Argyris gives the example of a thermostat. A single-loop system would be one in which a manager or leader decides that the room (company) functions best when the temperature is exactly 70 degrees and sets the thermostat accordingly. A single-loop process would be one in which the thermostat simply did the job of regulating the temperature to meet the leader's desired temperature. A double-loop process would be one in which a thermostat not only simply regulated the temperature, but could provide feedback to the manager/leader about the observed effects of different temperatures on actual performance. Imagine how successful a leader might be if a thermostat might observe that when working on certain projects, a lower (or higher) temperature was desirable. In this sense, the leader learns from the system, not just the other way around. Go back to your Organizational Identity chart. Focus on one of your current organizations (e.g., your track team, your sorority, your dorm, etc.) and think about a question you have related to that organization (e.g., "Why do our team meetings always start 20 minutes late?" "Why do the same people get elected to office?"). Make a list of how you might go about getting answers to your question that involve you learning about the organization. Whom would you talk to? What questions would you ask? What are your biggest concerns in terms of seeking answers?

Bridge the Knowing-Doing Gap

Pfeffer and Sutton bluntly pose the question, "Why do so much education and training, management consulting, and business research and so many books and articles produce so little change in what managers and organizations actually do?"[42] Companies spend more than $60 billion on training each year and $43 billion on managerial consulting.[43] Each year, more than 80,000 students are awarded an MBA degree and even more earn an undergraduate degree in a business-related field. Yet, not much ever seems to change. Most managers are experts at knowing; but, when it comes to action (doing), they are complete buffoons. In short, there is a tremendous gap between knowing and doing. Five culprits act as leading causes of the knowing-doing gap:

1. *When talk substitutes for action,* for example, planning meetings, making presentations, rehearsing for meetings, and so on. Basically, smart people love to talk about ideas and knowledge, but avoid action.
2. *When memory substitutes for thinking.* In short, organizations rely on what they have done in the past.

3. *When fear prevents acting on knowledge.* Even though most companies claim that they are interested in human learning, many are intolerant of mistakes.
4. *When measurement obstructs good judgment.* Over time, companies bureaucratize management procedures, resulting in organizational arthritis.[44]
5. *When internal competition turns friends into enemies.* People are often threatened by the best and the brightest in their own organization.[45]

Conclusion

You began this chapter by creating your own Organizational Identity chart. We defined OB as the study of how people are influenced by organizations and in turn, how people affect their organizations. We identified three key content areas of OB: thoughts or cognition, affect (or emotion, which also includes motivation), and behavior. We introduced four levels of analysis for studying OB that will reoccur throughout this book: the individual level, the interpersonal (one-on-one level), the team (or small group or department level), and finally, the most general level, that of the entire organization. We pointed out that a person's behavior in organizations is partly a function of the person and partly determined by the situation, such as norms and policies. We introduced five key skills people should develop: technical skills, decision-making (or judgment) skills, interpersonal skills, ethical and moral skills, and self-knowledge skills. We outlined six key tensions that represent dilemmas for most organizational actors: the pursuit of self versus organizational interest; focusing on the work to be done (task) or the people; putting work or family first; exploration or exploitation; promotion versus prevention; and dilettantism versus narrow focus. We ended the chapter by discussing how the science of OB progresses via seven different methodologies: field studies, laboratory studies, classroom studies, case studies, meta-analysis, surveys and polls, and business pundits.

Notes

1. Rix, S. (2004). *Aging and work—A view from the United States.* AARP Public Policy Institute.
2. McCuan, J. (2004, April 1). Guard your exits! *Inc. Magazine,* 44.
3. Trunk, P. (2007). *Brazen careerist: The new rules for success.* New York: Business Plus.
4. Amat Corporation. Retrieved from http://www.ruleof72.net/rule-of-72-learn.asp.
5. Farrell, C. (2004, July 26). No need to hit the panic button. *Business Week,* 78.
6. Caumont, A. (2004, June 20). Moving on: Before you jump to a new job, take a look at the options and yourself. *Washington Post,* p. 5.
7. Hammonds, K. (2004, July 1). We, incorporated. *Fast Company,* 67.
8. Weintraub, A. (2006, April 24). Eyes wide open. *Business Week,* 78–79.
9. Chan, S. (2006, May 9). Fire department tries a softer, gentler approach. *New York Times.*
10. Buchanan, L. (2006, April 1). The office: The three-corner office. *Inc. Magazine,* 112.
11. Associated Press. (2005, September 6). Retrieved from http://www.foxnews.com/story/0,2933,168638,00.html.
12. Emily, J. (2005, September 14). Holding out hope for missing kids—As evacuees move, reuniting families increasingly difficult. *Dallas Morning News,* p. 7.
13. Thomas, E. (2005, September 14). The lost city. *Newsweek,* 42–52.
14. Campo-Flores, A. (2006, March 13). Katrina's latest damage. *Newsweek.* Retrieved from www.msnbc.msn.com/id/11677333/site/newsweek/.
15. CNN. (2005, March 14). Ex-hostage: "I wanted to gain his trust." Retrieved from http://www.cnn.com/2005/LAW/03/14/smith.transcript.
16. Lewin, K. (1951). *Field theory.* New York: Harper & Row.
17. Miller, G. A. (1956). The magical number seven, plus or minus two. Some limits on our capacity to process information. *Psychological Review, 63,* 81–87.
18. Chi, M. T. H., Feltovich, P. J., & Glaser, R. (1981). Categorization and representation of physics problems by experts and novices. *Cognitive Science, 5,* 121–152.
19. Goleman, D., Boyatzis, R. E., & McKee, A. (2002). *Primal leadership: Realizing the power of emotional intelligence.* Boston: Harvard Business School Press.
20. Zagorin, A. (2005, February 14). The Abu Ghraib scandal you don't know. *Time,* 36–37.
21. One for the team. (2004, May 3). *Time,* 38–40.
22. Dauten, D. (2004, June 21). American dream isn't about money, but the wealth of possibilities. *St. Louis Post–Dispatch.*
23. Morris, B. (2003, December 8). When bad things happen to good companies. Schwab was the brokerage built on integrity and fair play. After 6,505 layoffs and a restructuring, can it save its soul? *Fortune,* 80.

24. Haddock, S., et al. (2001). Ten adaptive strategies for family and work balance. *Journal of Marital and Family Therapy, 27*(4), 445–458.

25. Belkin, L. (2003, November 9). Life's work: Sharing a life, a family, and a workweek. *New York Times,* Section 10, p. 1.

26. Collier, M. (2002). *Starting an eBay business for dummies.* New York: Wiley.

27. March, J. G. (1994). *A primer on decision making.* New York: Free Press.

28. Higgins, E. T. (2002). How self-regulation creates distinct values: The case of promotion and prevention decision making. *Journal of Consumer Psychology, 12,* 177–191.

29. Higgins, E. T. (1998). Promotion and prevention: Regulatory focus as a motivational principle. In M. P. Zanna (Ed.), *Advances in experimental social psychology* (Vol. 30, pp. 1–46). New York: Academic Press.

30. Higgins, E. T., Shah, J., & Friedman, R. (1997). Emotional responses to goal attainment: Strength of regulatory focus as moderator. *Journal of Personality and Social Psychology, 72,* 515–525.

31. Sternberg, R. J., & Grigorenko, E. L. (1999). In praise of dilettantism. *APS Observer, 12,* 37–38.

32. Weinberg, R., & Nord, W. (1982). Coping with "It's all common sense." *The Organizational Behavior Teaching Journal, 7*(2), 29–33.

33. Pfeffer, J. (1993). Barriers to the advance of organizational science: Paradigm development as an independent variable. *Academy of Management Review, 18*(4), 599–620.

34. Rafaeli, A., & Sutton, R. (1991). Emotional contrast strategies as means of social influence: Lessons from criminal interrogators and bill collectors. *Academy of Management Journal, 34*(4), 749–775.

35. O'Reilly, C. A., & Chatman, J. A. (1994). Working smarter and harder: A longitudinal study of managerial success. *Administrative Science Quarterly, 39,* 603–627.

36. Thompson, L., Kern, M., & Loyd, D. L. (2003). Research methods of micro organizational behavior. In C. Sansone, C. Morf, and A. Panter (Eds.), *Handbook of methods in social psychology.* Thousand Oaks, CA: Sage.

37. Loyd, D. L., Kern, M. C., & Thompson, L. (2005). Classroom research: Bridging the ivory divide. *Academy of Management Journal: Learning and Education, 4*(1), 8–21.

38. Ibid.

39. De Dreu, C. K. W., & Weingart, L. R. (2003). Task versus relationship conflict, team performance, and team member satisfaction: A meta-analysis. *Journal of Applied Psychology, 88,* 741–749.

40. Buckingham, M., & Coffman, C. (1999). *First break all the rules: What the world's greatest managers do differently.* New York: Simon & Schuster.

41. Argyris, C. (2002). Double-loop learning, teaching and research. *Academy of Management Learning and Education, 1*(2), 206–218.

42. Pfeffer, J., & Sutton, R. (2000). *The knowing knowledge gap—How smart companies turn knowledge into action* (p. 1). Cambridge, MA: Harvard Business School Press.

43. Ibid, pp. 1–2.

44. Katz, R. (1982). The effects of group longevity on project communication and performance. *Administrative Science Quarterly, 27,* 81–104.

45. Menon, T., Thompson, L., & Choi, H. (2006). Tainted knowledge versus tempting knowledge: People avoid knowledge from internal rivals and seek knowledge from external rivals. *Management Science, 52*(8), 1129–1144.

Chapter | 2

UNDERSTANDING PEOPLE AND THEIR BEHAVIOR

Everyone has a unique personality and as a consequence, a unique life story.[1] What has made you the person you are? Take 20 minutes to complete Dan McAdam's Life Story Exercise (you can do this on a sheet of paper or using the spreadsheet in the Self-Discovery section). Ideally, do this with a classmate so you can focus on the skills involved in understanding another person's life story. You may be surprised.

STEP 1: Think of your life as if it were a book and create chapters (at least two and no more than seven). Give each chapter a title and briefly summarize it.

STEP 2: Think about key events in your life, such as your peak experience, your "nadir" experience, a turning point, your earliest memory, and an important scene from your childhood, teenage, and college years.

STEP 3: Looking back over your life, describe the single greatest challenge you have ever faced.

STEP 4: Characters: Looking over your chapters, who are the key people in your life? (Think of these people as the heroes and villains in your story.)

STEP 5: The Future: Describe a positive future that is realistic. Then, describe a negative future in which something could happen, but you hope it does not occur.

STEP 6: Life Theme: Looking back over your entire life story, what is the central theme, message, or purpose of your life?

What Makes People Tick?

Hopefully you have taken the time to craft the first draft of your Life Story. And, if you have taken the time to listen to another person's Life Story, you can begin to understand just how complex people are. Most people find themselves at a loss at one time or another to explain why people behave the way they do—for example, why the plan they put into place has produced the opposite results they intended; why their attempt to give well-meaning feedback to a friend is met with defensiveness and retribution. By the same token, many people sometimes do not understand their own behavior, for example, why they are feeling uninspired or perhaps overly sensitive; why they can't bring themselves to have a much needed discussion about a failing course of action. This chapter focuses on understanding what makes people think and act the way they do. And understanding, as we will see, is the key toward changing our own and others' behavior.

Behavior Is a Function of Personality and the Situation

In Chapter 1, we noted that people's behavior is partly determined by their personality (traits, skills, and disposition) and partly determined by the norms and pressures of their situation. (Recall our example in Chapter 1 of Ashley Smith's encounter with gunman Brian Nichols.) Whereas your personality is largely invariant (i.e., fixed and stable), the "situation" is much more flexible and malleable, meaning that it can change suddenly. One implication is that it is easier for people to try to modify or change their environment than their basic instincts. The same is true for the other people in our lives: We will have more success if we change the situation rather than attempt to change a person's personality.

In Chapter 1, we introduced five skills (technical, decision making, interpersonal, ethical, and self-knowledge). In this chapter, we focus on three key aspects of people's personality: intelligence, temperament, and motivation. By personality, we focus on largely invariant aspects about people—factors that are very stable and hard to change. Then we focus on three key aspects of the situation: company culture, organizational norms, and psychological contracts. In this book, we will use the terms *internal attributions* and *external attributions* to refer to whether people think the cause of their own (and others') behavior is driven by their personality (internal) or the pressures of the situation (external). When we attempt to explain our own behavior or that of others, we need to consider both internal factors as well as external factors. As an exercise, think about your own Life Story and in particular, your "Life Theme." How much of what has happened in your life is a function of your internal factors (i.e., your personality, traits, disposition) versus situational factors (i.e., being in a particular place at a particular time)?

Intelligence

Most people would agree that intelligence is critical for success in organizations, and in many of life's enterprises. Intelligence is related to a number of life's pursuits, including income and education.[2] In *IQ and the Wealth of Nations,* Lynn and Vanhanen argue that IQ is an important determinant of educational attainment, salary, and a variety of economic success measures.[3] In the United States and the United Kingdom, the correlation between IQ and people's earnings is 0.35. In other words, IQ is associated with up to one third of a person's financial success.

However, few people would agree on what intelligence is and how to measure it. For example, Dunning asked people to define "intelligence," and their definitions were colored by what they excelled in.[4] In other words, creative people who got low academic grades defined intelligence as "creativity"; people who scored well on tests defined intelligence as "academic achievement." Moreover, incompetent people lack insight into their own failings. Most incompetent people do not know that they are incompetent. In short, incompetent people lack self-appraisal skills.

Most people think of intelligence as relatively invariant—that is, in a genetic capacity, you are what you are. However, Robert Sternberg vehemently disagrees. According to Sternberg intelligence is malleable, shaped and increased through our life experiences.[5] Think about your own Life Story. What "critical" event do you think had the greatest influence on your intelligence? "Successful intelligence" is the ability to achieve success in life, given one's personal standards and within one's sociocultural context.[6] The ability to capitalize on one's own strengths and leverage, correct, or compensate for one's own weaknesses is the real marker of intelligence.

Thus, when it comes to what intelligence means to scholars who measure it, there are two schools of thought. One school holds that intelligence is a single, unified trait; the other school of thought believes that there are several distinct types of intelligence. Before reading further, take a personal stand on this. In other words, if you had to say whether intelligence was a single, general trait, or a composite of several different, distinct things, what would you say? And why?

G-Factor Intelligence

One of the earliest views of intelligence (and still widely popular today) is that intelligence is a generalized trait. This unified view of intelligence argues that intelligence is reflected by one's **G-factor,** or "general" intelligence.[7] Several investigations of leadership have linked intelligence (measured via G-factor) and leadership success. However, it is not necessary for leaders to be geniuses to be effective. In fact, it is more important that leaders *appear* to be smart (rather than actually *be* smart).[8] General mental ability is positively associated with career success, as measured by income and occupational status.[9] However, when we start dealing with highly intelligent populations, such as students enrolled in advanced courses, intelligence has less predictive power, simply because there is not much variation in the sample. Simply put, suppose you are in a class in which all the students had been valedictorian of their high school. If this were the case, there would not be much variation on their ACT scores!

Multiple Intelligences

A more contemporary view of intelligence is that it is not best described as a single factor but, rather, as a panoply of several different types of intelligence. For example, Sternberg's triarchic theory of intelligence poses that there are three distinct types of intelligence: **componential intelligence** (the ability to think abstractly and process information effectively), **experiential intelligence** (the ability to formulate new ideas, and to combine seemingly unrelated facts or information), and **contextual intelligence** (the ability to adapt to changing environmental conditions and to shape the environment).[10] Similarly, Howard Gardner's theory of **multiple intelligences** challenges the traditional view that intelligence is a unitary capacity that can be adequately measured by IQ tests.[11] Gardner proposes that there are eight intelligences (see Exhibit 2.1). The intelligences identified by Gardner are ones that have distinct areas in the brain. Organizational behavior arguably involves each of the eight types of intelligence. (As an exercise, revisit the Organizational Identity exercise in Chapter 1. Which types of intelligence did you draw on in the different types of organizations you have been a part of?)

Emotional Intelligence

Emotional intelligence is "the ability to perceive emotions, to access and generate emotions so as to assist thought, to understand emotions and emotional knowledge, and to reflectively regulate emotions so as to promote emotional and intellectual growth."[12] The traditional view of emotion in organizations was that decision makers and leaders should not feel or express emotion. "Rule your feelings, lest your feelings rule you!"[13] According to theories of emotional intelligence (EQ), effective organizational actors have a brain as well as a heart. Look at your Life Story. Were there any chapters or episodes in your story that revealed emotional intelligence?

Peter Salovey and his research team at Yale began to wonder why some people who seemed to have everything going for them—high IQs and great careers—seem to sabotage

EXHIBIT 2.1 Multiple Intelligences

Type of Intelligence	Description	Example of a person who exemplifies this type of intelligence
Linguistic	Ability to communicate and make sense of the world through language; storytelling, great writers and orators	J. K. Rowling, author of the Harry Potter series
Musical	These people create and communicate sound	Miles Davis, Jimi Hendrix
Logical mathematical	These people use and appreciate abstract relations; scientists and mathematicians, statisticians	John Nash
Spatial	These people perceive visual and spatial information to create and transform space, e.g., graphic artists, designers, architects	Frank Lloyd Wright
Bodily kinesthetic	Control of one's own body, control in handling objects	Lance Armstrong, Mikhail Baryshnikov
Interpersonal	Awareness of others' feelings, emotions, goals, and motivations	Oprah Winfrey
Intrapersonal	Awareness of one's own feelings, emotions, goals, and motivations	Sylvia Plath
Naturalist	Recognition and classification of objects in the environment	Charles Darwin

Source: Gardner, H. (1983). *Frames of mind: The theory of multiple intelligences.* New York: Basic Books.

themselves at some point. Salovey and his colleagues began to dig deeply into areas of learning, development, and emotion to discover relationships between emotion and what was previously regarded as nonemotional activity. Thus, the new, enlightened view of management is that emotions are adaptive and functional, and they organize cognitive activity. Insights in learning theory suggest that emotions are necessary for intelligence. Interestingly, it was Charles Darwin himself who heralded the EQ movement more than 125 years ago with the publication of his book, *The Expression of Emotions in Man and Animals.*[14] In that book, Darwin sharply argued that emotional systems in people and animals ensure survival of the species by energizing required behaviors and signaling valued information.

Skill Areas of Emotional Intelligence

Emotional intelligence encompasses a variety of skills that can be summarized into four key abilities (see Exhibit 2.2).

■ **Self-awareness,** or the ability to understand emotions in ourselves, is the bedrock of an effective emotional sensory system. Think about your Life Story and in particular your critical incidents from childhood, adolescence, and adulthood. What have you learned about yourself as you reflect on those incidents?

■ **Other-awareness or empathy,** the ability to perceive emotions in others and to take their perspective, is not only critical to management but critical for any interpersonal relationship. For most relationships, such as marriage, friendship, and teamwork, empathy is associated with more positive relationship outcomes.[15] Most important, simply possessing a great deal of background information and facts about a person does not lead to greater empathic ability; rather, people must also acquire extensive information about another person's subjective (inner) experiences. In other words, we must get to know people from the inside instead of merely from the outside.

EXHIBIT 2.2

Emotional Intelligence Skills

Self-Awareness	**Other-Awareness**
• identifying emotions in ourselves • understanding emotional feelings • having the ability to understand what causes emotions, what the relationships among various emotions are, how they change	• identifying emotions in others • perceiving emotions • empathy • reading people • developing others
Self-Regulation	**Social Skills**
• managing emotions • showing appropriate emotional expression • "getting in the mood" • having the ability to incorporate one's feelings and the feelings of others into thinking	• using emotions skillfully • managing emotions in a way that enhances personal growth and social relations • collaboration and cooperation

Partially derived from: Goleman, D. (1998). *Working with emotional intelligence.* New York: Bantam Books; Caruso, D. R., & Salovey, P. (2004). *The emotionally intelligent manager: How to develop and use the four key emotional skills of leadership.* San Francisco: Jossey-Bass; Mayer, J. D., & Salovey, P. (1997). What is emotional intelligence? In P. Salovey & D. Sluyter (Eds.), *Emotional development and emotional intelligence: Implications for educators* (pp. 3–31). New York: Basic Books.

Moreover, several emotional disorders, such as autism and Asperger's syndrome (a mild form of autism), are characterized by an inability to perceive emotions in others or to take another's point of view.[16] (Take at least 30 minutes to listen to another person's Life Story to practice empathy.)

■ **Self-regulation** refers to the ability of a person to control emotions. In a general sense, self-regulation refers to the ability of people to control their impulses. This is incredibly important in organizational life, as leaders and managers who fail to exercise self-control may suffer disastrous consequences. As can be seen in Exhibit 2.3, Howard Dean failed to self-regulate during the 2004 presidential primary and as a result, the American public distrusted his ability to lead. However, as important as it is, we don't have an endless supply of self-control. It takes energy to control our temper (which Howard Dean did not do on that fateful night). In fact, exerting self-control reduces the amount of strength or control we can bring to other tasks.[17]

EXHIBIT 2.3

Failure to Self-Regulate?

When presidential candidate Howard Dean screamed almost incoherently at his troops in the 2004 Iowa caucus, this cost the former Democratic presidential candidate his chances in the 2004 Democratic primary. Dean committed a "red flag," raising the latent suspicion that he was psychologically unstable. Whereas passion is a good thing, it crossed over into anger.

Source: Hitt, G. (2004, January 23). Spin doctors prescribe dose of self-deprecation for Howard Dean ("Yeeeaaahh!"). *Wall Street Journal,* A11.

To assess how exercising self-control affects performance, in one investigation, food-deprived participants were exposed to "severe" temptation by leaving them alone in a room with cookies and chocolate candies.[18] (To add to the torture, the cookies had just been baked in the same room, so the aroma was wafting in the air!) Then, the participants got the bad news: They were told that they had been randomly assigned to eat from a bowl of radishes (considerably less appetizing than chocolate chip cookies). For comparison purposes, a "control" group was permitted to eat the cookies and another "control" group was not shown any food at all. All groups then were given a job-related task that measured their persistence. Everyone performed relatively well in terms of persistence with the exception of the radish group (i.e., the people who were told to resist eating the cookies and eat the radishes instead), who gave up much faster on the task. The upshot is that resisting temptation consumes another resource—the ability to apply oneself in a challenging organizational context; moreover, people exercising self-regulation have the negative experience of time being slowed down.[19]

■ **Social skills** refers to a large, complex set of abilities in terms of relating to other people, creating trust, and sustaining relationships. Think about the heroes and villains in your Life Story. Which of the four EQ skills did the heroes possess and the villains lack?

Emotions

There are several different kinds of emotions (see the circumplex in Exhibit 2.4). In general, emotions are divided into "positive" and "negative" branches. Note that there are many more negative emotions than positive ones. This is because negative emotions threaten the sustainability of relationships and consequently, we need to understand causes and consequences of negative emotions.

Measuring EQ

Measuring EQ is challenging. There are three primary ways: self-report (the least useful), peer and superior ratings (such as 360-degree evaluations), and behavioral measures, such as the MSCEIT (the Mayer-Salovey-Caruso Emotional Intelligence Test), which tests a person's ability to recognize nonverbal emotion, and the like.[20] Behavioral or actual performance measures often involve presenting pictures of people with different emotional expressions and asking the observers to identify the emotion that the person in the picture is feeling. Self-report tests, on the other hand, simply involve asking participants to

EXHIBIT 2.4   Distinct Emotions

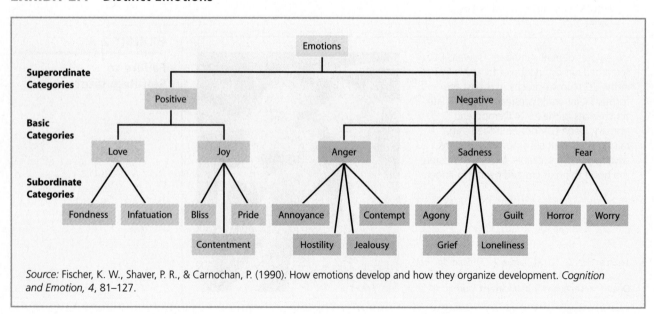

Source: Fischer, K. W., Shaver, P. R., & Carnochan, P. (1990). How emotions develop and how they organize development. *Cognition and Emotion, 4*, 81–127.

respond to a variety of questions about their emotional expressiveness (e.g., "It is hard for me to understand the way I feel") and their interest in the emotions of others (e.g., "I am sensitive to the feelings of others"). Peer and superior ratings might involve co-workers or teammates evaluating a given person on a variety of EQ skills and then comparing one's own self-rating to peer ratings.

Research Support for EQ

Research support for EQ is mixed. Many of the studies lack control groups and in a sense are "sampling on the dependent variable" (see Chapter 1). In other words, just by looking at a consequence you cannot infer the cause. For example, a famous study of EQ is the "marshmallow" investigation.[21] In this investigation, 4-year-old children either were offered a marshmallow to eat immediately or told they must wait for 15 minutes but then would receive two marshmallows. In short, by delaying gratification for 15 minutes, the children could double their utility. As would be expected, there was much variation in terms of ability to delay gratification: One third of the children took the marshmallow immediately; some waited a little longer; and one third waited the full 15 minutes. The dependent variable was effectiveness in life over the next 10 years. Ten years later, the differences between the two groups were dramatic: Those who had delayed gratification were described by their parents as more academically and socially competent. Specifically, the children who had been able to delay gratification were more verbally fluent, rational, attentive, thoughtful, and able to deal with frustration and stress. Moreover, those who were able to delay gratification had significantly higher SAT scores. However, this study is correlational, rather than causal. Much of the support is post-hoc (after the fact) in nature, rather than predictive. Thus, there is no way to establish a causal relationship between inability to delay gratification as a child and performance as an adult.

Only a handful of studies have examined the predictive validity of EQ, and many of these have used self-report measures.[22] In one investigation, the EQ of undergraduate students was used to predict year-end grades.[23] The predictive validity of emotional intelligence was compared to the predictive validity of traditional cognitive abilities and the five dimensions of personality (extraversion, neuroticism, conscientiousness, agreeableness, and openness to experience.) Only some measures of EQ predicted academic success, and none of the EQ measures showed incremental predictive validity for academic success over cognitive and personality variables. The authors conclude that the overlap between EQ measures and traditional measures of intelligence and personality limits the ability of EQ to predict above and beyond that.

One argument that supports why EQ should matter is the simple fact that if companies measure IQ or achievement and select on that variable, then IQ itself will not predict job success. In short, if there is no variation on a trait, then it cannot be predictive. Think of it this way: Universities and companies often "select" people on the basis of their intelligence (as measured by IQ or achievement or grades). Thus, the people who are admitted into prestigious companies and select graduate programs are *all* smart, and there is very little variation in terms of their IQ. For example, student grade point averages are not a good predictor of early career progress.[24] And Graduate Record Exam (GRE) scores are of limited use in predicting postgraduate performance.[25] EQ is more predictive of job success because it is normally distributed.

Skills for Building EQ

The skills for building EQ are strongly related to the four EQ competency areas. To be effective, people must practice the skills. Many typical MBA curriculums do not develop EQ competencies.[26]

- *Heightening self-awareness:* Self-awareness of one's own emotions is the first step in improving emotional intelligence. Indeed, people who have a "language" for talking about their emotions (and those in others) are less likely to "act out" in self-destructive and inappropriate ways.[27] In your Life Story, when did you show high self-awareness? When did you lack self-awareness?

■ *Understanding your triggers:* Once a person learns to identify different emotional states, the next step is to identify the causes or triggers of one's emotional states.

■ *Self-regulation:* The importance of self-regulation ability cannot be underestimated. People who effectively "manage their emotions" have better interactions with their friends and make better impressions on people.[28] However, effective self-regulation does not just mean "keeping a lid on it." The ability to display and suppress emotional expressions in accord with situational demands is key. In one investigation, students' adjustment in the first two years of college following September 11th was examined as a function of displaying *and* suppressing emotion.[29] Students who were better at enhancing as well as suppressing their emotions were less distressed during college and had better memory as well. We noted above that engaging in self-regulation is cognitively taxing and, in essence, depletes our ability to perform. However, people can ward off depletion if they view their self-control as helping others or even helping themselves.[30] In short, when self-regulation threatens to deplete you, you can ward off the effects of depletion if you are sufficiently motivated. Another way to ward off depletion is via reappraisal, or changing how we think about an event.[31]

■ *Journaling:* People who write about emotional topics have improved physical health compared to those who write about superficial topics.[32] For example, people who write about their feelings lower their blood pressure and heart rate, strengthen their immune system, and increase their coping skills. Most important, it is not efficacious to write about just anything; rather, it is important to integrate our emotions with the thoughts we have about the situations that produced them. Effective journaling involves:[33]

Using positive emotion words frequently
Using negative emotion words moderately
Using causal words like "caused me to" and "led me to"
Using insight words like "realize" and "understand"

Caruso and Salovey prescribe 20 minutes of journaling each day.[33]

■ *Rehearsing action plans:* It takes about two weeks for a behavior to become a habit. When a behavior becomes a habit, a person is able to use that behavior without thinking. Moreover, people who are clear with regard to how they want to express emotion, particularly negative emotion, have greater interpersonal success. One investigation examined the implications of people in conflict over emotional expression. People who were emotionally ambivalent (undecided about their emotions) were less effective in their communication ability, had less positivism in their relationships, and took a subordinate stance in their communications.[34]

■ *Bouncing back:* Lots of evidence indicates that resilient people are able to "bounce back" from stressful experiences (that we all encounter at one time or another) quickly and effectively. The broaden-and-build theory of positive emotions suggests that resilient people use positive emotions strategically to rebound from and find positive meaning in stressful situations.[35] Think about your Life Story, particularly your "nadir" experience. Did you bounce back?

■ *Practicing empathy:* Empathy is the ability to look at the world through the eyes of others. It is not sympathy. And it does not mean you need to agree with that person; it simply means taking that person's perspective. Perspective-taking is a skill that people can consciously turn off or turn on, and that powerfully affects a number of organizationally relevant outcomes, such as lessening prejudice and discrimination.[36]

■ *Sharing positive events:* Is it better to be social and communicative when good things happen? Yes: Communicating personal positive events with others increases personal well-being.[37] Moreover, when others respond positively, the benefits are magnified. Even if you don't directly share your positive experiences, your own mood is contagious—it affects others. For example, the positive mood of a leader is associated with improved group performance, job satisfaction, and job involvement.[38] Moreover, business customers themselves shape their own experiences with companies via their

EXHIBIT 2.5

Promotion, Prevention, and Emotional Experience

	Success Experience	Failure Experience
Prevention Focus	Relief	Anxiety
Promotion Focus	Happiness	Disappointment

Source: Based on Higgins, E. T. (1997). Beyond pleasure and pain. *American Psychologist, 52*(12), 1280–1300.

own mood; customers who are more "agreeable" increase the display of positive emotions in service providers.[39]

■ *Promotion-focus:* In Chapter 1, we distinguished prevention-focus from promotion-focus. As it turns out, these distinctions are related to emotional experience.

In Exhibit 2.5, we see that everyone, regardless of whether they are chronically prevention focused or promotion focused, will sometimes experience success in life's endeavors and sometimes experience failure. The prevention-focused person who experiences success will often feel relief. In contrast, the promotion-focused person who experiences the same success will feel happiness. Conversely, when the prevention-focused person experiences a failure, she will experience anxiety, but when the promotion-focused person experiences the same failure, she will feel disappointment. Thus, prevention-focused people often preclude themselves from feeling true happiness. As an exercise, look at Step 5 (The Future) in your Life Story. You created both a promotion focus and a prevention focus. Which focus do you think about most often?

■ *Forgiveness:* Forgiveness and generosity are associated with enhanced mental and physical well-being. The effects of forgiveness are particularly pronounced in strong commitment relationships (such as marriage and with one's supervisor).[40] Forgiveness lowers psychological tension; and failure to forgive works at cross-purposes with intentions to persist, long-term orientation, and psychological attachment.

Temperament and the Big Five

A person's personality or temperament has been endlessly fascinating to philosophers since the beginning of time. Plato and Aristotle argued that human nature arises from three parts or faculties of the soul.[41]

However, the task of understanding personality has been a rocky road for management theorists and personality theorists. For several decades, just about as many different personality tests and measures existed as there were people to measure. There was no common understanding or metric. In short, there was no intradisciplinary consensus. Then a breakthrough occurred when some researchers at different universities collaborated (just as in the case of the wildly successful Human Genome Project) and agreed on a set of core personality dimensions. They named the five key dimensions "the Big Five" or the "five-factor model" of personality.[42] Nearly all clusters of personality-relevant adjectives can be subsumed under the **Big Five.**[43]

According to Big Five researchers, there are five major dimensions of personality. The five factors are not types, but rather dimensions, meaning that people vary on them (i.e., people can be high or low on any dimension). It is easy to remember them because they spell the word OCEAN: Openness to experience, Conscientiousness, Extraversion, Agreeableness, and Neuroticism.[44] (See Exhibit 2.6.)

No personality test can perfectly predict actual behavior. If we consider the powerful fundamental attribution error, or the tendency for people to ascribe dispositional reasons for the behavior of others and discount the situation, then we have a situation ripe for the overreliance on personality tests. Even if personality could be accurately measured

EXHIBIT 2.6 **The Big 5 Personality Traits**

	Description	People who are high on this dimension:	People who are low on this dimension are:
O	Openness to experience	Make adjustments in activities in accordance with new ideas or situations	Aversive to change; insist on standardized rules and norms
C	Conscientiousness	Consider others when making decisions	Relatively oblivious to others
E	Extraversion	Show a keen interest in other people and external events, and venture forth with confidence into the unknown	Self-focused or self-absorbed; anxious when in presence of others
A	Agreeableness	Display compatibility with other people; are able to get along with others	Combative; argumentative
N	Neuroticism	Are unstable and highly anxious	Stable and low in anxiety

Source: Ewen, R. B. (1998). *Personality: A topical approach,* p. 140. Mahwah, NJ: Erlbaum. Reprinted by permission of Lawrence Erlbaum Associates, Inc. via Copyright Clearance Center.

(it often can't), there would still remain serious questions about whether personality actually predicts behavior (it often pales in comparison to situational pressures).

Motivation

Motivation counts for more than raw intelligence. This is why Thomas Alva Edison said that genius is 1 percent inspiration and 99 percent perspiration.[45] Motivation, unlike intelligence and temperament, can be controlled.

Intrinsic versus Extrinsic Motivation

There are two major types of motivation: intrinsic and extrinsic. Simply stated, a person is **intrinsically motivated** when he enjoys doing an activity or a job for the pleasure that it brings. A person is **extrinsically motivated** when he does a job or activity because it will bring rewards such as money or fame. A key way in which people misjudge others is that they assume that others are purely extrinsically motivated, whereas most people believe that they are uniquely intrinsically motivated. This is not to say that most people do not care about extrinsic rewards. They do. However, if we treat others as if they are purely extrinsically motivated, this can lead to problems.

For example, if positive feedback and praise are not carefully administered, they can undermine a person's intrinsic interest.[46] That is, employees may do something for purely intrinsic reasons, such as the joy of learning new things or expressing themselves, but if a supervisor praises the work and administers large extrinsic rewards for the work, this may lead employees to believe they are doing the work for the money. For example, pay-for-performance systems tend to make people less enthusiastic about their work.[47] (See Exhibit 2.7 for how managers can avoid the potentially deleterious effects of externally imposed deadlines.)

We are not suggesting that companies should never offer extrinsic (e.g., pay-based) rewards to their employees. Rather, when providing a reward, you should emphasize what you value about the work and how the company views the employee. Indeed, when high effort is rewarded, people are more industrious. Just as people can be reinforced for working hard, they can be reinforced for creativity.[48]

Maslow's Hierarchy of Needs

One of the most useful conceptions of human motivation is Maslow's **hierarchy of needs.**[49] Abraham Maslow, a clinical psychologist, reasoned that before people could care about such

**EXHIBIT 2.7   How Managers Can Avoid the Potentially Deleterious Effects
of Externally Imposed Deadlines**

Although deadlines set by supervisors are a fact of life, external goals and deadlines have been shown to demotivate people. Burgess et al. interviewed people to determine whether they devised and used strategies to offset the damaging effect that externally imposed deadlines have on intrinsic motivation. Across the board, if employees have either complete or partial self-determination, they remain motivated. Specifically, people who actively co-opt a deadline as their own, or who self-impose sub-deadlines within an overall externally imposed deadline, or who self-impose even more stringent deadlines than those their supervisor imposes, are all more motivated than employees who don't take any ownership of the externally imposed deadline.

Source: Burgess, M., Enzle, M. E., & Schmalz, R. (2004). Defeating the potentially deleterious effects of externally-imposed deadlines: Practitioners' rules of thumb. *Personality and Social Psychology Bulletin, 30*(7), 868–877.

things as making a difference and realizing their "dreams," they need to satisfy more basic goals, such as making a living. Thus, Maslow posited a "hierarchy" of needs, ranging from physiological needs at the most basic level (e.g., thirst, hunger, shelter) to self-actualization at the highest level (i.e., the fulfillment of one's potential; see Exhibit 2.8). According to Maslow, people could not recognize, much less pursue, the next higher level in the hierarchy until they dealt with the needs that supported it.

Maslow was first to suggest that people need to satisfy basic needs before striving for higher-order needs; Herzberg was first to put this idea in a management context.[50] Herzberg proposed a theory about job factors that motivate employees. Herzberg constructed a two-dimensional paradigm of factors that affect people's attitudes about work. Factors such as company policy, supervision, interpersonal relations, working conditions,

EXHIBIT 2.8   Maslow's Hierarchy of Needs

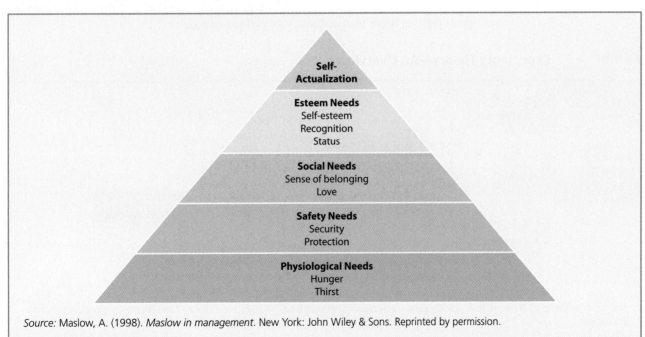

Source: Maslow, A. (1998). *Maslow in management.* New York: John Wiley & Sons. Reprinted by permission.

and even salary are hygiene factors rather than true motivators. According to the theory, the absence of hygiene factors can create job dissatisfaction, but their presence does not really motivate employees. The following factors strongly determine job satisfaction: achievement, recognition, the work itself, responsibility, and advancement.

Expectancy Theory

Expectancy theory focuses on the motivation people have to do work. In the workplace, people make many choices about what to focus on and how much effort to exert. Expectancy theory focuses on how people make choices among different types of behaviors and levels of effort. Expectancy theory is named for the fact that people are motivated to work when they expect that they will be able to achieve certain outcomes.

According to expectancy theory, a person's motivation to do work is a result of three different types of beliefs: **expectancy** (the belief that your efforts will result in performance), **instrumentality** (the belief that your performance will be rewarded), and **valence** (the perceived value of the rewards).[51] As can be seen in Exhibit 2.9, expectancy theory claims that motivation is a multiplicative function of all three components. This means that if any one of these factors is zero, the overall level of motivation will be zero.

As can be seen in Exhibit 2.9, the overall level of performance a person shows is not just a function of his or her motivation; skills and abilities matter as well. For example, a person may believe that he has medical expertise and can save lives, and he is highly motivated to do so; however, if he has never been to medical school, his job performance will be disastrous! In addition to skills and abilities, job performance is also affected by role perceptions, which is another way of saying what people believe is expected from them on the job.

Goal Setting

Employees who have specific, challenging goals perform at a higher level than employees with vague goals, such as "do your best."[52] (Think back to the Organizational Identity exercise in Chapter 1. Can you remember a time when you set a very high, particularly challenging goal?) Additionally, self-efficacy is important in goal setting.[53] People with high self-efficacy are more committed to assigned goals, find and use better strategies to attain their goals, and even respond more adaptively to negative feedback than do people with low self-efficacy. With respect to performing tasks, there are two goals that might guide your performance. On one hand, you might have a learning goal (which often involves engaging in a challenging task); on the other hand, you might have a performance goal, which involves the desire to demonstrate your competence.[54] People with learning goals perform better than do those with performance goals.[55]

EXHIBIT 2.9 Expectancy Theory—An Overview

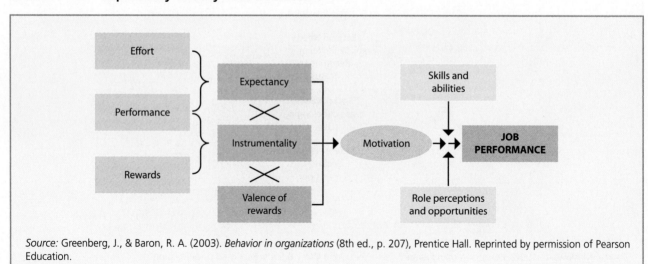

Source: Greenberg, J., & Baron, R. A. (2003). *Behavior in organizations* (8th ed., p. 207), Prentice Hall. Reprinted by permission of Pearson Education.

Motivations Vis-à-Vis Others

At any time, organizational actors might be concerned for themselves and their own welfare and concerned about the other party (see Exhibit 2.10).[56]

Of the several goals, three seem particularly relevant and common in most organizational enterprises: competitive goals (maximizing the difference between one's own and the other party's outcomes), self-interest goals, and cooperative goals.

Self-Efficacy

According to self-efficacy theory, people's beliefs in their own capabilities strongly influence how well they can perform a task, their persistence, and the choices they make. **Self-efficacy** is the belief in one's capabilities to organize and execute the sources of action required to manage prospective situations.[57] Self-efficacy is very situation-specific, meaning that a person might have very high self-efficacy when it comes to complex computer programming ability, but that same person might be low in self-efficacy for making a public speech. People with low self-efficacy in a particular domain will avoid behaviors and situations that call for that behavior. Most important, self-efficacy with regard to skill is something that can be learned. There are four sources of information that influence a person's self-efficacy:

- Performance accomplishments (e.g., experiences of successfully performing a given behavior)
- Vicarious learning or modeling (e.g., watching a role model perform a desired behavior)
- Verbal persuasion (e.g., a person might seek encouragement or support from others)
- Physiological arousal (e.g., a person's heartbeat and autonomic system might increase at the mere thought of performing a certain task, such as public speaking)

Self-efficacy is related to a variety of career-related behaviors[58] and also aids in understanding career development problems.[59] For example, the Occupational Self-Efficacy Scale

EXHIBIT 2.10 Messick and McClintock's Circumplex of Motivations

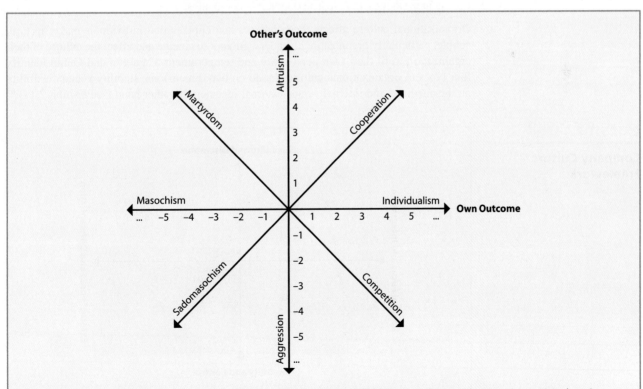

Source: McClintock, C. G., & van Avaermet, E. (1982). Social values and rules of fairness: A theoretical perspective. In V. Derlega & J. Grezlak (Eds.), *Cooperation and helping behavior* (pp. 43–71). New York: Academic Press. Reprinted by permission of Elsevier.

measures students' perceptions of self-efficacy with respect to the educational requirements and job duties of 20 occupations.

We now turn our attention to the other side of the behavior equation, focusing on the situational pressures that affect our behavior.

Organizational Culture

Corporate or organizational culture is essentially the personality of the organization. **Organizational culture** includes the values, norms, and outwardly visible signs of organizational members and their behaviors. Organizational culture reflects the shared beliefs of organizational members. Most people think that culture shapes organizational behavior; however, people (particularly organizational leaders) attempt to change the culture of their organizations to fit their own personality.[60] Consider four types of organizational culture:[61]

- *Academy culture:* Employees are highly skilled and tend to stay in the organization while working their way up the organizational hierarchy. The organization is a stable place where employees develop and exercise their skills. Examples include universities, hospitals, and large corporations that have been in existence for several decades.
- *Baseball team culture:* Employees are "free agents" who have highly valued skills. Individuals are in high demand and have options elsewhere. This type of culture characterizes fast-paced, high-risk organizations, such as investment banks, advertising agencies, and so forth.
- *Club culture:* In this culture, the key is to fit in. Usually employees start at the lowest ranks and work their way up the organization. The organization promotes from within and highly values senior members. Examples include the military and some law firms.
- *Fortress culture:* In this culture, there is often extensive and frequent reorganization and change is constant. Employees don't know if they will be laid off or promoted. There are opportunities for employees with timely, specialized skills. Examples include savings and loans and large car companies.

Organizational culture affects the behaviors and choices that individuals make; in turn, people, particularly organizational leaders, attempt to change and affect the culture of their organization to fit their own personality and temperament. Cameron and Quinn identify four types of organizational cultures based on two dimensions: stability versus flexibility on the one hand and internal versus external focus on the other hand (see Exhibit 2.11).[62]

EXHIBIT 2.11

Company Culture Framework

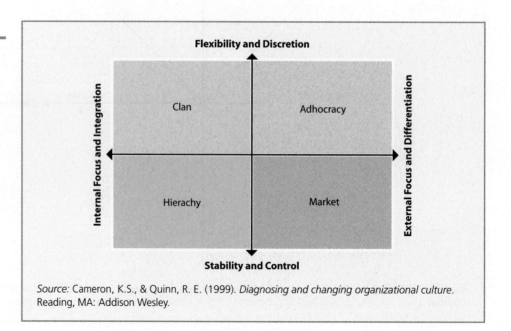

Source: Cameron, K.S., & Quinn, R. E. (1999). *Diagnosing and changing organizational culture.* Reading, MA: Addison Wesley.

As can be seen in Exhibit 2.11, the clan culture in the upper left is most similar to a family-type organization. Shared values and goals, a strong internal focus, cohesion, and participation all characterize organizations with clan cultures. These organizations often seem more like families than economic entities. Clan cultures believe that environments can best be managed through teamwork and employee involvement. One example of a clan culture is People Express Airlines in its first five years of operation.

The adhocracy culture in the upper right is the most responsive to hyper-turbulent conditions in volatile industries. The root of the word *adhocracy* is ad hoc, referring to a temporary, specialized, dynamic unit that assembles and then disbands around a particular goal. Aerospace, software, and think-tank consulting companies are all examples of adhocracy cultures.

The hierarchy culture in the lower left is the most traditional of company cultures in which bureaucratic decision making is in place (e.g., rules, specialization, and so on). Organizations such as McDonald's and Ford Motor Company are examples of the hierarchy culture. These organizations have strict rule manuals, very specific requirements for promotion, and well-articulated systems of command.

Finally, the market culture is in the lower right. The market refers to a type of organization that functions like a market itself. It is oriented toward the external environment (e.g., customers and clients); it is focused on transactions with external entities (such as suppliers and regulators); and unlike a hierarchy, which is maintained by rules, market cultures operate via market mechanisms, such as supply and demand, contracts, and competitive advantage. The core values in market cultures are competitiveness and productivity. GE (General Electric) is an example of a market culture company.

Organizational Norms

A **norm** is a generally agreed on set of rules that guides the behavior of people in organizations. Norms are not formal company rules; they differ from formal organizational policies in that they are unwritten. Because norms are expectations about appropriate behavior, they embody information about what people should do under various conditions. Often norms are so subtle that people are not consciously aware of them. Organizational norms regulate key behaviors such as honesty, manner of dress, punctuality, and emotional expression. Norms can either be **prescriptive**, dictating what should be done, or **proscriptive**, dictating behaviors that should be avoided. What are the norms in your current organization? Try to list five.

Norms are relevant to just about every aspect of organizational life, including dress as well as performance, and how much effort people generally apply to a problem. It is through the process of socialization that organizational members learn the roles they are expected to adopt and the norms they are expected to follow. And, if socialization tactics are not effective, group members often punish or ostracize those who fail to conform.

Psychological Contracts

Denise Rousseau began to see a pattern develop when studying organizational downsizing.[63] She realized that employees as well as companies hold a contract-like mental model of how people do work. A **psychological contract** is "an individual's subjective belief in the reciprocal nature of the exchange relationship between himself/herself and a third party, based on the promises made or implied in their interactions."[64] The psychological contract is predicated on the perception that an exchange of promises had been made (e.g., career opportunities, working conditions) to which both parties are bound. Even with the best of intentions from both the employee and employer, relationships can break down and the psychological contract can be violated. Think about your Organizational Identity exercise. In the full-time and part-time jobs that you have held, what were the psychological contracts?

EXHIBIT 2.12

Psychological Contracts

	Duration: short-term	Duration: long-term
Performance terms: clearly specified and articulated	Transactional: short-term, highly specified performance	Balanced: long-term, highly specified performance
Performance terms: unspecified	Transitional: no guarantees; short-term, unspecified performance	Relational: long-term, unspecified performance

Source: Rousseau, D. (1995). *Psychological contracts in organizations: Understanding written and unwritten agreements,* p. 34. Newbury Park, CA: Sage. Reprinted by permission of Sage Publications, Inc.

The key elements in a psychological contract are the expected time frame (short-term or long-term) and the performance (well specified and circumscribed versus unspecified and far-ranging; see Exhibit 2.12).

The PCI, or psychological contract inventory, is an instrument that assesses the existence of contracts held by employees and their companies. The **relational contract** is a long-term or open-ended employment arrangement based on mutual trust and loyalty. Rewards are only loosely conditioned on performance and derive from membership and participation in the organization. In contrast, the **transactional contract** characterizes employment arrangements with short-term or limited duration, primarily focused on economic exchange; specific, narrow duties; and limited worker involvement in the organization. The **transitional contract** is usually present when elements of an organization change, such as during a merger or acquisition, which often leads to uncertainty, distrust, and instability and potentially high levels of turnover. A **balanced contract** is the hybrid form of relational and transactional contracts where shared values and commitments are present alongside the need to attain specific business goals.

When performance requirements are clearly specified by employers and when employees hold realistic expectations of their organization, violations are less likely to occur. In virtual environments, in which employees are not physically co-located, there is an even greater need for communication about psychological contracts. There is a relationship between the Big Five and reactions to violations of psychological contracts.[65] In particular, people who are high in neuroticism are more likely to use transactional contracts, and people high in conscientiousness are more likely to use relational contracts.

Biases in Understanding Others

The biggest impediment to the accurate understanding of our own behavior and that of others is not the absence of measurement tools or the lack of scientific breakthroughs or models, but the person himself or herself. We also discuss some of these shortcomings in the chapter on decision making.

Fundamental Attribution Error

The fundamental attribution error is the tendency of people to ascribe dispositional reasons to explain the behavior of others and discount the impact of the situation.[66] People make internal attributions when they explain the behavior of others. For example, consider a boss attempting to understand why a particular employee is late to work. Using the concepts of this chapter, we know that there are several internal reasons that might explain this person's tardiness, such as not being motivated or being low in conscientiousness (one of the Big Five traits). However, there are also situational factors that might lead a person to be late for work, such as the fact that the company norms might dictate that late arrival is OK or that the psychological contract that the employee has with the company indicates that late arrival is acceptable. Of course, it is also possible that there was a transit strike and the train was late! Most people discount the powerful role of situational factors and make unwarranted dispositional attributions about a person's behavior (e.g., they assume the employee is unmotivated). This is problematic for several reasons. First, the person may be excessively relying on stereotypes about people to drive dispositional attributions. Second, when we make dispositional attributions for a person's behavior, we often treat the person in a way that engenders that very behavior. This process is known as the **self-fulfilling prophecy** or **behavioral confirmation** (see Exhibit 2.13).

Consistency Bias: Halos and Forked Tails

People's impressions of others have a high degree of internal consistency. What this means is that once we know one positive thing about someone, we tend to develop other positive beliefs about this person. For example, once we decide that someone is trustworthy, we also might decide that he or she is intelligent. So far, this sounds innocent enough. But consider that one of the most widely held biases is the physical attractiveness bias, the fact that physically attractive people are believed to be warmer and smarter than less attractive people.[67] The **halo effect** is the tendency to believe that people whom we trust and like are also intelligent and capable. The **forked tail effect** is the complementary bias: Once we have formed a negative impression about someone, we tend to view everything else about him or her in a negative fashion. (This is why it is so difficult to recover from making a bad impression.)

Primacy and Recency Bias

We form impressions of others on the basis of very limited information. Indeed, the entire process of forming an impression is largely automatic, using mostly the first pieces of information that we learn about someone.[68]

Bandwagon Bias

The bandwagon bias is the tendency for people to want to hold views similar to those of the people whom they believe represent the majority.

EXHIBIT 2.13   Self-Fulfilling Prophecy/Behavioral Confirmation

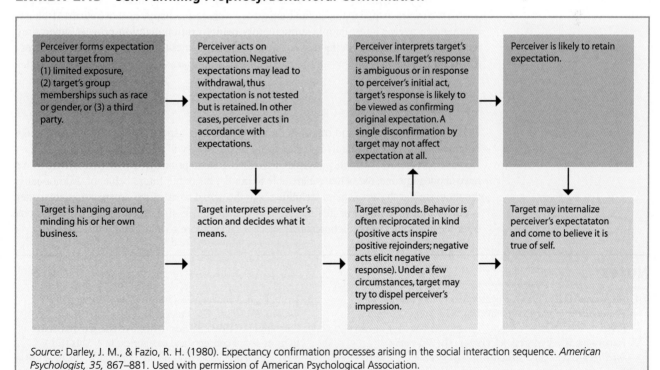

Source: Darley, J. M., & Fazio, R. H. (1980). Expectancy confirmation processes arising in the social interaction sequence. *American Psychologist, 35,* 867–881. Used with permission of American Psychological Association.

Roadblocks to Understanding Ourselves

In addition to the problems we encounter when attempting to understand the behaviors of others, we often lack insight into our own behaviors. There are five major ways that we delude ourselves.[69]

Unrealistic Optimism

Very smart people can act foolishly by thinking that they are too smart to be foolish. Unrealistic optimism is the tendency for people to believe that they are so smart that they can do whatever they want and not worry about the consequences. In short, people hold an inflated and erroneous view of themselves.

Self-Serving Bias/Egocentrism

Most people are motivated to maintain a favorable view of themselves, even if it means deluding themselves. In short, people give themselves more credit than others are willing to give them. This means, for example, that in a typical 360-degree evaluation, no matter how positive it may be, people will feel underappreciated by others.

Omniscience

Omniscience occurs when people believe they know everything and lack awareness of what they don't know. In short, they are unaware of their own limits.

Omnipotence

Omnipotence is the faulty belief people hold that they are all-powerful. Closely related is the illusion of invulnerability, in which people believe that they will get away with whatever actions they might engage in, no matter how inappropriate or irresponsible they may be.

The Powerful Process of Adaptation

As strange as it sounds, most people do not realize how much they are able to adapt to new situations. Most people severely underestimate their ability to adapt to both good news (e.g., winning the lottery) and bad news (e.g., being denied a job, a romantic breakup, an electoral defeat, negative personality feedback, or rejection by an employer).[70] For example, people who were denied tenure at their university were just as happy as those awarded tenure, when asked a year later. People immediately begin a rationalization process when they receive bad news, such as being denied tenure. When it comes to good news, people underestimate how much they will adapt to the good news. In this sense, people take it for granted.

Conclusion

Understanding ourselves and others is the most important aspect of management. We make judgments of people constantly and attempt to predict who will bring our organizations value. However, prediction is a highly complex task. As a general principle, the more information we have about someone, the better we are able to predict his or her future behavior. Additionally, the more similar the assessment technique is to the actual work of the organization, the better is our predictive ability. For this reason, assessment centers that simulate real organizations offer the possibility of predicting career success, much more so than does actual GPA.[71]

Notes

1. McAdams, D. P. (1985). *Power, intimacy and the life story: Personalized inquiries into identity.* New York: Guilford Press.
2. Herrnstein, R., & Murray, C. (1994). *The bell curve: Intelligence and class structure in American life.* New York: Free Press.
3. Lynn, R., & Vanhanen, T. (2002). *IQ and the wealth of nations.* Westport, CT: Praeger.
4. Dunning, D. (1993). Words to live by: The self and definitions of social concepts and categories. In J. Suls (Ed.), *Psychological perspectives on the self* (Vol. 4, pp. 99–126). Hillsdale, NJ: Lawrence Erlbaum.

5. Sternberg, R. J., & Kaufman, J. C. (1998). Human abilities. *Annual Review of Psychology, 49,* 479–502.

6. Sternberg, R. J., & Grigorenko, E. L. (1999, Spring). Myths in psychology and education regarding the gene-environment debate. *Teachers College Record,* 01614681, *100*(3).

7. Spearman, C. (1904). General intelligence, objectively determined and measured. *American Journal of Psychology, 15,* 201–293.

8. Rubin, R. S., Bartels, L. L., & Bommer, W. J. (2002). Are leaders smart or do they just seem that way? Exploring perceived intellectual competence and leadership emergence. *Social Behavior and Personality, 30,* 105–118.

9. Judge, T. A., Higgins, C. A., Thoresen, C. J., & Barrick, M. R. (1999). The Big Five personality traits, general mental ability, and career success across the life span. *Personnel Psychology, 52,* 621–652.

10. Sternberg, R. J. (1985). *Beyond IQ: A triarchic theory of human intelligence.* NewYork: Cambridge University Press.

11. Gardner, H. (1999). *The disciplined mind.* New York: Simon & Schuster.

12. Mayer, J. D., & Salovey, P. (1997). What is emotional intelligence? In P. Salovey and D. Sluyter (Eds.), *Emotional development and emotional intelligence: Implications for educators* (pp. 3–34). New York: Basic Books.

13. Publilius, S. (1961). Sententiae. In J.W. Duff & A. M. Duff (Eds.), *Minor Latin poets* (pp. 14–111). Cambridge, MA: Harvard University Press. (Original work written c. 100 BCE).

14. Darwin, C. (1872). *The expression of the emotions in man and animals.* New York and London: D. Appleton.

15. Flury, J., & Ickes, W. (2001). Emotional intelligence and empathic accuracy. In J. Ciarrochi, J. P. Forgas, and J. D. Mayer (Eds.), *Emotional intelligence in everyday life.* Philadelphia: Psychology Press.

16. James, R., & Blair, R. (2002). Theory of mind, autism and intelligence. In L. F. Barrett and P. Salovey (Eds.), *The wisdom in feeling.* New York: Guilford Press.

17. Muraven, M., & Baumeister, R. F. (2000). Self-regulation and depletion of limited resources: Does self-control resemble a muscle? *Psychological Bulletin, 126,* 247–259.

18. Baumeister, R. F., Bratslavsky, E., Muraven, M., & Tice, D. M. (1998). Ego-depletion: Is the active self a limited resource? *Journal of Personality and Social Psychology, 74,* 1252–1265.

19. Vohs, K. D., & Schmeichel, B. J. (2003). Self-regulation and the extended now: Controlling the self alters the subjective experience of time. *Journal of Personality and Social Psychology, 85,* 217–230.

20. Ciarrochi, J., Chan, A., Caputi, P., & Roberts, R. (2001). Measuring emotional intelligence. In J. Ciarrochi, J. P. Forgas, and J. D. Mayer (Eds.), *Emotional intelligence in everyday life.* Philadelphia: Psychology Press.

21. Mischel, W., Peake, P. K., & Shoda, Y. (1990). Predicting adolescent cognitive and self-regulatory competencies from preschool delay of gratification. *Development Psychology, 26,* 978–986.

22. Bar-On, R. (1997). *Bar-On Emotional Quotient Inventory (EQ-i): A test of emotional intelligence.* Toronto, Canada: Multi-Health Systems; Schutte, N. S., Malouff, J. M., Hall, L. E., Haggerty, D. J., Cooper, J. T., Golden, C. J., et al. (1998). Development and validation of a measure of emotional intelligence. *Personality and Individual Differences, 25,* 167–177.

23. Barchard, K. A. (2003). Does emotional intelligence assist in the prediction of academic success? *Educational and Psychological Measurement, 64*(3), 437.

24. Waldman, D. A., & Kobar, T. (2004). Student assessment center performance in the prediction of early career success. *Academy of Management Learning and Education, 3*(2), 151–167.

25. Sternberg, R. J., & Williams, W. M. (1997). Does the Graduate Record Examination predict meaningful success in the graduate training of psychologists? A case study. *American Psychology, 52,* 630–641.

26. Boyatzis, R. E., Stubbs, E., & Taylor, S. N. (2002). Learning cognitive and emotional intelligence competencies through graduate management education. *Academy of Management Journal on Learning and Education, 1*(2), 150–162.

27. Caruso, D., & Salovey, P. (2004). *The emotionally intelligent manager: How to develop and use the four key emotional skills of leadership.* San Francisco: Jossey-Bass.

28. Lopes, P. N., Brackett, M. A., Nezlek, J. B., Schutz, A., Sellin, I., & Salovey, P. (2004). Emotional intelligence and social interaction. *Personality and Social Psychology Bulletin, 30*(8), 1018–1034.

29. Bonanno, G. A., Papa, A., LaLande, K., Westphal, M., & Coifman, K. (2004). The importance of being flexible: The ability to both enhance and suppress emotional expression predicts long-term adjustment. *Psychological Science, 15,* 482–487.

30. Muraven, M., & Slessareva, E. (2003). Mechanisms of self-control failure: Motivation and limited resources. *Personality and Social Psychology Bulletin, 29,* 894–906.

31. Richards, J. M. (2004). The cognitive consequences of concealing feelings. *Current Directions in Psychological Science, 13,* 131–134.

32. Pennebaker, J.W. (1990). *Opening up: The healing power of confiding in others.* New York: Avon.

33. See note 27.

34. Mongrain, M., & Vettese, L. C. (2003, April). Conflict over emotional expression: Implications for interpersonal communication. *Personality and Social Psychology Bulletin, 29,* 545–555.

35. Tugade, M. M., & Frederickson, B. L. (2004). Resilient individuals use positive emotions to bounce back from negative emotional experiences. *Journal of Personality and Social Psychology, 86*(2), 320–333.

36. Galinsky, A. D. (1999). *Perspective-taking: Debiasing social thought.* Unpublished doctoral dissertation, Princeton University. Bazerman, M. H. & Neale, M. A. (1982). Improving negotiation effectiveness under final offer arbitration: The role of selection and training. *Journal of Applied Psychology, 67*(5), 543–548.

37. Gable, S. L., Reis, H. T., Impett, E. A., & Asher, E. R. (2004). What do you do when things go right? The intrapersonal and interpersonal benefits of sharing positive events. *Journal of Personality and Social Psychology, 87,* 228–245.

38. George, J. M. (1995). Leader's positive mood and group performance: The case of customer service. *Journal of Applied Social Psychology, 25,* 778–794.

39. Tan, H. H., Foo, M. D., & Kwek, M. H. (2004). The effects of customer personality traits on the display of positive emotions. *Academy of Management Journal, 47*(2), 287–296.

40. Karremans, J. C., Van Lange, P. A. M., Ouwerkerk, J. W., & Kluwer, E. S. (2003). When forgiveness enhances psychological well-being: The influence of interpersonal commitment. *Journal of Personality and Social Psychology, 84,* 1011–1026.

41. Hamilton, E., & Cairns, H. (Eds.) (1961). *The collected dialogs of Plato.* Princeton, NJ: Princeton University Press. Aristotle. (1976). *Ethics.* Trans. J. A. K. Thomason. London: Penguin.

42. Ewen, R. B. (1998). *Personality: A topical approach.* Mahweh, NJ: Erlbaum.

43. Saucier, G., & Goldberg, L. R. (1998). What is beyond the Big Five? *Journal of Personality, 66,* 495–524.

44. Whereas for most people the five-factor model and OCEAN are the same, among researchers, there are differences. They are treated similarly here for purposes of exposition.

45. Retrieved from http://edison.rutgers.edu/inventions.htm on May 8, 2006.

46. Freedman, J. L., Cunningham, J. A. & Krismer, K. (1992). Inferred values and the reverse-incentive effect on induced compliance. *Journal of Personality and Social Psychology, 62,* 357–368.

47. Kohn, A. (1993). *Punished by reward: The trouble with gold stars, incentive plans, A's, praise, and other bribes.* Boston, MA: Houghton Mifflin.

48. Eisenberger, R., & Selbst, M. (1994). Does reward increase or decrease creativity? *Journal of Personality and Social Psychology, 66,* 1116–1127.

49. Maslow, A. (1954). *Motivation and personality.* NewYork: Harper and Row.

50. Herzberg, F., Mausner, B., & Snyderman, B. (1959). *The motivation to work* (2nd ed.). New York: Wiley.

51. Porter, L. W., & Lawler, E. E. (1968). *Managerial attitudes and performance.* Homewood, IL: Irwin.

52. Locke, E, A., & Latham, G. P. (1990). *A theory of goal setting and task performance.* Englewood Cliffs, NJ: Prentice-Hall.

53. Locke, E. A., & Latham, G. P. (2002). Building a practically useful theory of goal setting and task motivation: A 35-year odyssey. *American Psychologist, 57,* 705–717.

54. Dweck, C. S., & Leggett, E. L. (1988). A social cognitive approach to motivation and personality. *Psychological Review, 95,* 256–273.

55. Seijts, G. H., Latham, G. P., Tasa, K., & Latham, B. W. (2004). Goal setting and goal orientation: An integration of two different yet related literatures. *Academy of Management Journal, 47,* 227–239.

56. Messick, D. M., & McClintock, C. G. (1968). Motivational basis of choice in experimental games. *Journal of Experimental and Social Psychology, 4,* 1–25.

57. Bandura, A. (1977). Self-efficacy: Toward a unifying theory of behavioral change. *Psychological Review, 84,* 191–215; Bandura, A. (1981). Self-referent thought: A developmental analysis of self-efficacy. In J. H. Flavell & L. Ross (Eds.), *Social cognitive development: Frontiers and possible futures* (pp. 200–239). Cambridge: Cambridge University Press.

58. Betz, N. E., & Hackett, G. (1981). The relationship of career-related self-efficacy expectations to perceived career options in college women and men. *Journal of Counseling Psychology, 28*(5), 399–410.

59. Hackett, G. (1995). Self-efficacy in career choice and development. In A. Bandura (Ed.), *Self-efficacy in changing societies* (pp. 232–258). New York: Cambridge University Press.

60. Bardkoll, G. L. (2001). *Individual personality and organizational culture* or *Let's change this place so I feel more comfortable.* Retrieved October 16, 2001, from www.pamij.com/barkdoll.html.

61. Sonnenfeld, J. (1988). *The hero's farewell.* New York: Oxford University Press.

62. Cameron, K., & Quinn, R. (1999). Diagnosing and changing organizational culture. Reading, MA: Addison-Wesley.

63. Harwood, R. (2002). The psychological contract and remote working: An interview with Prof. Denise M. Rousseau. *Ahoy Magazine.* Retrieved December 14, 2004, from http://www.odysseyzone.com/news/hot/rousseau.htm.

64. Rousseau, D. M. (1995). *Psychological contracts in organizations.* Thousand Oaks, CA: Sage.

65. Raja, U., Johns, G., & Ntalianis, F. (2004). The impact of personality on psychological contracts. *Academy of Management Journal, 47*(3), 350–368.

66. Ross, L. (1977). The intuitive psychologist and his shortcomings: Distortions in the attribution process. In L. Berkowitz (Ed.), *advances in experimental social psychology* (Vol. 10, pp. 173–220). Orlando, FL: Academic Press.

67. Dion, K., Berscheid, E., & Walster, E. (1972). What is beautiful is good. *Journal of Personality and Social Psychology, 24*(3), 285–290; Landy, D., & Sigall, H. (1974). Beauty is talent: Task evaluation as a function of the performer's physical attractiveness. *Journal of Personality and Social Psychology, 29,* 299–304.

68. Bargh, J. A., Lombardi, W. J., & Higgins, E. T. (1988). Automaticity of person x situation effects on impression formation: It's just a matter of time. *Journal of Personality and Social Psychology, 55,* 599–605.

69. Sternberg, R. J. (2004). Why smart people can be so foolish. *European Psychologist, 9*(3), 145–150.

70. Gilbert, D. T., Pinel, E. C., Wilson, T. D., Blumberg, S. J., & Wheatley, T. (1998). Immune neglect: A source of durability bias in affective forecasting. *Journal of Personality and Social Psychology, 75,* 617–638.

71. See note 24.

Chapter | 3

ETHICS AND VALUES

Everyone has encountered an ethical dilemma in life. Oftentimes, these dilemmas can be rather small, such as whether to inform a wait staff member that a restaurant has undercharged for a dinner. Other times, the dilemmas can be monumental, such as reporting a friend who has shoplifted or stolen property from a company. These situations are called "moments of truth."[1] Think about a moment of truth you have faced in your life. Focus on the exact point in time in which you felt that the situation transformed from "business as usual" into a situation in which a problem, temptation, or barrier arose. Who were the stakeholders involved? Next, focus on how you reacted once you recognized this "moment of truth." Did you act on impulse or emotion? Did you follow a recognized script or procedure? Or did you think through the situation, collect information, consider various courses of action, and act accordingly? Finally, what was the reaction of the stakeholders to your actions? Your analysis of how you behaved in the situation is the "moment of recognition" in which you hopefully gain insight into the ethical aspects of your behavior. As you read this chapter, think about how you might have reacted differently to this same situation.

Ethics and OB

Ethics is more important than ever because of the complexity of choice that we face in each decision we make. **Ethical thinking** is the cognitive means by which people reason when they are faced with situations that involve values. Ethical thinking is the systematic examination of ethical issues at a moment of truth to determine whether a person's actual or contemplated behavior is ethical or unethical. By this definition, altruism is not ethics. **Altruism,** or putting others' interests ahead of one's own interests, might be viewed as one type of ethical behavior, but ethics is a much larger domain than altruism.

Perhaps one reason why ethics is of monumental concern in organizations is that business people are considered highly self-interested and consequently willing to cut corners. For example, the business scandals such as that at Shell (described in Exhibit 3.1) have occurred across the corporate world, at companies that were once famous, but are now infamous: ImClone, Enron, Arthur Andersen, WorldCom, and the like.

In this chapter, we first define ethics. We return to our levels of analysis approach to make the point that ethical issues occur at all levels. Then we deal with the question of whether ethics can be taught. We discuss the conditions that often conspire to create perfect ethical storms. And, perhaps most important, we take up the question of how people can proactively deal with ethical decisions.

Moments of Truth

It is hard to go through a day without encountering something that might be considered to be an ethical issue or question. Every day we face "moments of truth." Exhibit 3.2 depicts the moment of truth and how our resulting behavior can be classified into three categories: unethical, normal, and praiseworthy.

Many times, moments of truth occur without our conscious realization that we have encountered them and certainly without deliberate ethical analysis. To help us better recognize and analyze moments of truth, let us identify four key phases in any given moment of truth (see Exhibit 3.3).

Exhibit 3.3 shows that the first phase is "business as usual" during which one or more people (moral agents) are pursing their own self-interests in a normal way. These people are in a steady state and face no particular crucial challenges (e.g., they might studying in the library). In the second phase, an opportunity or threat arises in an agent's field of action to which he or she must respond. This may come in the form of a barrier, problem, or

---

EXHIBIT 3.1 **Business Scandals at Shell**

For many decades, Royal Dutch Shell group had a culture of respect and formalism, perhaps to the point of lacking humor and appearing somber. In the 1990s, the Anglo-Dutch company embraced a new kind of management style that included meetings in which managers were told to shake their bodies and arms in energizer exercises, reveal personal secrets to their colleagues in trust-building games, blare rock music during business retreats, and enact skits based on Jerry Springer shows. But bad taste was not the only problem. Creative bookkeeping methods made it appear that Shell had vast energy reserves and such bookkeeping antics clearly violated SEC guidelines. The company used several accounting maneuvers to hide its failure to find energy and dramatically overstated its oil and gas reserves. Finally, Shell Exploration Chief Walter van de Vijver told his boss via e-mail that he was "sick and tired about lying" about reserves. Ultimately, Shell had to pay fines totaling over $150M. By most accounts, this cultural revolution led Shell into one of the worst business and ethical crises of its 115-year history. Although hindsight is 20–20, and it will never be possible to determine whether the new culture was indeed the causal factor in Shell's debacle, the company saw a strong connection and became hell-bent on changing it. As of 2004, Shell began attempts to restore the standards that made them the elite of the industry in the 1970s.

Source: Cummins, C., & Latour A. (2004, November 2). Changing drill: How Shell's move to revamp culture ended in scandal. *The Wall Street Journal*, A1.

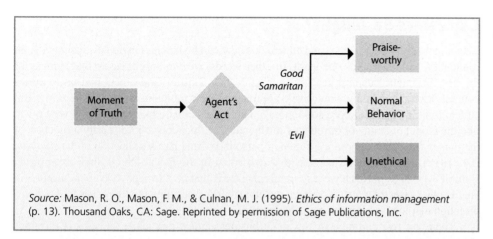

Source: Mason, R. O., Mason, F. M., & Culnan, M. J. (1995). *Ethics of information management* (p. 13). Thousand Oaks, CA: Sage. Reprinted by permission of Sage Publications, Inc.

EXHIBIT 3.2

Model of Ethical Consequences

temptation in the agent's way that forces the agent to respond to it (e.g., you might be tempted to tear out the pages of a library book because the copy machine is broken). This new situation involves a group of stakeholders, people who are affected or could be affected by the decision and who have an interest in its outcome (e.g., the library, future students who might want to check out the book). The point in time at which this challenge occurs is your moment of truth. It is the trigger point for change. The ultimate choice that a person makes will determine the final outcome and will also affect the stakeholders. This is the point at which ethical decisions are made. At the moment of truth, a person can respond in one of three ways: (1) act on impulse or emotion; (2) act based on habits or scripts; (3) act on the basis of decision and deliberate thought. Following the action, the stakeholders and the environment react. This feedback rebounds to the organizational actor and the ethical significance of his or her choices are revealed. This process results in a "moment of recognition," in which the agent gains insight into the ethical aspects of his or her behavior. Finally, there is a resolution during which the stakeholders and the actor come to terms with the action.

In summary, there are four key components: the agents and stakeholders, the moment of truth, the moment of recognition, and the resolution in which the ethical behavior may be analyzed. An ethical person is able to recognize moments of truth when confronted with them, reflect (versus simply react) when confronted with them, anticipate the moment of recognition (i.e., the impact on stakeholders), and arrive at an ethically defensible decision.

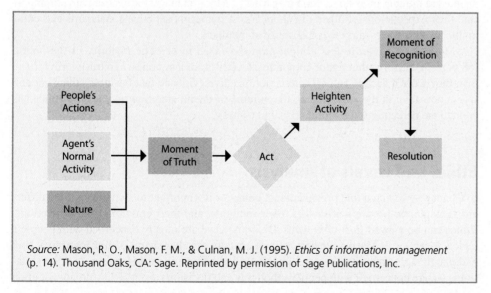

Source: Mason, R. O., Mason, F. M., & Culnan, M. J. (1995). *Ethics of information management* (p. 14). Thousand Oaks, CA: Sage. Reprinted by permission of Sage Publications, Inc.

EXHIBIT 3.3

Moment of Truth Model of Ethical Behavior

Can Ethics Be Taught?

Like almost everything, ethics and ethical thinking can be taught. Obviously, having a great foundation certainly helps one learn. In other words, we can only imagine that if many of the now infamous business leaders such as Jeffrey Skilling and others had taken ethics courses, then maybe they would have approached their moments of truth differently. But ethical thinking is not simply good morals. Our view is that ethical thinking is very much like the model of behavior introduced in Chapter 2: Ethical behavior is partly a function of the *person* (i.e., their upbringing and their personality) and partly a function of the *situation* (i.e., the company culture, such as that described in the Royal Dutch Shell example in Exhibit 3.1). The approach we take in this chapter is that people need to keep themselves in check; otherwise, they may be subject to "ethical drift," meaning that they start to move in a direction that they are not consciously aware of.

There are five common myths about business ethics that make the subject of ethics difficult to teach:[2]

Myth #1: It's easy to be ethical: A common misperception is that ethical decision making is clear and simple. Mantras such as "If it stinks, don't do it" pervade ethical thought. Such mantras do not do justice to the complexity surrounding ethical decision making. Ethical decisions often involve multiple stages, with the first being "moral awareness," then "moral judgment" (i.e., deciding that a specific action is morally justifiable), followed by "moral motivation" (i.e., the commitment to take the moral action), and finally "moral character" (persistence or follow-through).

Myth #2: Unethical behavior in business is simply the result of "bad apples": Or, "bad people do bad things and good people do good things." This myth arises from the fundamental attribution error: the tendency to attribute behavior to a person's disposition, and severely underplay the powerful situational pressures involved.

Myth #3: Ethics can be managed through formal ethics codes and programs: Most organizations have formal ethics and legal compliance programs that include written standards of conduct that are communicated and disseminated to employees, ethics training classes, and systems for reporting misconduct. For example, the Sarbanes-Oxley law, passed in 2002, requires corporations to set up an anonymous system for employees to report fraud and other unethical activities. However, it is important to realize that the presence of a formal program in no way guarantees effective ethics management; employees must believe that formal policies actually guide behavior, not just exist in unopened rulebooks.

Myth #4: Ethical leadership is mostly about the leader's integrity: The myth of ethical leadership focuses attention narrowly on individual character and qualities such as integrity, honesty, and fairness. Leaders must be moral people and moral managers. Moral people are thought of as honest and trustworthy. Moral managers are those who communicate their expectations of others. In short, moral managers set ethical standards and communicate ethical messages to organizational members.

Myth #5: People are less ethical than they used to be: The majority of the public (68 percent) believes that senior corporate executives are less honest and trustworthy today than they were a decade ago.[3] There is no objective evidence that business ethics are any worse now than in the past. Rather, the volume of media attention on business ethics has created the perception of a moral crisis in business.

Ethics and Levels of Analysis

In Chapter 1 we noted that organizational behavior is important to study from three different standpoints: people's behaviors, their thoughts, and their emotions and motivations. Ethics can be viewed in similar ways. Obviously, we are mostly concerned with people's ethical behavior. If Martha Stewart had not actually sold her shares of ImClone stock (but had just thought about it), she would not have served time in jail! However, in other situations, we are concerned with people's thoughts and decisions, even if they do not act upon them. Consider, for example, the radio DJ for the New York radio station that played a parody song regarding the victims of the 2004 tsunami.[4] The songwriter's harsh, inhumane comments undoubtedly reflected negatively on the radio station. Finally, we are concerned with emotion and motivation as well. We find ourselves disturbed when someone seems to take pleasure in another's ill fortune.

Keeping in mind the behavior, judgment, and emotion analysis, we can also use our four levels of analysis (also introduced in Chapter 1) to analyze ethical behavior. First, from an *intrapersonal standpoint,* do we think clearly and honestly about ethical situations or do we rationalize? A person's personal ethical standards represent the foundation of a much more complex ethical system. Perhaps of greatest concern to most people is **interpersonal ethics,** or how we treat others. Lying, cheating, stealing are all obvious examples of unethical behavior that directly harm others. Of greater concern to many people are behaviors that are on the borderline, such as "white lies." Group-level ethical behavior is played out every day in organizations, such as when people find themselves unable to speak up in a group meeting in which others are minimizing relevant concerns. In the 1990s, consultants at the Arthur Andersen consulting firm were pressured by colleagues to pad their prices. **Organizational ethics,** such as those depicted in the new culture at Royal Dutch Shell, are the norms that people are exposed to every day in their organization. In many senses, this has the most powerful impact on behavior. Our discussion of levels of analysis does not seem complete unless we consider a broader set of ethics, one that might apply to communities or indeed, to the world. This type of ethical thinking is "beyond a firm's boundaries."[5]

In organizations, people should consider four spheres of morality: (1) commitments of private life; (2) commitments of economic agents; (3) commitments of company leaders; and (4) responsibilities beyond the company's boundaries (see Exhibit 3.4).[6]

The commitments of private life consist of basic things that most people take for granted, such as telling the truth, keeping promises, not hurting others, and so on. The idea is that unless we are first a moral person, it is hard or impossible for us to be a moral manager. The commitments of economic agents transport the individual from private life to organizational life. Companies entrust their managers to work for shareholders' interests. And in this sense, market standards and the rational expectations model usually apply. Another sphere of responsibility is that of the company leader. As managers grow in power in their organizations, their influence over others increases dramatically. And such power requires responsibility—a topic we discuss in detail in Chapter 5. Finally, Badaracco's model suggests that managers' responsibilities do not stop at their firm's boundaries. Companies have complex relationships with government agencies, other firms, competitors, suppliers, customers, and so on.

The costs of ethical failures extend outward to consider a variety of stakeholders.[7] Exhibit 3.5 depicts three levels of business costs associated with ethical failures.

The level 1 costs of ethical failures are the easiest to calculate because they concern stakeholders of which executives are clearly aware: themselves, the company, and the government. In short, level 1 costs are the fines and penalties that result from a lawsuit or

Commitments of **private life** (as a person)	Commitments of **an economic agent** (as a manager)
Commitments of **company leadership** (as a leader and spokesperson)	Commitments **beyond the firm's boundaries** (as an embassador)

EXHIBIT 3.4

Four Spheres of Morality

Source: Badaracco, J. L. (1992). Business ethics: Four spheres of executive responsibility. *California Management Review, 34*(3), 64–79. Copyright © 1992, by The Regents of the University of California. Reprinted from the CALIFORNIA MANAGEMENT REVIEW, Vol. 34, No. 3. By permission of The Regents.

EXHIBIT 3.5   Business Costs of Ethical Failures

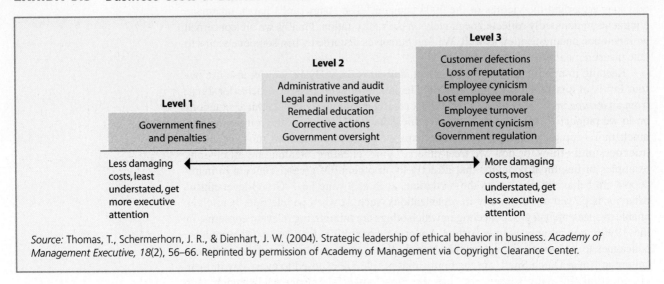

Source: Thomas, T., Schermerhorn, J. R., & Dienhart, J. W. (2004). Strategic leadership of ethical behavior in business. *Academy of Management Executive, 18*(2), 56–66. Reprinted by permission of Academy of Management via Copyright Clearance Center.

government decree. For example, in the Enron business scandal, the company's accounting firm received a fine of $500,000 in its sentencing for obstruction of justice. Level 1 costs are the least serious and most survivable burdens. Level 2 costs are primarily administrative in nature and refer to "cleanup" costs, including such costs as attorney and audit fees, investigative costs, and remedial actions. Level 3 costs are the most difficult to quantify and the most likely to be underappreciated by executives. They involve such things as customer distrust and defection, reputation loss, brand damage, morale loss, and ultimately increased government regulation. Can you think of a situation in which you suffered a cost because of somebody else's ethical failure?

Unethical Behavior as Incremental Descents into Wrongdoing

First, let's set the record straight: The great majority of people are good and intend to do good (obviously, there are exceptions). There is no one moment when an organizational actor sits down, draws the shades, and conspires to commit wrongdoing. Rather, "there is an incremental descent into poor judgment."[8] It would be naïve for anyone to believe that he or she will never face an ethical challenge or that ethical behavior is black and white. Ethical behavior is shades of gray. We cannot control what will happen to us (e.g., a sour business market, failure to obtain a desired patent), but we do have choices when it comes to how we react to events. We divide our discussion into cognitive mechanisms and social-situational mechanisms. The cognitive and social-situational factors that we discuss conspire to lead people astray.

Cognitive Mechanisms

Cognitive mechanisms reflect the way in which most people reason about situations that usually lead to effective decision making, but can sometimes lead people astray.

RATIONALIZATION   How could the unethical behavior of business leaders of Enron, WorldCom, and Parmalat have been committed by upstanding community members, givers to charity, and caring parents—hardly the profile of criminals.[9] Each was fully capable of **rationalization,** or "mental strategies that allow employees (and others around them) to view their corrupt acts as justified."[10] People may use rationalizations privately or collectively to neutralize any regrets or negative feelings resulting from unethical behavior. Six of the most common rationalizations that may lead to unethical behavior by business leaders include:[11]

- *Denial of responsibility:* A person perceives that there is no other choice than to participate in the (unethical) behavior.
- *Denial of injury:* A person convinces himself or herself that no one is harmed by their actions.
- *Denial of victim:* A person can vehemently argue that injured parties deserve whatever negative outcomes befall them (i.e., "they should not trust everyone").
- *Social weighting:* A person condemns the condemner and points to others that are worse in their behaviors (e.g., "You have no right to criticize me"; "Others have done worse things than me").
- *Appeal to higher loyalties:* A person argues that the violation of norms is due to their attempt to attain higher-order values (e.g., "I was trying to be loyal"; "I did not want to create hysteria").
- *Metaphor of the ledger:* A person rationalizes that he or she is entitled to indulge in unethical behaviors because they have accrued credits (time and effort) in their demanding leadership position ("I gave my life to the company").

NORM OF SELF-INTEREST The **norm of self-interest** refers to the pervasive *belief* that people are self-interested. In most business programs, the fundamental assumption of human behavior (and indeed the standard of rational thought) is the rational expectations model. The rational behavior model (which is reviewed in Chapter 7) holds that people should act in a way that maximizes their own utility. Most people construe the maximization of **utility** to be synonymous with the maximization of **self-interest,** and even more narrowly, the maximization of monetary gain. However, utility, as we clearly note in Chapter 6, can encompass the welfare and benefit of others. Yet, most people believe that others are motivated by self-interest and thus, they treat self-interest as a norm. As a case in point, people were asked why they contribute to charity.[12] In reality, many people contribute to charity or help victims of disasters because they want to engage in acts of goodness. However, people often explain their decisions to contribute to charity using the language of self-interest (e.g., a charitable donation improved their tax status and allowed beneficial write-offs).

When people suspect that others are motivated by self-interest, their own behavior changes in a way that is much more competitive. For example, negotiators who gain a reputation as tough bargainers meet with tougher demands by their peers.[13]

PLURALISTIC IGNORANCE **Pluralistic ignorance** refers to the fact that people are often completely unaware that others feel exactly the same way that they do. Perhaps the most well-known fable that depicts pluralistic ignorance is the story of the emperor with no clothes.[14] Recall in this Hans Christian Andersen story that an emperor is duped by a greedy clothier who charges the emperor exorbitant prices to make a grand set of new clothes. The clothier does not actually make any clothes for the emperor, but creates the illusion that only men of high intelligence and royalty can see the elegance of the clothes. When the emperor parades naked in the street, the entire town pretends to see the beautiful clothes. Each person privately cannot see the clothes, but falsely believes everyone else does—hence, pluralistic ignorance. (In the story, a small child emerges as a whistle-blower.)

In companies, similar situations occur at an ethical level when certain company employees act in an unethical fashion. Everyone privately regards the behavior to be questionable (such as the analyst in the Royal Dutch Shell Company). Yet, no one takes action.

Related to pluralistic ignorance is the bystander effect.[15] The **bystander effect** refers to the tendency for any given individual to not intervene as the number of perceived other social factors increases. This phenomenon was first applied to account for why no one in a densely populated neighborhood in New York City did anything to help a woman who was murdered outside her apartment building. The woman, Kitty Genovese, was stabbed to death with over 30 "witnesses" failing to help her. In the classic study testing the bystander effect, participants who believed a person was having an epileptic seizure were more likely to go for help when they thought they were alone than when they thought there were other people that also heard the man having a seizure. The bystander effect is attributed to the diffusion of responsibility, where responsibility is not explicitly assigned and as a result individuals feel a sense of responsibility to help in the situation.

DESENSITIZATION **Desensitization** refers to the fact that people's sensitivity to almost anything may decay over time. For example, consider how people might react to a loud noise. A person sitting in a quiet library might be extremely startled to hear a cell phone ringing. However, if the library contained other noises, particularly loud ones, that person may be desensitized to the sound of a cell phone. Now consider ethical behavior. A person in an organization that has extremely high standards might experience a great deal of shock to witness someone falsely reporting an earnings statement. However, the same person might have a more muted reaction to a false earnings statement if there is a great deal of "questionable" behavior and actions taking place in the organization.

Social-Situational Mechanisms

Social-situational mechanisms are often triggered by certain cues in the environment, with the most notable being peer pressure.

SOCIALIZATION   Unethical acts in organizations are usually accompanied by socialization tactics in which newcomers entering corrupt units or departments are induced to accept and practice the same unethical behaviors. Three common socialization practices based on a review of white-collar crime include (1) co-optation; (2) incrementalism; and (3) compromise.

In **co-optation** rewards are used to change attitudes regarding unethical behaviors. This might be in the form of incentives, either financial or social. Co-optation is often subtle, and the persons affected may not realize that they have changed their standards so that they can benefit from the rewards associated with unethical behavior.

Incrementalism involves the socialization, particularly of newcomers, in unethical behavior. Usually, a newcomer is first encouraged to engage in an act that may be only slightly unethical. Engaging in this act creates cognitive dissonance (i.e., a person's beliefs about what is right conflict with his or her actual behavior). To relieve the dissonance, the person rationalizes.[16]

Finally, in **compromise,** people essentially resolve their concerns about ethical standards and their own behavior by adopting a midpoint. These three forms of socialization are not mutually exclusive and often occur in combination and reinforce one another.

CONFORMITY PRESSURE   Conformity occurs when people bring their behavior in alignment with what they believe to be a group's expectations and beliefs. **Conformity pressure** occurs when a group persuades an individual to agree with them in belief and in behavior. For example, employees of Arthur Andersen consulting firm were trained to adopt the "Andersen Way," which in the early days contained strong ethics. Andersen himself often told employees, "Think straight, talk straight."[17] Thus, conformity pressure when it aligns around ethical principles can actually be a good thing. However, the same social-psychological principles, when based on unethical principles, can be extremely problematic. Conformity pressure on the individual manager is greatest when the rest of the group is unanimous.[18] Conformity pressure is greater when people value and admire their teams.[19] Most people underestimate the conformity pressures that operate in groups. Perhaps this is because they like to think of themselves as individuals.

RESOURCE SHORTAGES AND COMPETITION When people encounter scarce resources, they experience realistic group conflict.[20] When resources are scarce, people are especially likely to "cut corners." An elaborate business computer game challenge played by University of Texas business students showed how competition can bring out the worst in business managers. During the first phase of the multi-day computer game, students made righteous and idealistic choices, such as investing in collaborative team training and reducing their own executive compensation. However, when a revenue race began between three competitor companies, students' behaviors changed: They concealed the fact that their employees were using pirated software, they postponed action in a sexual harassment suit in their own company, and they put their own employees at risk by failing to evacuate them when they had knowledge of an imminent terrorist attack—all in a race to make their numbers. One student, who actually role-played an ethics officer in a simulated company, said, "I never thought I'd make choices that way. But it was as if the business was yelling at me, 'You've got to get production . . . you've got to get production' . . . I made the wrong choice."[21]

Ethical Breaches

We've been talking about unethical behavior as though it were of one, consistent, broad type. However, unethical behavior can vary in kind and intensity. Unethical behavior can be small or large in scale. And, its effects can be minuscule or far-reaching. For example, the scandals that occurred at Sunbeam, Enron, Global Crossing, Qwest, and WorldCom cost investors more than $300 billion and put tens of thousands of people out of work.[22]

In an effort to understand why people may "bend the rules," over 100 executives from Academy of Management's Advisory Panel were asked to indicate why management bends rules and what they risk in doing so.[23] Three key rationales emerged from the data: performance-based judgment calls, faulty rules, and socially embedded norms. **Performance-based judgment calls** (which 74 percent of the executives surveyed admit to) are managerial decisions to bend the rules for the purpose of enhancing individual or organizational performance. People tell themselves that by bending the rules, the outcome will be more fair, more efficient, and more beneficial for the company in the long run. One of the most commonly observed performance-based judgment calls are company travel policies, which seem to be viewed as a type of recognition or reward for outstanding performance. **Faulty rules** (which 70 percent of executives admit to) are company policies that are ambiguous, out-of-date, or simply wrong in the eyes of the manager and therefore, subject to creative revision. Well-known "loopholes" in company policies are often exercised for the sake of convenience. **Socially embedded norms** (47 percent of executives report this) primarily reflect a perceived lack of respect for rules by people in the company. The adage "No one expects strict adherence to the rules" and an outright disdain for playing by the rules are examples.

Prescriptive Ethical Models

Ethical behavior, like almost anything else, involves constant practice. We've discussed ethical drift, but the world is constantly changing and we are confronted with new technologies that create unprecedented ethical challenges. We believe that people who have prepared properly are in the best position to approach the unannounced ethical challenges with the most effectiveness. We introduce three ethical models here. Ideally, you should adopt one to serve as your guide in organizational life.

Mason, Mason, and Culnan's Six Questions

Mason, Mason, and Culnan put forth a six-step prescriptive model for resolving ethical issues (see Exhibit 3.6).

As can be seen in Exhibit 3.6, the first question we should ask when we sense a moment of truth is, "What are the facts?" This step involves identifying the key people

EXHIBIT 3.6

Prescriptive Model for Resolving an Ethical Issue

1. What are the facts?
2. What ethical principles, standards, or norms should be applied?
3. Who should decide?
4. Who should benefit from the decision?
5. How should the decision be made?
6. What steps should be taken to prevent this issue from occurring again?

Source: Mason, R. O., Mason, F. M., & Culnan, M. J. (1995). *Ethics of information management.* Thousand Oaks, CA: Sage. Reprinted by permission of Sage Publications, Inc.

involved and, more importantly, the stakeholders and their motivations. The second question asks, "What ethical principles, standards, or norms should be applied?" In this step, the relevant ethical considerations are applied to the facts. Steps 1 and 2 provide the basis for corrective vision and for resolving a given issue: The ethical principles brought forward for consideration can be used to interpret the facts of the case and arrive at a preliminary moral judgment. The third question, "Who should decide?" focuses on two key considerations: the need for participation by all the relevant parties and issues of legitimacy. There is a tendency for organizational leaders to make ethical decisions in isolation from other parties. So a first consideration is whether all the relevant players are participating. Many executives play out an internal dialogue by imagining what their mother or father would say to them. The fourth question, "Who should benefit from the decision?" focuses on identifying the several stakeholders that are affected by the decision and appropriately weighting their interests. Decision makers need to balance each of these concerns. Question 5, "How should the decision be made?" reflects the important issue of procedural justice. The method by which any ethical decision is made must be fair and follow established procedures. Ideally, organizations should establish a set of procedures before an ethical crisis arises. Such procedures identify the parties who have authority to comment and veto decisions. Finally, question 6, "What steps should be taken to prevent this issue from occurring again?" is often overlooked. Organizational leaders must realize that all decisions they make will become part of their organization's historical transcript. In short, ethical decision makers must ask themselves how they want to affect the future (as well as rectify the past).

Badaracco's Four Enduring Questions

According to Badaracco, people who hold power in organization need to think carefully about four key questions when attempting to resolve a difficult dilemma (see Exhibit 3.7):[24]

- Which course of action will do the most good and the least harm?
- Which alternative best serves others' rights, including shareholders' rights?
- What plan can I live with, which is consistent with the basic values and commitment of my company?
- Which course of action is feasible in the world as it is?

The first question, "What will do the most good and the least harm?" focuses on the morality of consequences and is John Stuart Mills's question based on utilitarianism (morally good actions bring the best consequences for everyone they affect and do so with the least cost, risk, and harm). Consider the consequences relating to use of the drug RU-486: the survival of the Roussel Uclaf company, the health and safety of millions of women who might use RU-486, the health of people with diseases that might be treated with RU-486, and issues of the morality, politics, and regulation of abortion.

The second question focuses on the morality of rights and is reflective of Thomas Jefferson's Declaration of Independence: Human beings have inalienable rights to life, liberty, and the pursuit of happiness. Business executives, in a complementary fashion, have duties to respect the rights of their stakeholders.

EXHIBIT 3.7

Badaracco's Four Enduring Questions

John Stuart Mill:
Consequences

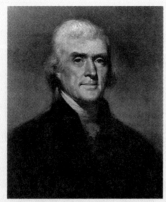

Thomas Jefferson:
Rights

Aristotle:
Integrity

Machiavelli:
Practicality

Source: Badaracco, J. L. (1992). Business ethics: Four spheres of executive responsibility. *California Management Review, 34*(3), 64–79. Copyright © 1992, by The Regents of the University of California. Reprinted from the CALIFORNIA MANAGEMENT REVIEW, Vol. 34, No. 3. By permission of The Regents.

The third question is rooted in Aristotle's philosophy: What kind of human community are we seeking to create? This question asks executives who face difficult decisions to search their consciences, and to ask how they want to be remembered.

The fourth question is Machiavelli's question and is purely pragmatic: What will work in the world as it is? What is actually feasible, given the current constraints? For some people, this question is amoral because it focuses on the ends, not the means, and it does not consider the morality of the means.

Anand, Ashforth, and Joshi's Method for Dealing with Rationalization and Socialization of Unethical Behavior

Companies need to understand how to combat rationalization and socialization before they become ingrained in the corporate culture. Prevention and cure strategies are depicted in Exhibit 3.8.

In terms of prevention, fostering awareness among employees is an act of consciousness-raising. Once employees are made aware of the rationalization and socialization tactics they can identify these behaviors in themselves and others more readily. The "headline" or "front-page" test is the mental simulation in which an employee imagines that all of his or her actions are reported in the newspaper for all to see.

EXHIBIT 3.8

Prevention and Cure of Rationalization and Socialization of Unethical Behavior

Focus on Prevention

- Foster awareness among employees
- Use performance evaluations that go beyond numbers
- Nurture an ethical environment in the organization
- Have top management serve as role models

Reversing Rationalization and Socialization

- Avoid denial and move quickly
- Involve external change agents
- Remain aware and vigilant

Source: Anand, V., Ashforth, B., & Joshi, M. (2004). Business as usual: The acceptance and perpetuation of corruption in organizations. *Academy of Management Executive, 18*(2), 39–53.

The use of performance evaluations that go beyond numbers is often thought to be too difficult and too messy. However, evaluations based on numeric outcomes only (such as sales quotas) significantly increase the likelihood of unethical activity in organizations. This prescription suggests that companies pay attention not only to whether the numbers are met, but how the numbers are met.

Nurturing an ethical environment in the organization is a matter of organizational culture. Many companies have adopted an explicit code of ethics; but to be effective, the code of ethics must be supported by organizational structures and policies. Employees who have misgivings or uncertainties about a course of action should have access to mechanisms that allow them to discuss the issues with an independent corporate representative (e.g., ombudsperson or ethics officer). The ombudsperson does not maintain names in his or her records. Second, an organization should have strong verification procedures in place for code-compliance during key activities. For example, Shell managers are required to certify that "neither the company nor its authorized representatives has been party to the offering, paying, or receiving of bribes."[25]

Ethical Rules of Thumb

In addition to the multi-step prescriptive models described above, we introduce several rules of thumb that the organizational actors should consider.

Front-Page Test

The front-page test, or light-of-day test, poses the following ethical challenge: Would you be completely comfortable if your actions and statements were printed in full on the front page of your city's newspaper or reported on the TV news? If not, then your behavior or strategies in question may be regarded as unethical. Another version: How would you feel if you had to stand before your organization's board of inquiry and describe what you have done?

Role Modeling

Would I advise others to do what I am doing? Would I be proud to see my child act the way I have acted in my organization? What if everyone acted this way? Would the resulting organizational culture be desirable?

Third-Party Advice

Too often, people struggle silently with ethical issues. It is appropriate and educational to consult third parties about ethical issues.

Policies

Often the best place to start resolving an ethical issue is by educating yourself with the current, relevant organizational policies and procedures. Ask questions. Ask for information.

Accountability

Organizational actors who view themselves as accountable to their organization and its stakeholders start to hold a view more like that of the CEO.

Conflicts of Interest

Educate yourself about the most common forms of conflict of interest before you are faced with an actual situation. Ask business partners and colleagues how they experience conflicts of interest and how they handle the situation. Create a personal standard before you are confronted with an actual situation.

Conclusion

Too often, students of OB think that ethical issues are relegated to the top management office. In this chapter, we've made the point that ethical issues and challenges arise every day. It is not a question of whether you will face an ethical issue (you will), it is a question of how you will respond to that situation. We've argued that awareness of the most common ethical breaches is worth a pound of cure. We've taken the point of view that ethics can be taught. Moreover, ethics is not simply "being a good person." It certainly helps to be a "good person," but that is no guarantee that managers will behave in an ethical fashion when faced with a moment of truth. We've argued that unethical organizational behavior is insidious and that there is no one moment when people conspire to commit wrongdoing. In fact, most people do not even perceive a situation as an ethical challenge: therefore, part of ethics education is raising awareness. We discussed cognitive mechanisms that lead to unethical behavior (rationalization, pluralistic ignorance, desensitization) and social-situational mechanisms (socialization, conformity pressure, resource shortages, and stress). We outlined perspective models for dealing with ethical issues.

Notes

1. Mason, R. O., Mason, F. M., & Culnan, M. J. (1995). *Ethics of information management.* Thousand Oaks, CA: Sage.
2. Trevino, L., & Brown, M. (2004). Managing to be ethical: Debunking five business ethics myths. *Academy of Management Executive, 18,* 69–83.
3. Big majority believes tough new laws needed to address corporate fraud; modest majority at least somewhat confident that Bush will support such laws. (2002, July 27). *PR Newswire.*
4. NAPABA denouces morally and racially radio programming in NYC. (2005, February 5). *Asianconnections.com.* Retrieved from http://www. asianconnections.com/news. php?news_id=56.
5. Badaracco, J. L. (1995). *Business ethics: Four spheres of executive responsibility.* Chicago: Richard D. Irwin, Inc.
6. Ibid., p. 229.
7. Thomas, T., Schermerhorn, J. R., & Dienhart, J. W. (2004). Strategic leadership of ethical behavior in business. *Academy of Management Executive, 18*(2), 56–66.
8. Charan, R., & Useem, F. (2002). Why companies fail. *Fortune, 145*(11), 50–62.
9. Anand, V., Ashforth, B., & Joshi, M. (2004). Business as usual: The acceptance and perpetuation of corruption in organizations. *Academy of Management Executive, 18*(2), 39–53.
10. Ibid., p. 39.
11. Ibid., p. 41.
12. Miller, D. T. (1999). The norm of self-interest. *American Psychologist, 54*(12), 1053–1060.
13. Tinsley, C. H., O'Connor, K. M., & Sullivan, B. A. (2002). Tough guys finish last: The perils of a distributive reputation. *Organizational Behavior & Human Decision Processes, 88*(2), 621–642.
14. Andersen, H. C. (1837, 1948). The emperor's new suit. In H. C. Andersen, *Shorter Tales* (trans. Jean Hersholt). New York: Heritage Press.
15. Latane, B., & Darley, J. M. (1968). Group inhibition of bystander intervention in emergencies. *Journal of Personality and Social Psychology, 10*(3), 215–221.
16. Ashforth, B. E., & Anand, V. (2003). The normalization of corruption. *Research in Organisational Behavior, 25,* 1–52.
17. Trevino, L. K., & Brown, M. E. (2004). Managing to be ethical: Debunking five business ethics myths. *Academy of Management Executive, 18,* 74.
18. Asch, S. (1956). Studies of independence and conformity. A minority of one against a unanimous majority. *Psychological Monographs, 70*(9, Whole No. 416); Allen, V. L., & Wilder, D. A. (1977). Social comparison, self evaluation, and conformity to the group. In J. M. Suls & R. L. Miller (Eds.), *Social comparison processes: Theoretical and empirical perspectives* (pp. 187–208). New York: Hemisphere.
19. Back, K. W. (1951). Influence through social communication. *Journal of Abnormal and Social Psychology, 46,* 9–23.

20. Campbell, D. T. (1965). Ethnocentric and other altruistic motives. In D. Levine (Ed.), *Nebraska symposium on motivation* (pp. 283–301). Lincoln: University of Nebraska Press.

21. McCartney, S. (2004, May 10). Business simulation tests ethical decision-making. *The Wall Street Journal.*

22. Byrne, J. A. (2002b, August 12). Fall from Grace. *Business Week,* 51–56.

23. Veiga, J. F., Golden, T. D., & Dechant, K. (2004). Why managers bend company rules. *Academy of Management Executive, 18*(2), 84–91.

24. Badaracco, J. L. (1992). Business ethics: Four spheres of executive responsibility. *California Management Review, 34*(3), 64–79.

25. Berenbeim, R. (2000). Global ethics. *Executive Excellence, 17*(5), 7.

Chapter
4

COMMUNICATION

Think about an important event in your life (such as graduation, a major performance, a special trip, etc.). First, write a narrative account for that event, being very careful to focus on how time unfolded and what you were doing at each point in time. Focus also on how you were feeling at each point in time. Second, write a new paragraph about the same event, but this time, write it in third person and be as fact-based as you can. Don't refer to feelings, but instead, use descriptive words to describe how things look, much as a scientist would. Then, tell your first story (the narrative account) to someone and make a note of how engaged the listener is. Tell your scientific account to a different person. Make a note of how interested the person is when listening to you. Do the same thing for the lecture in one of your classes. First, create an "account" of the lecture that is based on narrative and includes much story. Second, create an "account" of the lecture that is totally fact-based. Give both accounts to a friend who missed the lecture. Ask your friend which account he or she got more out of.

Most people find that the first account—the personal narrative—is more engaging and interesting. Why, then, do so many public speakers resort to boring, dry speeches when given the chance to communicate? In this chapter, we focus on the principles of communication in organizations.

Communication is the dynamic process of transmitting and receiving meaningful information.[1] Whereas most of us want communications to be clear and effective in business organizations, we don't want the wrong people to effectively communicate. Or, put another way, there is an implicit assumption that communication should be used for constructive purposes, rather than destructive purposes (such as the failed terrorist plot described in Exhibit 4.1).

People in organizations may choose to make decisions, choose to negotiate, or select a change management program, but communication is something that we don't have the luxury of engaging in or not. Communication is ubiquitous and fundamental, and people who join organizations are expected to be proficient at it. Although we communicate in organizations, it is not a guarantee that we are effective or skilled communicators.

We begin this chapter by introducing the fundamental communication model. We then introduce a dynamic communication model based on social construction. We analyze communication challenges at each of the critical levels of analysis used in this book: individual, interpersonal, group, and organizational. We focus also on nonverbal communication. We broach the topic of communicating via information technology in Chapter 14, "The Virtual Workplace."

Basic Communication Model

The basic model of communication, introduced by Shannon and Weaver, describes how information is directly and linearly transmitted from the sender to the intended recipient.[2] The only disruption in the process is "noise."[3] This basic communication model essentially describes communication as a conduit model. The fundamental communication model involves several key elements: the message source (or sender, encoder), the message (or code, information, meaning), a channel (or medium), and a receiver (target, decoder, or listener). See Exhibit 4.2.

In the model, communication progresses from one stage to the next in a relatively linear process. The linear communication model allows for various refinements and elaborations, such as in the case where the sender and receiver give each other feedback regarding the effectiveness of the communication attempt.[4] Further, various social-contextual factors, including characteristics of the receiver and sender, goals of the interactants, and various aspects of the situation affect the success of the communication attempt.[5] Communication is a disjunctive task, such that if there is a breakdown in one step or process, the final outcome suffers. In short, communication is only as strong as the weakest link.

Sender

The **sender** is the individual, group, or organizational unit that needs or wants to share information with some other individual, group, or organization to accomplish a

EXHIBIT 4.1   The Communication of Terrorism

In June of 2003, Iyman Faris, an Ohio trucker, admitted to working with al Qaeda to plan a terrorist attack in the United States. Faris plotted to destroy New York's Brooklyn Bridge and derail a passenger train. Faris disguised himself as a truck driver but he actually led a secret life. The plot to blow up the Brooklyn Bridge by cutting the suspension cables supporting the bridge involved an intense series of communications between Faris and key al Qaeda operatives, including Khalid Sheikh Mohammed. Because Faris and his al Qaeda operatives suspected that their communication might be intercepted, they developed a code to convey key aspects of their plan: "gas cutters" (which could be used to burn through the bridge cables) were referred to as "gas stations"; similarly tools for derailing trains were referred to as "mechanics shops." After scouting the bridge and determining its security and structure would not allow Feris to complete the terrorist mission he passed a message to al Qaeda that simply said, "The weather is too hot."

Source: CNN.com, June 19, 2003.

EXHIBIT 4.2   Basic Communication Model

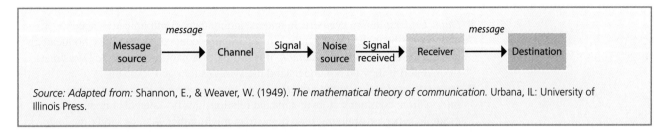

Source: Adapted from: Shannon, E., & Weaver, W. (1949). *The mathematical theory of communication.* Urbana, IL: University of Illinois Press.

communication goal. The sender originates the message and is responsible for the initial transmission of a message.

Receiver

The **receiver** (or decoder) is the individual, group, or organizational unit for which the information is intended. The receiver may be obvious, as in the case of a memo or letter addressed to a specific person, or it may be implicit, such as when a "general departmental memo" is circulated, but the topical matter deals with the actions of a certain person. The receiver needs to decode the message.

Message or Information

The **message** is the information that a sender needs or wants to share with other people. The message includes the details, language, and nuance of the communication. Effective communication depends on messages that are as clear and complete as possible. A message is *clear* when it contains information that is easily interpreted or understood. A message is *complete* when it contains all the information necessary to achieve a common understanding between the sender and receiver.

INTELLECTUAL BANDWIDTH The greater the intellectual bandwidth a person has, the more he or she can successfully encode messages. Consider Exhibit 4.3.

EXHIBIT 4.3

The Hierarchy of Understanding

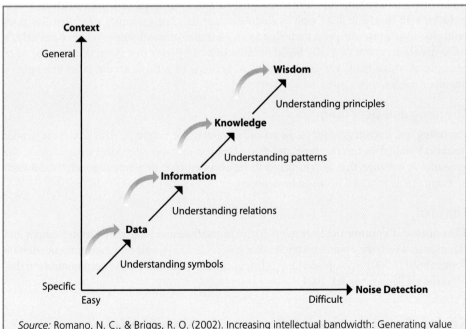

Source: Romano, N. C., & Briggs, R. O. (2002). Increasing intellectual bandwidth: Generating value from intellectual capital with information technology. *Group Decision and Negotiation, 11*(2), 69–86. Reprinted by permission.

In Exhibit 4.3, we see that the process of understanding a message depends on the degree of noise detection and the context.

- *Data: Understanding symbols.* In understanding data, communicators need to understand the meaning of symbols in a particular context, as data have no meaning outside the context. As an example, it is difficult for people to read the Dow Jones stock report if they do not understand the symbols for each company.
- *Information: Understanding relationships among symbols.* In understanding information, communicators understand relationships between data items. As an example, a person applying for a home loan might notice that the larger the loan applied for, the higher the interest rate.
- *Knowledge: Understanding patterns in information.* In understanding knowledge, people must understand the patterns that emerge from information. For example, a female executive might notice a pattern in which women's advancement in the organization is blocked at certain levels of performance review.
- *Wisdom: Understanding principles.* Wisdom entails understanding the causes and consequences in patterns. As an example, Nobel laureate Daniel Kahneman and collaborator Amos Tversky developed a theory of loss aversion to explain why decision makers exhibit preference reversals evaluating certain kinds of gambles.

To create value for the organization, communicators must be able to share their ideas, knowledge, and wisdom. A person's **intellectual bandwidth,** then, is a function of her or his capacity to transform data into wisdom.[6]

Communication Medium

The **communication medium** refers to the mode or method of communication (e.g., print, speech, video, electronic, etc.). There are nearly endless possibilities, ranging from face-to-face to computer-mediated. As a general principle, there are more potential channels of information available to a person who communicates face-to-face. Therefore, understanding is often greater in a face-to-face situation. We focus on the topic of communication modality in Chapter 14, "The Virtual Workplace."

Noise

Noise refers to anything that blocks a signal or makes a signal difficult to detect. Noise includes both mechanical as well as linguistic barriers. For example, a fax that has poor print due to a worn-out print cartridge is an example of mechanical noise. Similarly, a voice mail that cannot be easily heard because of a cell phone that is out of area is another example. A voice mail that cannot be heard because of a thick accent is an example of linguistic noise.

Encoding and Decoding

Encoding and **decoding** refer to the terms, symbols, and language with which the sender (encoder) embodies the message and those that the receiver (decoder) uses to parse the message. A message that is sent needs to be encoded (put in a language, etc.), and each message that is received needs to be decoded.

Context

The **context of communication** refers to the immediate and long-term circumstances and situation in which the communication takes place. Certainly, cell phone communication on September 11, 2001, took place in a different context than cell phone communication that occurred on September 10, 2001.

Social-Constructionist Communication Model

Many people believe that the mechanistic communication model described above does not adequately capture the true essence of communication.[7] Instead of a one-way flow of information through discrete steps, the "new look" at communication views it as a much more social-dynamic process involving the creation of meaning between interactants, shared understanding, mutual socialization and adaptation, and the creation of personal and social identities.[8]

Social Meanings Model

The **social meanings model** examines how nonverbal cues, such as gestures, touch, interpersonal distance, and eye gaze, are used along with verbal language in social interaction.[9] Burgoon and colleagues distinguish between structure and function of nonverbal communication in their treatment of unspoken dialogue.[10] Examining one cue (e.g., eye gaze) in isolation from others (e.g., touch, forward lean, etc.) cannot provide as much insight into the meaning of the communication as would examining cues that work in concert.

Collaborative Model

The **collaborative model** of communication focuses on how both parties of the conversation work together to ensure that they have a common understanding of each utterance in a conversation before they move on to the next utterance.[11] Thus, each utterance in a conversation has two stages: First the speaker makes an utterance; then the listener signals an understanding of that utterance by using back-channel responses (e.g., "uh-huh"; "mm-hmm"), providing a relevant next turn, or by simply remaining attentive. If we consider the fact that people tend to match or reciprocate the communication they receive from the other person, this propels people toward a mutual socialization process.

Grice's Communication Maxims

Grice approached communication from a practical standpoint and presumed that people approach every conversation with an expectation that information will be meaningfully exchanged.[12] He proposed four communication principles or maxims that communication should have: *honesty* (i.e., high quality), *quantity* (i.e., provide a sufficient amount of information), *relation* (speak to the topic at hand), and *manner* (i.e., be direct). Violations or clashes between any of these four basic maxims require additional work on the part of the listener to decipher the message. Many people suggest that violations of Grice's maxims occur quite often, but not for the reasons one might think (i.e., dishonesty). Rather, it is people's desire to be excessively polite that causes the problems.[13] According to Brown and Levinson, politeness strategies range along a continuum of indirectness, ranging from direct, blunt statements to on-record acts (e.g., politely worded statements that refer to the issue at hand) to off-record acts (i.e., ambiguous statements).[14]

Whorfian Hypothesis

The **Whorfian hypothesis** is the idea that the language people use determines (to some degree) the way in which they think and behave. As a case in point, monolingual speakers of an American Indian language called Zuni—a language that does not recognize any difference between yellow and orange—had more difficulty in re-identifying objects of these colors. More recently, a study of deaf infants raised by hearing parents reveals that language has a strong impact on cognition.[15] Specifically the children's understanding of terms that referred to mental states (e.g., anxious, preoccupied) was more limited. With regard to organizational behavior, we conjecture that organizations, which develop many names, terms, and even acronyms for key concepts, will in some sense create organizations in which people are much more sensitized to these things.

Communication Model and Levels of Analysis

It is important to keep in mind that communication must operate at each level of analysis described earlier: individual, interpersonal, group, and organizational.

Individual Communication: Challenges and Competencies

We begin our discussion of the communication model's levels of analysis by examining the challenges and competencies of the individual communicator in the organization.

GPA Theory: Goals–Plans–Action Theory

According to **GPA theory,** speakers produce messages to accomplish goals, and thus develop and enact plans for pursuing goals.[16] Interaction goals are states of affairs that speakers desire to attain or maintain through talk, and communicators often attempt to pursue and coordinate multiple goals during a conversation. Moreover, their goals can change during a conversation.

Similarly, Wilson's **cognitive rules,** or CR, model[17] assumes that people possess cognitive rules that they employ to match a given situation. For example, a supervisor might associate the goal of "giving advice" with a situation in which a subordinate is considering a new project or process.

Communicators may be judged incompetent for pursuing goals that others view as inappropriate. Consider O'Keefe's analysis of regulative communication situations[18] in which someone must correct another person's problematic behavior—very typical in organizations! They created a group project situation in which one team member, whom they called "Ron," repeatedly failed to do his part and called to say that he would be late again with his work. How did the students respond? Some of the students responded with what O'Keefe viewed as "goalless" communications: "Look, I can't handle this any more. Why do you keep doing this to me? Just go away!" Or, more agitatedly, "You A-hole. I knew you would not do your work. I am going to see that you are fired."

These messages are goalless because they failed to pursue goals that were relevant to the task. That is, neither message does anything to encourage or help Ron finish his part of the group assignment. A better response to Ron would have been something like, "Ron, your absence is delaying the company report. I need you to suggest a way that we can make sure we meet the deadline."

Developing Communication Skills

There are many things that an individual communicator can do to improve the quality and effectiveness of her or his communication.

SPEED   It is widely recognized that faster speech rates are associated with perceptions of intelligence.[19] In the rapid pace of organizational life, people monitor their time and evaluate the return of conversations. Kuiper analyzed the verbal fluency of announcers of horse races—announcers who may serve many years in an apprentice capacity while developing their ability to deliver rapid-fire descriptions of fast-changing events.[20] However, under certain conditions, people with the greatest experience may actually have lower rates of speech because they make effective use of pauses to assist their listeners in comprehending the message. For example, Neil, Worrall, Day, and Hickson contrasted the speech fluency of professional broadcasters, student broadcasters, and people with no broadcasting experience while they were reading news stories and editorials.[21] When reading news stories, the professionals had higher speech rates and fewer and shorter silent pauses than the other two groups. When delivering an editorial, however, it was the student broadcasters who were the fastest, because the more experienced broadcasters were using pauses to their advantage. Thus, people with more experience have the ability to speak with greater rapidity, but they may choose not to do so in the interest of maximizing listener comprehension.

ACCURACY   Expert communicators don't make as many mistakes as novices do, when measured against a criterion of accuracy or appropriateness.[22] And communicators who practice exhibit far fewer speech errors and disfluencies.

FLEXIBILITY Another behavioral skill that characterizes expert communicators is their ability to adjust and change in response to situational factors. The ability to make behavioral adjustments is a central component of communication competence. For example, people who are more effective in cross-cultural contexts are those who have been able to adjust both their encoding and decoding abilities—such as using empathy, displaying respect, speaking more slowly, and so forth.[23]

COMMUNICATION ANXIETY OR APPREHENSION As people gain experience in communicating, one-on-one and in groups, they are less likely to experience communication anxiety or apprehension. People who are nervous when they communicate with others often have distracting thoughts and are concerned about the impression they are making. This intensive self-focus can often "backfire" and only make the communicator more likely to suffer disfluency. The mental act of trying to suppress certain thoughts actually makes them come to mind at a greater rate.[24] Specifically, the very act of trying not to think about something requires that a person erect a mental mechanism to recognize the particular unwanted thoughts. This requires control and vigilance. When a person becomes preoccupied with another task, she or he becomes less vigilant and the unwanted thoughts are more likely to occur. This explains why people who suffer from anxiety and use thought suppression actually become more anxious[25] and why people become involved in secret relationships.[26] This suggests that communicators who attempt to rid themselves of feelings of anxiety may actually become more anxious than if they did not consciously think about repressing anxious thoughts.

STYLE OR ACCENT Of all the communication characteristics described in this section, a person's communication style (or accent) is perhaps the least controllable by the speaker. The most popular method for examining people's attitudes toward speech style is based on the **matched-guise technique.**[27] In this technique, respondents listen to tape-recordings of speakers using different speech characteristics and evaluate the speaker on particular dimensions. By using the same speaker and the same message, vocal characteristics and content are completely controlled. Across the board, people who use "standard speech" are more favorably evaluated than nonstandard speakers, particularly on intelligence and competence.[28] In contrast, speakers using nonstandard speech are perceived more positively than standard speakers on solidarity, kindness, and attractiveness.[29] In employment interviews, speakers of standard styles are more likely to be hired for higher-status jobs; and nonstandard speakers are more likely to be hired for lower-status jobs.

CONTROL OR DOMINANCE **Control,** or dominance, refers to the constellation of constraints people place on one another by what they say and how they structure their conversations. Persuasive and powerful communication unambiguously defines the situation, targets particular individuals, and pinpoints desired actions.[30] In contrast, powerless speech is tentative and often uses hedges (e.g., "kind of"), intensifiers ("totally"), tag questions ("that's interesting, isn't it?"), rising intonation, and hesitations. People who hear messages in a powerful speech style are more in favor of the message than of the same message in a less powerful style.[31] Lakoff suggested that powerless speech is a female speech register.[32]

Interpersonal Communication: Challenges and Competencies

We've focused on a number of communication challenges for the individual. What about the communication challenges that crop up at the interpersonal level?

Message Tuning

Message tuning refers to how senders tailor messages for specific recipients. People who send messages (e.g., "Finish the report"; "Let me give you some feedback") adjust their messages in ways they think best suit the recipient. This tuning is so powerful that it actually colors people's own perceptions. For example, in one investigation, people were asked to form their own independent impressions of a target person and then to communicate either positive, negative, or neutral information about the target to another person. Communication goals completely determined what information people conveyed to the audience, so much so that it overrode people's own impressions. Participants actually reformulated their own impressions in the direction of the positive, negative, or neutral impression they had been instructed to convey![33] Message tuning also means that senders will construct messages that match the characteristics of their audience. For example, gubernatorial candidate Claire McCaskill pronounced her state's name "Missou-rah" in TV ads aimed at rural areas; but she pronounced the same name "Missou-ree" in TV ads that aired in urban areas and cities.[34] People send shorter, less complete messages to one another when they believe that they can capitalize on an existing shared knowledge base. However, people overestimate the commonality of information they share with others. Consequently, the messages they send become less clear.

Another example: Performance-appraisers give substantially higher ratings when they have to give face-to-face feedback to a poorly performing employee, as opposed to making a tape-recorded message.[35] (In all cases, objective information about the poor-performing employee was identical.)

Message Distortion

If message tuning refers to how senders "spin" messages to suit the receiver, **message distortion** refers to how senders will distort information outright, because they have a bias to present information that they believe will be favorably received by the recipient.[36] For example, when people send a message to an audience whom they believe has either a "pro" or "anti" stance on a particular topic, they err in the direction of adopting the audience's point of view. A former senior executive at Xerox said, "I was never allowed to present to the board unless things were perfect. [I] could only go in with good news. Everything was prettied up."[37]

Biased Interpretation

Message senders are not the only ones who distort messages. Recipients often hear what they want to hear when receiving messages, especially ambiguous ones. When people are more ego-involved, they are more likely to make "excuses" for poor performance, so that they can preserve a favorable view of themselves.[38] For example, the lower a person's GMAT score is, the lower the score is that the person believes can qualify as "intelligent."[39]

Curse of Knowledge

The **curse of knowledge** is the tendency for an informed, knowledgeable person, such as an expert, not to be able to communicate their knowledge to others.[40] For example, in one simulation, traders who possessed privileged information, which could have been used to their advantage, behaved as if their trading partners also had access to the privileged information. Speakers overestimate the commonality or overlap between their own knowledge base and that of others. Successful communication depends on the ability of people to anticipate miscommunication.[41] Most people overestimate their ability to send a clear message—they expect the recipients to understand more than they actually do.

Illusion of Transparency

People believe that their thoughts, attitudes, and reasons are much more **transparent**—i.e., obvious to others—than is actually the case.[42] For example, when people were told to wear an embarrassing (Barry Manilow) T-shirt in a group meeting, the person wearing the T-shirt (falsely) believed that everyone else was aware of the T-shirt.[43] Thus, most communicators overestimate their effectiveness. People expect others to understand them more often than others actually do.

Proximity Effect

People are more likely to communicate with people that are physically close to them. For example, even when students are seated alphabetically in a classroom, friendships are significantly more likely to form between those whose last names begin with the same or a nearby letter.[44] This may not seem particularly noteworthy until you consider the fact that you may meet some of your closest colleagues or perhaps even a future business partner, merely because of an instructor's seating chart. If an instructor changes seat assignments once or twice during the semester, each student becomes acquainted with additional colleagues.[45] To further see the power of the **proximity effect,** consider the entering class of the Maryland State Police Training Academy. Trainees were assigned to their classroom seats and to their dormitory rooms by the alphabetical order of their last names. Some time thereafter, trainees were asked to name their three best friends in the group. The results followed the rules of alphabetization almost exactly. Caplans were friends with Carsons; not with Werners or Samuels, even though they were separated by only a few yards (see also Byrne and Kipnis[46]). In a carefully controlled investigation, Allen examined the likelihood that team members would communicate at least once per week, solely as a function of the number of feet between their offices. The result was a near-perfect correlation: The shorter the distance, the greater the likelihood of communication.[47]

In Exhibit 4.4, Allen measured the distance (in feet) between people's offices in an organizational setting. He then plotted the number of times each week that various people in the office communicated with one another—e.g., at the water cooler, over lunch, and so on. The results were striking: The probability of two people communicating at least once per week was nearly perfectly correlated with how far apart their offices were. And, for those with offices 30 feet apart (or closer), this had the greatest effect on communication.

Indirect versus Direct Communication

Each statement a communicator makes to another has an intended meaning that is couched in casual conversation. **Indirect speech acts** are the ways in which people ask others to do things—but in indirect ways. For example, consider the various ways of requesting that a person resign from a project team. (See Exhibit 4.5.)

Each statement can serve as a request to comply with the demand, even though (except for, "Dan, leave the project team") the sentence forms are assertions and questions rather than requests. Thus, statements 2 through 9 are indirect speech acts; a listener's

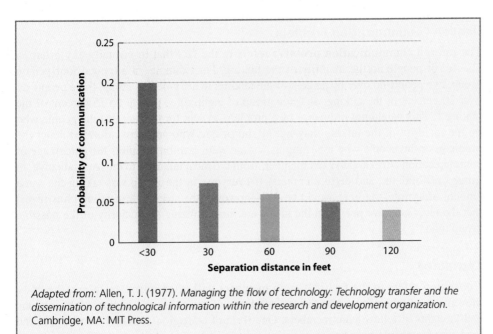

EXHIBIT 4.4

Probability of Communicating at Least Once per Week

Adapted from: Allen, T. J. (1977). *Managing the flow of technology: Technology transfer and the dissemination of technological information within the research and development organization.* Cambridge, MA: MIT Press.

EXHIBIT 4.5   **Different Ways to Make a Request That Requires Progressively More Inferences and Assumed Common Knowledge on the Part of the Receiver**

- ■ "Dan, leave the project team."
- ■ "Dan, we're wondering whether it might be best if you left the team."
- ■ "Dan, we're thinking that we don't need your involvement in the team at this point."
- ■ "Dan, we're wondering if your talents might be best utilized elsewhere."
- ■ "Dan, we're thinking that the team is ahead of schedule and does not require its original staffing."
- ■ "Dan, have you thought about involving yourself in some of the new projects and lessening your involvement in others?"
- ■ "Dan, many of the original projects are being reconfigured; yours might be one that is affected."
- ■ "Dan, the team has been able to take on the project, thanks to your early involvement."
- ■ "Dan, can you help us out with some of these new projects?"

Adapted from: Krauss, R. M., & Fussell, S. R. (1996). Social psychological models of interpersonal communication. In E. T. Higgins & A. W. Kruglanski (Eds.), *Social psychology: Handbook of basic principles* (pp. 655–701). New York: Guilford.

understanding of the intention behind the communicators' message requires an extra cognitive step or two, and can often fail, especially under stress.

Indirect speech acts are a function of the magnitude of the request being made (i.e., trivial requests, such as asking an employee for the time of day, are easy to accommodate; terminating someone is much more difficult to accommodate), the power the recipient has over the sender, and the social distance in the culture.[48] Thus, as the magnitude of requests increases, the power distance increases, and the social distance increases, requests made by organizational actors will become more indirect.

Group and Team Communication: Challenges and Competencies

We've discussed the challenges of two-party communication. There are additional challenges that arise at the level of the team and small group.

Uneven Communication Problem

The **uneven communication problem** refers to the fact that in virtually any group, a handful of people do the majority of the talking. For example, in a typical four-person group, two people do over 60 percent of the talking; in a six-person group, three people do over 70 percent of the talking; and in a group of eight, three people do 75 percent of the talking.[49] This would not ordinarily be a problem, except for the fact that the people who do the majority of the talking may not be the people who are most informed about the problem, or the people who are using their time well. Exhibit 4.6 plots the percentage of communication attributed to each member, from the most talkative to the least talkative, in groups of four, six, and eight members. If everyone in the group was taking the same amount of airtime, the lines would be flat—however, the steeply descending plots reveal that the most talkative people in the group are monopolizing the majority of the possible group time.

Contagion

Contagion refers to the fact that team members will often mirror or mimic the body movements of others (e.g., mannerisms and tones of voice) as well as mimic the emotions and thoughts of fellow team members. One form of contagion is **bodily mimicry,** or the tendency for people who are communicating to mirror one another's bodily movements

EXHIBIT 4.6

Distribution of Participation as a Function of Group Size

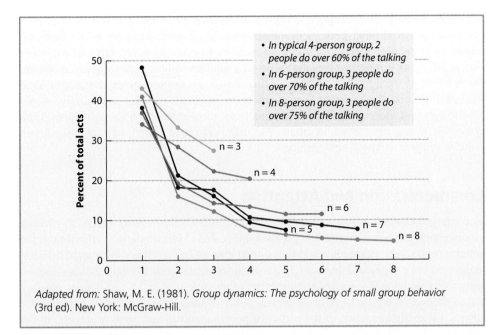

- In typical 4-person group, 2 people do over 60% of the talking
- In 6-person group, 3 people do over 70% of the talking
- In 8-person group, 3 people do over 75% of the talking

Adapted from: Shaw, M. E. (1981). *Group dynamics: The psychology of small group behavior* (3rd ed). New York: McGraw-Hill.

and posture. Most of the time, people are not aware that they are mirroring one another's movements; conversations seem to be smoother and communication easier when people are coordinating their movements.

Minimizing Communication Errors in Groups

Given the large number of ways that people in groups and teams can miscommunicate, it is not surprising that increasing the accuracy and efficiency of communication is paramount for successful interaction. The following strategies increase the effectiveness of communication (but cannot prevent disastrous miscommunication).

ROLE ASSIGNMENTS AND ROLE CLARITY One of the key ways that successful teams operate is through clear roles and responsibilities. The assignment of roles and responsibilities should not be left to chance. Indeed, groups who have high consensus about roles and responsibilities perform better than those who don't.[50]

DISCUSS GROUP PROCESS The ability of a group to communicate about how they communicate is known as **meta-communication.** Michael West refers to this as "group reflexivity"[51]—the skill with which team members are able to analyze and reflect upon the group's process. Groups whose members understand the group's process are more effective than groups who don't.

Groups who fail to discuss process, or the means by which they will conduct meetings, communicate, and so on, will often be driven by **pseudo-cues**—they pay attention to cues that may not be very meaningful. One pseudo-cue for determining who gets to speak in a group is gender (men speak more than women in face-to-face groups); another pseudo-cue is seating arrangement at a table (people at the head of a table speak more, and are more likely to be elected as a leader, than others—even when the seating has been random). Groups who discuss their process are more likely to be conscious of pseudo-cues.

TRAIN PEOPLE AS A TEAM Simply put: People who must work together should train together. Teams whose members work and train together perform better than teams whose members are equally skilled but do not train together.[52] Team training allows members of the group to develop common perceptions of a problem and a common language for treating the problem.

PERSPECTIVE TAKING **Perspective taking** is the ability to look at a situation from the point of view of another person. In a team situation, communication would be much improved if people "tuned" their communication to take the perspective of the other person. **Message tuning** involves the ability of a sender to adjust a message to a recipient. For example, if an engineer is communicating details of a project design, it would be ideal to know if the message recipient is an engineer or a psychologist. Not surprisingly, people give longer and more elaborate street directions to people whom they presume to be unfamiliar with a city.[53] And, in groups, old members spend more time explaining group policies and procedures to new members.

Communication and Attention

According to Ocasio, decisions in organizations are often influenced by which information gets attention and what information gets communicated.[54] Ocasio defines **attention** as the noticing, encoding, interpreting, and focusing of time and effort by organizational decision makers on both issues and answers. In his attention-based view of organizations, Ocasio argues that attention is a limited resource, such that organizational actors cannot possibly attend to everything that might be of relevance in their organization. What gets our attention is partly a function of the particular people involved and partly a function of the situation itself. Organizations distribute and regulate the attention of their decision makers in three ways:

- *Focus of attention:* What decision makers do depends on what issues and answers they focus on. Sometimes, organizational actors attend to things in a deliberate and controlled fashion; in other instances, attention is automatic, and not under a person's direct control.
- *Situated attention:* What issues and answers decision makers focus on and what they do depends on the particular context or situation they find themselves in.
- *Structural distribution of attention:* What particular context or situation decision makers find themselves in, and how they attend to it, depends on how the organizations' rules and resources and social relationships regulate the allocation of issues, answers, and decision makers into specific communications.

As an example, Ocasio and Joseph examined how Jack Welch, the long-time CEO of General Electric, relied on the organization's formal communication channels to selectively focus attention in a way that profoundly affected GE's corporate decision making.[55] In their analysis of GE over 50 years, they show how Welch focused attention through corporate-level strategy initiatives rather than bottoms-up strategic planning.

Nonverbal Communication

It is estimated that up to 60 percent of the meaning in any social situation is communicated nonverbally.[56] Furthermore, in cases where nonverbal and verbal messages conflict, people rely on nonverbal cues to interpret messages.[57] In one investigation, students viewed 30-second video clips (with the sound turned off) of professors' lectures and then rated the professors on a variety of personal qualities.[58] Students' ratings were remarkably accurate in terms of consensus and in terms of how the professors were actually rated by the students who took their classes. Nonverbal information is informative because it is relatively irrepressible, in that people cannot control it.

Types of Cues

Nonverbal communication is anything that is not words. Thus, it includes the following:

- *Vocal cues or paralinguistic cues:* such as pauses in speech, intonation, and fluency, as well as vocal cues, such as tone and inflection and speech volume, pace, and fluency.

- *Facial expression:* smiling, frowning, or expressing surprise. Darwin noted that people mimic the distress that others are actually feeling.[59] This mimicry is an expression of sympathy for the victim.
- *Eye contact:* Often, a high level of gazing can be interpreted as a sign of interest or liking; however, in some contexts, eye contact is a sign of dominance and aggression.[60]
- *Interpersonal spacing:* the distance between people when they talk or communicate. In general, the more a person likes another, the closer they will stand. Friends stand closer than strangers.[61]
- *Posture:* the most common being whether a person's posture is "open" or "closed" (open posture, such as uncrossed arms, body in full view, etc.).
- *Body movements:* such as crossing and uncrossing one's legs.
- *Gesture:* The three classes of gestures for embellishing a verbal message include (1) **illustrators** (such as drawing a circle with one's hands to signify something that is round); (2) **emblems,** which symbolize certain messages (such as the North American thumbs-up for "OK," and the finger on the lips for "quiet"); and (3) **adaptors** (which are not related to speech and include such things as touching one's nose, scratching one's head, etc.). Media experts who coach political candidates often train their clients as much on their nonverbal communication as they do their verbal communication. During the 1988 U.S. presidential campaign season, Roger Ailes, George Bush's media consultant, was quoted in *Newsweek*[62] as telling Bush before one of his televised debates, "There you go with that f-ing hand again. You look like an f-ing pansy."

  Gesture does much more than simply convey meaning. It *makes* meaning. For example, people who are blind from birth never see people moving their hands as they talk and have no model for gesturing. Yet congenitally blind speakers gesture despite their lack of a visual model, and do so even when speaking to a blind listener![63] Moreover, the spontaneous hand movements that co-occur with speech are not random. In fact, gestures that co-occur with speech may facilitate the speaker's ability to think and process information.[64] Moreover, gesture plays a real role in the learning process: People learn more deeply when they gesture than when they don't.
- *Touching:* Touching another person in an appropriate way, such as on the hand, often leads to positive reactions, but it can backfire, too.

Lying and Deception

Probably nothing is more top-of-mind in communication among organizational actors than the extent to which people feel that they can "trust" the other person. If we feel that another is deceiving us, it can damage relationships and wreak havoc on organizational culture. Most people look at nonverbal communication as a promising way to detect deception. In virtually all communication, a key goal (implicitly or explicitly) is the detection of deception. (See Exhibit 4.7 for how the FBI teams up with psychologists to improve detection of deception.)

In many situations, such as with a trusted friend, we don't worry about deception. But should we? College students report telling about two lies a day during the course of normal interactions with others.[65] Other investigations suggest that as many as one third of people's daily social interactions involve some form of deception.[66] Lies are a "deliberate attempt without forewarning to create in another a belief which the communicator considers untrue."[67] Thus, this could range from small "white" lies (e.g., "I love your suit," when in fact you do not) to more serious lies (e.g., falsifying sales information).

Accuracy in Detecting Deception

Most people are not very good at detecting deception. A meta-analysis of 253 studies of people distinguishing truths from lies revealed an overall accuracy rate of 53 percent—not

EXHIBIT 4.7 **FBI Teams with Psychologists to Zero In on Human Deception**

In June 2004, the FBI and the National Institute of Justice teamed up with the American Psychological Association to offer an exclusive workshop for top law enforcers on detecting deception. Although polygraph tests seem rampant in movies, they are based on autonomic reactions and are considered unreliable. In fact, a scientific study of polygraph effectiveness revealed "no evidence of polygraph validity."* Paul Ekman, a renowned nonverbal communication expert, developed the Institute for Analytic Interviewing, which trains people to detect deception. According to Ekman, skilled interrogators build rapport with their interviewers.

Source: Adelson, R. (2004). Detecting deception. *APA Monitor on Psychology, 35*(7), 70.

* Saxe, L., Dougherty, D., & Cross, T. (1983). *Scientific validity of polygraph testing: A research review and evaluation—A technical memorandum* (No. OTA-TM-H-15,). Washington, DC: U.S. Congress Office of Technology Assessment.

much better than chance.[68] Merely warning people to be wary of deception is not particularly helpful, either—it just makes people more suspicious of everyone.[69]

People who are specially trained, such as CIA agents, can be effective in detecting decision. Certain specific behaviors reliably distinguish lies from truth: Liars blink more, hesitate more, and make more speech errors. Liars have higher pitched voices and their pupils are more dilated. They fidget more, speak with hesitation, and make more negative statements. A good source of information regarding decision is the person's motivation to lie. When people are motivated to lie, their lies actually become more obvious to observers.[70]

Nonverbal Leakage

A key theory of deception detection is the idea that a liar needs to monitor his or her face, voice, and body—an entire host of potential cues. According to deception theory, liars cannot possibly monitor everything, and so something leaks out and is revealed to the recipient. **Nonverbal leakage** refers to the nonverbal signals that a person emits that he or she is not even aware of. According to Ekman and Friesen,[71] liars pay attention to what they are saying more than how they are saying it. Consequently, liars often betray themselves through paralinguistic expressions of anxiety. For example, voice pitch is higher when someone is lying than when she or he is telling the truth.[72]

Detecting Deception and the Written Word

When we think about detecting deception, we often think about how we might scrutinize a person talking to us. James Pennebaker developed computer software known as Linguistic Inquiry and Word Count.[73] The software analyzes written content and can with some accuracy (67 percent) detect when someone is lying. In several investigations, people are told to write—as persuasively as possible—truthful or deceptive essays about their views on a hot topic, such as abortion. Deceivers commit three telltale signs in their written communication:

- *Fewer first-person pronouns.* Liars tend to avoid statements of ownership (e.g., "I," "me," "mine"), distance themselves from their stories, and avoid taking responsibility for their actions.
- *More negative-emotion words.* No matter what the subject, liars are more likely to use words such as "hate," "worthless," "sad"; perhaps because they feel anxious and guilty.
- *Fewer exclusionary words,* such as "except," "but," or "nor." **Exclusionary words** distinguish what they know from what they do not know. Liars seem to have a problem with this complexity, and it shows when they write something.

Deception and Information Technology

Analyzing how to detect a liar who communicates via written messages or e-mail naturally raises the question of whether the communication medium affects the incidence of lying. In one investigation, participants kept a diary for a week, in which they recorded all of their social interactions, including lies.[74] People lied most on the telephone and least in e-mail; lying rates in face-to-face and instant messaging (via e-mail) were about equal.

The Organizationally Competent Communicator: Taking Yourself to the Next Level

Although there are several threats to the effectiveness of communication in organizations, there are several steps that you can take to improve your ability to communicate.

Overt Practice

There may be no observation about communication skills that is more fundamental, and more far-reaching in its implication, than that they are developed and refined over time through implementation.[75] However, simple repetition or use of a skill, even over an extended time period, is not sufficient to bring about maximal performance. Rather, people need to focus attention on the details of their behavior with an eye toward modifying and reorganizing their actions.

Mental Practice

A typical conception of practice is that it involves actual execution of the behavioral skills one is seeking to master. However, simple mental rehearsal of the target behaviors can also improve performance and is particularly pronounced for skills that involve cognitive components.[76]

Direct Instruction and Coaching

An example of direct instruction or coaching might involve explaining the function and use of eye contact.[77] Eye contact is one of the ways that people show interest and attention to other people. People could be "coached" about the implications of someone who shows too much or too little eye contact. There are situations in which it is important to make eye contact, such as when making a request, when listening to someone who is making an important report, and so on.

Modeling

Bandura noted that "virtually all behavioral, cognitive, and affective learning from direct experience can be achieved vicariously by observing people's actions and the consequences for them."[78] The most effective way to teach complex social behavior and communication skills is via modeling and imitation. Modeling can be presented either on videotape or live depiction. People are more likely to feel that they can perform a behavior if they see people model that behavior. And the more similar the model is to the person, in terms of sex, age, and other characteristics, the more likely the protégé is to model the behavior.

Role-Playing

Whereas coaching and modeling are passive techniques in that people simply absorb information presented by others, role-playing calls for production and practice of actual behaviors. The purpose of role-playing is to practice desired, optimal behaviors in controlled settings where they can be observed and where feedback can be offered. It is desirable for an expert to provide feedback to the target in role-playing; feedback that is focused on effect rather than appearance is ideal. For example, it is better to tell someone, "You made me feel that you did not know what you were talking about," rather than, "You looked confused."[79]

Storytelling and Narrative

Recall the opening exercise of this chapter. Narrative or storytelling is a powerful way of communicating. Stories affect people more than when the same information is presented in a list-like structure.[80] Nussbaum, Comadena, and Holladay studied three award-winning professors and discovered that all of them used narrative as a way of instructing.[81] The ability to tell stories is critical for effective communication. Bruner compared two ways of knowing or communicating: (1) the narrative mode of knowing, and (2) the logo-scientific model.[82] It is the narrative mode of knowing and communicating that makes communication more interesting and intense. Organizational actors engage in competitive narrative contests, attempting to circulate stories that enable themselves and their allies, and that pollute their enemies. Not only is telling a story more interesting for the audience, narratives are easier for people to comprehend and remember. For example, the wisdom of cultures is passed from generation to generation through story and narrative.[83] And the plots and themes in theses stories reflect the conflicts, solutions to problems, humor, and values of the culture. As a case in point, consider Nordstrom department stores, long known for their impeccable customer service. Part of Nordstrom's corporate culture is reflected in stories about a customer who received a cash reimbursement for returning snow tires without a receipt—which could not possibly have been purchased from Nordstrom, as they do not sell snow tires. Yet, in the story, Nordstrom aims to please even the most irrational of customers. (See Exhibit 4.8 for how a Hollywood screenwriter uses stories to coach boring business executives to be more interesting.)

Questioning

Excellent communicators take full advantage of the dynamic, double-loop opportunity of communication. They ask questions, checking their understanding, during the conversation. They don't try to lead the witness to a particular conclusion, but rather, show their genuine understanding.

Process Consultation and Active Inquiry

Edgar Schein's **process consultation method**[84] is a model of nondirective counseling applied to organizations. It is a process of helping. The key assumption of process consultation is that in order to be helpful to one's colleagues, one's team, and one's organization, it is necessary to establish effective relationships, understand the "real"

EXHIBIT 4.8   Screenwriting Coach Works with Executives to Help Them Communicate via Stories

According to screenwriting coach Robert McKee—whose students have written, directed, and produced hundreds of hit films, including *Forrest Gump, Erin Brockovich,* and *Sleepless in Seattle*—the typical business manager gets lost in boring company-speak, which includes PowerPoint slides, dry memos, etc. McKee coaches these leaders to engage listeners through telling stories.

McKee explains that a good story has an "inciting incident" that throws life out of balance (e.g., a new job, someone close dies, or a company is forced into bankruptcy). The protagonists' expectations crash into "uncooperative objective reality," meaning that things don't work their way. Then, the light comes—but only after struggle.

McKee explains how even the driest of situations, such as a biotech start-up attempting to persuade Wall Street bankers to invest, can be a powerful story. The manager could tell the potential investors how the company has discovered a chemical compound that prevents heart attacks and show them slides. Or the manager could begin with a story about his own father, who died of a heart attack.

Source: McKee, R. (2003). Storytelling that moves people. *Harvard Business Review, 81*(6), 51–55.

concerns, and offer help. According to Schein, people in organizations must be continual helpers in order for organizations to function effectively.

The **active inquiry process**[85] is a method of helping and coaching that embodies effective communication. Schein outlines three key phases of the active inquiry model: pure inquiry, exploratory diagnostic inquiry, and confrontative inquiry. In the following paragraphs we work through the three phases of the model and refer to the helper as the coach and the helpee as the coachee.

PURE INQUIRY   Pure inquiry ironically begins with silence, where the coachee controls the process and the content of the interaction. The coach's role is to prompt the coachee to tell his or her story. The coach listens carefully and above all, remains neutral. Schein notes that listening is a:

> rather complex activity that can be pursued very actively or very passively. If we are to go with the flow and access our ignorance, it would appear at first glance that we should be fairly passive and attentive to let the coachee develop the story in his or her own way. But in many situations, the coachee just asks a question or two and then falls silent with an expectant look. It is at this moment that the coach must be careful not to fall into the trap of taking on all the power that is offered.[86]

The coach's approach is guided by the following "pure inquiry" questions:

- What is the situation?
- What is going on?
- Describe the situation . . .
- Tell me more . . .
- Please go on . . .
- Give me examples of x . . .
- What are the details?
- How can I help?

It is very important for the coach not to prompt with questions that presuppose a problem, because that is what the coachee may wish to deny. Further, Schein advises that the coach avoid "why" questions. Why questions stimulate diagnostic (cause-effect thinking), which may get ahead of the story of what brought the coachee to the coach in the first place.

EXPLORATORY DIAGNOSTIC INQUIRY   In this phase, the coach begins to influence the coachee's way of thinking about the organization and herself by deliberately focusing on issues other than the ones the coachee has presented. These questions do not influence the content of the story, but rather, the focus of attention within the story. During this phase, the coach manages the process of analyzing the content of what the coachee has said. The coach does not insert or suggest content ideas, advice, or the like. Schein outlines three types of questions: feelings and reactions (e.g., "how did you feel about that?", "what was your reaction?"); hypotheses about causes (e.g., "why do you think that happened?", "why did others have the reaction they did?"); and actions taken or contemplated (e.g., "What are your options?").

CONFRONTATIVE INQUIRY   During the last phase, the coach shares his or her own ideas and reactions about the process and content of the situation. Instead of merely prompting the coachee to elaborate, the coach now makes suggestions or offers options that may not have occurred to the coachee. The goal of this phase is for the coachee to get a new perspective on the problem. Examples of questions during this phase would include, "Could you have done x?" "Have you considered the following course of action?" and so forth.

Conclusion

We've discussed several types of levels of communication in this chapter. We've pointed to the most common failures of communication that occur at all levels. Moreover, we've discussed how communication competencies and challenges change when different modalities are employed (e.g., face-to-face versus telephone versus e-mail). Most people don't consciously think about their communication style or effectiveness. Communication is a skill and therefore, people may learn to improve their ability to effectively send and interpret messages.

Notes

1. Krauss, R. M., & Chiu, C. (1998). Language and social behavior. In D. T. Gilbert, S. T. Fiske, & G. Lindzey (Eds.), *Handbook of social psychology* (4th ed., Vol. 2, pp. 41–88). New York: Oxford University Press.
2. Shannon, C. E., & Weaver, W. (1949). *The mathematical theory of communication.* Urbana, IL: University of Illinois Press.
3. Berlo, D. K. (1960). *The process of communication.* New York: Holt, Rinehart and Winston.
4. Schramm, W. (1973). *Men, messages, and media: A look at human communication.* New York: Harper & Row.
5. Parks, M. R. (1994). Communicative competence and interpersonal control. In M. L. Knapp & G. R. Miller (Eds.), *Handbook of interpersonal communication* (2nd ed., pp. 589–618). Thousand Oaks, CA: Sage.
6. Nunamaker, J. F., Jr., Romano, N. C., Jr., and Briggs, R. O. (2002, March). Increasing intellectual bandwidth: Generating value from intellectual capital with information technology. *Group Decision and Negotiation, 11*(2), 69–86.
7. Noels, K. A., Giles, H., & Le Poire, B. (2003). Language and communication processes. In M. A.Hogg & J. Cooper (Eds.), *The Sage handbook of social psychology* (pp. 232–257). Sage.
8. Delia, J. G., O'Keefe, B. J., & O'Keefe, D. J. (1982). The constructivist approach to communication. In F. E. X. Dance (Ed.), *Human communication theory: Comparative essays.* New York: Harper & Row.
9. Burgoon, J. K. (1980). Nonverbal communication research in the 1970s: An overview. In D. Nimmo (Ed.), *Communication Yearbook 4.* New Brunswick, NJ: Transaction Books.
10. Burgoon, J. K., Buller, D. B., & Woodall, W. G. (1996). *Nonverbal communication: The unspoken dialogue* (2nd ed.). New York: McGraw-Hill.
11. Clark, H. H. (1985). Language use and language users. In G. Lindsay & E. Aronson (Eds.), *Handbook of social psychology* (Vol. II, pp. 179–231). New York: Random House; Clark, H. H. (1996). *Using language.* Cambridge, MA: Cambridge University Press.
12. Grice, H. P. (1975). Logic and conversation. In P. Cole & J. L. Morgan (Eds.), *Syntax and semantics: Speech acts.* New York: Academic Press.
13. Holtgraves, T. (2001). Politeness. In P. Robinson and H. Giles (Eds.), *The new handbook of language and social psychology.* John Wiley & Sons.
14. Brown, P., & Levinson, S. C. (1987). *Politeness: Some universals in language use.* Cambridge, England: Cambridge University Press.
15. Skoyles, J. R. The Sapir-Whorf hypothesis: New surprising evidence. Retrieved from: www.users.globalnet.co.uk/~skoyles/swh.html;

Skoyles, J. R. (1998). Speech phones are a replication code. *Medical Hypotheses, 50,* 167–173. http://cogprints.soton.ac.uk/abs/psyc/199901003.
16. Berger, C. R. (1997). *Planning strategic interaction: Attaining goals through communicative action.* Mahwah, NJ: Erlbaum; Dillard, J. P. (1990). The nature and substance of goals in tactical communication. In M. J. Cody & M. J. McLaughlin (Eds.), *The psychology of tactical communication* (pp. 70–91). Philadelphia, PA: Multilingual Matters.
17. Wilson, S. R. (1990). Development and test of a cognitive rules model of interaction goals. *Communication Monographs, 57,* 81–103; Wilson, S. R. (1995). Elaborating the cognitive rules model of interaction goals: The problem of accounting for individual differences in goal formation. In B. Burleson (Ed.), *Communication Yearbook 18* (pp. 3–25). Thousand Oaks, CA: Sage.
18. O'Keefe, B. J. (1988). The logic of message design: Individual differences in reasoning about communication. *Communication Monographs, 55,* 80–103.
19. Greene, J. O. (2003). Models of adult communication skill acquisition: Practice and the course of performance improvement. In Greene, J. O., & Burleson, B. R. (Eds.). *Handbook of communication and social interaction skills.* Lawrence Erlbaum.
20. Kuiper, K. (1996). *Smooth talkers: The linguistic performance of auctioneers and sportscasters.* Mahwah, NJ: Lawrence Erlbaum.
21. Neil, E., Worrall, L., Day, A., & Hickson, L. (2003, March). Voice and speech characteristics and vocal hygiene in novice and professional broadcast journalists. *Advances in Speech Language Pathology, 5*(1), 1–14.
22. Newell, A., & Rosenbloom, P. S. (1981). Mechanisms of skill acquisition and the law of practice. In J. R. Anderson (Ed.), *Cognitive skills and their acquisition.* Hillsdale, NJ: Erlbaum. (Also available as Carnegie-Mellon University Computer Science Tech. Rep. #80–145.); Proctor, R.W., & Dutta, A. (1995). *Skill acquisition and human performance.* Thousand Oaks, CA: Sage.
23. Martin, J. N., & Hammer, R. M. (1989). Behavioral categories of intercultural communication competence: Everyday communicator's perception. *International Journal of Intercultural Relations, 13,* 302–332.
24. Wegner, D. (1994). Ironic processes of mental control. *Psychological Review, 101,* 34–52.
25. Wegner, D. M., & Wenzlaff, R. M. (1996). Mental control. In E. T. Higgins & A.W. Kruglanski (Eds.), *Social psychology: Handbook of basic principles.* New York: Guilford Press.
26. Wegner, D. M., Lane, J. D., & Dimitri, S. (1994). The allure of secret relationships. *Journal of Personality and Social Psychology, 66,* 287–300; Wegner, D. M., Shortt, J.W., Blake, A.W., & Page, M. S. (1990). The suppression of exciting thoughts. *Journal of Personality and Social Psychology, 58*(3), 409–418.

27. Lambert, W., Hodgeson, R. C., Gardner, R. C. & Fillenbaum, S. (1960). Evaluational reactions to spoken languages. *Journal of Abnormal and Social Psychology, 60,* 44–51.

28. Ryan, R. M. (1982). Control and information in the intrapersonal sphere: An extension of cognitive evaluation theory. *Journal of Personality and Social Psychology, 43,* 450–461.

29. Cargile, A. C., & Bradac, J. J. (2001). Attitudes towards language: A review of speaker-evaluation research and a general process model. In W. B. Gudykunst (Ed.), *Communication yearbook 25* (pp. 347–382). Mahwah, NJ: Erlbaum.

30. Ng, S., & Bradac, J. (1993). *Power in language.* Newbury Park, CA: Sage.

31. Holtgraves, T. M., & Lasky, B. (1999). Linguistic power and persuasion. *Journal of Language and Social Psychology, 18*(2), 196–205.

32. Lakoff, G. (1973). Hedges: A study in meaning criteria and the logic of fuzzy concepts. *Journal of Philosophical Logic, 2,* 458–508.

33. Skowronski, J. J., Carlston, D. E., Mae, L., & Crawford, M. T. (1998). Spontaneous trait transference: Communicators take on the qualities they describe in others. *Journal of Personality and Social Psychology, 74,* 837–848.

34. Young, V. (2004, June 15). McCaskill airs her first two TV ads—one for rural areas, one for cities. *St. Louis Post-Dispatch,* p. B.3.

35. Waung, M., & Highhouse, S. (1997). Fear of conflict and empathic buffering: Two explanations for the inflation of performance feedback. *Organizational Behavior and Human Decision Processes, 71*(1), 37–54.

36. McCann, C. D., & Higgins, E. T. (1992). Personal and contextual factors in communication: A review of the communication game. In G. R. Semin & K. Fiedler (Eds.), *Language, interaction, and social cognition* (pp. 144–172). Newbury Park, CA: Sage.

37. Charan, R. & Useem, J. (2002, May 27). Why companies fail. *Fortune,* p. 50.

38. Miller, D. T. (1976). Ego involvement and attributions for success and failure. *Journal of Personality and Social Psychology, 34,* 901–906.

39. Dunning, D., & Cohen, G. L. (1992). Egocentric definitions of traits and abilities in social judgment. *Journal of Personality and Social Psychology, 63,* 341–355.

40. Keysar, B. (1998). Language users as problem solvers: Just what ambiguity problem do they solve? In S. R. Fussell & R. J. Kreuz (Eds.), *Social and cognitive psychological approaches to interpersonal communication* (pp. 175–200). Hillsdale, NJ: Erlbaum.

41. Keysar, B., & Henly, A. S. (2002). Speakers' overestimation of their effectiveness. *Psychological Science, 13,* 207–212.

42. Gilovich, T., Savitsky, K., & Medvec, V. H. (1998). The illusion of transparency: Biased assessments of others' ability to read one's emotional states. *Journal of Personality and Social Psychology, 75,* 332–346.

43. Gilovich, T., Medvec, V. H., & Savitsky, K. (2000). The spotlight effect in social judgment: An egocentric bias in estimates of the salience of one's own actions and appearance. *Journal of Personality and Social Psychology, 78,* 211–222.

44. Segal, M. (1974). Alphabet and attraction: An unobtrusive measure of the effect of propinquity in a field setting. *Journal of Personality and Social Psychology, 30,* 654–657.

45. Byrne, D. (1961). Interpersonal attraction and attitude similarity. *Journal of Abnormal and Social Psychology, 62,* 713–715.

46. Kipnis, D. M. (1957). Interaction between members of bomber crews as a determinant of sociometric choice. *Human Relations, 10,* 263–270.

47. Allen, T. J. (1977). *Managing the flow of technology: Technology transfer and the dissemination of technological information within the research and development organization.* Cambridge, MA: MIT Press.

48. See note 14.

49. Shaw, M. E. (1981). *Group dynamics: The psychology of small group behavior* (3rd ed.). New York: McGraw-Hill.

50. Katzenbach, J. R., & Smith, D. K. (1993). *The wisdom of teams.* Watertown, MA: Harvard Business School Press.

51. West, M. A., Sacramento, C. A., & Fay, D. (2005). Creativity and innovation implementation in work groups: The paradoxical role of demands. In L. Thompson & H S. Choi (Eds.), *Creativity and innovation in organizational teams.* Mahwah, NJ: Lawrence Erlbaum.

52. Hollingshead, A. B. (1998). Group and individual training: The impact of practice on performance. *Small Group Research, 29,* 254–280; Littlepage, G. E., Robison, W., & Reddington, K. (1997). Effects of task experience and group experience on group performance, member ability, and recognition of expertise. *Organizational Behavior & Human Decision Processes, 69,* 133–147.

53. Krauss, R. M, & Fussell, S. R. (1991). Perspective-taking in communication: Representations of others' knowledge in reference. *Social Cognition, 9,* 2–24.

54. Ocasio, W. (1997). Towards an attention-based view of the firm. *Strategic Management Journal, 18,* 187–206.

55. Ocasio, W., & Joseph, J. (2006). Governance channels and organizational design at General Electric: 1950–2001. In R. M. Burton, B. Eriksen, D. D. Haakonsson, & C. C. Snow (Eds.), *Organization design: The dynamics of adaptation and change.* Information and Organization Design Series. Boston, MA: Springer.

56. Birdwhistell, R. (1955). Background to kinesics. *ETC, 13,* 10–18; Philipott, J. S. (1983). *The relative contribution to meaning of verbal and nonverbal channels of communication: A meta-analysis.* Unpublished master's thesis. University of Nebraska, Lincoln.

57. Burgoon, J. K. (1985). The relationship of verbal and nonverbal codes. In B. Dervin & M. J. Voight (Eds.), *Progress in communication sciences, Vol. 6* (pp. 263–298). Norwood, NJ: Ablex; Burgoon, J. K., Buller, D. B., & Woodall, W. G. (1996). *Nonverbal communication: The unspoken dialogue* (2nd ed.). New York: McGraw-Hill.

58. Ambady, N., & Rosenthal, R. (1993). Half a minute: Predicting teacher evaluation from thin slices of nonverbal behavior and physical attractiveness. *Journal of Personality and Social Psychology, 64,* 431–441.

59. Darwin, C. (1872). *The expression of emotions in man and animals.* New York: Philosophical Library.

60. Ellsworth, P. C., & Carlsmith, J. M. (1968). Effects of eye contact and verbal content on affective response to dyadic interaction. *Journal of Personality and Social Psychology, 10,* 15–20.

61. Aiello, J. R., & Cooper, R. E. (1972). The use of personal space as a function of social affect. *Proceedings of the American Psychological Association, 7,* 207–208.

62. Warner, M., & Fineman, H. (1988, September). Bush's media wizard. *Newsweek,* p. 19.

63. Iverson, J. M., & Goldin-Meadow, S. (1998, November 19). Why people gesture when they speak. *Nature, 396,* 228.

64. Goldin-Meadow, S., Alibali, M., & Church, R. B. (1993). Transitions in concept acquisition: Using the hand to read the mind. *Psychological Review, 100,* 279–297.

65. DePaulo, B. M., Kashy, D. A., Kirkendol, S. E., Wyer, M. M., & Epstein, J. A. (1996). Lying in everyday life. *Journal of Personality and Social Psychology, 70,* 979–995.

66. Camden, C., Motley, M., & Wilson, A. (1984). White lies in interpersonal communication: A taxonomy and preliminary investigation of social motivations. *Western Journal of Speech Communication, 48*(4), 309–325.

67. Voida, A., Wendy, C., Newstetter, W. C., & Mynatt, E. D. (2002, April 20–25). When conventions collide: The tensions of instant messaging attributed. Proceedings of the SIGCHI conference on human factors in computing systems: Changing our world, changing ourselves. Minneapolis, MN.

68. Bond, C. F., Jr, & DePaulo, B. M. (2004). Accuracy and truth bias in the detection of deception. Manuscript in preparation.

69. Toris, C., & DePaulo, B. M. (1984). Effects of actual deception and suspiciousness of deception on interpersonal perceptions. *Journal of Personality and Social Psychology, 47,* 1063–1073.

70. DePaulo, B. M., LeMay, C. S., & Epstein, J. A. (1991). Effects of importance of success and expectations for success on effectiveness at deceiving. *Personality and Social Psychology Bulletin, 17,* 14–24.

71. Ekman, P., & Friesen, W. V. (1974). Nonverbal behavior and psychopathology. In R. J. Friedman & H. M. Katz (Eds.), *The psychology of depression: Contemporary theory and research* (pp. 203–224). New York: Wiley.

72. Ekman, P., Friesen, W. V., & Scherer, K. (1976). Body movement and voice pitch in deceptive interaction. *Semiotica, 16,* 23–27.

73. Pennebaker, J. W., Francis, M. E., & Booth, R. J. (2001). *Linguistic inquiry and word count (LIWC): LIWC2001.* Mahwah, NJ: Erlbaum.

74. Hancock, J. T., Thom-Santelli, J., & Ritchie, T. (2004, April 24–29). *Deception and design: The impact of communication technology on lying behavior.* Proceedings of the SIGCHI conference on human factors in computing systems, pp.129–134. Vienna, Austria.

75. See note 19.

76. Feltz, D. L., & Landers, D. M. (1983). The effects of mental practice on motor skill learning and performance: A meta-analysis. *Journal of Sport Psychology, 5,* 25–57.

77. Segrin, C., & Givertz, M. (2003). Methods of social skills training and development. In J. O. Greene & B. R. Burleson (Eds.), *Handbook of communication and social interaction skills* (pp. 135–176). Mahwah, NJ: Erlbaum.

78. Bandura, A. (1999). Social cognitive theory: An agentic perspective. *Asian Journal of Social Psychology, 2*(1), 21–41.

79. See note 77.

80. Pennington, N., & Hastie, R. (1992). Explaining the evidence: Tests of the story model for juror decision making. *Journal of Personality and Social Psychology, 62,* 189–206.

81. Nussbaum, J. F., Comadena, M. E., & Holladay, S. J. (1987). Classroom verbal behaviors of highly effective teachers. *Journal of Thought, 22,* 73–80.

82. Bruner, J. (1986). *Actual minds, possible worlds.* Cambridge, MA: Harvard University Press.

83. Rubin, D. C. (1995). *Memory in oral traditions: The cognitive psychology of epic, ballads, and counting-out rhymes.* New York: Oxford University Press.

84. Schein, E. H. (1969). *Process consultation: Its role in organization development.* Reading, MA: Addison-Wesley. Schein, E. H. (1999). Empowerment, coercive persuasion and organizational learning: Do they connect? *The Learning Organization, 6*(4), 163–72.

85. Schein, E. H. (1999). Empowerment, coercive persuasion and organizational learning: Do they connect? *The Learning Organization, 6*(4), 163–72.

86. Ibid., p. 42.

POWER AND INFLUENCE IN ORGANIZATIONS

Think about a time when you had power over someone. In a paragraph, describe the situation in as much detail as you can remember. What type of power did you exert over the other person? Would you describe your use of power as based on your subject expertise (such as when you were skilled in a domain and others weren't?). Would you describe your use of power as benevolent or malevolent? How did the other person react? What happened as a result of his or her reactions? How would the person have reacted and how would the results have been different had you used a different source of power?

Now, think about a time when someone had power over you. What was the basis of that person's power? In other words, did that person have control over scarce resources? Or threaten you? Would you describe that person's use of power as benevolent or malevolent? How did you react? What happened as a result of your reactions? How would you have reacted and how would the results have been different had the other person used a different source of power?

After you have thought about these two situations, take a moment to complete the Personal Power exercise (Exercise 5.1) in the self-discovery section.

Power and Influence

Power is a dynamic in any relationship (whether it is business or personal). And, in any relationship, one person has more power than the other at a given point in time. **Power** is the ability of a person to control the actions of another person in a relationship.[1] Power is the ability of a person to get someone else to do something they might not otherwise have done.[2] For example, in Exhibit 5.1, a complete stranger calling on a telephone had the power to induce people to ask others to take off their clothes!

Many times, power may exist but may not be actually used. Think of power as a capacity or a potential. Power involves dependency of one person on another. As a general principle, in a relationship between A and B, the greater A's dependency on B, the greater the power B has over A. Dependency is increased when the resource a person controls is important and scarce.[3] For example, a person who is solely responsible for determining merit raises in his or her organization is very powerful. Control over others' outcomes can be direct or indirect. For example, direct power might be the case in which a professor selects certain students to be on a highly desirable group project; indirect power occurs when a group of teaching assistants, working under a professor's supervision, make selection decisions. In this sense, the power that the professor has is indirect. Control can be unilateral or bilateral (i.e., one-sided or two-sided). For example, in an organization in which supervisors provide performance ratings of subordinates, power is one-sided. If an organization seeks to obtain 360-ratings of how subordinates rate their boss in addition to how supervisors rate their subordinates, power is bilateral, particularly if it has implications for remuneration and advancement. Power can be used deliberately (consciously) or preconsciously. For example, a person may not be consciously aware of using power in a meeting to show approval or rejection of ideas via subtle, nonverbal behaviors, such as frowning, shrugging, or averting the eyes.

Influence is the ability of a person to change the behavior of another person. There are three types of influence: conformity, compliance, and obedience to authority. **Conformity** occurs when people change their beliefs or behaviors in ways that are consistent with what they believe to be the group's standards. **Compliance** occurs when people do what they are asked to do, even though they might prefer not to do it. Compliance differs from conformity in that a person voluntarily conforms, but needs to be asked—and agree—to comply. In some situations, such as the story of the hoax caller, people agree to comply because they view the requester (in this case the caller describing himself as a police officer) to have legitimate authority. Organizational and social norms permit people with authority to make requests and dictate that subordinates should obey them (e.g., security personnel have enormous amounts of authority because of their dress and position).

Power in organizations, and especially in social relationships, is often hidden or not discussed. For most people, having power and using power is not something they readily

EXHIBIT 5.1   Pseudo-Power

The caller to the Phoenix-area Taco Bell said he was a police officer and told the manager that there was a thief in the establishment. Apparently, someone's purse was missing. The caller commanded the manager to perform a strip search of a female customer in the back office. Most of the managers of the several establishments contacted by the caller, including Taco Bell, McDonald's, Wendy's, Burger King, Ruby Tuesday, Applebee's, Perkins, and Hardee's, complied with the request to perform the strip search. However, the whole thing was a giant hoax. The caller has successfully commanded unsuspecting managers to pull the same stunt dozens of times in the United States for more than five years. The searches have included males and females, lawsuits by employees and customers have been filed, and managers have faced criminal charges. The managers caught up in the hoax believed that the caller was an authority figure and, consequently, did not question his authority, even if it meant performing bizarre and unethical acts. An assistant manager at Hardee's in Rapid City, South Dakota, was charged with kidnapping and second-degree rape after he detained and forced one of his female employees to strip, as directed by the caller. Some, such as Sheriff Joseph Arpaio, think that managers are "ignorant" to fall for the scam and should face criminal charges. "It's mind-boggling. How can a responsible person . . . ever do [this] just because some guy calls them on the telephone and tells them he's a cop?"

Source: Adapted from Associated Press, 2004, April 9.

admit. It would seem that leadership and power would be closely connected. However, using power usually has negative connotations, whereas exercising leadership usually has positive connotations. What are the differences between leadership and power? There are three key points of difference. First is **goal-compatibility,** or the extent to which the leader and his or her followers share the same goals. Using power does not require that the followers have the same goals as the power user. Rather, using power requires a dependent relationship. In contrast, for leaders to be effective, they usually have to set goals that are aligned with those of the people who are expected to follow the leader. Second, the ability to lead involves a relationship between the leader and those who are led that is not necessarily based on an immediate exchange of resources. In contrast, the use of power often involves an exchange of resources—even if the resources involve the use of threat or punishment. Finally, leadership is a relatively long-term relationship between the leader and the led, whereas the use of power is often very short-term and fluctuates across situations.

Power and Politics in Organizations

Power is not evenly distributed among people and teams in organizations, meaning that some people enjoy a great deal of power whereas others do not have much power at all. People in power often make rules and put systems into place that secure and enhance their power. Consequently, people in organizations are (un)consciously motivated to secure power. The other organizational members and groups not in power may consider these rules unfair and dictatorial. Each of us is more vulnerable to the temptation to (ab)use power than we realize.

The use of power in organizations creates "politics." In terms of organizations, "when people get together, power will be exerted."[4] And, when people in organizations are using their power, they are engaged in politics. According to Pfeffer, "Organizational politics comprises activities taken within organizations to acquire, develop, and use power and other resources to obtain one's preferred outcomes in a situation in which there is uncertainty or disagreement about choices."[5] Political action in organizations focuses on how people use power to affect decision making. Political behavior in organizations refers to "those activities that are not required as part of one's formal role in the organization, but that influence, or attempt to influence, the distribution of advantages and disadvantages within the organization."[6] Certain organizational cultures tend to promote a greater amount of political behavior, including cultures characterized by low trust, role ambiguity, unclear performance evaluation systems, zero-sum reward allocation practices, democratic decision making, performance pressure, and self-serving senior managers.[7]

Playing Organizational Politics

What are the tactics and strategies that people within organizations use to increase their chances of winning political battles as they are commonly played out? Jennifer George and Gareth Jones suggest seven strategies.[8] (For another view of political influence strategies, see Exhibit 5.2.)

- *Increase indispensability.* If your contributions to an organization are valuable and if you are the only one who has such skills, then you are probably indispensable. However, if your work is undervalued (i.e., people don't appreciate it) and/or others can easily perform your work, then you are easily dispensable. Consider, for example, a computer programmer who is the only person who knows the computer passwords and who is the only one capable of rebooting the company's computer when it crashes. Short of hoarding passwords, how does a person demonstrate that he or she is indispensable for their company? We do not suggest hoarding knowledge or information. It will only make others angry. Rather, and somewhat ironically, perhaps the best way to become indispensable is to give away information. In other words, people who are always helpful and generous with their knowledge come to be regarded as "indispensable."

- *Increase nonsubstitutability.* Closely related to indispensability is non-substitutability. In other words, if no one else is perceived to be capable of bringing what you bring to the organization, this means you are nonsubstitutable.

EXHIBIT 5.2   Political Influence Strategies

According to the Hay Group, managers often use one or more of nine different influence strategies to have impact or influence in their organizations. Most important, there is no single best influence style; rather, each style is effective in different situations.

Influence Strategy	Definition
Empowerment	Making others feel valued by giving them praise, credit, and recognition; and by involving them in decision making and in the planning and implementation of ideas
Interpersonal Awareness	Identifying other people's concerns and positioning one's ideas to address these concerns
Bargaining	Gaining support by offering to exchange favors or resources, by making concessions, or by negotiating to a mutually satisfactory outcome
Relationship Building	Taking the time to get to know others personally and to maintain friendly communication with them so that they will be inclined to support one's ideas in the future
Organizational Awareness	Building support for one's ideas by identifying and getting the support of the key people who can influence others within the organization
Common Vision	Showing how one's ideas support the organization's broader goals or values, or appealing to higher principles such as fairness
Impact Management	Thinking carefully about the most interesting, memorable, or dramatic way to present ideas in order to gain people's support
Logical Persuasion	Using logical reasons, facts, and data to convince others, or using knowledge or expertise to persuade
Coercion	Using threats, punishments, or pressure to get others to do what you want

Source: Hay Group. (2005). *Influence strategies exercise—Profile and interpretive notes,* pp. 3–4. Boston: Hay Group. Copyright © 2005 by Hay Acquisition Company, Inc. All rights reserved. Reprinted by permission.

- *Increase centrality.* **Centrality** refers to how much your work and contributions are part of the core values and activities of the organization. For example, suppose that you are a professor and you teach a "core" course that all students need to take before they can enroll in elective courses. Your course is "central." However, if your course is an elective course that only a few students take and it is not a prerequisite for other classes, then you are less central. By centrality, we don't mean that people should be part of every team. Rather, they should be connected to the key decision makers in the organization and, most importantly, should be the connectors who bring together unique talents in the organization.
- *Associate with powerful managers.* You may not enjoy a lot of power yourself, but if you are connected to powerful people, this can indirectly increase your power in an organization. Top managers often mentor aspiring lower level managers.[9]
- *Build and manage coalitions.* A coalition is a group of people who join together to try to influence a decision. People form coalitions when no one person is powerful enough to achieve their goals single-handedly. Ideally, coalitions should contain as few members as possible to achieve a given objective. This often means recruiting people on a one-on-one, person-by-person basis.
- *Influence decision making.* By influencing decisions, people change the direction of an organization. Ideally, it is important to be unobtrusive and to influence decisions in a way that does not suggest you are self-interested.
- *Control the agenda.* Agendas shape decisions. So, by controlling the agenda, a manager exerts control even before decisions are formulated.

EXHIBIT 5.3 *p*Power, the Personal Power Scale

Directions: For each of the following statements, choose a number on a 7-point scale to indicate your agreement with that statement as it pertains to you. Note: 1 = not true at all; not characteristic of me, and 7 = very true; very characteristic of me.

1. **I can get people to listen to what I say.**
2. **Even when I try, I am not able to get my way. *(R)***
3. **I think I have a great deal of power.**
4. **Even if I voice them, my views have little sway. *(R)***
5. **I can get others to do what I want.**
6. **My ideas and opinions are often ignored. *(R)***
7. **I have a great deal of influence or control.**
8. **If I want to, I get to make the decisions.**
9. **My wishes don't carry much weight. *(R)***

Note: The items with an "R" are reverse-scored, such that 1 = 7, 2 = 6, 3 = 5, 5 = 3, 6 = 2, and 7 = 1. Your total score after reverse-scoring indicates your overall personal power. Higher scores indicate greater personal power.

Source: O'Neill, P., Duffy, C., Enman, M., Blackmer, E., Goodwin, J., & Campbell, E. (1988). Cognition and citizen participation in social action. *Journal of Applied Social Psychology, 18,* 1067–1083.

Power as an Individual Difference

Many people think of power as a personality trait, in which some people possess a greater need to exercise power than do others. For example, the personal power scale in Exhibit 5.3 measures a factor called personal power, or *p***Power**—the degree to which a person desires to use and have power.

How does the use of personal power affect the three key aspects of organizational behavior—people's thoughts, feelings, and behavior? People who use or have power are more likely to be action-oriented, particularly with respect to their goals. For example, in one simulation, some people who were given power in a group task were more likely than others to take a card in a simulated game of blackjack than those who lacked power.[10] Power activates a person's behavior approach system and therefore leads to action.[11] In short, people who have been empowered are not passive; they like to take action. Power can lower a person's inhibitions and natural constraints, which can give rise to disobedience. For a summary of how personal power affects people's judgment, emotion, and behavior, see Exhibit 5.4.

EXHIBIT 5.4 **How Power Affects Judgment, Emotion, and Behavior**

High Power People:	Low Power People:
• Are more sensitive to rewards *(e.g., overestimate how much people positively gossip about them; overestimate how happy people are; feel more positive emotion after watching films, interactions, etc.)*	• Are more sensitive to threats *(e.g., overestimate how much people negatively gossip about them; overestimate how angry people are; feel more negative emotions after watching films, interactions, etc.)*
• Express their ideas more	• Suppress themselves
• Are more likely to pursue goals and resources	• Show greater risk-aversion
• Express greater optimism	• Feel more negative emotion
• Engage in more risk-seeking behavior	• Are less likely to pursue resources
• Engage in greater escalation of commitment	• Believe others are "intrinsically motivated"
• Show greater "hindsight" bias	
• Believe that others are "extrinsically motivated"	
• Devalue others	
• Attempt to increase social distance	

Based on: Keltner, D., Gruenfeld, D. H., & Anderson, C. (2003, April). Power, approach, and inhibition. *Psychological Review, 110*(2), 265–284.

Power and Perception

What is the effect of power on those who actually use it?[12] People are attracted to power, and using power is rewarding and stimulating. People who use power are often egocentric in their perceptions. For example, they believe they are more fair and generous than others regard them to be. It would seem that leaders would be hypervigilant about their styles, seeking constant feedback as to the effectiveness of their approach. Paradoxically, the opposite appears to be true. People in positions of power are less motivated to scan their environment or to process information.[13] In short, they are less dependent on others and, therefore, less motivated to pay attention to the actions of others. In contrast, people who lack power (i.e., are resource dependent on others) have an incentive to pay careful attention to those in power. For example, graduate students (who are dependent on professors to obtain their degree) spend an inordinate amount of time recalling and processing behaviors and activities engaged in by faculty members.[14] Similarly, those who have more power show more variability in their behaviors—in short, they engage in a broader array of behaviors.[15] Similarly, people who lack power are hypervigilant.[16] They are often distrustful of those who have power.[17] People regard power-seeking people to be unethical and question the motives of those who seek to enhance their control.

Sources of Power

David Kipnis asked managers in business organizations how they try to influence their coworkers to do things.[18] Managers said,

- "I simply order him to do what I ask."
- "I act very humble while making my request."
- "I explain the reasons for my request."

These examples suggest that people use different sources of power when attempting to influence people. Most people use one or more of six basic types of power when attempting to influence someone.[19] The six key sources of power include legitimate power, expert power, coercive power, reward power, referent power, and informational power (see Exhibit 5.5).

EXHIBIT 5.5   Sources of Power

(Example: Supervisor Correcting How Subordinate Does Job)	
Source of Power	**Definition**
Legitimate Power	Based on a person's holding of a formal position; other person complies because of belief in legitimacy of power holder (e.g., "I'm your boss")
Reward Power	Based on a person's access to rewards; other person complies because of desire to receive rewards (e.g., promotions)
Coercive Power	Based on a person's ability to punish; other person complies because of fear of punishment (e.g., negative performance evaluations)
Expert power	Based on personal expertise in a certain area; other person complies because of belief in power holder's knowledge (e.g., "I know what is best")
Referent power	Based on a person's attractiveness to others; other person complies because of respect and liking for power holder (e.g., "The company needs you")
Informational power	Based on the higher power person having information that the lower power person does not possess (e.g., "Here's the data that prove it")

Source: French, J. R. P., & Raven, B. (1959). The bases of social power. In D. Cartwright (Ed.), *Studies in social power* (pp. 150–167). Ann Arbor: Institute for Social Research, University of Michigan. Reprinted by permission.

Exhibit 5.5 illustrates six ways that a superior may try to correct how a subordinate does her job. Notice that the six sources of power are ones that anyone might engage in, depending upon the circumstances. **Reward power** is the ability to provide positive outcomes for another person to help that person accomplish a desired goal or offer a valued reward. Rewards could be economic (e.g., a raise), but they can also be subjective (e.g., a smile of approval). **Coercive power** is the use of force, threats of punishment or disapproval to influence someone. **Expert power** is when a person uses special knowledge, training, and expertise to influence others. **Informational power** is the use of data, logical arguments, or persuasive messages to influence another person. **Referent power** occurs when people comply with a request or change because they admire someone or identify with a team. **Legitimate power** is the use of a person's status, job title, or position to influence another. There are many ways that people in organizations signal their authority in a situation.

What kinds of leaders are liked best? In other words, what types of power should a leader choose to use to gain the respect and compliance of others in the organization? The effectiveness of influence strategies used by teachers in U.S. classrooms was investigated as a case in point.[20] Two forms of influence—expert power and referent power—were especially effective. A teacher who uses expert power emphasizes her experience and knowledge so that students comply with requests out of respect for the teacher's expertise. Two other forms of influence, coercion and legitimate authority, are distinctly less effective. Coercion and legitimate authority produce immediate changes in behavior, but in the long run, they do not motivate students. Exhibit 5.6 illustrates that leaders who use coercive power are liked least, whereas leaders who use informational power or referent power are liked most. Leaders who use reward power are liked less than leaders who use legitimate or expert power. Too often, leaders believe that subordinates are responsive to material gains, when in fact subordinates are motivated by intrinsic factors. As we noted in Chapter 2, the prolonged use of material rewards over time can actually undermine an employee's intrinsic interest in performing a task.

Power Motivation

Power has negative connotations in U.S. culture (even in business). Most people do not like to admit that they enjoy using power, and people are highly suspect of individuals who report liking power or using power. Whereas it is considered admirable to be concerned about doing things well (achievement), or making friends (affiliation), it is considered reprehensible to desire to have influence over others (power motivation). Thus, people do

EXHIBIT 5.6

What Kinds of Leaders Are Liked Best?

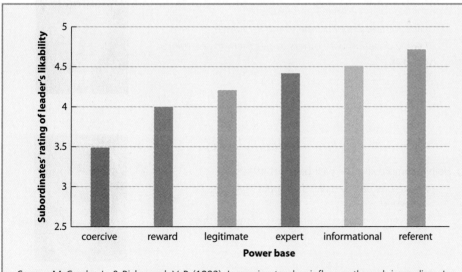

Source: McCrosky, J., & Richmond, V. P. (1992). Increasing teacher influence through immediacy. In V. P. Richmond & J. C. McCrosky (Eds.), *Power in the classroom: Communication, control, and concern, 45,* 200–211. Reprinted by permission of James C. McCrosky.

not readily admit (and are not even aware of) their need for power in their relationships with others. McClelland distinguishes two types of power: **personal power** (which we have talked about as a basic need to be dominant; also known as direct power) and **socialized power** (which is a type of rechanneled power).[21]

Distinction: *p*Power versus *s*Power

If *p*Power (personal power) is a person's need to exercise direct control or influence over others, then *s*Power (socialized power) is a person's need to express power in socially acceptable ways. Many people with power motivation express it through *s*Power. Examples would include people who choose a profession or occupation such as teaching or counseling as a career. Similarly, some people choose to be visible in "prestige professions," including talk show hosts, radio commentators, masters of ceremony, and so on. Some people consistently display **agentic** (i.e., task-oriented) behavior with their friends, such as taking charge of a situation. Other people engage in "mentoring" behavior and roles, another form of "socialized" power. Indeed, a person's power motivation predicts his or her mentoring behavior.[22] And the higher the power motivation of mentors, the more likely they see mentoring behavior as increasing their own reputation.

The power-motivation scale assesses the three motivations that underlie a person's use of power: leadership, prominence, and helping. **Leadership** is assessed by a person's desire to take control and to set direction. **Prominence** is a person's desire to be admired or respected. **Helping** is a person's desire to improve the well-being of others. (See Exhibit 5.7 for examples

EXHIBIT 5.7

Power Motivation

Leadership (taking control, setting direction)
> *I enjoy planning things and deciding what other people should do.*
> *I like to have a lot of control over the events around me.*

President George W. Bush

Prominence (being admired and respected)
> *I like to have people come to me for advice.*
> *I enjoy debating with others to get them to see things my way.*

President Bill Clinton

Helping (improving the well-being of others)
> *I hope one day to make an impact on others or the world.*
> *I am very concerned about the welfare of others.*

President John Kennedy

Source: Adapted from McClelland, D. (1987). *Human motivation.* New York: Cambridge.

of different power motivations.) President George W. Bush exemplifies the leadership power motivation. In April 2006, Bush declared himself the "decider" about the issue of Donald Rumsfeld remaining as the Secretary of Defense.[23] In a very different fashion, former president Bill Clinton exemplified the prominence power motivation. Clinton enjoyed debating his point of view and providing advice for others. He has said that "disagreement is freedom's privilege."[24] In contrast, former president John F. Kennedy exemplified the helping power motivation. Kennedy wanted to profoundly change the world. As an example, recall his inaugural address to the American public on January 20, 1961, in which Kennedy said, "Ask not what your country can do for you, ask what you can do for your country."[25]

Benevolent and Malevolent Power

Power is not a universally corruptive force. Like fire, it is not power that is bad, it is how people use it. How power is used reflects one's personal values and beliefs. For example, power is an opportunity to better the lives of others and improve society (e.g., Abraham Lincoln, Nelson Mandela, and Martin Luther King, Jr.). Alternatively, power is a license to pursue selfish and hostile goals (e.g., Adolf Hitler and Osama Bin Laden). How might we distinguish whether a person's use of power is inherently benevolent or malevolent? The misuse of power scale is one way of examining malevolent and benevolent power.[26] (See Exhibit 5.8 for examples of benevolent and malevolent power.) Another example of the malevolent use of power is the hostile boss or supervisor (see the *New York Times* article on the hostile boss).[27]

Crimes of Obedience

Crimes of obedience are immoral or illegal acts that are committed in response to orders from an authority.[28] For example, when soldiers obey orders to torture or kill unarmed civilians, they are engaging in crimes of obedience. When the prison abuse

EXHIBIT 5.8   Benevolent and Malevolent Power

Malevolent power

"If I had enough money to sue another person, I would sue for all the money she or he was worth."

"The best way of getting your way with someone is to make him or her feel guilty."

Adolf Hitler   Osama Bin Laden

Benevolent power

"It is not acceptable for people in high positions to take liberties with their company's fringe benefits as a form of extra compensation."

"Rules are not meant to be broken, even if no one finds out, and no one is directly hurt."

Mother Teresa   Nelson Mandela   Abraham Lincoln

Source: Lee-Chai, A. Y., & Bargh, J. A. (2001). *The use and abuse of power.* Philadelphia, PA: Psychology Press. Reprinted by permission of Taylor & Francis via Copyright Clearance Center.

EXHIBIT 5.9 Iraq Prison Abuse Scandal

The scandal at Abu Ghraib erupted after the CBS television station broadcast images on April 28, 2004, depicting Iraqi prisoners at Abu Ghraib, near Baghdad, being subjected to a wide range of physical and psychological abuses by U.S. soldiers. Among other things, prisoners were stripped and kept naked in darkened cells without any bathroom facilities and in at least one case, beaten to death. Another picture revealed a U.S. soldier using violence and urinating on a hooded Iraqi captive. Another picture revealed an Iraqi prisoner standing on a box with his head covered, wires attached to his hands. He was told that if he fell off the box, he would be electrocuted. In most of the pictures, Americans are laughing, posing, pointing, or giving the camera a thumbs-up (indicating approval).

The key question is, "Why?" One view is that the abuse was confined to a few ill-disciplined soldiers. Another view is that U.S. leadership, much like the Holocaust in World War II, endorsed the abuse and instructed soldiers to engage in acts of violence and abuse. One soldier, Army Reserve Staff Sergeant Chip Frederick (charged with maltreatment of a prisoner), said, "We [soldiers] had no support, no training whatsoever. And I kept asking my chain of command for certain things like rules and regulations. . . . Military intelligence has encouraged and told us, 'great job.'"

Source: Abuse of Iraqi POWs by GIs probed, 60 Minutes II has exclusive report on alleged mistreatment (2004, April 28). *CBS News.*

scandal at Abu Ghraib, a prison in Iraq, broke in 2004, people were horrified because the conditions at Abu Ghraib deviated so sharply from the Geneva Convention, which has guidelines for the appropriate treatment of prisoners of war (see Exhibit 5.9).

In the 1960s Stanley Milgram designed a series of laboratory experiments to understand the issues involved in obedience to authority.[29] The Milgram studies involved two people, a "learner" and a "teacher." The study was set up so that that a confederate (an accomplice of the experimenter) was always the "learner"; the real subject was always the "teacher." The study was described to "teachers" as an exploration of the benefits of punishment on learning. The teacher's job was to read aloud pairs of words that the learner was supposed to memorize. Each time the learner made a mistake, the teacher was to administer an electric shock. For realism, a large shock machine was put on the table to be controlled by the teacher. The range of voltage was from 15 to 450 volts. The learner was strapped in a chair in another room. The teacher could not see the learner, but could hear the learner. During the testing, the learner made errors in memorizing the words. The learner would groan with each supposed shock and when they reached high levels would actually scream. As the shocks intensified, the learner would beg the teacher to stop, pound the table, and kick the wall. Finally, he simply stopped responding altogether, suggesting he had fallen unconscious or died. (Exhibit 5.10 indicates the percentage of people who obeyed the experimenter's orders.)

As can be seen in Exhibit 5.10, all 40 subjects delivered the 240-volt shock (labeled as intense), and 65 percent of the group, which included business people and other professionals, continued to the highest level of shock (labeled "Danger: Severe Shock"). No one anticipated the levels of obedience that Milgram observed. Psychiatrists, for example, predicted that most people would quickly stop giving shocks once the learner protested. In a series of 18 studies, Milgram identified the conditions that increase or decrease obedience.[30] (This is summarized in Exhibit 5.11.) Situations that make people feel more responsible (i.e., accountable) for their own actions or that stimulate the teacher to take the perspective of the victim (and his or her suffering) are less likely to produce blind obedience. And the physical presence of the authority figure is key. Obedience is greatest when the authority figure (i.e., CEO or general manager) is in the same room. In short, it is harder to disobey your boss when he or she is in the same room. The message from Milgram's studies is that normal people can be led to perform destructive acts when exposed to strong pressure from a legitimate-appearing authority.

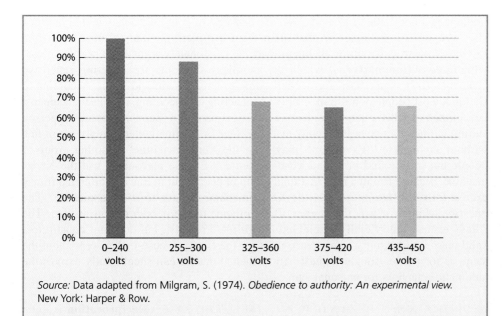

Source: Data adapted from Milgram, S. (1974). *Obedience to authority: An experimental view.* New York: Harper & Row.

EXHIBIT 5.10

Percentage of Subjects Who Obeyed the Experimenter's Orders to Administer Electric Shock

Influence Strategies

We've discussed the types and uses of power extensively. What about influence? Influence is different from power in that, whereas power stems from an underlying need and is usually chronic (long-lasting), **influence** is a tactic, and of a more temporary nature, varying from situation to situation.

Weapons of Influence

Robert Cialdini, a social psychologist, went undercover for several years to study how various organizations use influence with their employees and their customers. For example, Cialdini got a job as a used car salesman to study how organizations train their employees about the use of influence, particularly with customers. He published his

EXHIBIT 5.11   Conditions That Increase Obedience to Authority

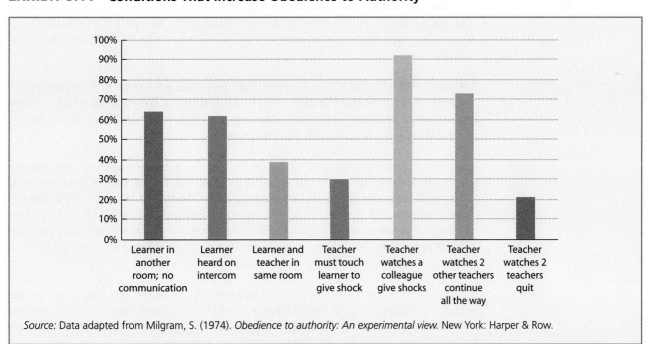

Source: Data adapted from Milgram, S. (1974). *Obedience to authority: An experimental view.* New York: Harper & Row.

findings in a book titled *Influence: Science and Practice.* In his book, Cialdini outlined six "weapons of influence"[31] that stem from a typical person's almost robot-like responses to particular buttons being pushed. He passionately argued that people operate with **fixed-action patterns,** which are mindless shortcuts for enacting repetitive behaviors, such as purchasing groceries, going to a restaurant, and so on. According to Cialdini, most people don't think deeply about acting and deciding, they just engage in a tape of their own behavior. Consider one investigation of how people respond to a person cutting in line in a queue for a copy machine: One of the line-cutters simply cut in line without any excuse ("Excuse me, may I use the Xerox machine"); another group of people cut in line and provided a valid excuse ("Excuse me, may I use the Xerox machine, because I'm in a rush"); a final group of people cut in line and offered a flimsy excuse ("Excuse me, may I use the Xerox machine, I have to make copies").[32] The question of interest was the degree of compliance to the person cutting in line. The flimsy excuse superficially resembled a legitimate request, but does not constitute a valid reason. Shockingly, compliance rates for the flimsy excuse-maker were about the same as for the legitimate request. An influence master can successfully exploit the automatic behaviors for personal gain.

RECIPROCATION: "THE OLD GIVE AND TAKE—AND TAKE" **Reciprocation** is quite simply the irrepressible urge for people to repay others what has been given to them. In one investigation, people had much more success in selling raffle tickets if they had given a cola drink to the target person.[33] People who had been offered soft drinks purchased twice as many raffle tickets, whether or not they had accepted the drink.

COMMITMENT AND CONSISTENCY: "HOBGOBLINS OF THE MIND" People feel enormous pressure to behave in a consistent fashion. Once people have proclaimed an attitude or engaged in a behavior, they are under personal and social pressure to act in a way that is consistent with it. Thus, one way of influencing another person to do what you want is to get them to verbally agree to something before you ask them to engage in a particular behavior, such as buying something.

SOCIAL PROOF: "TRUTHS ARE US" People look to others as a benchmark for what is normal and acceptable. In short, if we are confused or uncertain as to how to behave or think about a certain situation, we watch how other people are reacting. If everyone else is doing something, such as arriving five minutes early (or late) to weekly business strategy meetings, we assume it is the right thing to do. The people to whom we pay closest attention to determine our own behavior are people with high status in the organization.

LIKING: "THE FRIENDLY THIEF" People are more likely to agree to something when someone they know and like asks them to do it. But it is not even necessary to know someone or to like them on the basis of having spent time with them. If we think someone is similar to us, we automatically like them more.

AUTHORITY: "DIRECTED DEFERENCE" As the opening example in this chapter illustrates, most people can be influenced to do something they would not ordinarily do if a powerful authority figure directs them to do so. There are two types of authority: legitimate authority figures (such as doctors in a medical setting, CEOs in a business setting) and pseudo-authority figures, which are people who are not actual authorities, but attempt to be treated as such by the way they dress and their mannerisms. (Exhibit 5.1 is an example of someone who used pseudo-authority.)

SCARCITY: "THE RULE OF THE FEW" **Scarcity** refers to the fact that when people perceive something to be in short supply or available for a limited time only, they become more intent on securing it. In this sense, things (and people) that are hard to get are perceived to be more valuable than things that are within easy reach.

Impression Management

Impression management is the means by which organizational actors try to convey the impressions that others develop of them.[34] By controlling the impressions that others develop of us, we can then influence our access to valued organizational resources, such as jobs, funding, opportunities, and so on. In a political context, such as an organization, impression management might influence the allocation of resources. Broadly speaking, there are seven major self-presentation behaviors that people use to manipulate information (and hence, the impression they convey to others):

- *Self-descriptions:* Statements that describe personal characteristics, such as temperament, traits, opinions, hobbies, and personal life (e.g., "I am trustworthy").
- *Conformity:* Agreeing with someone else's opinion so as to gain his or her approval (e.g., "Yes, I know what you mean and I feel the same way too").
- *Accounts:* Providing excuses, justifications, or other explanations for a troublesome event (such as showing up late to work) in an attempt to minimize the severity and negativity of the event.
- *Apologies:* Admitting responsibility for an undesirable event and at the same time, seeking to be forgiven for the action (e.g., "I am sorry about that. Thanks for your understanding").
- *Acclaiming:* Explaining favorable events to maximize the desirable implications (e.g., "The room was filled to capacity when I was listed as one of the speakers for the new product launch")
- *Flattery:* Complimenting others to gain favor. Strategically, it is best to flatter targets on an aspect of themselves that is very important to them, but that they feel somewhat insecure about.
- *Favors:* Doing something nice for someone to gain approval or a special favor.

All in all, impression management attempts are remarkably successful.[35] In several investigations, many involving job interviewing simulations, job applicants who used IM (impression management) techniques performed better in job interviews than did those who did not use IM, and the interviewers were more inclined to hire the people who used IM.

Why Do People Conform?

There are two main reasons why people conform. People conform because they want to be right or because they want to be liked.

Informational Influence

Informational influence or the "desire to be right" refers to the fact that most people want to see themselves as rational (even if they are not); thus, they can be influenced by relevant information, such as facts and figures, but also testimonials and emotional information. For example, a summer intern on her first day in a new organization may carefully observe the dress and behavior of the managers in the company to determine what is appropriate and expected. Observing others is a key way that we gather information. The tendency to conform to informational influence gained by observing others depends on two things: (1) how well informed we believe the group is (e.g., it may not be helpful to observe the behavior of other summer interns or of part-time consultants), and (2) how confident we are in our own independent judgment (if we are less confident in ourselves, we are more open to influence).

Social Influence

One of the most powerful forms of social influence is our fundamental desire to be liked and admired, especially by the groups we belong to. And we want to avoid being teased or embarrassed.[36] Most people seek membership in social groups (e.g., their departmental units and communities), and if they believe that their group values something, they often bring their own beliefs around as well. Thus, **social influence** (sometimes called normative influence) occurs when people change their beliefs so as to gain acceptance and approval by a valued group. For example, the summer intern described earlier may overstate her interest in golf if she believes that the other people in the organization are golfing aficionados.

When Do People Conform?

Conformity is most likely to occur when critical factors operate, particularly when the group is large, the group is unanimous, and it is committed.

Group Size

Conformity is greater when there are more people present. For example, two other people in agreement produce more conformity in someone than does one person. And three people lead to much more conformity than do two. However, increasing the size of a group past four does not dramatically increase conformity.[37]

Group Unanimity

A person who attempts to stand up to a unanimous group is under an enormous amount of pressure. If the group is not united, however, there is a serious downturn in the degree of conformity. One other dissenter (in an otherwise unanimous group) drops conformity to about one fourth its levels. Moreover, it does not matter who the nonconformer is—highly knowledgeable expert or crackpot![38] It does not even matter if the other nonconformer is right. A nonconformer who advocates for an openly wrong decision can effectively "release" others in the group to move away from the majority. Although it might be annoying to have loudmouths and naysayers in a group, the important fact is that they can improve the group's process.

Group Commitment

The more people feel committed (loyal) to their group, the more likely they are to conform. For example, people are more likely to defer to authorities such as an employer if they receive benefits from belonging to the group or organization.[39] Compliance with authorities is also more likely to occur when people believe they are being treated fairly, trust the motives of authorities, and identify with the group or organization.[40]

Social impact theory suggests that influence is a multiplicative combination of three factors: the number of influence sources, their relevance (and immediacy) to the influence target, and their strength.[41] As an example, consider how social impact theory might predict a person's response to the behavior and dress of his colleagues. If several of his new colleagues are engaging in a particular behavior (such as checking e-mail during meetings, or interrupting others during a discussion), the likelihood is greater that the new hire will begin to do the same (illustrating the *size* principle). If these colleagues are also part of the new hire's project team, their potential influence is greater (illustrating the *commitment* principle). Finally, if the influence attempts are strong and clear, this makes it even more likely that the new hire will conform.

Conclusion

In this chapter, we examined power as a personal characteristic of people that may stem from any of three motives: achievement, affiliation, or control. We looked at power in terms of benevolent and malevolent desires. We discussed several influence tactics, and we then turned the tables and examined the conditions under which powerful people and influential managers are most likely to gain conformity. Throughout this chapter we've argued that the use of power is at the heart of organizational politics. Most people recoil from political organizational environments. However, it would be naïve to believe that power is not a part of all organizations. The student of organizational behavior understands how to analyze power in herself and others, and how to use different types of power and influence effectively and responsibly.

Notes

1. Kelley, H. H., & Thibaut, J. (1978). *Interpersonal relations: A theory of interdependence.* New York: Wiley.
2. Dahl, R. (1957, July). The concept of power. *Behavioral Science,* 202–203.
3. Minzberg, H. T. (1983). *Structure in fives: Designing effective organizations.* Englewood Cliffs, NJ: Prentice-Hall.
4. Robbins, S. (2003). *Organizational behavior* (p. 157). Upper Saddle River, NJ: Prentice Hall.
5. Pfeffer, J. (1981). *Power in organizations* (p. 7). Boston: Pitman.
6. Farrell, D., & Petersen, J. C. (1982). Patterns of political behavior in organizations (p. 405). *Academy of Management Review, 7*(3), 403–412.
7. Ibid.
8. George, J., & Jones, G. (2004). *Understanding and managing organizational behavior* (4th. ed.). Upper Saddle River, NJ: Prentice Hall.
9. Jennings, E. (1967). *The mobile manager.* East Lansing, MI: Michigan State University Press.
10. Galinsky, A. D., Gruenfeld, D. H., & Magee, J. C. (2003, September). From power to action. *Journal of Personality & Social Psychology, 85*(3), 453–466.
11. Keltner, D., Gruenfeld, D. H., & Anderson, C. (2003). Power, approach, and inhibition. *Psychological Review, 110,* 265–284.
12. Fiske, S. T. (1993). Controlling other people: The impact of power on stereotyping. *American Psychologist, 48,* 621–628.
13. Fiske, S. T., & Neuberg, S. L. (1990). A continuum of impression formation from category-based to individuating processes: Influences of information and motivation on attention and interpretation. In M. P. Zanna (Ed.), *Advances in experimental social psychology* (Vol. 23, pp. 1–74). New York: Academic Press.
14. Kramer, R. M. (1996). Divergent realities and convergent disappointments in the hierarchic relation: The intuitive auditor at work. In R. M. Kramer & T. R. Tyler (Eds.), *Trust in organizations* (pp. 216–45). Thousand Oaks, CA: Sage.
15. Guinote, A., Judd, C. M., & Brauer, M. (2002). Effects of power on perceived and objective group variability: Evidence that more powerful groups are more variable. *Journal of Personality and Social Psychology, 82,* 708–721.
16. Kramer, R. M. (1998). Paranoid cognition in social systems: Thinking and acting in the shadow of doubt. *Personality and Social Psychology Review, 2,* 251–75.
17. Lind, A., & Tyler, T. (1988). *The social psychology of procedural justice.* New York and London: Plenum Press.
18. Kipnis, D. (1984). The use of power in organizations and in interpersonal settings. In S. Oskamp (Ed.), *Applied social psychology annual 5* (p. 186). Beverly Hills, CA: Sage.
19. French, J. R., & Raven, B. (1968). The basis of social power. In D. Cartright & A. Zander (Eds.), *Group dynamics.* New York: Harper & Row. Cited in Carlopio, J., Andrewartha, G., & Armstrong, H. (1997). *Developing management skills in Australia.* South Melbourne, Australia: Longman.
20. McCroskey, I. C., & Richmond, V. P. (1992). Increasing teacher influence through immediacy. In V. P. Richmond and I. C. McCroskey, *Power in the classroom: Communication, control, and concern* (pp. 101–119). Hillsdale, NJ: Lawrence Erlbaum.
21. McClelland, D. (1987). *Human motivation.* New York: Cambridge.
22. Schmidt, L. C. (1997). A motivated approach to the prediction of mentoring relationships satisfaction and future intention to mentor. Research report summarized in: Frieze, I. H., & Boneva, B. S. (2001). Power motivation and motivation to help others. In A.Y. Lee-Chai & J. A. Bargh (Eds.), *The use and abuse of power.* New York: Psychology Press.
23. Garden, R. (2006, April 18). President Bush nominates Rob Portman as OMB director and Susan Schwab for USTR (The White House, Office of the Press Secretary). Retrieved May 17, 2006 from http://www.whitehouse.gov/news/releases/2006/04/20060418-1.html.
24. Remarks at a Memorial Day ceremony at the Vietnam Veterans Memorial, Bill Clinton's speech. (1993, May 31). Retrieved May 15, 2007 from www.usmemorialday.org/speeches/President/may31c93.txt.
25. Kennedy Inaugural Ceremony. John Fitzgerald Kennedy, Robert Frost and others. (1961, January 20). *National Recording Preservation Board,* The Library of Congress.
26. Lee-Chai, A.Y., & Chartrand, T. L. (2000). *MOP: The misuse of power scale.* Technical Report #2000A. Research Center for Human Relations. New York University.
27. Carey, B. (2004, June 22). Fear in the workplace: The bullying boss. *New York Times.*
28. Kelman, H. C., & Hamilton, V. L. (1989). *Crimes of obedience: Toward a social psychology of authority and responsibility.* New Haven, CT: Yale University Press.
29. Milgram, S. (1963). Behavioral study of obedience. *Journal of Abnormal and Social Psychology, 67,* 371–378.
30. Milgram, S. (1974). *Obedience to authority.* New York: Harper & Row.
31. Cialdini R.B. (1993). *Influence: Science and practice.* New York: HarperCollins.
32. Langer, E., Blank, A. & Chanowitz, B. (1978). The mindlessness of ostensibly thoughtful action: The role of "placebic" information in interpersonal interaction. *Journal of Personality and Social Psychology, 36*(6), 635–642.

33. Regan, D. T. (1971). Effects of a favor and liking on compliance. *Journal of Experimental Social Psychology, 7,* 627–639.

34. Schlenker, B. R. (1980). *Impression management: The self-concept, social identity, and interpersonal relations.* Monterey, CA: Brooks/Cole.

35. Baron, R. A. (1989). Impression management by applicants during employment interviews: The "too much of a good thing" effect. In R. W. Eder & G. R. Ferris (Eds.), *The employment interview: Theory, research, and practice* (pp. 204–215). Newbury Park: Sage.

36. Janes, L. M., & Olson, J. M. (2000). Peer pressure: The behavioral effects of observing ridicule of others. *Personality and Social Psychology Bulletin, 26*(4), 474–85.

37. Asch, S. E. (1955). Opinions and social pressure. *Scientific American, 193,* 31–35.

38. Morris, W. N., & Miller, R. S. (1975). The effects of consensus-breaking and consensus-preempting partners on reduction of conformity. *Journal of Experimental Social Psychology, 11,* 215–223.

39. Tyler, T. R. (1997). The psychology of legitimacy. *Personality and Social Psychology Review, 1,* 323–345.

40. Huo, Y. J., Smith, H. J., Tyler, T. R., & Lind, E. A. (1996). Superordinate identification, subgroup identification, and justice concerns: Is separatism the problem, is assimilation the answer. *Psychological Science, 7,* 40–45.

41. Latane, B. (1981). The psychology of social impact. *American Psychologist, 36,* 343–356.

Chapter 6

RELATIONSHIPS AND SOCIAL NETWORKS

The world of organizations is fundamentally about relationships. Getting work done depends on having a good relationship with your co-workers. Fortunately, there is a science to relationships. To facilitate study of the central principles of business and personal relationships, complete the Relationship Interdependence analysis in the Self-Discovery section. There are seven steps in this analysis that we will refer to in this chapter. Step 1 asks you to think about a current relationship. Step 2 asks you to think about the rewards you derive from being in this relationship. As with any relationship, there are often costs or burdens, and thus step 3 asks you to indicate the costs involved in maintaining this relationship. In step 4, indicate your overall level of satisfaction and commitment to the relationship. In step 5, try your best to imagine how the other person in the relationship would answer these same questions. Steps 6 and 7 ask you to reflect on how much you are getting out of the relationship and to speculate on what you would do if the relationship were to end.

EXHIBIT 6.1   Dealing with Conflict in a Business Relationship

Letter sent to *Inc. Magazine:* *Two years ago, I started a business with two partners. Most, if not all, of our growth has come on the backs of just two of us; the third partner doesn't do much and we would prefer to get rid of him. Can we simply vote him out of the company?*

Answer: *If only business partnerships were like Survivor. Alas, a better source of reality-show guidance is Court TV, because that's where you'll end up if you mishandle your legal relationships. Nor is a lawsuit all your risk. Extricating yourself from a bad [business] partnership is like defusing a bomb. Sudden moves (plotting a coup or storming into his office flanked by lawyers) can set the whole thing off. Try talking to your partner: He may be unhappy and looking for a graceful exit. If he wants to stay, consider restructuring the partnership to address your unequal contributions.*

Source: McCuan, J. (2004, April 1). Guard your exits! *Inc. Magazine, 4,* 44. Reprinted by permission of Mansueto Ventures LLC via Copyright Clearance Center.

If there is one thing that people in big and small companies, both public and private, self-owned or publicly traded, stress about, it is their relationships—with their bosses, their peers, their subordinates, and even their customers. By all counts, relationships in business are more difficult than relationships in personal life. In our personal life, we can simply follow Francis Edward Smedley's maxim, "All's fair in love and war."[1] Yet, as the example in Exhibit 6.1 indicates, you can't just "walk out" if a business relationship has gone sour. If you do, you risk losing money or even going to court! In this chapter, we examine relationships, trust, and social networks in organizations.

Fundamental Building Blocks of Dyadic Relationships

Dyadic, or two-party, relationships are the fundamental building blocks of all organizational behavior and all social behavior. Dyadic relationships are the second level of analysis in the four levels we introduced in Chapter 1. The one-on-one relationship can be analyzed using interdependence theory and its derivatives, social exchange theory, and equity theory.

Interdependence theory

Thibaut and Kelley argued that the essence of any interpersonal relationship is interaction.[2] They defined **dyadic interaction** as occurring when two people emit behavior in each other's presence. For example, when two roommates plan a party together by asking questions and making plans, they are "emitting" behaviors. The behavior emitted must have the possibility of affecting the other person. For example, if your roommate says that she won't allow anyone to borrow her CDs for the party, this has an effect on you. And each person has an extensive repertoire of behaviors that might be emitted in a given interaction. A **behavior sequence** consists of things that people say and do that are directed at some goal. Some of the responses within this sequence are **instrumental,** in that they move the individual towards the goal; others are **consummatory,** in that they engender the individual's enjoyment of the goal state. For example, making a list of party items to buy is instrumental; joking about what to wear is consummatory. **Interdependence theory** analyzes the pattern of interaction between people in terms of outcomes that people incur in the form of rewards and costs. **Rewards** are the satisfactions that a person receives from interacting with another. **Costs** are the negative consequences of emitting a sequence of behavior. Exhibit 6.2 depicts the different types of resources that people can "exchange" (give and receive) in any relationship. Note that the resources vary in terms of particularism. Resources that are high in **particularism** depend a lot on who is providing the resource (e.g., a kiss from a complete stranger is not as valuable as one from your own child). The value of resources that are low in particularism, such as money, don't change depending on who gave it to you (e.g., $50 from an uncle has as much market value as does $50 received from the lottery). The other dimension is how concrete or tangible the resource is; goods and services (such as a bicycle or housekeeping service) are more tangible than information or status. In general, people try to maximize their rewards and minimize their costs.

EXHIBIT 6.2

**Resources That May
Be Exchanged in
a Relationship**

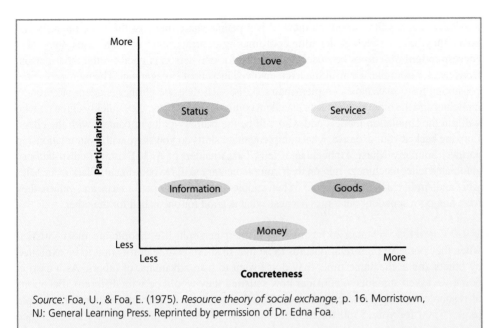

Source: Foa, U., & Foa, E. (1975). *Resource theory of social exchange,* p. 16. Morristown, NJ: General Learning Press. Reprinted by permission of Dr. Edna Foa.

Social Exchange Theory

According to **social exchange theory,** people in relationships exchange rewards and costs.[3] Simply said, when two people are in a relationship, they either might reward or punish each other, or satisfy or frustrate each other. People exchange rewards and costs with each other and subsequently earn profits or incur losses. People in relationships attempt to maximize the goods they receive and minimize the costs they pay in their relationships. These rewards and costs are relative in two senses: (1) relative to what each partner has come to expect out of the relationship in general, and (2) relative to the rewards and costs they could find in some other relationship (e.g., working for a different company or finding another friend to spend time with and confide in).

EVALUATING OUTCOMES People keep track of the rewards and costs they incur in a given relationship. They don't keep Excel spreadsheets, as in the exercise at the beginning of the chapter, but most people make informal assessments of the value they derive from relationships. (As an exercise, ask a friend to describe his or her current personal relationship and note whether he/she refers to costs.) People are concerned with two key indices: the **satisfaction** they derive from their relationships and how **committed** they are to the relationship.[4] When it comes to satisfaction and commitment, people "add up" and "evaluate" their relationship with their boss.[5]

Thibaut and Kelley introduced two measures that drive our satisfaction and commitment to a given relationship: CL and CLalt. **CL,** or **comparison level,** refers to what a person believes he or she is entitled to in a given relationship. This is often influenced by the relationships this person has had in the past and what she has come to expect. Think about the Relationship Interdependence exercise you completed. In step 4, how much "satisfaction" did you indicate? **CLalt,** or **comparison level for alternatives,** refers to the alternatives that a person has to his or her current situation. For example, suppose that an employee, George, has been working for a company, but feels that his supervisor is not allowing him to grow as a leader. George recently received a call from a rival company that has offered him a more exciting job. The other company then becomes George's CLalt. According to Rusbult,[6] the better the "deal" that a person can get elsewhere, the less committed that person will be to a particular relationship. Again, think about the Relationship Interdependence exercise. In step 7, you were asked to indicate how easy it would be to find a different relationship. This is your CLalt.

COORDINATING OUTCOMES In all relationships, people try to coordinate their activities to maximize the benefits to both partners. When people share many of the same interests and goals, they have a much easier time coordinating their actions.[7] In such cases, they have **correspondent outcomes** because what is good for one person is good for the other person. Consider, for example, a consulting team involved in a client engagement. The members of the consulting team may have complementary skills, such that one partner is adept at complex modeling and the other partner is an excellent communicator. Thus, they quickly agree on who will run the simulation models and who will be the primary point of contact with the client. Looking back at your exercise, what complementary skills do you share with your relationship partner? Similarly, Marty Ambuehl and Neil Clark, founders of ATM Express (a distributor of automated teller machines), rely on their complementary skills to coordinate: Clark is the sales whiz and Ambuehl is the manager.[8] When people have different preferences and values, they have non-correspondent outcomes because what is good for one is bad for the other.

SOCIAL UTILITY Whether in business or in their personal life, people are most satisfied when they perceive their relationships to be fair. In short, people don't want to be exploited by others and at the same time, they don't want to take advantage of others. As a case in point, we asked students to consider how satisfied they would be with different allocations of resources (money) to themselves and another person—a business partner, for example (e.g., "$500 for you; $300 for the other person").[9] We paid attention to the difference between how much the self got versus how much the other person got and found that, most of the time, people do not want to make more money than the other person. This explains why the highest point of satisfaction in Exhibit 6.3 is when the difference is zero! As people considered how satisfied they felt when the other person earned significantly more or significantly less, satisfaction dropped—Exhibit 6.3 looks like a tent, draping down. Notice, however, that the tent is more steep (and dissatisfaction is more strong) when we see ourselves as under-benefiting in a relationship. Stated another way, although we like things being equal in our relationships, if it has to be unequal, we'd rather earn more than the other person than have them earn more than us.

In any relationship, we have many choices with respect to how we divide or allocate resources with the most common being equality, equity, and need. **Equality** refers to dividing resources exactly equally between people. For example, suppose you hired some students to

EXHIBIT 6.3

Difference between Own and Other Payoff and Relationship to Satisfaction

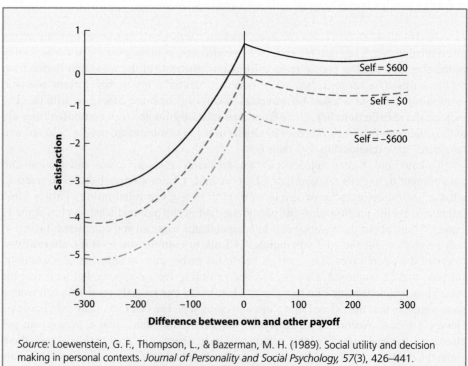

Source: Loewenstein, G. F., Thompson, L., & Bazerman, M. H. (1989). Social utility and decision making in personal contexts. *Journal of Personality and Social Psychology, 57*(3), 426–441. Used by permission of American Psychological Association.

grade papers for a course you were teaching. Imagine that some students work very fast and grade a lot of papers; others work slower and grade fewer papers. The equality rule states that you pay the students equally—without regard to how much they accomplished. In contrast, the **equity rule** states that you pay the students based on how much work they did. Finally, the **needs-based rule** states that you pay the students according to how much they need the money. For example, suppose that some of the students are work-study or co-op students who really need extra money to support themselves in college and buy books.

Communal versus Exchange Relationships

Many people in relationships, particularly personal relationships, such a friendship, dating, or marriage, reject the idea that they keep track of who contributes to the relationship. Rather, people in personal relationships feel that they should contribute what they can and trust that others are doing the same. However, we might not feel this way about a business relationship. For example, if your boss told you that he or she could not pay you, you would probably be upset. Clark and Mills distinguish two types of relationships, exchange relationships and communal relationships.[10] In **exchange relationships,** people give and receive benefits (such as money, time, energy, etc.) with the expectation of receiving comparable benefit in return soon afterward. In exchange relationships, people do not feel a long-term responsibility for others in the business. In contrast, in **communal relationships,** people feel a personal responsibility for the needs of the other people. The idea is that if a person has been a part of an organization, the organization should stand by this person in their time of need. (For an example, see Exhibit 6.4.) There are four key differences between communal and exchange relationships:[11]

■ People in communal relationships pay more attention to the needs of their partners and associates than those in exchange relationships. For example, you are probably more aware of your best friend's needs than your boss's needs.

EXHIBIT 6.4   Communal or Exchange Relationship?

When Lance Armstrong was diagnosed with an extremely aggressive stage IV testicular cancer in 1995, his team, Cofidis, dropped him like a hot potato. Cofidis used a part of their contract with Armstrong to drop his sponsorship on their elite race team. At the same time, Lance Armstrong enjoyed a communal relationship with Nike. Lance did not have insurance. No one ever imagined that he would race again; he was in a fight for his life. Longtime friend Phil Knight of Nike picked up the phone to Nike's benefits department and said, "Give him full coverage." In his book, Armstrong talks about his communal relationship with Nike, "I'll spend the rest of my life trying to adequately convey what it meant to me and I'll be a Nike athlete for as long as I live. They paid my contracts in full, every single one—even though each of them had the right to terminate the deal—and none of them ever so much as asked me about when I would ride a bike again. In fact, when I went to them and said, "Hey, I've started this cancer foundation and I need some money to stage a charity bike race," every single one of them stepped forward to help. So don't talk to me about the cold world of business."

Source: Armstrong, L. (2000). *It's not about the bike: My journey back to life* (pp. 124–125). New York: Berkley Publishing Group.

■ People in communal relationships prefer to talk about emotional topics, such as what makes them happy or sad, whereas people in exchange relationships prefer unemotional topics, such as the weather or stock prices. Think about what topics you feel comfortable discussing with your best friend versus your employer.

■ A person is perceived as more altruistic if she or he offers to help someone in an exchange relationship (because help is only offered unconditionally in communal relationships).

■ A person is seen as more selfish if she or he does not offer to help someone in a communal relationship.

Social Identity and Organizational Identity

As you might imagine, in long-term relationships, people's sense of who they are is intimately tied to the people in their own organizations. In short, people come to see the organization as a part of themselves and vice versa. Moreover, our "social identities" provide us with a buffer against threats and setbacks: When our self-esteem is shaken by a failure experience, our organizational affiliations provide us with reassurance and identity.[12] Indeed, people who think about what they stand for and what their organizations stand for are more cohesive.[13]

Two Types of Ties: People and Group

There are at least two types of bonds that people can have with their group or organization: They can be attracted to the particular individuals in the group (person-based bonds) or they can be attracted to the group, regardless of the specific members (organization-based bonds). The implications might be important for organizations. People who are attracted to their organization might be more unlikely to quit, if a key group of their closest colleagues have been relocated, terminated, or resigned. Think back to the organizational identity exercise in Chapter 1. For each of the organizations you identified, was it the particular people in the organization itself that was meaningful for you? Or was it the group itself?

Improving Relationships

How can people improve their relationships with subordinates, peers, and superiors? To address this issue, we first consider how to develop rewarding relationships. Then, we take up the question of how to address problems in relationships.

Developing Relationships

Many people desire to improve the relationships that they have with their colleagues. However, it is often not easy for people to do this. A first, critical step is to honestly evaluate the status of the relationships you have with others. List 10 of your most important relationships (this includes your friends, bosses, etc.). For each one, consider where your relationship falls along the dimensions outlined in Exhibit 6.5. People who have more varied and flexible perspectives about their relationships are in a better position to handle relationship disappointments. People who have highly "compartmentalized" views of their relationship partners (e.g., they have mostly positive perceptions with a few "red flags" here or there) are most vulnerable to being disappointed with their partners or terminating their relationships.[14] Simply put, if you tend to view your relationships in black-and-white terms (e.g., as highly positive or highly negative), you're likely to be more disappointed and disillusioned about those relationships than if you hold a more complex view of your relationships. It is far better to have an "integrated" view of your relationship partners, where you have struggled to balance the positive qualities of your friends and co-workers in light of their foibles and created a sophisticated, nuanced understanding.

EXHIBIT 6.5   **Dyadic Dimensions Along Which Relationships Develop**

Dimension	From	To
Openness and Self-Disclosure	Limited to "safe," socially acceptable topics	Disclosure goes beyond safe areas to include personally sensitive, private, and controversial topics and aspects of self
Knowledge of Each Other	Surface, "biographic" knowledge — impressionistic in nature	Knowledge is multifaceted and extends to core aspects of personality, needs, and style
Predictability of Other's Reaction and Responses	Limited to socially expected or role-related responses, and those based on first impressions or repeated surface encounters	Predictability of other's reactions extends beyond stereotypical exchange and includes a knowledge of the contingencies affecting the other's reactions
Uniqueness of Interaction	Exchanges are stereotypical, guided by prevailing social norms or role expectations	Exchanges are idiosyncratic to two people, guided by norms that are unique to the relationship
Multi-modality of Communication	Largely limited to verbal channels of communication and stereotypical or unintended nonverbal channels	Includes multiple modalities of communication, including nonverbal and verbal "shorthand" specific to the relationship or the individuals involved; less restrictiveness of nonverbal
Substitutability of Communication	Little substitution among alternative models of communication	Possession of and ability to use alternative modes of communication to convey the same message
Capacity for Conflict and Evaluation	Limited capacity for conflict; use of conflict-avoidance techniques; reluctance to criticize	Readiness and ability to express conflict and make positive or negative evaluations
Spontaneity of Exchange	Interactions tend to be formal or "comfortably informal" as prescribed by prevailing social norms	Greater informality and ease of interaction; movement across topical areas occurs readily and without hesitation or formality

Adapted from: Galegher, J., Kraut, R. E., & Egido, C. (1990). *Intellectual teamwork: Social and technological foundations of cooperative work.* Mahwah, NJ: Lawrence Erlbaum.

Friendship and Work

Although most people avoid office romance (see Exhibit 6.6 for an exception), most people might actually seek to make friends in the office. Is it a good idea? Does it help you and the workplace? *Gallup Management Journal* set out to see: They surveyed 1,003 employees across the United States.[15] The key finding was that employees who are "actively engaged" at work—meaning that they are involved and excited—are the ones most likely to indicate that their workplaces encourage close friendship (55 percent), compared with only 21 percent of those not engaged and only 9 percent of those actively disengaged. And, apparently, when employees are engaged (and making friends with others at work), this has a positive effect on the bottom line. Interestingly, the most important personal relationship that surfaced was the one that employees have with their manager. The managers who are most beloved are described as those who "set others up for success."

Choices in Relationships: Voice, Loyalty, Neglect, and Exit

Carol Rusbult investigated the diverse ways that people react when they are dissatisfied with their relationships.[16] (Rusbult's model has been applied to marriage as well as job satisfaction.) She identified four common reactions to dissatisfaction: voice, loyalty, neglect, and exit.

EXHIBIT 6.6   Office Romance and Office Spouses

Most people have been trained, told, or otherwise warned to not get involved romantically with people at work. The key reason is that when it ends, someone has to lose or be uncomfortable or bitter.

However, the folks at the *Princeton Review* actually encourage office romance. In fact, 6 of the top 10 executives, including the CEO and president, are married to employees who work at the company. Over 40 couples met at the company and have gotten married and 20 children have been born.

More widely speaking, 32% of people have an "office spouse," defined as someone who is of the opposite sex that they bond with out of mutual respect and common interests. In fact, office spouses spend more time with each other than they do with their actual spouses!

Sources: Gossage, B. (2004, February). Fishing off the company pier. *Inc. Magazine* (pp. 17–18); Johne, M. (2006, April 5). Wedded work bliss: The office spouse. *The Globe and Mail* (p. C1). Toronto, Canada.

Consider Exhibit 6.7. As can be seen, there are two critical dimensions to consider, the first being whether the person takes constructive (helpful) action in a relationship or destructive (hurtful) action. The second dimension focuses on whether the person's intervention is active or passive. **Voice** is a constructive, active intervention. Voice occurs when a person actively discusses problems, seeks help, tries to change some aspect of the situation, or is otherwise positively engaged. Voice is most often used when a person has been satisfied with a relationship and invested in the relationship. To illustrate voice, consider the person writing the letter to the editor of *Inc. Magazine* in Exhibit 6.1: He could sit down with the partner, explain his point of view, and suggest a course of action for positive change (voice). Think about the Relationship Interdependence exercise you completed at the outset of this chapter. When have you exercised "voice" in that relationship? What effect did it have?

Loyalty is a constructive, but passive course of action. This person passively waits for things to improve. For example, an employee might publicly support her organization and

EXHIBIT 6.7

Voice, Loyalty, Neglect, and Exit in Relationships

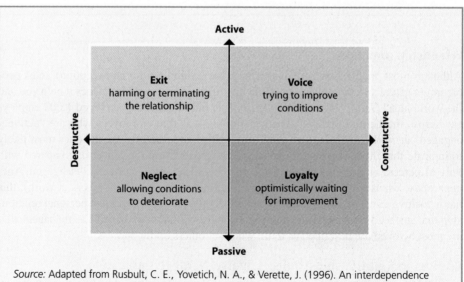

Source: Adapted from Rusbult, C. E., Yovetich, N. A., & Verette, J. (1996). An interdependence analysis of accommodation processes. In G. J. O. Fletcher & J. Fitness (Eds.), *Knowledge structures in close relationships: A social psychological approach.* Mahwah, NJ: Lawrence Erlbaum.

perform her job well, but be privately dissatisfied and waiting patiently for things to change. Loyalty would involve a rationalization process in which the letter-writer to *Inc.* would patiently wait for things to get better. Again, think about your own relationships. When have you exercised loyalty?

Neglect is a destructive, passive course of action. The person engaging in neglect is passively allowing the relationship to deteriorate. In an organization, this may mean that a manager is letting conditions worsen through a lack of effort, or calling in extra sick days. This response is most common when a person has not been satisfied in the relationship and has made low investments in the relationship. Neglect would involve the letter-writer in Exhibit 6.1 not doing anything and continuing to be upset and complaining to others. On what occasions have you neglected a relationship? Were you consciously aware that you neglected the relationship?

Exit is a destructive, active course of action. Exit refers to actively ending a relationship. For example, in a business situation, a person might search for a different job, a transfer, or quit. The partner could simply exit the relationship (the *Inc.* editor hints that this is often tricky to do for legal and financial reasons). When have you exited a relationship?

Types of Trust

Trust is the cornerstone of all relationships. **Trust** is an expression of confidence in another person (or group of people) that you will not be put at risk, harmed, or injured by their actions.[17] Trust is a positive expectation that another person will not act opportunistically.[18] To trust someone means that we could be exploited by that person. And most relationships hold some incentive for people to behave in an untrustworthy fashion.[19] Schindler and Thomas identify five key dimensions of trust in relationships: integrity, competence, consistency, loyalty, and openness.[20]

- **Integrity** refers to honesty and truthfulness.
- **Competence** encompasses our belief that someone possesses the technical and interpersonal skills to carry through with his or her promise.
- **Consistency** relates to a person's reliability, predictability, and judgment in handling situations.
- **Loyalty** is the willingness to protect and save face for another person.
- **Openness** is our belief that the other person is not misrepresenting himself or herself and is neither omitting information nor committing falsehoods.

In the world of organizations (as well as in personal relationships), people form three types of trust in their relationships with others: deterrence-based trust, knowledge-based trust, and identification-based trust.[21]

Deterrence-Based Trust

Deterrence-based trust is predicated on fear of reprisal if trust is violated. People in deterrence-based trust relationships follow through on their promises because they fear the consequences if they violate the trust. Deterrence-based trust is effective to the extent that someone has the ability to make credible threats and carry out punishments. Many people believe that most new relationships—whether personal or business—begin on a base of deterrence. The consequences most often used are punishments, sanctions, incentives, rewards, and legal implications. Deterrence-based trust often involves contracts and various forms of bureaucracy and, sometimes, surveillance. For example, Milton Hershey and Henry Ford both hired detectives to keep an eye on their employees outside of work.[22] Ford even created a "sociological department" inside Ford, staffed by 50 inspectors to keep tabs on autoworkers' behavior off the job. Today, with the advent of sophisticated information technology, the incidence is even greater: Global positioning systems track long-haul truckers' speed on distant highways, unnecessary stops, and non-normal routes. Car sales personnel are fitted with RFID tags to monitor their test drives.

Deterrence-based trust mechanisms are more common than you might think. The vice president of Indianhead Insurance Agency, Inc., in Wisconsin, did not think he had a problem in his office because everyone was always working hard—or so it appeared until Stellar Internet Monitoring revealed that 25 percent of his 40 employees were abusing instant messaging. He says, "We don't have a problem anymore." Overall, 22 percent of companies in the United States have terminated at least one employee for e-mail infractions. However, you don't have to work at a large company to enter into deterrence-based trust relationships. Installing hidden cameras to "spy" on childcare providers is another example of deterrence-based trust. Similarly, a student who asks a friend to "spy" on a dating partner is another example.

It is usually a good idea to formalize even the most trusting of business relationships. For example, Marty Ambuehl and Neil Clark were college friends who owned a piano-moving company. They formed their first partnership with a handshake and a wink. But when they founded their company, ATM (a distributor of automated teller machines), in 1999, they established a more formal structure.[8] Attorneys brought up unthinkable, tough issues right from the start, such as, "What happens if the two of you don't want to be partners anymore?" Exit strategies should always be discussed at the outset of a partnership. Prenuptial agreements (an example of deterrence-based trust) are at an all-time high.[23]

Knowledge-Based Trust

As you can imagine, deterrence-based trust relationships are difficult to maintain for a variety of reasons, not the least of which is that continual monitoring is expensive. Moreover, deterrence-based trust does not produce the kind of loyalty that many organizations wish to engender in their employees. For this reason, many relationships are rooted in **knowledge-based trust,** or trust that derives from a person's history of interaction with someone. Knowledge-based trust is based on a personal repository of information about another person. For example, if a person has been helpful and predictable in the past, then we have more reason to believe that he or she will continue to be helpful and predictable in the future. We acquire knowledge of another person over time and such knowledge is based on a combination of first-hand as well as second-hand (or reputational) information.

Identification-Based Trust

The highest level (and most rewarding level) of trust is achieved when there is an emotional connection between the parties. **Identification trust** is trust that is based on a person's ability to empathize with another person. In essence, it allows one person to act as an agent for another person. The idea is that people understand one another so well and have such aligned interests that each can act on behalf of the other. Transaction costs are much lower in organizations that are characterized by trust, and high-trust societies have an enormous competitive advantage over legalistic societies.

Building Trust: Instrumental and Emotional Mechanisms

The keys for building trust are not that different from those involved in building relationships. Here we identify two routes or paths for building trust. One route is based on instrumental strategies. The other route is based more on relational strategies. Relational trust-building strategies center primarily on building knowledge-based trust, which is largely based on competency and consistency. For an interesting look at how companies try to build trust with customers using relational (instead of instrumental) strategies, see Exhibit 6.8. What are the key ways that people build trust in their relationships within and between organizations?

- *Be consistent:* Consistency is a cornerstone of trust. If you are consistent, people trust you more.
- *Be open-minded:* People don't like others who won't listen to different points of view. Better yet, tell others what it takes to persuade you.
- *Demonstrate competence:* Remember that knowledge-based trust is based on a person's repository of information about your effectiveness in a number of situations.

EXHIBIT 6.8 **Wooing Customers with Relational (Rather Than Instrumental) Strategies**

Customer retention is an issue of paramount concern to companies; it is the single biggest concern for CEOs, according to a Conference Board survey.

Companies have historically been simply too rational and have assumed that their customers are cool-headed rational utility maximizers. Apparently, companies are figuring out that customer loyalty is driven by a meaningful, emotional relationship with a brand (not cool-headed rational calculus).

As one case in point, the taste of food does not predict which customers return to eat fast food at a franchise. Rather, it is the quality of interactions that customers have with the people who take their orders and serve them that are the main predictors. The customers who have pleasant interactions are five times more likely to return.

Source: Adapted from Gopal, A. (June 10, 2004). Customer satisfaction isn't good enough: How to build emotional connections that will keep your customers coming back. *Gallup Management Journal.*

So, even if you have faltered because of ignorance, show that you care enough to bring yourself up to speed.

- *Self-disclosure (up to a point):* Trust builds as people come to know one another. Self-disclosure is the means by which people get to know one another.
- *Get near them:* Also known as the propinquity effect, or the proximity effect: we grow to like the people we find ourselves physically close to.
- *Similarity:* Find points of meaningful similarity between yourself and colleagues.
- *Good mood:* Good moods are contagious and attract people to you.
- *Reciprocity:* If someone does a favor for you, repay it, not with money, but with another favor.

Recovering from Breaches of Trust

Sometimes, despite your best efforts, a breach of trust will occur in a relationship. The question is not so much how to "defend" yourself when trust has been violated, but how to save the relationship (assuming it is worth preserving). What are the best broken-trust-repairing strategies?

- *Apologize without an excuse.* People love apologies but they don't want to hear flimsy excuses or rationalizations.
- *Focus on the future.* You can't change the past, but you can do something about the future. Stop dallying. Say what is going to be different and what you can do.
- *Do something symbolic.* People often remember symbolic displays more than mere words. If your problem was failing to return a call or e-mail, then consider sending "instant message" flowers or a gourmet basket—whatever suits.
- *Be active, not passive.* Don't say, "I don't know what to do." Come up with a plan, and ask for feedback about it.

Networks

So far, we've discussed relationships primarily as a one-on-one concept. However, in organizations, we are part of several one-on-one relationships, and people in those relationships introduce us to others. In this sense, organizations contain networks of one-on-one relationships. Most companies publish organizational charts, which depict formal reporting relationships. The top line of the organizational chart reveals who has the power of position in the company. However, actual relationships do not always necessarily follow those prescribed by formal organizational charts. Informal networks built through trust and relationships between people are actually more informative and predictive of who actually talks to whom and how the work gets done. The organization chart shows the formal rules. But how an organization really works is determined by the human network. For this reason, many companies treat informal networks as an "invisible enemy."[24] Because informal networks are largely invisible, and therefore ungovernable, they represent a threat to some. However, more enlightened companies and their leaders can use networks to achieve far more than they otherwise might. In fact, a study from the Conference Board in New York revealed that the information technology (IT) approach isn't the most successful way to share knowledge or to transform knowledge into action. The study surveyed 200 executives at 158 large global companies and found that the most successful methods for turning knowledge into practical results came from informal employee networks.[25]

Social Capital versus Human Capital

Most of us know correctly what is meant by human capital. Your **human capital** is a composite of your education, skills, and experience. It is a summation of your talent and expertise. Most of us have invested a number of years improving our human capital. Presumably, we think this investment will allow us to bring our organizations more value and will directly influence our compensation. Indeed, there is a strong, positive relationship between the number of years in school (and degrees attained) and the average starting salaries that people make.

A different type of capital is what is known as social capital. If human capital is *what* you know, then social capital is *whom* you know. Social capital is not what you personally bring to the organization in the way of experience, skill, and expertise. Rather, **social capital** refers to your web of personal and business networks of people, information, ideas, leads, business opportunities, and so on. In his book, *Achieving Success through Social Capital,* Baker notes that the "social" in the term "social capital" emphasizes that these resources are not personal assets; no single person owns them.[26] Rather, the resources reside in the networks of relationships. Whereas human capital refers to individual ability, social capital refers to opportunity created through interactions of people. According to Baker, it is a myth that people in organizations can achieve greatness via individual action; rather, what is inevitably necessary for success at the individual and organizational levels are networks of relationships. Baker asserts:

> Success is social: It depends on our relationships with others. All the ingredients of success that we customarily think of as "individual"—natural talent, intelligence, education, effort, and luck—are intricately intertwined with networks. This reconsideration of success demonstrates why it's useful to unlearn the lessons of individual achievement, revising our perspective of the world and how it operates.[27]

The most central people in a network are people bestowed with an extraordinary level of trust. People know what to expect from the "hubs." They return calls. They attend key meetings. They follow through. They are consistent. Their informational bandwidth is enormous. They convey news.

Measuring Social Capital

There are a variety of techniques to measure social capital. Consider Exhibit 6.9. First, let's imagine that Gregory and Berta are the same age, they have the same degree, from the same university, and graduated at the same time—in short, their human capital is nearly indistinguishable.

Next, imagine that each of the dots in the diagrams represents a business contact or colleague. The lines that connect the dots indicate who trusts whom. The dark lines indicate a very strong, interpersonal connection—a trusting, mutual relationship.

Gregory has a network of relatively close colleagues; the key people in Gregory's network all know and trust one another. This is called a **clique network.** Ron Burt notes that all organizational networks contain **structural holes,** or gaps between different people and groups.[28] Gregory spans one structural hole.

Now, consider Berta. First, we immediately notice that her network is much less tightly knit than is Gregory's network. Second, Berta's network spans what appears to be more groups or clusters than does Gregory's network. Berta does not know more people than does Gregory, rather, Berta knows more people who don't know each other. Third,

EXHIBIT 6.9 Social Networks of Two People within the Same Company

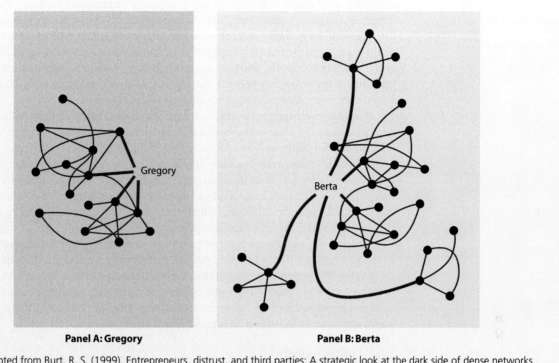

Panel A: Gregory   **Panel B: Berta**

Source: Adapted from Burt, R. S. (1999). Entrepreneurs, distrust, and third parties: A strategic look at the dark side of dense networks. In L. Thompson, J. Levine, & D. Messick (Eds.), *Shared cognition in organizations: The management of knowledge.* Mahwah, NJ: Lawrence Erlbaum.

Berta's network is structurally more unique than is Gregory's network. Berta's network spans 10 structural holes! Berta is a boundary-spanner in her organization. She helps bridge organizational divides.

Exhibit 6.10 summarizes the advantages and disadvantages of boundary-spanning versus clique networks. First, let's consider the typical clique network. The key advantage is the high degree of cohesion that membership in exclusive clique networks affords. Members are emotionally drawn to each other, and it is very reassuring to be a member of a clique network. Another closely related aspect is loyalty and support. If cohesion refers to the mutual attraction that members feel for one another, then loyalty and support is the behavioral extension of cohesion. Finally, another advantage of clique networks is that it is very easy to make decisions because the members of the network have access to similar information.

	Clique Network	Boundary-Spanning Network
Advantages	✓ High cohesion ✓ Loyalty and support ✓ Increased efficiency of decision making	✓ Leverages diversity ✓ Capitalizes on opportunity ✓ Greater innovation ✓ Earlier promotions ✓ Higher salaries
Disadvantages	✓ Redundant communication ✓ Biased communication ✓ Groupthink ✓ Dispensable members	✓ Greater conflict in both task and relationships ✓ Power struggles

EXHIBIT 6.10

Advantages and Disadvantages of Clique and Boundary-Spanning Networks

The disadvantages of clique networks center on the usefulness and timeliness of information. Because members of clique networks are not centrally located in organizational networks, the information they are privy to is often redundant, meaning that it is simply rehashed. Further, because members of clique networks do not have the benefit of alternative points of view, their perspectives could be biased. Under such conditions, groupthink could occur, as in the case in which group members value cohesion over the integrity of the group's decision. Finally, and perhaps most crudely, members of clique networks are dispensable in the sense that because they do not occupy organizationally unique networks, they do not bring an information advantage to their organization.

Boundary-spanning networks, like Berta's network, offer a number of advantages that nicely navigate the disadvantages of a typical clique network. Because boundary-spanners have access to people who are not members of the same network, this increases informational diversity. Moreover, boundary spanners are more likely to be on the leading edge of opportunity—they are more likely to hear "breaking news" before their counterpart clique networkers do. They are more likely to innovate because the greater diversity of ideas can stimulate out-of-the-box thinking. Finally, as we will review next, they are more likely to be promoted and they make higher salaries.

However, boundary-spanning is hard work. Boundary spanners are going to be at the nexus of more conflict—between people, different groups, and different ideas—much more often and more intensely felt than their sequestered clique networkers. Accordingly, boundary-spanners need to be conformable with managing conflict. Because of their powerful informational role in the organization, they may pose a status threat to those who might appear to be higher on an organizational chart.

Types of Networks

Cross and Prusak analyzed the networks at more than 50 large organizations and identified four common network types whose performance is critical for the organization:[29]

Central connectors link most people with one another. They are unlikely to be "formal leaders" but they know who knows what.

- *Boundary-spanners* connect the network with other parts of the company. They step out of their functional comfort zone and consult with different kinds of people.
- *Information brokers* keep the different subgroups in the network together.
- *Peripheral specialists* hold the specialized expertise in the company.

Karen Stephenson suggests that any organization (or any society, for that matter) has at least six different types of networks operating at any given point in time.[30] The six different types of networks represent six core layers of knowledge, each with its own informal network of people exchanging information:

- *Work network:* With whom do you exchange information as part of your daily work? The more structurally diverse your network is—in terms of knowledge and information—the better. For example, a field study of 182 work groups in a Fortune 500 telecommunications firm examined the effectiveness of groups who were diverse in terms of geographic location, functional assignments, and business units.[31] When groups were more diverse, groups performed better when they shared their knowledge.
- *Social network:* With whom do you "check in" at the office to find out what is going on?
- *Innovation network:* With whom do you kick around new ideas or think about wild courses of action?
- *Expert knowledge network:* To whom do you turn for expertise and advice?
- *Career guidance network:* Who do you go to for advice about your future?
- *Learning network:* Whom do you seek out to improve what you are doing? In one investigation, the networks that students use for their own learning was examined.[32] Broadly speaking, students used one of two types of networking behaviors—one targeting professors (vertical networking) and another targeting fellow students (horizontal networking). Both vertical and horizontal networking had a positive impact on grade performance.

Evidence for the Value of Social Capital

Baker makes a powerful business case for the assertion that social capital improves business performance. Baker points to several key indicators, including getting a job, pay and promotion, influence and effectiveness, venture capital funding, organizational learning, word-of-mouth marketing, strategic alliances, mergers and acquisitions, and democracy.[33]

GETTING A JOB Most people do not get jobs via formal mechanisms, such as responding to advertisements or headhunters, Web site postings, and the like. More people find jobs through personal contacts. Granovetter investigated how a group of men in Newton, Massachusetts, found their jobs and discovered that people usually get jobs through others they do not know well.[34] This phenomenon illustrates what Granovetter calls the "strength of weak ties." In the same study, Granovetter also found that people who got jobs through informal networks were paid higher and had a higher degree of job satisfaction, compared to those who got their jobs through formal mechanisms.

PAY AND PROMOTION People with greater social capital are paid more, promoted faster, and promoted at younger ages.[35]

VENTURE CAPITAL AND FINANCING The U.S. Small Business Administration sponsored a series of surveys to examine how start-ups and new businesses get venture capital: 75 percent of start-ups and new businesses secure financing through the "informal investing grapevine"—social networks.[36]

CUSTOMER COMMITMENT In one investigation, customers' trust in their banks was measured separately from their beliefs about their banks' purely self-interested motivations.[37] Customers were less likely to switch banks if they had trust in their banks. The key to customers putting trust in their banks was the extent to which the bank had a customer orientation and bank manager continuity. If banks were not customer focused and if there were too many points of contact between the customers and the bank (i.e., less continuity), the customers did not trust the bank as much and were more likely to switch banks.

QUALITY OF LIFE People with more developed and diverse networks live longer,[38] are less susceptible to the common cold,[39] and are happier than people with less developed networks.

Knowledge of Your Own Network

Krackhardt provides powerful evidence that managers who are cognitively aware of their own networks are more successful than those who are less cognitively aware.[40]

Ethics of Social Capital

A cursory reading of network theory and social capital would seem to suggest that people can manipulate others for their own gain—i.e., they cultivate relationships for their own selfish purposes. Many people believe that such behavior—adding and dropping people from their network—is just plain unethical. According to Baker, every organizational member has an obligation to deliberately manage relationships; anyone who does not is behaving unethically. Moreover, even if you are not aware of it, you manage the size and inclusiveness of your network every day. Baker says, "You can't avoid deliberate decisions about your networks of relationships."[41] Anyone who has gotten married, divorced, and remarried has made a conscious decision about their network. Moreover, anyone who has hired someone, built a project team, fired someone, invited a new hire to a social function, or introduced someone to a colleague has also engaged in network shaping.

Conclusion

We've discussed the importance of relationships in organizations. Many people think that relationship building comes naturally. People who fail to think about, understand, and improve their business relationships are doing a disservice to themselves, their team, and their organizations. To not be conscious of the choices we are making in relationships—whether they be voice, loyalty, neglect, or exit—is to not be aware of the most important aspect of organizational life. People in relationships are not so much self-interested as they are interested in fairness. We discussed how the motive for equity is so strong that people feel compelled to restore it. We discussed how one-on-one relationships compose a person's social network in an organization. Most people are part of tightly organized, highly redundant clique networks. Fewer people are boundary spanners.

Notes

1. Smedley, F. E. (1850). *Frank Fairlegh*. London, U.K.: A. Hall Virtue.

2. Thibaut, J. W., & Kelley, H. H. (1959). *The social psychology of groups*. New York: John Wiley and Sons and Kelley, H. H., & Thibaut, J. W. (1978). *Interpersonal relations: A theory of interdependence*. New York: John Wiley and Sons.

3. Homans, G. C. (1961). *Social behavior: Its elementary forms*. New York: Harcourt, Brace & World.

4. See note 2.

5. Buckingham, M., & Coffman, C. (1999). *First, break all the rules: What the world's greatest managers do differently*. New York: Simon & Schuster.

6. Rusbult, C. E. (1983). A longitudinal test of the investment model: The development (and deterioration) of satisfaction and commitment in heterosexual involvements. *Journal of Personality and Social Psychology, 45,* 101–117.

7. Surra, C. A., & Longstreth, M. (1990). Similarity of outcomes, interdependence, and conflict in dating relationships. *Journal of Personality and Social Psychology, 59,* 501–516.

8. Kessenides, D. (2004, November 1). Happy together. *Inc. Magazine, 11,* 54.

9. Loewenstein, G. F., Thompson, L., & Bazerman, M. H. (1989). Social utility and decision making in interpersonal contexts. *Journal of Personality and Social* Psychology, *57*(3), 426–441.

10. Clark, M. S., & Mills, J. (1979). Interpersonal attraction in exchange and communal relationships. *Journal of Personality and Social Psychology, 37,* 12–24.

11. Mills, J., & Clark, M. S. (2001). Viewing close romantic relationships as communal relationships: Implications for maintenance and enhancement. In J. Harvey & A.Wenzel (Eds.), *Close romantic relationships: Maintenance and enhancement* (pp. 13–25). Hillsdale, NJ: Erlbaum.

12. Meindl, J. R., & Lerner, M. J. (1984). Exacerbation of extreme responses to an outgroup. *Journal of Personality and Social Psychology, 47,* 71–84.

13. Prentice, D. A., Miller, D.T., & Lightdale, J. R. (1994). Asymmetries in attachments to groups and to their members: Distinguishing between common-bond and common-interest groups. *Personality and Social Psychology Bulletin, 20,* 484–493.

14. Showers, C. J., & Zeigler-Hill, V. (2004). Organization of partner knowledge: Implications for relationship outcomes and longitudinal change. *Personality and Social Psychology Bulletin, 30,* 1198–1210.

15. Crabtree, S. (2004, June 10). Getting personal in the workplace. *Gallup Management Journal.*

16. Drigotas, S. M., Whitney, G. A., & Rusbult, C. E. (1995). On the peculiarities of loyalty: A diary study of responses to dissatisfaction in everyday life. *Personality and Social Psychology Bulletin, 21,* 596–609.

17. Axelrod, R. (1984). *The evolution of cooperation.* New York: Basic Books.

18. Boon, S. D., & Holmes, J. G. (1991). The dynamics of interpersonal trust: Resolving uncertainty in the face of risk. In R. A. Hinde & J. Groebel (Eds.), *Cooperation and prosocial behavior* (pp. 190–211). Cambridge, England: Cambridge University Press.

19. Kramer, R. M. (1999). Trust and distrust in organizations: Emerging perspectives, enduring questions. *Annual Review of Psychology, 50,* 569–598; Kramer, R. M., Brewer, M. B., & Hanna, B. (1996). Collective trust and collective action. In R. M. Kramer and T. R. Tyler (Eds.), *Trust in organizations* (pp. 331–356). Thousand Oaks, CA: Sage.

20. Schindler, P. L., & Thomas, C. C. (1993). The structure of interpersonal trust in the workplace. *Psychological Reports, 73,* 563–573.

21. Shapiro, D., Sheppard, B. H. & Cheraskin, L. (1992). Business on handshake. *Negotiation Journal, 8,* 365–77; Lewicki, R. J., & Bunker, B. (1996). Developing and maintaining trust in work relationships. In R. Kramer & T. Tyler (Eds.), *Trust in organizations: Frontiers of theory and research* (pp. 114–139). Newbury Park, CA: Sage.

22. Hammonds, K. (2004, July 1). We, incorporated. *Fast Company,* 67.

23. Kirkman, A. (2005, February/March). Why prenups are on the rise. *Modern Bride Magazine* (pp. 323–326).

24. Cross, R., & Prusak, L. (2002). The people who make organizations go—or stop. *Harvard Business Review, 80*(6), 105–112.

25. The Conference Board. (2000). *Beyond knowledge management: New ways to work* (Report No. 1262–00RR). New York: National Industrial Conference Board.

26. Baker, W. E. (2000). *Achieving success through social capital: Tapping hidden resources in your personal and business networks.* San Francisco, CA: Jossey-Bass.

27. Ibid., p. 9.

28. Burt, R. (1999). Entrepreneurs, distrust, and third parties. In L. L.Thompson, J. M. Levine, & D. M. Messick (Eds.), *Shared cognition in organizations* (pp. 213–243). Mahwah, NJ: Lawrence Erlbaum.

29. Cross, R., & Prusak, K. (2002, June). The people who make organizations go—or stop. *Harvard Business Review,* 5–12.

30. Kleiner, A. (2002). Karen Stephenson's quantum theory of trust. *Strategy & Business, 4th Quarter,* 29.

31. Cummings, J. (2004). Work groups, structural diversity, and knowledge sharing in a global organization. *Management Science, 50*(3), 352–364.

32. Hwang, A., Kessler, E. H., & Francesco, A. M. (2004). Student networking behavior, culture, and grade performance: An empirical study and pedagogical recommendations. *Academy of Management Learning & Education, 3,* 139–150.

33. See note 26.

34. Granovetter, M. (1995). *Getting a job: A study of contacts and careers* (2nd ed.). Chicago: University of Chicago Press.

35. Burt, R. (1992). *Structural holes.* Cambridge, MA: Harvard University Press. (cf. 34).

36. Reynolds, P. D., Bygrave, W. D., & Autio, E. (2003). *Global entrepreneurship monitor: 2003 executive report.* London, U.K.: London Business School and Babson College.

37. Saparito, P. A., Chen, C. C., & Sapienza, H. J. (2004). The role of relational trust in bank–small firm relationships. *Academy of Management Journal, 47*(3), 400–410.

38. Mignone, J. (2003). *Measuring social capital: A guide for First Nations communities.* Canadian Institute for Health Information. Retrieved from: secure.cihi.ca/cihiweb/en/ downloads/MeasuringSocialCapital2003_e.pdf.

39. Cohen, S., Doyle, W. J., Skoner, D. P., Rabin, B. S., & Gwaltney, J. M., Jr. (1997). Social ties and susceptibility to the common cold. *Journal of the American Medical Association, 277,* 1940–1944.

40. Krackhardt, D. (1987). Cognitive social structures. *Social Networks, 9,* 109–134.

41. See note 26.

Chapter 7

DECISION MAKING

Before reading this chapter, complete the Rational Model of Decision Making exercise on the Web site for this chapter (Exercise 7.1). Part of making good decisions is accurately stating decisions that need to be made. Think about a decision you must make in your life right now. People who are able to make rational decisions in their lives—i.e., decisions that are well researched, well evaluated, and implemented in a timely fashion—are in an ideal position to make good decisions for their organizations.

**Herbert Simon
1978 Nobel prize**
for his pioneering research into
the decision-making process
within economic organizations

**Daniel Kahneman
2002 Nobel prize**
for integrating psychological
research into economic science,
particularly concerning
judgment and decision making
under uncertainty

Decision making is the foundation of all organizational activity and the core of a manager's job. Most people think they are superior at making decisions. For example, most people believe that they are in the top quartile on decision-making ability, though it is of course impossible for everyone to be in the top quartile.[1] Thus, most people are under an illusion of superiority when it comes to making decisions.[2] Most people fail to make decisions using full information; and when they do have full information, they often make flawed decisions.

Thus, decision making represents a paradox. Most people regard themselves to be above-average decision makers, but of course it is impossible that everyone is "above average." The challenge of decision making is so difficult and important that the only two Nobel prizes in economics ever awarded to psychologists were for their work on decision making.[3] Herbert Simon, a member of Carnegie Mellon's psychology faculty for over five decades, took the world by storm in 1960 when he published *The New Science of Management Decision*. In 2002, Daniel Kahneman, a psychologist at Princeton, received the Nobel Prize for his work (see Exhibit 7.1).

In this chapter, we introduce decision making at four different levels of analysis, corresponding to the levels introduced in Chapter 1: intrapersonal decisions, interpersonal decisions, group decisions, and organizational-level decisions. We then review three broad types or domains of decisions: decision making under certainty, uncertainty, and risk. Next, we discuss descriptive, normative, and prescriptive Models. In this section, we introduce a compendium of human biases that threaten decision making. We conclude by introducing several methods to improve decision making.

Decision Making: Levels of Analysis

There are four distinct types of decisions, following the four levels of analysis we introduced in Chapter 1:

■ *Intrapersonal decisions:* also known as individual decision making; decisions we make on our own.

■ *Interpersonal decisions:* two-party decision making, such as when a couple purchases a car or house; also, situations in which two people, such as buyer and seller, negotiate.
■ *Group decisions:* decisions that we make in a group or team, are more complex than interpersonal (two-party) decisions.
■ *Organizational-level decisions:* decisions that occur at an organizational level.

Intrapersonal Decisions

Intrapersonal decisions are decisions that we make by ourselves. They can be ordinary (such as deciding which entrée to order from a restaurant menu) or monumental (such as which person to marry, or which job offer to take). Intrapersonal decisions would seem to be the most straightforward decision, but they are often the most difficult because people struggle with evaluating costs and benefits. For example, the stuffed burrito would taste great, but is high in fat; the salad is healthy, but not appetizing.

WANT–SELF VERSUS SHOULD–SELF   One of the most vexing intrapersonal decisions is when we must choose between "wants" and "shoulds."[4] Decision makers essentially have two selves that they must deal with at every decision stage: the want-self and the should-self.[4] *Wants* represent choices that are highly desirable in the short term to the decision maker and often bring immediate gratification, such as indulging in a calorie-laden dessert or perhaps delaying the writing of a report. *Shoulds*, on the other hand, represent choices that are less desirable in the short term, but in the long term will be more beneficial to the decision maker. A good example is physical exercise; many people do not like devoting one hour a day to physical exercise, but in the long run they will be healthier if they do. Unless people are wary, their behavior is going to be driven by their wants (instead of shoulds). In short, a "want" orientation leads to short-term pleasure, but long-term loss.

CONFLICT: APPROACH AND AVOIDANCE   Intrapersonal decisions often involve approach and avoidance. There are three major kinds of intrapersonal approach-avoidance decisions: approach-approach, avoidance-avoidance, and approach-avoidance.[5] Sometimes, people find themselves in an **approach-approach conflict.** These lucky people must choose between two or more attractive options, such as which weekend invitation to accept, which party to attend, which date to accept, or which car to buy. Sometimes people are in **avoidance-avoidance conflict.** Think of this as choosing from among two necessary evils. For example, when cyclist Lance Armstrong was diagnosed with advanced testicular cancer he faced two (undesirable) choices: a radical chemotherapy treatment combining the strongest of drugs that would effectively attack the cancer cells, but would mean that he would never be able to compete again; or a less radical (but experimental) treatment of chemotherapy (that might not be as effective in combating cancer) that might "save" his lungs—necessary for elite athletic performance. Finally, **approach-avoidance conflict** involves choosing options that have both desirable as well as undesirable aspects. For example, a change in job might promise greater remuneration (approach), but would also involve considerable uncertainty and a move that would adversely affect one's family (avoidance).

Interpersonal Decisions

Interpersonal decision making involves two people making joint choices. Whenever two people are interdependent and neither can make a unilateral choice, then they must make an interpersonal decision. Most interpersonal decision making involves a combination of two motives: cooperation and competition.[6] In the relationships chapter, we discussed independence theory and social exchange theory, which involve balancing these two motives.

EXHIBIT 7.2

Interdependence Matrix

In this interpersonal choice situation, the pleasure you / your roommate experience is on a 1–10 scale. The outcomes we receive depend on what the other person (our roommate) decides to do. As we see, the best outcomes are ones in which our behavior is coordinated with that of our roommate.

	Roommate goes to party	Roommate stays home and studies
You go to party	Both of you have a good time and possibly feel some guilt. You: +8 Roommate: +10	You don't enjoy the party as much without your friend and feel some guilt about not studying. You: +5 Roommate: +5
You stay home and study	You do well on the test, but feel that your social life is suffering. You: +6 Roommate: +6	Both of you make A's on the test; studying is easier because you can quiz one another and you are not reminded of the party you are missing. You: +10 Roommate: +8

COORDINATION The clearest way of modeling interpersonal decision making is with an interdependence matrix.[7] For example, consider the interdependence matrix in Exhibit 7.2. In Exhibit 7.2, we see that two roommates must each choose between going to a party or studying for an exam. Notice that each person's outcomes are affected not only by the choice they make, but also by what the other person decides to do. The numbers assigned to each possible outcome represent the pleasure or satisfaction each person feels (hypothetical, of course!) on a 1–10 scale. For illustrative purposes, assume that your roommate is more of a party animal than you. As we can see, both people are more satisfied when they do the same thing than when each person does something different. However, for you, the best situation is for both of you to stay home and study. Your roommate feels the best situation is for both of you to go to the party.

PRISONER'S DILEMMA Albert Tucker coined the term **prisoner's dilemma** to refer to the classic two-party interpersonal decision-making situation.[8] To show the organizational relevance of the prisoner's dilemma, we consider a situation in which two people are suspected of committing a serious crime. However, there is not enough direct evidence to convict the partners in crime. The law enforcement officials would like, ideally, for one or both parties to confess—and therefore, this would provide enough evidence for a conviction. As a first step, the district attorney at the law enforcement office separates the two suspects so that they will not talk or communicate. She then presents the suspects with two choices: They can confess to the crime or remain silent (i.e., not confess). She further explains that their fate (outcome) will be determined not only by what they decide to do, but also by what their partner chooses to do. Obviously, the suspects would be better off if they could coordinate their choices (like the roommates in the previous example). However, unlike our example with the roommates, the district attorney informs the suspects that they cannot communicate with each other. Thus, each of the suspects faces a dilemma: to confess or not to confess. As we can see in Exhibit 7.3, if neither suspect confesses, their jail time is the lowest; thus, this is obviously the best outcome for both of them. But, remember, they cannot talk and coordinate their behavior. So, what should they do, given that they don't know what their partner is going to do?

Many people believe that each suspect should simply not confess and hope that their partner would also not confess. However, it is not that easy. As a way of analyzing the situation, imagine that you are one of the suspects and you have learned that your partner is not going to

EXHIBIT 7.3

Prisoner's Dilemma

		Friend	
		Cooperate (not confess) **C**	**Defect** (confess) **D**
Cooperate (not confess)	**C**	Friend: 2 yrs You: 2 yrs	Friend: 0 yrs You: 10 yrs
Defect (confess)	**D**	Friend: 10 yrs You: 0 yrs	Friend: 5 yrs You: 5 yrs

You (label for rows)

confess. You aren't supposed to know this, but suppose that you have an accurate "insider tip." Thus, your choice boils down to confessing, which would leave you with 0 years in jail, or not confessing, which would leave you with 2 years in jail. If we knew (for sure) that the other person was not going to confess, we would confess so that we would not have to spend any time in jail. Now, let's change the situation and imagine that we have perfectly good information that our partner is going to confess. Our choices then are to confess and go to jail for 5 years or to not confess and go to jail for 10 years. It does not take us long to realize that confessing is better for us, given this situation. Then, we have a realization: We don't need to have an "inside tip" to figure out what we should do. No matter what our partner decides to do, it is always better for us to confess. This is known as **dominance detection**—when we detect a strategy that is uniformly better across situations than any other strategy. Then, we have another disturbing realization: Our partner's dominant strategy is to confess as well. That means that in this situation, both people will confess and go to jail for 5 years—a lose-lose outcome. It would be far better for both parties not to confess. But not confessing requires both parties to suspend self-interest—in other words, it requires people to make themselves highly vulnerable. This is why the situation is called a prisoner's dilemma: The rational pursuit of what is best for us leads to a situation that is worse for everybody.

Tit for Tat. Before you conclude that prisoners' dilemmas only pertain to the decisions faced by criminals, think again. Many everyday situations may be reliably modeled as a prisoner's dilemma situation. For example, consider a situation in which two colleagues, Mac and Mike, are considering how much credit to give their co-worker for their joint work. If they both give the other person credit in public for their work and accomplishments, it gives the impression that both of them are working hard, and ultimately, serves both of them well. If neither of them gives the other credit in public forums, then this does not serve either of them well. Now, consider the possibility that one of them, Mac, gives Mike credit, but Mike does not give Mac credit. This makes Mike look good to superiors and serves Mike (at the expense of Mac). In a parallel fashion, Mike might give Mac credit and Mac might not give Mike credit. The point is: Both colleagues might have an incentive to want to receive credit, but not want to give the other credit. This is the essence of the prisoner's dilemma: the fact that the rational pursuit of self-interest leads to mutually suboptimal outcomes.

Note that the prisoner's dilemma could also be used to study price competition between two airline companies, or brand competition between two beer companies. Not surprisingly, understanding how to deal effectively with prisoner's dilemma situations is paramount for organizational behavior. (As an exercise, visit the Web sites of Miller Beer and Budweiser Beer—these rivals regularly engage in negative advertising.) Robert Axelrod thought the situation was important enough to involve the brains of esteemed scientists from all over the world. He arranged for a computer tournament in which he invited members of the scientific community to participate in a 200-round prisoner's dilemma.[9] To participate in the tournament, every entrant had to submit a "strategy" (i.e., a plan that would guide a decision maker in what to do in every round under all possible conditions). He further explained that the strategies would be evaluated in terms of the maximization of gains across all opponents they faced. Hundreds of strategies were submitted by eminent scholars from around the world.

The winner of the large tournament was the simplest strategy submitted. The computer code was only four lines long. The strategy was called tit-for-tat and was submitted by Anatol Rapoport. Tit-for-tat accumulated the greatest number of points (profits) across all trials with all of its opponents. The basic principle of tit-for-tat is simple: Tit-for-tat always cooperates on the first round and in subsequent rounds does whatever its opponent did on the previous trial. For example, suppose that tit-for-tat played against someone who cooperated on the first trial, defected on the second trial, and then cooperated in the third round. Tit-for-tat would cooperate on the first and second trials but defect on the third round, and resume cooperation in round 4.

Tit-for-tat never beat any of the strategies it played against. Because tit-for-tat is always trusting (and therefore vulnerable) on the first round, it can never do better than its opponent. The most tit-for-tat can do is to earn as much as its opponent. Its tremendous advantage is attributable to the ability of tit-for-tat to induce cooperation in the other party.

Group Decisions

Group decisions build on the analysis of two-party decisions. For example, a **social dilemma** is a multiperson extension of the prisoner's dilemma. Garrett Hardin, a prominent sociologist, described a vexing situation in which members of a community shared a common pasture.[10] Each farming family was allowed to let one cow graze in the grassy commons area. This would allow the family a source of nutrition. Moreover, 100 families sharing the pasture would represent a sustainable level for the commons area (any more cows would threaten the ultimate viability of the natural resource). However, each farmer was motivated to maximize his or her utility by allowing two cows to graze. In this sense, that farmer's utility would be doubled and the difference between 100 and 101 cows grazing in the pasture would be imperceptible. However, if every farmer were to do this, this would result in 200 cows in the pasture, an unsustainable level. Hardin referred to this situation—dilemma—as a social dilemma. There are some critical points of difference between a social dilemma (also known as a multiparty prisoner's dilemma) and a two-party prisoner's dilemma. First, whereas each party in a prisoner's dilemma can directly control the outcomes of the other person, this is not true in a social dilemma. Second, social dilemmas in organizations often render the actions of others anonymous. For example, one common social dilemma in nearly any organization is the supply cabinet. Most organizations don't want go to the trouble of locking the supply cabinet and having to get a key every time a person needs a pad of paper or a box of staples. So they leave it open and unlocked. A highly self-interested person might take most of the supplies from the cabinet for his own use and leave nothing behind. Other office members may not know who is raiding the supply cabinet. Third, social dilemmas are riskier than are prisoner's dilemmas. If you are the only trusting person in an organization of self-interested players, this results in a disastrous outcome for you.

TYPES OF SOCIAL DILEMMAS   Exhibit 7.4 considers two aspects of social dilemmas. On the one hand, social dilemmas can occur within an organization or between organizations, such as in the case of a price war. Internal social dilemmas are those that occur within a given organization. Also known as intraorganizational dilemmas, examples include two colleagues fighting over a corner office, or a single staff member. External social dilemmas, or interorganizational dilemmas, involve competition between companies, such as price competition (such as when airlines drop prices to compete with one another). Another distinction between social dilemmas concerns whether they involve taking too much or failing to contribute.[11] "Taking" dilemmas involve situations in which organizational actors

EXHIBIT 7.4

Social Dilemmas: Multiparty Prisoner's Dilemma Game

	Taking	Contributing
Internal (*Intra-organizational*)	• **Resources (money, real estate, staffing)** • **Budget-fudging**	• **Committee work** • **Recognition**
External (*Inter-organizational*)	• **Price competition** • **Brand competition** • **Overharvesting** • **Pollution**	• **Paying taxes** • **Public television**

Based on: Messick, D. M., & Brewer, M. B. (1983). Solving social dilemmas: A review. In L. Wheeler and P. Shaver (Eds.), *Review of Personality and Social Psychology* (Vol. 4, pp. 11–44). Beverly Hills, CA: Sage.

are overharvesting. "Contributing" social dilemmas involve situations in which people are failing to contribute their fair share, such as in the case of not giving enough recognition to others or failing to pay taxes or support a public good. As an exercise, make a list of all the "public goods" you have enjoyed today, such as public radio, public TV, and so forth. Have you contributed to supporting these goods?

FOSTERING COOPERATION IN SOCIAL DILEMMAS A key question is how to facilitate cooperation in social dilemmas. There are two broad types of strategies (see Exhibit 7.5). One type of strategy involves "structural" solutions. Structural solutions are those that involve significant infrastructure to build. For example, in most U.S. cities, tollbooths have camera-monitoring devices. This is a form of enforcement. Regulation, privatization, and tradable permits are all structural mechanisms that are designed to minimize cheating and self-interested behavior. A number of psychological strategies exist that also are extraordinarily effective in encouraging cooperation in social dilemmas, but that, unlike structural strategies, are not enforceable. Psychological contracts are implicit agreements in which organizational actors agree to cooperate. Handshakes are examples of psychological contracts. Other psychological strategies for increasing cooperation include identifying a superordinate identity, such as a shared common cause; communication (competitive behavior often arises when people are out of touch); personalizing others; and publicizing commitments that people make to cooperate.

Organizational-Level Decisions

Organizational decision making involves decisions made by a collective of individuals. There have been several extensions of interpersonal and group decision making to the level of organizational decision making.

EXHIBIT 7.5   How to Encourage Cooperation in Social Dilemmas

Structural Solutions	*Psychological Solutions*
• Align incentives—enforcement	• Psychological contracts—norm of reciprocity; accountability
• Regulation	• Superordinate identity
• Privatization—putting public lands in private hands	• Communication—clarifies others' behaviors
• Tradable permits—U.S. solution to air pollution	• Personalize others—name contributors (in-group)
	• Publicize commitments—increase risk of social sanctions

Source: Adapted from Brett, J., & Thompson, L. (2007). *Negotiation Strategies for Managers*. Kellogg Executive Program.

CARNEGIE MODEL OF DECISION MAKING   The Carnegie model is the organizational parallel to the bounded rationality approach at the individual level. An important concept in the Carnegie model is **bounded rationality,** or the idea that people have a limited capacity to process information. Another concept is **coalitional activity**, or bands of managers that essentially negotiate and compromise with each other in the decision-making process. Specifically, the Carnegie model suggests that decision makers are highly desirous of making rational decisions, but because they lack time and energy, they cannot devote infinite resources to decision making. Moreover, coalitions of managers are often formed to overpower other managers and thus, decisions become political in organizations. The result is that managers often engage in **satisficing behavior** (quick and dirty solutions) rather than optimizing behavior. For example, the availability bias states that the more prevalent a group or category is judged to be, the easier it is for people to bring instances of this group or category to mind[12] (e.g., it is easier to think of words that begin with the letter "R" as opposed to words that have "R" as the third letter, even though the second group is more common).

GARBAGE CAN MODEL   The **garbage can model** of organizational decision making argues that instead of problems leading to solutions in organizations, organizations create solutions even before they have defined a problem.[13] The garbage can model characterizes organizations in terms of organized anarchy, in which there is high uncertainty in both the ability to identify problems and to solve problems. Organized anarchies have three characteristics:

1. *Ill-defined preferences:* There is lack of consensus among organizational actors on what the goals should be.
2. *Unclear technologies and capacities:* The technology is poorly understood.
3. *Fluid participation:* There is rapid turnover of employees.

The garbage can model is meant to symbolize how organizations tend to solve problems using the most recently used solution or technology (i.e., the one that is at the current top of the heap). Thus, the garbage can model predicts that, among other things, organizations provide solutions to situations that actually don't have problems, create problems that they can solve with currently available solutions, and fail to solve problems that actually exist. Thus, the solutions that are brought to bear on organizational problems do not necessarily fit with the actual environment. Rather, they often reflect internal dynamics, politics, historical accidents, and so on.

The "garbage can" refers to decision making in which problems, solutions, and coalitions mix and compete with each other for organizational attention and action. Chance, luck, and timing are important determinants of what organizations decide to do. It would be far better, of course, for organizations to make decisions based on fact, merit, and appropriate timing.

ORGANIZATIONAL SENSE-MAKING   Daft and Weick suggested that people in organizations attempt to make sense of events around them.[14] They proposed that people are highly motivated to reduce ambiguity and uncertainty. Daft and Weick suggest that rational action in organizations is relatively rare or nonexistent; what really occurs is that reasons to explain behaviors are created after the fact. Thus, the organizational sense-making model argues that people create stories or reasons after the fact in their attempt to explain ambiguous results.

INSIDER VERSUS OUTSIDER VIEWS   Kahneman and Lovallo argue that decision makers in organizations have two distinctly different vantage points for analyzing every organizational problem—the *insider* view and the *outsider* view.[15] The insider view is the biased decision maker who looks at each problem as unique. The outsider view is capable of putting the decision in perspective of the organization's previous decisions and outcomes. Kahneman and Lovallo suggest that organizational decision makers have a strong tendency to consider

EXHIBIT 7.6   Insider/Outsider Views in Decision-Making

In 1976 one of us (Daniel Kahneman) was involved in a project designed to develop a curriculum for the study of judgment and decision making under uncertainty for high schools in Israel. The project was conducted by a small team of academics and teachers. When the team had been in operation for about a year, with some significant achievements already to its credit, the discussion at one of the team meetings turned to the question of how long the project would take. To make the debate more useful, I asked everyone to indicate on a slip of paper their best estimate of the number of months that would be needed to bring the project to a well-defined completion: a complete draft ready for submission to the Ministry of Education. The estimates, including my own, ranged from 18 to 30 months. At this point I had the idea of turning to one of our members, a distinguished expert in curriculum development, asking him a question phrased as follows:

"We are surely not the only team to have tried to develop a curriculum where none existed before. Please try to recall as many such cases as comparable to ours at present. How long did it take them, from that point, to complete their projects?" After a long silence, something much like the following answer was given, with obvious signs of discomfort: "First I should say that not all teams that I can think of in a comparable stage ever did complete their task. About 40% of them eventually gave up. Of the remaining, I cannot think of any that was completed in less than seven years, nor of any that took more than ten." In response to a further question, he answered: "No, I cannot think of any relevant factor that distinguishes us favorably from the teams I have been thinking about. Indeed, my impression is that we are slightly below average in terms of our resources and potential."

Source: Kahneman, D., & Lovallo, D. (1993). Timid choices and bold forecasts: A cognitive perspective on risk taking. *Management Science, 39*(1), 17–31. Reprinted by permission of INFORMS.

problems unique, when in fact problems in organizations reoccur and repeat themselves regularly. Managers tend to view the current problem in isolation and discount or neglect statistics of the past (which could be very useful) in evaluating current decisions. Overly optimistic forecasts result from an insider view of problems, which anchors predictions about the future on plans and scenarios. (See Exhibit 7.6 for an example of one group's failure to look at a decision from the outside.) Left to their own instincts, decision makers uniformly gravitate toward the inside view. Kahneman and Lovallo caution decision makers to adopt an outsider view of problems that brings relevant data and information to bear and allows the decision maker to dispassionately disassociate himself from a problem.

Domains of Decisions

There are three main types of decisions that people and organizations make. We refer to these different types as *domains of decisions:*

- Decision making under certainty
- Decision making under uncertainty
- Decision making under risk

Riskless Choice: Decision Making under Certainty

Riskless choice, also known as decision making under certainty, focuses on how organizational actors choose from among two or more readily available courses of action. For example, consider a student choosing from among three possible cars to purchase, or a company choosing a new logo. There is no risk involved for the most part because the choices and their consequences are largely known. Rather, the decision maker simply needs to weigh each aspect of the decision.

The main model of riskless choice is the multiattribute theory, also known as MAUT. Here is how it works: Consider a student who is attempting to choose from among three jobs, one at a large packaged goods company, another at a small start-up company, and the

EXHIBIT 7.7

Multiattribute Decision Making

Job	Salary (weight = 3)	Location (weight = 1)	Career Advancement (weight = 5)
A: (large packaged goods company)	3	3	2
B: (small start-up company)	1	5	3
C: (medium-sized consulting firm)	4	1	4

third at a medium-sized consulting firm (see Exhibit 7.7). Also, assume that the only relevant dimensions of each job are the salary, the location, and the chances for career advancement. (Obviously, actual career choices are more complex.) Next, assume that the student currently holds an offer from each company and that she effectively "rates" or "evaluates" each job on a 1–5 scale on each of these dimensions, with higher numbers signifying more attractive options.

According to MAUT, a quick and easy way of choosing among these three attractive options is to simply imagine that salary, location, and career advancement are equally important aspects and add up the value of each job. This would yield a value of 8 for the packaged goods company, a value of 9 for the start-up, and a value of 9 for the consulting firm. At this point, the MAUT model prescribes that choice A should be eliminated and the student should choose between B (start-up) and C (consulting firm). However, suppose that further analysis indicates that the student cares more about career advancement than anything else. Presume that (on a 1–5 scale of importance) career advancement is a 5, salary is a 3, and location is only 1. MAUT allows us to reevaluate the alternatives by simply multiplying the value of the alternatives by their relative importance, producing a "weighted" average. This would yield a total value of 22 for the packaged goods company, 23 for the start-up, and 33 for the consulting firm. Suppose, then, that the student tells us that she neglected to consider another key aspect of her job—flexible scheduling. She tells us that flexible scheduling is the most important aspect. This would mean that she should insert another column in her decision-making matrix, give that aspect the most weight, and then recalculate the decision. The important aspect to realize about decision making is that the outcome produced by the multiattribute decision-making model is only as valid as the data that are entered into the decision.

Decision Making under Uncertainty

Sometimes we must make decisions when the alternatives are uncertain or unknown. In such decision situations, the decision maker does not know what the future will bring, nor can she assign meaningful probabilities to it. For example, suppose you are a student choosing a major. It would be great to know if biomedical engineering will be a much-needed skill 15 years hence or whether organizational sociology (your other option) will be more in demand. There are simply too many variables to consider before you can assign probabilities to such a choice. For another example, what is the probability that hiring a new employee will yield an increase in business productivity?

Risky Choice: Decision Making under Risk

The third type of decision making is risky choice, or decision making under risk. Unlike decision making under uncertainty, in which the decision maker cannot assign reasonable probabilities to a decision, in decision making under risk the decision maker has the benefit of knowing the exact odds. The outcomes of risky choice situations are referred to as **prospects.**

EXHIBIT 7.8   Understanding Risk and Probability

Millions of people purchase lottery tickets and gamble—every week and every day. But do they really understand the stakes? Consider these statistics:

- If you toss a coin 26 times, your odds of getting 26 heads in a row are greater than the chance that your Powerball ticket will win you the jackpot.

- To have a reasonable chance of winning the Massachusetts lottery by purchasing a lottery ticket each week, you would need to persist for 1.6 million years.

- If you are an average British citizen who buys a ticket in Britain's National Lottery on Monday, you are 2,500 times more likely to die before the Saturday draw than to win the jackpot. Viewers of the lottery draw are 3 times more likely to die during the 20-minute program than to win.

- If you drive 10 miles to buy a Powerball ticket, you are 16 times more likely to die en route in a car crash than to win.

Source: Myers, D. (2003). The odds on the odds. *Across the Board, 46*(6), 6. Reprinted by permission.

Many people are not accurate at computing risk, even when the odds are perfectly known, as in the case of gambling (see Exhibit 7.8, "Understanding Risk and Probability").

EXPECTED UTILITY THEORY **Expected utility theory,** or EU, dates back to the 16th century, when French noblemen commissioned their court mathematicians to help them choose among gambles or parlor games. Modern utility theory is expressed in the form of gambles, probabilities, and payoffs. EU theory prescribes a theory of rational behavior. Behavior is rational if a person acts in a way that maximizes his or her decision utility or the anticipated satisfaction from a particular outcome. (Note that the maximization of utility is often equated with the maximization of monetary gain, but people obviously care about things other than money.)

UTILITY FUNCTION   A **utility function** is the quantification of a person's preferences with respect to certain objects such as jobs, dating partners, and food—nearly anything. It is possible to assign some score or number to any of several objects (or outcomes). For example, a person's decision to stay at his or her current job may be assigned a value of 6 on a 10-point scale. The possibility of a new job might be assigned either a value of 10 or 3, depending on how things work out at the new organization.

EXPECTED VALUE PRINCIPLE   The **expected value principle** is quite simply the sum of the value of a particular object (or outcome) multiplied by the probability of its occurrence. For example, suppose you have a choice between receiving $10,000 for sure or flipping a coin, with the stakes that tails will result in $0 and heads will result in $20,000. The expected value of the coin flip is $20,000 × .5 = $10,000. Thus, the gamble in this situation has an expected value identical to the sure course of action (i.e., receiving $10,000 for sure). This would normally mean that decision makers would be psychologically indifferent between a sure $10,000 and a risky $20,000. However, they aren't! The vast majority of decision makers prefer the sure thing over the gamble, despite their equivalent expected values.

EXPECTED UTILITY PRINCIPLE   Bernoulli proposed the St. Petersburg paradox to challenge the faultiness of the expected value principle: How much money would you be willing to pay to play a game with the following two rules: (1) An unbiased coin is tossed until it lands on heads. (2) The player of the game is paid $2 if heads appears on the opening toss; $4 if heads first appears on the second toss; $8 on the third toss; $16 on the fourth toss, and so on.[16]

EXHIBIT 7.9 Disease Dilemma: "Gain Version" (*Glass half-full*)

Imagine that the United States is preparing for the outbreak of an unusual Asian disease, which is expected to kill 600 people in the United States alone. Two alternative programs to combat the disease have been proposed. Assume that the exact scientific estimates of the consequences of the programs are as follows:

PLAN A: If program A is adopted, 200 people will be saved.

PLAN B: If program B is adopted, there is a 1/3 probability that 600 people will be saved; and a 2/3 probability that no people will be saved.

Question: *If forced to choose, which plan would you select?*

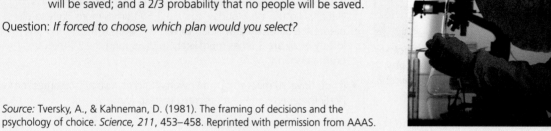

Source: Tversky, A., & Kahneman, D. (1981). The framing of decisions and the psychology of choice. *Science, 211*, 453–458. Reprinted with permission from AAAS.

First, let's calculate the expected value of the game by multiplying the payoff for each possible outcome by the probability of it occurring. Although the probability of the first head appearing on toss *n* becomes progressively smaller as *n* increases, the probability never becomes zero. The implication is that the value of the game is infinite![17] However, this is absurd; most people will not pay more than a few dollars to play.

The reactions that people have to the St. Petersburg paradox suggest that the psychological value of money does not increase proportionally as the objective amount increases. That is, we do not necessarily like $20 twice as much as $10. And the difference in our happiness when a $50,000 salary is raised to $100,000 is not the same as when a $500,000 salary is raised to $550,000. The concept of diminishing marginal utility suggests that additions to monetary amounts result in less increased utility.

Prospect Theory

Prospect theory predicts that people are risk averse for gains and risk-seeking for losses. Gains and losses, according to prospect theory, are defined by reference points.[18] As an example, consider the problem described in Exhibits 7.9, 7.10, and 7.11 (the disease

EXHIBIT 7.10 Disease Dilemma: Loss Version (*Glass half-empty*)

Imagine that the United States is preparing for the outbreak of an unusual Asian disease, which is expected to kill 600 people in the United States alone. Two alternative programs to combat the disease have been proposed. Assume that the exact scientific estimates of the consequences of the programs are as follows:

PLAN A: If program A is adopted, 400 people will die.

PLAN B: If program B is adopted, there is a 1/3 probability that nobody will die; and a 2/3 probability that 600 people will die.

Question: *If forced to choose, which plan would you select?*

Source: Tversky, A., & Kahneman, D. (1981). The framing of decisions and the psychology of choice. *Science, 211*, 453–458. Reprinted with permission from AAAS.

EXHIBIT 7.11 Framing Bias

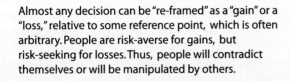

Almost any decision can be "re-framed" as a "gain" or a "loss," relative to some reference point, which is often arbitrary. People are risk-averse for gains, but risk-seeking for losses. Thus, people will contradict themselves or will be manipulated by others.

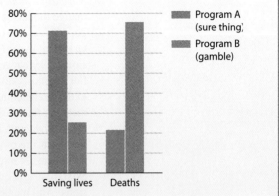

Source: Tversky, A., & Kahneman, D. (1981). The framing of decisions and the psychology of choice. *Science, 211*, 453–458.

dilemma). Most people, when given this problem, choose the sure course of action when they focus on "lives saved" (Exhibit 7.9); yet, when given the identical problem worded in terms of "lives lost" (Exhibit 7.10), the majority of people choose the risky course of action. This inconsistency reveals what Kahneman and Tversky refer to as the **framing effect.**

Descriptive, Normative, and Prescriptive Models

There are at least three purposes for understanding decision making as it occurs in organizations and in life. One purpose of studying decision making is to elaborate on what people "ought" to do. In other words, **normative models** present an ideal method by which people should make decisions. If normative decision making is the study of what people should do, then **descriptive models** investigate what people actually do. The study of people's actual (rather than idealized behavior) is **descriptive research.** Descriptive models tell us what people do particularly well and their key areas of weakness. A final purpose for understanding decision making is to actually help, improve, or otherwise coach people to improve their decision making. The purpose of **prescriptive models** is to address the question: "How can real people—as opposed to imaginary, idealized, super-rational people without psyches—make better choices in a way that does not do violence to their deep cognitive concerns?"[19] Thus, prescriptive analyses leverage some of the key results of normative theories and build on the empirical findings of descriptive studies.

Normative Models

Before we launch into a discussion of what normative decision-making models are and why they are important as a benchmark or an ideal, let's begin by raising the simple question: Why is it important for a decision maker to be rational? In other words, who cares if someone conforms to some ideal standard? Isn't decision making in the "eye of the beholder," so to speak? Stated another way, what is wrong with pure intuition or "gut feel"? *Plenty,* say scholars who study the disastrous effects of making decisions purely by gut feel. Here is a five-pronged argument for why it is desirable for decision makers to be rational:

■ *Normative models provide an ideal.* Models of rational behavior are based on the principle of maximization, such that the course of action followed guarantees that the decision maker will maximize his or her interest (whether that interest is monetary gain, career advancement, prestige, etc.). Normative models are based on the principle of utility maximization, such that the course of action followed guarantees the decision maker will maximize his or her chosen interest.

■ *Normative models are amoral, not immoral.* A very common misconception of normative models is that they induce managers to focus on money rather than on doing good. This is wrong. Normative models are not based on the maximization of monetary gain; they are based on the principle of utility maximization. Whatever the decision maker cares about—the sick, the elderly, goodwill—can be put into the model. For the most part, normative models help the decision maker follow a process; it is up to the decision maker what to put in the model. Thus, normative models are amoral, meaning that they don't involve morals; the decision maker brings those to bear.[20]

■ *Normative models provide ideal benchmarking.* Because normative models are based on a measure of decision-making perfection, they provide an excellent benchmark for managers interested in improving their performance. If rational models did not exist, managers would have no way of evaluating how well they are making decisions. And management theory could not offer any advice on how to help them because there would not be a consensus on what process to follow. In this sense, normative models serve a useful diagnostic purpose because they often reveal where decision makers make mistakes.

■ *Intuition is fundamentally flawed, unless you are an expert.* Too often, people claim that they make decisions based on gut feel. The difference between an expert's gut feel and a novice's gut feel, however, is enormous. First, the expert is able to analyze data at a level that she is not even consciously aware of—much like an expert chess player, who sees entire patterns and games. In contrast, novices who use gut feel are at the mercy of hundreds of human decision-making biases. Just about anything is better than gut feel when it comes to making decisions.[21]

■ *Normative models increase consistency.* The most oft-cited criticism leveled at decision makers is that they are inconsistent in how they make decisions. Indeed, whenever people believe that a leader's decisions are arbitrary, they become angry. Normative models, because of their strong, clear process, allow decision makers to be consistent. Normative models are systematic and consistent, meaning that they produce the same outcome; decision makers whose choices are arbitrary may be accused of ill-will or prejudice. Indeed, one of the insights of normative models is that decision makers would be well-advised not to make decisions themselves, but to model how they make decisions and use their own model to make decisions. As a case in point, Robyn Dawes studied how universities make admission decisions for graduate schools. According to Dawes, when making any kind of decision— whether selecting students for graduate school or choosing a partner—a decision maker is much better off using a linear model to predict likely outcomes. The expected value models and subjective expected utility models are all examples of normative models.[22]

Descriptive Models

More studies have documented how managers make decisions than almost any other aspect of managerial behavior. The results are disturbing: Left to their own devices (i.e., without the use of decision aids or awareness), managers fall prey to a number of decision-making errors and biases. This has led many scholars to conclude that managers are downright irrational.

It helps to define what we mean by rational versus irrational. Bell, Raiffa, and Tversky stated it best when they said,

> When we speak of nonrational people, we do not mean those with diminished capacities; we refer instead to normal people who have not given thought to the process of decision making, or even, if they have, are unable, cognitively, to implement the desire process. Decision makers are not economic automatons; they make mistakes, have remorse, suffer anxieties, and cannot make up their minds.[23]

EXHIBIT 7.12

Decision Biases

Faulty Perceptions about Ourselves	Faulty Perceptions of Others	Using Too Little Information or Invalid Information or Superficial Processing
• Self-serving bias • Egocentric bias • False uniqueness • Illusion of control • Overconfidence	• Halo effect • Forked tail effect • Primacy effect • Negativity effect • Fundamental attribution error • Confirmation bias	• Hindsight bias • Baserate fallacy • Insensitivity to sample size • Representativeness • Anchoring and adjustment

Herb Simon characterized decision makers as "satisficers"—meaning that they do just enough calculation and analysis to make decisions that will satisfy basic organizational criteria.[24] Simon suggested that decision makers, in their worst light, are cognitive misers that hoard their time and effort—preferring not to expend too much effort. Simon challenged decision makers to optimize their decision making.

So, what are these egregious errors that decision makers commit? They fall into three major classes: (1) the tendency to put ourselves in a good light and failure to evaluate ourselves critically, even if it means having double standards; (2) the tendency to form inaccurate impressions of other people, either focusing on the wrong thing or seeing what we want to see; and (3) the tendency to use too little information and jump to conclusions rather than systematically process information (see Exhibit 7.12).

Faulty Perceptions about Ourselves

As strange as it may seem, many people do not have accurate perceptions about themselves. Perhaps this fact explains the popularity of 360-degree feedback and peer feedback. As a way of thinking about yourself in terms of how others view you, consider the Johari Window[25] (see Exhibit 7.13). The aspects of ourselves that we are aware of but others are not is known as the **private self.** The aspects of ourselves that we are aware of and that others are aware of as well is the **transparent self.** The aspects that others see in us, but we fail to see in ourselves is the **unaware self.** Finally, the aspects of us that are hidden from ourselves as well as others is the **hidden self.** Here we consider the key ways in which our self-perceptions do not square with how others see us.

EXHIBIT 7.13

Johari Window

	Things that others see	Things that others don't see or know
Things we know about ourselves	Transparent self	Private self
Things we do not know about ourselves	Unaware self	Hidden self

Source: From *Group processes: An Introduction to group dynamics* by Joseph Luft, © 1984. Reprinted by permission of The McGraw-Hill Companies.

SELF-SERVING BIAS Most people are highly motivated to maintain a positive view of themselves, even if it means turning a blind eye to relevant information or having a double standard. The **self-serving bias** refers to the tendency for people to view themselves in a positive light. For example, upwards of 90 percent of people rate themselves as above average in terms of being intelligent, driving ability, etc.[26] However, it is mathematically impossible that 90 percent of people could be better than "average."

Another form of self-serving bias is how we explain successes and failures. Most people attribute their successes to internal qualities and failures to circumstances beyond their control.[27] As an example, Hyland examined CEOs' annual letters to shareholders.[28] If the company had a bad year, CEOs made significantly more references to unfavorable market conditions (a fact beyond their control); if it had been a good year, CEOs made more references to their own leadership.

EGOCENTRIC BIAS Consider the following situation: You and your roommate or your significant other are presented with a list of various responsibilities, such as "doing housework," "arranging social events," and so forth. You are each asked to (privately) estimate how much you contribute to this responsibility on a 0–100 percent scale, such that if you are the person solely responsible for making social arrangements in your household, you would rate yourself as 100 percent, and so on. Now, imagine that in a relationship, the two numbers (one obtained from each roommate or spouse) are summed together for any given responsibility. If there were complete agreement and accuracy on who was responsible for what, then the two numbers should add up to exactly 100 percent. However, in reality the totals are much higher.[29] People in relationships are guilty of an **egocentric bias**—they see themselves as contributing more. We give ourselves more credit than others give us and we give ourselves more credit than we give others.

ILLUSION OF CONTROL The **illusion of control** refers to the tendency for people to believe that they exert more influence over situations than they actually do.[30] Moreover, people often believe that they can influence purely random events. And the illusion of control extends to events that are totally out of our control. For example, most people believe that good things (such as winning the lottery) are more likely to happen to them than to others; and they believe that unfortunate things (such as being in a flood or car accident) are more likely to happen to others than themselves.[31]

OVERCONFIDENCE Many organizational situations call for us to assess the likelihood that our judgments about someone or something will be correct. ("What is the likelihood, Stan, that the advertising strategy that you propose will increase enrollments in our program?"; "Susan, how confident are you in your sales projections for next quarter?") In such situations, we often put a probability on how likely it is that we will be right. The tendency for people to place unwarranted confidence in their judgment of their abilities is the **overconfidence bias.** For example, disputants in conflict situations were asked the probability that a neutral judge would rule in their favor.[32] Whereas it would seem that the modal response would be 50 percent, respondents were significantly overconfident in believing they would prevail if the situation were to go to trial. Overconfidence does not serve us or our organizations well.

FALSE UNIQUENESS People not only want to see themselves favorably, they want to see themselves as unique. In fact, most people view themselves as more unique than others—again, this is statistically impossible. The **false uniqueness bias** is the tendency to view oneself as different (in a positive direction) from others.[33]

Faulty Perceptions about Other People

Given the importance and value in forming accurate impressions of others, it is surprising, then, that we often arrive at the wrong impression or fail to use all the data when evaluating others.

EXHIBIT 7.14   The Card Problem

Look at the numbers/letters below. Each number/letter represents a card. On each of the 4 cards, a letter appears on one side and a number on the other. Your task is to judge the validity of the following rule: *"If a card has a vowel on one side, then it has an even number on the other side."* Your task is to turn over only those cards that have to be turned over for the correctness of the rule to be judged. What cards will you turn over?

Source: Wason, P. C. (1966). Reasoning. In B. M. Foss (Ed.), *New horizons in psychology* (pp. 135–151), p. 146. Harmonsworth, Middlesex, England: Penguin Books. Reprinted by permission.

FUNDAMENTAL ATTRIBUTION ERROR   The fundamental attribution error is the powerful tendency for people to believe that others' behavior is determined by enduring personality traits and to discount the role of situational factors.[34] For example, believing that if someone comes late to work that they are irresponsible (rather than having missed the bus) is an example of the fundamental attribution error.

CONFIRMATION BIAS   Look at Exhibit 7.14 (the card problem) and answer the question before reading further. Most people (89 percent) turn over the E, which is a correct choice. It is necessary to turn over the E to support the rule. E is a vowel, and if it had an odd number on the other side, this would falsify the rule. A total of 62 percent of people also turn over the 4, which is not an informative choice because a 4 with a K on the other side would neither confirm nor disconfirm the rule. Only 25 percent of people turn over the 7, which is vitally important because, if the 7 has an even number on the other side, the rule is disconfirmed. Thus the correct answer is E and 7. This simple example makes the point that people have a strong tendency to seek information that confirms what they already know (or want to believe). This is called the **confirmation bias.**[35] The confirmation bias is extremely powerful; even trained scientists need to take special steps to ward off its powerful effect.

HALO EFFECT   The halo effect is the tendency for most people to believe that if a person possesses one desirable trait (e.g., good looks or intelligence), then they also possess other attractive traits. As a case in point, attractive people are judged to be nicer and more intelligent than people of average attractiveness.[36]

FORKED TAIL EFFECT   The forked tail effect is the opposite of the halo effect: If we meet a person who possesses one undesirable trait (e.g., physical unattractiveness, or short-temperedness), then we believe that they possess other negative traits. There is a pervasive belief that unattractive people are evil or unintelligent. Consider, for example, how many movies depict villains as physically scarred or deformed.

PRIMACY EFFECT   The **primacy effect** refers to the fact that the first pieces of information we learn about someone can dramatically alter our impression of them. Consider the description of Joe in Exhibit 7.15. When people read paragraph A before B, the great majority rate Joe as friendly. However, if they read paragraph B before Paragraph A, most rate Joe as unfriendly. This occurs despite the fact that the total amount of information about Joe is identical.

EXHIBIT 7.15   The Primacy Effect

A: Joe entered his office and opened his windows to let the bright sunlight in. He opened his office door wide and placed the cookies he'd picked up from the bakery on the community table. He turned on his computer and read through his e-mails. He responded to some pressing e-mails before opening the document that he needed to present to his GM (general manager) on Wednesday. He said "hello" to the secretarial staff when they entered the workroom next to his office.

B: On the way back from the cross-functional team meeting, Joe avoided conversation with the other members. A few times, people made eye contact, but Joe averted his eyes. Some people talked about going out for lunch later in the week, but Joe declined.

Question: Is Joe "friendly"?

Based on: Anderson, N. H., & Jacobson, A. (1965). Effect of stimulus inconsistency and discounting instructions in personality impression formation. *Journal of Personality and Social Psychology, 2,* 531–539.

NEGATIVITY EFFECT The **negativity effect** refers to the fact that once we have learned negative information about someone, we tend to put a lot of weight on that negative information. For example, one character flaw in an otherwise perfect résumé might cause more damage than having an average résumé (with no serious character flaws). In short, we pay more attention to negative information about someone or something than positive information.

Flawed Decision Making

Much of the time, we are not merely forming judgments of ourselves or others; we are attempting to make decisions about our company or to understand a complex sequence of events.

HINDSIGHT BIAS The **hindsight bias** is the tendency for people to believe that something was inevitable after it happened, though they could not predict it.[37] This leads to the "Monday morning quarterback" phenomenon.

BASERATE FALLACY Suppose you are making a tough decision about which video game console to purchase. There are lots of options, and *Consumer Reports* has detailed information about them based on thousands of data points. Your neighbor owns one model and although it is the highest one rated by *Consumer Reports*, she is unhappy with its performance. According to the **baserate fallacy,** people choose to rely on single, vivid data points, rather than much more reliable data.

INSENSITIVITY TO SAMPLE SIZE Look at Exhibit 7.16 (the hospital problem) before reading further. Most people choose "C" (about the same). However, it is much more likely that the average percentage of boys will stray from 50 percent if you have a small sample size. Another example: Which do you think is more likely to happen if you flip a coin, getting 6 heads in 10 flips of a coin or getting 6,000 heads in 10,000 flips of a coin? Certainly, it is not that strange if you get 6 heads in 10 coin flips; but if you got 6,000 heads in 10,000 flips, you would start to suspect an unfair coin. Consider the implications of this bias in advertising (e.g., "Four out of five dentists surveyed recommend sugarless gum for their patients who chew gum").

REPRESENTATIVENESS BIAS The **representativeness bias** comes into play when people attempt to predict the success or outcome of a new product or new hire, or when attempting to judge which category a person or thing best fits. People tend to make judgments on the

EXHIBIT 7.16   Hospital Quiz

A certain town is served by two hospitals. In the larger hospital, about 45 babies are born each day; and in the smaller hospital, about 15 babies are born each day. As you know, about 50 percent of all babies are boys. However, the exact percentage varies from day to day. Sometimes it may be higher than 50 percent, sometimes lower.

For a period of 1 year, each hospital recorded the days in which more than 60 percent of the babies born were boys. Which hospital do you think recorded more such days?"

A. The larger hospital

B. The smaller hospital

C. About the same (*that is, within 5% of each other*)

Source: Kahneman, D., & Tversky, A. (1974). Judgment under uncertainty: Heuristics and biases. *Science, 185*(4157), 1124–1181.

basis of stereotypical cues or information rather than by using more deliberate processing.[38] This can often lead to an accurate prediction. For example, suppose you are trying to predict whether a given MBA student is an accounting major or a marketing major, just based on their appearance and dress. The student in question wears a simple, white button-down shirt and carries a programmable calculator. You further know that at this university, approximately 40 percent of the graduating MBAs are marketing majors and less than 10 percent are accounting majors. What do you think this student's major is? Most people believe the student is an accounting major—based on appearance. However, it is far more likely that the student is a marketing major—based on the odds of 4:1.

ANCHORING   **Anchoring** comes into play when people attempt to extrapolate an estimate, based on some initial starting value.[39] For example, suppose that you are asked to indicate what would yield a larger sum: (a) being given $100,000 on the first day of a 30-day month; or (b) receiving only 1 cent on the first day of the month; 2 cents on the second day of the month, 4 cents on the third day, 8 cents on the fourth day, and so on, such that each day, your money doubles in a cumulative fashion for 30 days. Most people believe that option (a) is clearly better financially. However, they are wrong. By the end of day 30, the cumulative value of receiving a penny on the first day that doubles each consecutive day for 30 days would yield well over $10 million dollars! The payment on day 30 would be $5M! Most people are completely astounded at how this could add up so quickly, because they are psychologically anchored on the minuscule one cent.

Postscript on Human Bias

How do people manage to do anything right, if they are so busy making terrible decisions? First, the human biases and shortcuts identified in this chapter do not always lead to the wrong answer. Sometimes, they lead us to the right answer. Most of us make decisions that are good enough to get us by in everyday life, but probably not good enough to ensure the survival of our organizations. Second, people who see themselves in an overly positive light and have an inflated self-image actually have better psychological health and well-being.[40] Feeling good about ourselves sustains motivation and engagement in productive and creative work.[41] Moreover, positive self-regard fosters good social relationships as well, and it means we are less likely to be negative about others.[42]

Prescriptive Models

The key question is: How we should improve decision making? Fortunately, there are several options.

RATIONAL PROCESS MODELS   Bazerman outlines six steps in a rational decision-making model: (1) define the problem, (2) identify the criteria, (3) weight the criteria, (4) generate alternatives, (5) rate each alternative on each criterion, and (6) compute the optimal decision. Similarly, Hammond, Keeney, and Raiffa (1999) suggest eight steps: (1) work on the right problem, (2) specify your objectives, (3) create imaginative alternatives, (4) understand the consequences, (5) grapple with your trade-offs, (6) clarify uncertainties, (7) think hard about risk tolerance, and (8) consider linked decisions.[43]

AWARENESS OF BIASES Awareness of human biases is a first step in warding off poor decision making. In some cases, simply learning about a potential problem is enough to avoid it. For example, people who learn about entrapment (i.e., escalation of commitment) are less likely to become ensnarled in the "Big Muddy."[44]

DEBIASING AND PROBABILITY THEORY **Debiasing** refers to a procedure for reducing or eliminating biases from the decision maker. Fischhoff proposed four steps that decision makers can follow in debiasing training: (1) offer warnings about the possibility of bias; (2) describe the direction of the bias; (3) provide a dose of feedback; and finally, (4) offer an extended program of training with feedback and coaching. However, debiasing in no way guarantees success. Even when the bias is explicitly described to participants and they are instructed to avoid it, the bias remains.[45] According to Hastie and Dawes, one of the best ways to think systematically and avoid bias is to learn the fundamentals of probability theory and statistics, and apply those concepts systematically to judgments.[46]

EXPERIENCE, FEEDBACK, AND EXPERTISE It is a fallacy to believe that just because a person is a manager, banker, or even accountant, that they are immune to decision bias. In fact, several investigations have found the existence of biases in several highly experienced and expert populations, including real estate agents,[47] stockbrokers, medical doctors[48], and Ph.D.s in statistics and economics.[49] Tversky and Kahneman argued that basic judgmental biases are unlikely to correct themselves over time. The key to experience and learning is feedback.[50]

People can become experts in just about anything. Technically, it takes about 10 years of dedicated, intensive study to become an expert in anything, ranging from sports to physics.[51] If you figure that your organizational career will span 40 years or so, there is ample time to become an expert decision maker.

However, even experts make mistakes. For example, bias and overconfidence has been found to be remarkably high among professionals, including physicians[52] and financial experts.[53]

DECISION SUPPORT MODELS AND GROUP STRUCTURING TECHNIQUES Dawes demonstrates that it is not necessary to use statistically optimal weights in linear models (such as MAUT) to outperform experts. To prove this, Dawes asked a research assistant to go to several data sources and to construct linear models (like MAUT) with weights determined randomly except for sign (i.e., positive or negative). After the first 100 such models outperformed human judges (such as selecting graduate students for programs of study), Dawes constructed 20,000 such "random linear models" using three data sets: (a) final diagnoses of neurosis versus psychosis of 860 psychiatric inpatients; (b) first-year graduate school grade point averages; and (c) faculty ratings of performance of graduate students. All three predictions had been made both by linear models and by human experts, ranging from senior graduate students to eminent clinical experts. On average, the random linear models accounted for 150 percent more variance between criteria and predictions than did the holistic, clinical evaluations of the trained experts. The take-away point is that almost anything is better than letting an expert (much less novice) make a decision!

ACCOUNTABILITY There is some suggestion that when people make decisions that involve significant stakes, they are less likely to succumb to bias, presumably because they process information more carefully. For example, decision makers who feel accountable for their actions show less overconfidence than those who do not.[54]

Conclusion

We used the levels of analysis approach to analyze decision making at the intrapersonal, interpersonal, group, and organizational levels. At the intrapersonal level, we distinguished wants from shoulds, and approach-approach, approach-avoidance, and avoidance-avoidance conflicts. At the interpersonal level of analysis, we analyzed the prisoner's dilemma and concluded that the rational pursuit of self-interest leads to mutually unsatisfying outcomes. We introduced Axelrod's tit-for-tat strategy as a way of extricating oneself from the prisoner's dilemma, assuming that the situation is not a one-shot encounter. We then moved up a level of analysis to group decision making and considered social dilemmas. We distinguished social dilemmas from prisoner's dilemmas. Finally, we analyzed organizational-self decision making and discussed the Carnegie model and the garbage can model of decision making. We also described Weick's sense-making model. Throughout the chapter, we distinguished prescriptive models of decision making from descriptive models. The last part of the chapter considered the most common types of decision biases and methods for minimizing or eliminating bias.

Notes

1. Fischoff, B., Slovic, P., & Lichtenstein, S. (1977). Knowing with certainty: The appropriateness of extreme confidence. *Journal of Experimental Psychology: Human Perception and Performance, 4,* 552–564.
2. Messick, D. M., & Bazerman, M. H. (1996). Ethical leadership and the psychology of decision making. *Sloan Management Review, 37*(2), 9–22.
3. Herbert Simon received his Ph.D. in political science, but he held a position in psychology and published mainly in cognitive psychology journals.
4. O'Connor, K. M., deDreu, C. K. W., Schroth, H., Barry, B., Lituchy, T., & Bazerman, M. H. (2002). What we want to do versus what we think we should do. *Journal of Behavioral Decision Making, 15,* 403–418.
5. Lewin, K. (1935). *A dynamic theory of personality: Selected papers.* New York: McGraw-Hill; Coombs, C. H., & Avrunin, G. S. (1988). *The structure of conflict.* Hillsdale, NJ: Lawrence Erlbaum; Miller, N. E. (1944). Experimental studies of conflict. In J. McV. Hunt (Ed.), *Personality and the behavior disorders* (Vol. 1, pp. 431–465). New York: Ronald Press.
6. Walton, R., & McKersie, R. (1965). *A behavioral theory of labor negotiations: An analysis of a social interaction system.* New York: McGraw-Hill; Deutsch, M. (1973). *The resolution of conflict.* New Haven and London: Yale University Press; Kelley, H. H., & Thibaut, J. W. (1969). Group problem solving. In G. Lindzey & E. Aronson (Eds.), *The handbook of social psychology* (Vol. 4, pp. 1–101). Reading, MA: Addison-Wesley.
7. Thibaut, J. W., & Kelley, H. H. (1986). *The social psychology of groups.* New Brunswick, NJ: Transaction.
8. Tucker, A.W. (1950). *A two-person dilemma.* Mimeo, Stanford University. Published under the heading: On jargon: The prisoner's dilemma. *UMAP Journal, 1*(1980), 101.
9. Axelrod, R. (1981). The emergence of cooperation among egoists. *American Political Science Review, 75,* 306–318.
10. Hardin, G. (1960). Competitive exclusion principle. *Science, 131,* 1292–1297.
11. Messick, D. M., & Brewer, M. B. (1983). Solving social dilemmas: A review. In L. Wheeler & P. Shaver (Eds.), *Review of Personality and Social Psychology* (Vol. 4, pp. 11–44). Beverly Hills, CA: Sage.
12. Kahneman, D., & Tversky, A. (1982). Subjective probability: A judgment of representativeness. In D. Kahneman, P. Slovic, & A. Tversky (Eds.), *Judgment under uncertainty: Heuristics and biases* (pp. 32–47, Ch. 3). New York: Cambridge University Press.
13. Cohen, M., March, J. G., & Olsen, J. P. (1972). A garbage can theory of organizational choice. *Administrative Science Quarterly, 17,* 1–25.
14. Daft, R. L. & Weick, K. E. (1984). Toward a model of organizations as interpretation systems. *Academy of Management Review, 9*(2), 284–295.
15. Kahneman, D., & Lovallo, D. (1993). Timid choices and bold forecasts: A cognitive perspective on risk taking, *Management Science, 39,* 17–31.
16. Bernoulli, D. (1954). Exposition of a new theory of the measurement of risk (L. Sommer, Trans.). *Econometrica, 22,* 23–26. (Original work published 1738.)
17. Lee, W. (1971). *Decision theory and human behavior.* New York: Wiley.
18. Kahneman, D., & Tversky, A. (1979). Prospect theory: An analysis of decision under risk. *Econometrica, 47,* 263–291.
19. Bell, D., Raiffa, H., & Tversky, A. (Eds.). (1988). *Decision making: Descriptive, normative, and prescriptive interactions* (p. 9). New York: Cambridge University Press.
20. Tetlock, P. E., Peterson, R. S., & Lerner, J. S. (1996). Revising the value pluralism model: Incorporating social content and context postulates. In C. Seligman, J. Olson, & M. Zanna (Eds.), *The psychology of values* (pp. 25–51). Mahwah, NJ: Erlbaum.
21. Meehl, P. E. (1954). *Clinical versus statistical prediction.* Minneapolis, MN: University of Minnesota Press.
22. Dawes, R. M. (1979). The robust beauty of improper linear models. *American Psychologist, 34,* 571–582.
23. Ibid., p. 9.
24. Simon, H. A. (1965). *The shape of automation for men and management.* New York: Harper & Row.
25. Named after Joseph Luft and Harrington Ingram.

26. Taylor, S. E., & Brown, J. D. (1988). Illusion and well-being: A social psychological perspective on mental health. *Psychological Bulletin, 103,* 193–210.

27. Miller, D. T., & Ross, M. (1975). Self-serving biases in the attribution of causality. *Psychological Bulletin, 82,* 213–25.

28. Hyland, K. (1998). *Hedging in scientific research articles.* Amsterdam/Philadelphia: John Benjamins.

29. Ross, M., & Sicoly, F. (1979). Egocentric biases in availability and attribution. *Journal of Personality and Social Psychology, 37,* 322–336.

30. Langer, E. (1975). The illusion of control. *Journal of Personality and Social Psychology, 32,* 311–328.

31. Harris, P. (1996). Sufficient grounds for optimism? The relationship between perceived controllability and optimistic bias. *Journal of Social and Clinical Psychology, 15,* 9–52; Weinstein, N. D., & Klein, W. M. (1996). Unrealistic optimism: Present and future. *Journal of Social and Clinical Psychology, 15,* 1–8.

32. Bazerman, M. H., & Neale, M. A. (1982). Improving negotiation effectiveness under final offer arbitration: The role of selection and training. *Journal of Applied Psychology, 67,* 543–548.

33. Snyder, C. R., & Fromkin, H. L. (1980). *Uniqueness: The human pursuit of difference.* New York: Plenum.

34. Ross, L. (1977). The intuitive psychologist and his shortcomings. In L. Berkowitz (Ed.), *Advances in experimental social psychology* (Vol. 10, pp. 173–220). New York: Academic Press.

35. Wason, P. C. (1960). On the failure to eliminate hypotheses in a conceptual task. *Quarterly Journal of Experimental Psychology, 12,* 129–140.

36. Snyder, M., Tanke, E. D., & Berscheid, E. (1977). Social perception and inter-personal behavior: On the self-fulfilling nature of social stereotypes. *Journal of Personality and Social Psychology, 35,* 656–666.

37. Fischhoff, B. (1975). Hindsight = Foresight: The effect of outcome knowledge on judgment under uncertainty. *Journal of Experimental Psychology: Human Perception and Performance, 1,* 288–299.

38. Nisbett, R., & Ross, L. (1980). *Human inference: Strategies and shortcomings of social judgment.* Englewood Cliffs, NJ: Prentice Hall.

39. Kahneman, D., & Tversky, A. (1974). Judgment under uncertainty: Heuristics and biases. *Science, 185*(4157), 1124–1181.

40. Regan, P. C., Snyder, M., & Kassin, S. M. (1995). Unrealistic optimism: Self-enhancement or person positivity? *Personality and Social Psychology, 21,* 1073–1082.

41. Brown, J. D., & Dutton, K. A. (1995). The thrill of victory, the complexity of defeat: Self-esteem and people's emotional reactions to success and failure. *Journal of Personality and Social Psychology, 68,* 712–722.

42. Ybarra, O. (1999). Misanthropic person memory when the need to self-enhance is absent. *Personality and Social Psychology Bulletin, 25,* 261–269.

43. Bazerman, M. H. (2005). *Judgment in managerial decision making* (6th ed.). New York: John Wiley & Sons.

44. Nathanson, S., Brockner, J., et al. (1982). Toward the reduction of entrapment. *Journal of Applied Social Psychology, 12*(3), 193–208.

45. Fischhoff, B. (1982). For those condemned to study the past: Heuristics and biases in hindsight. In D. Kahneman, P. Slovic, & A. Tversky (Eds.), *Judgment under uncertainty: Heuristics and biases.* Cambridge, UK: Cambridge University Press.

46. Hastie, R., & Dawes, R. (2001). *Rational choice in an uncertain world.* Thousand Oaks, CA: Sage.

47. Neale, M., & Northcraft, G. (1986). Experts, amateurs, and refrigerators: Comparing expert and amateur decision making in novel tasks. *Organizational Behavior and Human Decision Processes, 38,* 305–317.

48. Christensen-Szalanski, J. J. J., & Beach, L. R. (1982). Experience and the base-rate fallacy. *Organizational Behavior and Human Performance, 29,* 270–278.

49. Ball, S. B., Bazerman, M. H., & Caroll, J. S. (1991). An evaluation of learning in the bilateral winner's curse. *Organizational Behavior and Human Decision Processes, 48,* 1–22.

50. Hogarth, R. M. (1981). Beyond discrete biases: Functional and dysfunctional aspects of judgmental heuristics. *Psychological Bulletin, 90,* 197–217.

51. Ericsson, K. A., Krampe, R. Th., & Tesch-Roemer, C. (1993). The role of deliberate practice in the acquisition of expert performance. *Psychological Review, 100,* 363–406.

52. Christensen-Szalanski, J. J. J., & Bushyhead, J. B. (1981). Physician's use of probabilistic information in a real clinical setting. *Journal of Experimental Psychology: Human Perception and Performance, 7,* 928–935; Centor, R. M., Dalton, H. P., & Yates, J. F. (1984, November). *Are physicians' probability estimates better or worse than regression model estimates?* Paper presented at the Annual Meeting of the Society for Medical Decision Making, Washington.

53. Staël von Holstein, C. S. (1972). Probabilistic forecasting: An experiment related to the stock market. *Organizational Behavior and Human Performance, 8,* 139–158.

54. Tetlock, P. E., & Kim, J. I. (1987). Accountability and judgment processes in a personality prediction task. *Journal of Personality and Social Psychology, 52,* 700–709.

CONFLICT MANAGEMENT AND NEGOTIATION

Think about a conflict you are currently involved with or a negotiation that you are contemplating. For example, you may be experiencing a conflict with a roommate about expenses or housekeeping. Similarly, perhaps you are attempting to buy some merchandise at less than list price. Next, open up the Negotiation Worksheet (Exercise 8.1 on the Website for this chapter). We will refer to that worksheet during this chapter as a way of understanding conflict and negotiation skills.

Conflict is inevitable in organizations. Consequently, a person's ability to deal with conflict is essential to be successful. This chapter addresses responses to conflict. We identify three types of conflict that occur in organizations, how they affect performance, and how best to deal with them. Next, we turn to the art and science of negotiation. We conclude by examining third-party intervention.

Managerial Grid

A common belief is that people respond to conflict by flight (escaping and avoiding) or by fight (engaging and battling). This is only partially correct. According to Blake and Mouton, there are at least five courses of action that people can take when they find themselves involved in conflict.[1] Their model focuses on the extent to which people are concerned for themselves and the extent to which they are concerned with the other party (see Exhibit 8.1).

To help understand the model, let's use it to analyze a conflict involving Time Warner and the SEC (Securities and Exchange Commission). See Exhibit 8.2.

First, let's imagine that in the scenario described in Exhibit 8.2, involving Richard Parsons (Time Warner) and the SEC, that Parsons did not have great concern for his own company (self), or concern about the SEC. These circumstances would have led him to be extremely passive and perhaps seek to avoid conflict. Now, imagine that Parsons has high concern for the SEC and relatively low concern for himself and his own company, Time Warner. This pattern would predict that he would simply accommodate or capitulate to the demands of the SEC—in other words, he would have restated the Bertelsmann deal, as the SEC wanted him to. Now, imagine that the opposite were true: high concern for the self (own company) and relatively low concern for the other party. This pattern would lead to force or use of threats (his actual strategy). If he had moderate concern for himself and the other party, we would predict him to compromise, that is, reach a midpoint, perhaps by agreeing to do some more markdowns on ads. Finally, in the situation in which Parsons has high concern for himself (own company) coupled with high concern for the other party, we would expect the most collaborative type of conflict resolution, often involving the creation of new alternatives aimed at satisfying both parties. Think about the conflict you described in the opening exercise of this chapter. Which one of the 5 styles did you employ?

EXHIBIT 8.1

Managerial Grid

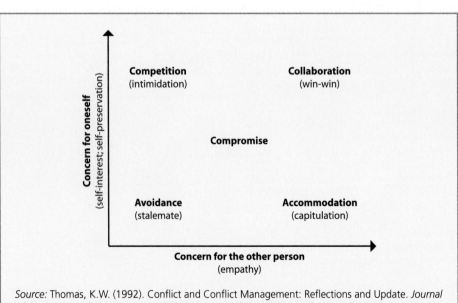

Source: Thomas, K.W. (1992). Conflict and Conflict Management: Reflections and Update. *Journal of Organizational Behavior, 13,* 265–274. Reprinted by permission of John Wiley & Sons Limited.

EXHIBIT 8.2 Conflict Between Time Warner and the SEC

In 2003, Richard D. Parsons, chairman and chief executive officer of Time Warner Inc., was in a conflict with the Securities and Exchange Commission that had lasted for more than 18 months. At the heart of the conflict was the question of whether Time Warner had "properly booked" a number of advertising deals negotiated by America Online Inc. before it merged with Time Warner (the Securities and Exchange Commission is chartered to ensure that companies do not benefit from insider information). Parsons had already revised downward AOL's reported ad revenues by $190 million over a two-year period. However, he refused to capitulate to the SEC's demands that he restate even more by marking down an unusual $400 million advertising deal AOL had reached with German media conglomerate Bertelsmann in 2001. The SEC suspected that AOL gave Bertelsmann the funds that it used to buy AOL ads—something called a "round trip" deal—which seriously violates securities regulations unless disclosed. Parsons dealt with the conflict through a risky, competitive tactic: He challenged the SEC enforcement director, Stephen M. Cutler, that he would "restate immediately" if any outsider auditor or financial professional found anything wrong with the Bertelsmann deal. For several months, a panel of hired guns sifted through AOL documents, e-mails, and databases. Ultimately, they could find nothing blatantly unusual. However, the SEC remained unconvinced.

Source: Dwyer, P., & Yang, C., in Washington, Ewing, J., in Frankfurt, and Lowry, T., in New York (2004, June 7). Showdown at Time Warner. *BusinessWeek,* p. 37.

Types of Conflict

Most people instinctively regard conflict to be a bad thing, and they often try to suppress it. However, conflict can actually be conducive to creative thinking and higher performance in teams (see Chapter 9). The key is to know what kinds of conflict are healthy and how to stimulate those types of conflict. See Exhibit 8.3 for three different types of conflict that can characterize any relationship.[2] (See Exhibit 8.4 for a description of the actual questions that determine which type of conflict characterizes a team or relationship.)

EXHIBIT 8.3

Three Types of Conflict

Type of conflict	Description	Examples
Relationship conflict	Involves disagreements based on personalities and issues that are not directly related to work	• "I hate the sight of his face" • "She is such a loser and she always will be"
Task conflict	Involves disagreements about the work that is being done in a group	• "I don't think we should be changing the name of our group at this point" • "Why should we abandon the marketing campaign that we have all agreed upon up until now?"
Process conflict	Centers on task strategy and delegation of duties and resources	• "We should discuss the candidates first before we vote on them" • "I think we should rotate the role of scribe because it is a lot of work to do"

Based on: Jehn, K. (1995). A multimethod examination of the benefits and detriments of intragroup conflict. *Administrative Science Quarterly, 40,* 256–282; Jehn, K. A., & Mannix, E. A. (2001). The dynamic nature of conflict: A longitudinal study of intragroup conflict and group performance. *Academy of Management Journal, 44*(2), 238–251.

EXHIBIT 8.4

Team Conflict Questionnaire

In thinking about the team you are most involved with at the present time, please answer the following questions on a scale of 1 to 7 with 1 = never, not at all, 4 = somewhat, sometimes, 7 = always, constantly.

Task Conflict

To what extent does your team discuss different ideas or opinions when completing assignments?

How often do your team members discuss evidence for alternative solutions when formulating team recommendations?

How much do your team members consider the pros and cons of each others' opinions when discussing work?

How frequently does your team debate the merits of different ideas when analyzing information or making decisions?

Relationship Conflict*

To what extent is there emotional disagreement among members of your team?

How much tension is there among members of your team?

How often is there personal friction among members of your team?

Process Conflict

People Coordination Conflict

How often is there tension in your team caused by member(s) not performing as well as expected?

How often does your team experience frustration because member(s) do not come prepared for team meetings?

To what extent is there friction in your team caused by member(s) not completing their assignment(s) on time?

How much tension is there in your team caused by member(s) arriving late to team meetings?

Task-Coordination

How much tension is there in your team caused by disagreements about how much time to spend on different parts of team work?

How often do disagreements about the optimal amount of time to spend in meetings occur in your team?

How frequently do members of your team disagree about what the purpose of team meetings should be?

Satisfaction**

How satisfied are you working with this team?

To what extent are you glad you are a part of this team?

How satisfied are your fellow team members with being a member of this team?

Source: Adapted from: Behfar, K. (2003). *The team exchange contract in autonomous work groups: Behaviors and work strategies for sustainable performance.* Doctoral dissertation, Cornell University.

* Jehn, K. (1995). A multimethod examination of the benefits and detriments of intragroup conflict. *Administrative Science Quarterly, 40,* 256–282.

** Peterson, R. (1997). A directive leadership style in group decision making can be both virtue and vice: Evidence from elite and experimental groups. *Journal of Personality and Social Psychology, 72*(5), 1107–1121.

Task Conflict

Task conflict, or cognitive conflict, is conflict about the issues, not about the people behind the issues. In this sense, it is depersonalized. Arguments about the merits of ideas, plans, and projects, and even utilization of scarce resources, are all examples of task conflict. In certain cases, task conflict improves the functioning of teams.[3] Task conflict stimulates creativity because it forces people to rethink problems and arrive at outcomes that everyone can live with.

Process Conflict

Process conflict centers on disagreements that people have on how to approach a task, and specifically who should be doing what. Process conflict is centered on how the group is achieving its goal. To this extent, it often centers on the nitty-gritty of conflict, such as members' pet peeves about the process, such as, "You never invite me to meetings" and "You always arrive 15 minutes late."

Relationship Conflict

Relationship conflict is also known as personality conflict or affective (emotional) conflict.[4] Relationship conflict does not always manifest itself in shouting matches; many people actively avoid conflict and when they do, the conflict is latent. Compared to the other types of conflict, relationship conflict is the most damaging and detrimental to group functioning.

Conflict and Productivity

De Dreu and Weingart conducted a meta-analysis of the association between different types of conflict (e.g., task conflict, relationship conflict, and a variety of measures of performance, such as team performance and team satisfaction). Results revealed strong negative correlations between relationship conflict and team performance. Moreover, the results indicated a negative relationship between task conflict and team performance and team satisfaction. Peterson and Behfar studied 67 teams and found that when groups receive negative performance feedback early on, relationship and task conflict increases.[5] However, groups that have high levels of trust early on are buffered from experiencing future relationship conflict (see Exhibit 8.5).

Resolving Conflict

The key is to not eliminate or suppress conflict—it is completely natural for conflict to emerge in organizations. Rather, it is better to transform unhealthy relationship conflict into a healthier version of conflict. Here, we discuss effective conflict management strategies.[6]

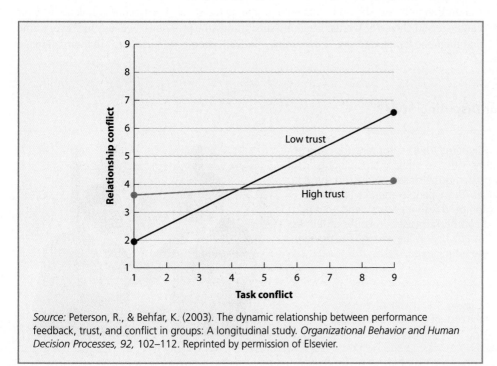

EXHIBIT 8.5

Trust Tempers Negative Conflict

Source: Peterson, R., & Behfar, K. (2003). The dynamic relationship between performance feedback, trust, and conflict in groups: A longitudinal study. *Organizational Behavior and Human Decision Processes, 92,* 102–112. Reprinted by permission of Elsevier.

AGREE ON A COMMON GOAL OR SHARED VISION People in conflict may not be able to agree about what is going on in their work group, but they may agree to an overarching goal, such as the sustainability of their group in the organization. For example, two colleagues may quarrel about office space, but will both wholeheartedly agree that their working relationship is worth preserving. To the extent that parties in conflict can agree on higher-order goals, conflict is reduced and people are more cooperative.[7] Sometimes, it is even effective for groups to be united by a common enemy.[8]

FOCUS ON CONTENT, NOT STYLE Conflict often begins as task conflict or process conflict, but then festers into relationship conflict—which is the unhealthiest type of conflict. As we noted above, relationship conflict is about personality and style. Behfar et al. examined conflicts in 51 project teams and found that the most successful teams were ones that rose above style issues and focused on content (see Exhibit 8.6 for a discussion of three disputing styles: interests, rights, and power).[9]

MODEL THE BEHAVIOR YOU WANT TO ELICIT Conflicts are like forest fires; they escalate quickly and can do a lot of damage quickly. Thus, it is important to effectively stop the conflict escalation cycle. There are three key ideas to keep in mind—all based on behavioral theory:

Model the behavior in yourself that you want to see in the other party. In short, due to the power of contagion and reciprocity, people tend to behave in ways that are similar to the ways that they are treated by others.

Use reinforcement to reward behaviors that you want to increase. If the other person has showed some sign of being reasonable, immediately reinforce that behavior with a verbal or nonverbal reward (such as a smile, eye contact or nod).

Do not react to behaviors that you want to extinguish. One of the most effective ways to extinguish behavior in another person is to simply not react.

SEPARATE THE PEOPLE FROM THE PROBLEM This sounds easy, but it is very difficult for most people in conflict to do. So it is useful to put at least three modalities into play to help you separate the people from the problem: seating position, language, and voice. First, you may not be able to change the fact that you are angry and feel misunderstood; however, it is harder to be angrier at someone if you are sitting next to them or side-by-side, as opposed to sitting across from them.[10] If you are standing up, the same principle applies; standing shoulder-to-shoulder puts both of you on the same side. Second, think about your language and choice of words. Begin by substituting the pronouns "we, us, our" every time you might be tempted to say "I, me, mine." Indeed, people who use "we" in their language

EXHIBIT 8.6   **What's Your Disputing Style?**

According to Ury, Brett, and Goldberg (1988), disputants use one of three styles when they are angry with one other: interest, rights, or power. The interest-based approach is the closest to the task-based conflict that we discussed earlier. These people attempt to uncover both parties' concerns, and attempt to fashion agreements that both can live with. The rights-based approach focuses on issues of fairness, entitlement, who's in the right and who's in the wrong. The power-based approach uses threats and intimidation.

Source: Ury, W. L., Brett, J. M., & Goldberg, S. B. (1988). *Getting disputes resolved: Designing systems to cut the costs of conflict.* San Francisco: Jossey-Bass.

are more likely to behave in a cooperative fashion.[11] Third, people in any dispute or conflict situation desire to be heard and to be understood.[12] Giving voice to another person does not mean you are giving in or agreeing with them. You are simply listening.

FOCUS ON THE FUTURE, NOT THE PAST People in conflict may never agree on what happened in the past, but they might very well agree on what should happen in the future. Thus, agree to disagree about what happened in the past and put the focus on the future. Behfar et al. caution that successful teams communicate the reason behind their decisions when accepting and distributing work assignments. Don't leave too many things unsaid.

ASSIGN WORK BASED ON EXPERTISE, NOT CONVENIENCE When it comes to conflict, it is important to stay focused on your interests. You are most likely to satisfy your interests by focusing on factors that can be implemented. In other words, it is not very constructive to ask the other person to "start behaving like a human being," as they will only take offense. A far better strategy is to ask the other person to "copy me on e-mails pertaining to the project" or "turn in the group work on time," and so on. Behfar et al. found that successful teams structure conflict productively by communicating the reasons behind their decisions when making group assignments and by assigning work to members based on expertise, not by convenience.

Negotiation: A Mixed-Motive Enterprise

Conflict is different from negotiation. Conflict often (but not always) involves: (1) negative emotions, such as anger; (2) misunderstanding or miscommunication between people; or (3) factors that are outside of the realm of pure economic concerns. Negotiation is a mutual decision-making process in which two or more parties make mutual decisions about what resources each will give and take. As such, negotiation is considered "transactional" and conflict is often considered to be "relational." In negotiation, we assume that parties are goal-directed and interdependent, such that neither can unilaterally assert their will.

Negotiation does not just occur on car lots, or among superpowers; it is woven into the fabric of day-to-day life. Negotiation is necessary any time you cannot achieve your own objectives without the cooperation of others. Negotiation is a necessity whenever people are interdependent. People in organizations are expected to know how to negotiate—for themselves, their teams, and their companies. Negotiation is a key communication and influence tool inside and outside the company. Your negotiation ability is directly related to leadership and promotion. Negotiation is not just about making more money—it's about building relationships and trust.

Unfortunately, most people are not nearly as effective as they could be when it comes to negotiation. They often reach **lose-lose outcomes** instead of **win-win outcomes;** they walk away from the table, even when they don't have attractive alternatives; they unnecessarily escalate conflict; and they sour, or damage, their relationships.[13] More than 80 percent of corporate executives and CEOs leave money on the table. However, they don't realize this. Fortunately, improving negotiation skills is not only possible to do, it is a well-developed science. This remainder of this chapter covers the theory and practice of effective negotiation. The two key skills of negotiation are:

- Creating value (integrative negotiation)
- Claiming value (distributive negotiation)

There are at least two major reasons why it is desirable to be a better negotiator. The reasons center upon both *economic* and *social* benefits.[14] As the Time Warner example in Exhibit 8.2 suggests, people who are effective and comfortable when they negotiate are more likely to achieve their *economic* goals, including a better price, a larger office, higher salary, or bigger budget, and they are also more likely to achieve their *interpersonal* goals, such as building trust in business relationships, effective teamwork, and peace of mind. Next, we define the mixed motives of cooperation and conflict that underlie negotiations and discuss negotiation styles; we then introduce two overarching sets of skills derived from negotiation theory: value creation and value claiming. We outline the major ways in which negotiators fall short.

Balancing Mixed Motives

Negotiation is a decision-making process in which two or more people make mutual agreements concerning the allocation of scarce resources. There are two motives always present in any negotiation: *cooperation* and *competition*. In short, in nearly any negotiation, people desire to cooperate with each other so that they can actually reach a deal and work together. That is, people know that they are better off working together rather than at odds with each other. At the same time, each party to a negotiation ultimately is interested in furthering their own interests (e.g., someone interviewing for a job no doubt wants to bring value to the company, but also wants a paycheck as well!). The competitive motive refers to the desire of each person to protect their own interests and goals.

These two motives define negotiation as a "mixed-motive" enterprise.[15] These two motives are also known as creating and claiming value.[16] In other words, when we want to create value, we often work with others in a cooperative fashion. However, even when people work cooperatively to expand the pie, they always need to divide the pie, or allocate resources, and that is claiming—an inherently self-interested motive. Think about the negotiation you described in the opening exercise. Were you aware of the two motives?

Negotiation Styles

Given that cooperation and competition are the two key underlying motives in any negotiation, it is not surprising that people naturally develop one skill more than the other. Some people believe it is necessary to choose to be either purely cooperative or competitive. This gives rise to two distinct negotiation styles: the too-soft negotiator and the too-tough negotiator. We'll ultimately argue that you should be neither one!

Many people believe that they need to cooperate fully by making unilateral concessions to the other party. Whereas cooperation is an important skill for successful negotiation, it is important not to lose sight of your own interests and goals. People in the business world bemoan the fact that they believe that they are too cooperative and that they give in too easily. Signals that might indicate that someone has a purely cooperative style include:

- Immediately caving in to the demands that other people make
- Being the first person to make a concession
- Revealing too much information so as to keep a relationship pleasant or get another person to like you

The flip side of the coin is to err on the side of being completely competitive. Signals that might indicate that someone has a purely competitive style include:

- Never revealing any information at all
- Always asking for more, no matter what you are offered
- Threatening to walk out in a negotiation unless your demands are met

Negotiators should not be purely competitive nor purely cooperative. Rather, negotiators should balance both motives. Bazerman and Neale suggest that negotiators should be *rational* rather than either too soft or too hard.[17] We will walk through exactly how to do this by focusing on the two key skills in negotiation: expanding the pie (also known as win-win negotiation) and slicing the pie (also known as power in negotiation).

Opportunistic Negotiation

Many negotiations in the business world are necessary or obligatory. For example, a merger or acquisition requires that companies negotiate. Similarly, buying a car usually requires that people negotiate. The same is true for buying a house, hiring new staff, negotiating a job offer, and choosing a roommate. However, most negotiations are not obligatory, but rather, opportunistic in the sense that people seize an opportunity to negotiate. Yet people differ in terms of their willingness to negotiate. For example, people from individualistic, egalitarian cultures, such as the United States, are more likely to feel comfortable negotiating with their supervisor or boss, more so than people from collectivistic, hierarchical cultures, such as Hong Kong.[18] Similarly, men are more likely to negotiate a job offer than are women.[19] Plus, men mention money earlier in a negotiation than do women.[20] For example, Lisa Barron videotaped men and women during a mock job interview (i.e., nothing was mentioned about a negotiation).[21] Men were more likely to spontaneously negotiate the offer during the mock job interview. This difference in the proclivity to negotiate can have a compounding effect on one's salary and wealth.[22]

If you are the type of person who is reluctant to negotiate, you are not trapped in that style forever. You can become more comfortable negotiating. As we shall find out, the first offer that negotiators put on the table has a huge impact on their ultimate success in the negotiation.[23] And nothing has a more dramatic impact on your success at the negotiation table than excellent preparation.

Next, we focus on the two essential skills involved in negotiation: creating value and claiming value. We outline the key strategies that can help negotiators improve their value-creation and value-claiming abilities.

Creating Value: Integrative Negotiation

Integrative negotiation is the art and science of leveraging interests so as to improve the outcomes of both parties.[24] Integrative negotiation is the opposite of fixed-sum or zero-sum negotiation. To take a simple example, imagine that two people are negotiating the price of a car. Price is the only issue. The seller demands $20,000. The buyer only wants to pay $15,000. They haggle and eventually agree to split the difference—at $17,500. This is an example of a **compromise agreement** and it is also an example of a **fixed-sum negotiation,** such that whatever one party gains, the other party loses in a direct one-to-one fashion.

Integrative negotiation involves creating value where it does not immediately or obviously exist. In the car example, imagine that the seller has a luxury model from the previous year that she or he needs to sell for inventory purposes. The seller places a huge value on clearing last year's inventory, and this is worth about $5,000 to her or him. The buyer, however, is much more concerned about extra amenities as well as price. The buyer would be delighted to get a luxury model of the car at a slightly higher price, and the seller would be happy to sell last year's model for a reduced cost. This is an example of an integrative agreement, because both parties are better off with this deal.

Integrative agreements create value for both parties. However, most negotiators are not adept at expanding the pie. They leave money on the table. Less than 4 percent of managers reach win-win outcomes when put to the test and the incidence of lose-lose outcomes is 20 percent.[25] In theory, it is far easier to expand the pie than it is to persuade the other negotiator to give you more resources. It is always in a negotiator's own interest to expand the pie, whether dealing with someone from their own company or the other party's company. The reason is simple: When you expand the pie, there is more to go around!

Separate Positions from Interests

In their classic book, *Getting to Yes,* Fisher and Ury explain the difference between *positions* and *interests* like this: "Interests motivate people; they are the silent movers behind the hubbub of positions. Your position is something you have decided upon. Your interests are what caused you to decide."

Interests are the underlying reasons why people even bother to negotiate. Moreover, interests are not necessarily always financial. Roger Fisher describes a negotiation between a company president selling a building he owned and a potential buyer.[26] "He was retiring and wanted $2 million, which he considered a fair price. He had a buyer, but the buyer wouldn't pay that price. I asked the seller, 'What's the worst thing about selling this building?' And he said, 'All of my papers for 25 years are mixed up in my corner office. When I sell the building, I can't throw everything away. I've got to go through that stuff. That's the nightmare I have.'" Then Fisher asked the buyer why he wanted the building. The buyer explained he hoped to use it for a hotel. This gave Fisher the idea of suggesting that the seller offer the buyer a lease with an option to buy with one contingency: that the president's name be on the corner office for three years. The buyer agreed. In this example, Fisher separated positions (sale price) from the underlying interests (access to papers and hotel business).

According to Fisher, Ury, and Patton, the most powerful interests are basic human needs:[27]

- Security
- Economic well-being
- A sense of belonging
- Recognition
- Control over one's life

The heart of any successful negotiation centers on resolving underlying interests. The key is to understand your own interests and, more important, taking the time and effort to understand the interests of the other party. It is almost inevitable that parties' positions will be opposed; yet their interests are not necessarily opposed. The **fixed-pie perception** is the belief that one's own interests are at complete odds with those of the other party. A whopping 68 percent of negotiators hold fixed-pie perceptions when they enter negotiations. Moreover, even when vast potential exists to leverage differences in priorities and interests, and thereby expand the pie, most negotiators fail to realize this. Thompson and Hastie measured negotiators' fixed-pie perceptions at the outset of negotiation and found that they reliably predicted whether negotiators could create value. Those who held fast to their erroneous fixed-pie perceptions created the smallest pies![28]

Prioritize and Weight the Issues

Successful win-win negotiation requires that negotiators have more than one thing to negotiate. In other words, if two people are simply haggling about the price of a good, there is no potential for win-win negotiation because whatever one person wins, the other person loses, in a direct, zero-sum fashion. In contrast, the minute that there are two or more issues on the table, then it is possible for a win-win solution to occur. Let's take a simple case in which two people are negotiating about a job, and the issues include salary, signing bonus, and vacation time. Obviously, the recruiter wants to minimize all three of these issues, and the job candidate would want the maximum possible salary, moving expenses, and signing bonus. Each party's position, then, is clear: "Give me everything I want." The parties might agree to compromise and arrive at a middle range on salary, moving expenses, and signing bonus. However, it behooves parties to prioritize the issues so that they can best focus on what is good for themselves. In our example, the employee may be relatively more concerned with signing bonus than vacation time. In contrast, the recruiter may be more concerned with vacation time than signing bonus. And so it would make sense for the parties to "trade off" these issues. Thus, prior to entering any negotiation, negotiators should prepare by creating their own list of the issues and their relative importance. Medvec suggests that negotiators create a "scoring system" to represent how they feel about the issues identified.[29] There is no single best way to do a scoring system. One method is to simply allocate 100 points to different possible options, giving more points to options that are most important. Raiffa coaches negotiators to be as explicit as possible about expressing their utilities. Medvec has three rules when it comes to scoring systems: (1) Everything that a negotiator cares about should be represented on the score card; (2) the negotiator should be sure to check for indifference—meaning that things that add up to the same amount of points should really represent equal utility; and (3) the scoring system should be dynamic, meaning that as information changes, the negotiators should be able to quickly update the information.

Unbundle the Issues

Negotiators should unbundle or fractionate the issues. Integrative agreements require a minimum of two issues. In other words, people can potentially reach a win-win agreement if they are negotiating price, service, terms, and delivery date. But a win-win agreement is not possible if negotiators merely bargain over price.

When negotiators prioritize and weight the issues, they can effectively trade one issue off for another. This is crucially important so as to prevent negotiators from enacting a sub-optimal compromise solution.[30] Consider the classic fable of the sisters and the orange. In this story, two sisters are quarrelling bitterly over a single orange. To resolve the conflict, they agree to compromise and cut the orange in half. Subsequently, one sister uses the juice (to make fresh-squeezed orange juice) and throws the peel away; the other sister uses only the peel (to make classic orange scones) and throws the juice away. Obviously, this is a tragicomic agreement that typifies how the sisters failed to exploit their true, underlying interests. Had they unbundled the issues—and negotiated the juice as well as the peel— they might have reached the integrative, value-added agreement of giving all the juice to one sister and all the peel to the other sister.

Negotiators are often concerned about revealing their preferences and priorities because they fear that this information will be used against them by the other party. To test this possibility, we conducted an investigation in which we randomly divided people into three groups: In some groups both negotiators were "coached" to exchange information about interests; in other groups, only one negotiator was told to ask information; in the third group, no specific coaching was given.[31] Groups in which one or both parties sought information about interests performed dramatically better. Moreover, negotiators who revealed information were not disadvantaged. Revealing information about your interests and priorities does not hinder your bargaining strength. It helps expand the pie and create more value.

Ask for the Right Information

Negotiators who ask for information are not only more likely to get it, but they are more effective at expanding the pie, as compared to negotiators who do not ask for information. The key is to ask for the right kind of information. Asking the other party how much they will pay you (if you are a seller) or how cheap can you buy it for (if you are a buyer) is not likely to be effective. In contrast, asking for information about the other party's interests can dramatically open possibilities for expanding the pie.

One stumbling block that negotiators may face is that the other party may be reluctant or unwilling to share information about his or her priorities. In this instance, a negotiator should reveal his or her own interests, thereby setting the stage for a reciprocity effect.[32] The **reciprocity effect** tends to occur when people emit cooperative behavior; when they are competitive or dominant, this leads the other party to be submissive.[33] However, under certain circumstances, when the other party behaves aggressively, this leads to an escalation of conflict. Rothbart and Hallmark examined how people respond to being attacked by others.[34] During World War II, the American journalist Edward R. Murrow broadcast nightly from London, reporting on the psychological and physical consequences of the Nazi bombing of British cities. Contrary to Nazi intent, the bombing did not move the British toward surrender. It had the opposite effect: strengthening, rather than diminishing British resolve to resist German domination. Shortly after the United States entered World War II, the Americans joined the British in launching costly bombing raids over Germany. The intent was to decrease the German people's will to resist. Later research reported by the Office of Strategic Services that compared lightly and heavily bombed areas found only minimal differences in civilians' will to resist. People often attempt to use coercion to attempt to get the other party to concede, but it nearly universally backfires.

EXHIBIT 8.7a

Simplified Job Negotiation

Issue	Alternatives	Candidate (Points)
Salary	$90,000 $85,000 $80,000	6,000 3,000 0
Bonus	10% 7.5% 5%	4,000 2,000 0
Vacation time	3 weeks/yr 2 weeks/yr 1 weeks/yr	2,000 1,000 0

Create a Superset of Issues

The most effective negotiators complicate, rather than simplify things. Effective negotiators expand the issue set and are truthful to themselves and the other party about which issues are most important. To the extent that the negotiators learn about the other party's preferences and priorities, they can fashion value-added trade-offs.

Propose Value-Added Trade-Offs

Once the negotiator has identified his or her interests, unbundled the issues, and prioritized his or her interests, the negotiator is now in a position to propose value-added trade-offs. For example, look at the chart in Exhibit 8.7a. As you can see, this negotiator (whom we will call the "candidate") has created a scoring system for a new job in which the following issues have been given points: salary, bonus, and vacation time. As can be seen, this negotiator is primarily concerned with salary and bonus, and relatively less concerned with vacation time (as reflected by the relatively larger number of points the negotiator assigned to those issues). We strongly caution negotiators not to offer concessions on a given issue unless they simultaneously ask for something in return. Rather, negotiators should link a concession to a request for a gain on a more important issue. For example, the negotiator whose preferences are depicted in Exhibit 8.7a might propose that she be given a 10 percent bonus but only 1 week of vacation time. If the negotiator has correctly ascertained that the other party (presumably the hiring firm) is more interested in vacation time and less concerned with signing bonuses, this would constitute a value-added trade-off.

In Exhibit 8.7b, the candidate tries to speculate about the recruiter's interests. Again, the story of the sisters and the orange is relevant. One of the sisters is more interested in the

EXHIBIT 8.7b

What About the Recruiting Firm?

Issue	Alternatives	Candidate (Points)	Recruiter (Points)
Salary	$90,000 $85,000 $80,000	6,000 3,000 0	?
Bonus	10% 7.5% 5%	4,000 2,000 0	?
Vacation time	3 weeks/yr 2 weeks/yr 1 weeks/yr	2,000 1,000 0	?

EXHIBIT 8.7c

Compromise Agreement

Issue	Alternatives	Candidate (points)	Recruiter (points)	
Salary	$90,000	6000		Total value to
	$85,000	3000	?	Candidate
	$80,000	0		= 6,000
Bonus	10%	4000		
	7.5%	2000	?	
	5%	0		
Vacation time	3 weeks/yr	2000		
	2 weeks/yr	1000	?	
	1 weeks/yr	0		

fruit, and the other is more interested in the rind. Suppose that the candidate believes that the recruiter's interests are directly opposed (fixed-pie perception).

The candidate might propose a compromise solution, such as that depicted in Exhibit 8.7c, in which the candidate requests the mid-range salary, the mid-range bonus, and the mid-range vacation time. Exhibit 8.7d depicts the recruiter's actual preferences (note that the job candidate would never know this, but in our example, it is useful to analyze the negotiation outcome when both parties' preferences are perfectly known). Exhibit 8.7e reveals the outcome of a compromise approach. Each party gains 6,000 points, for a joint value of 12,000.

Exhibits 8.7f and 8.7g reveal two different integrative (value-creating) strategies. In both integrative agreements, the recruiter and candidate trade off or logroll bonus and vacation time. Notice that the candidate values the bonus whereas the recruiter needs to minimize vacation days. Finally, Exhibit 8.8 depicts the theoretical integrative frontier of negotiations. In integrative negotiations, both parties attempt to move northeasterly along the integrative frontier.

Make Multiple Offers of Equivalent Value Simultaneously

Most naïve negotiators negotiate the same way they play tennis: They make one offer, wait for the return, and then make another offer. And usually, the naïve negotiator makes a steady series of gradual concessions. This is sometimes known as the negotiation dance, which typically involves meeting the other party halfway. This type of concession making is ineffective because it leads to suboptimal compromise. The **multiple offer strategy** involves presenting the other party with at least two (and preferably more)

EXHIBIT 8.7d

Other Party's True Preferences

Issue	Alternatives	Candidate (Points)	Recruiter (Points)
Salary	$90,000	6,000	0
	$85,000	3,000	3,000
	$80,000	0	6,000
Bonus	10%	4,000	0
	7.5%	2,000	1,000
	5%	0	2,000
Vacation time	3 weeks/yr	2,000	0
	2 weeks/yr	1,000	2,000
	1 weeks/yr	0	4,000

EXHIBIT 8.7e

Compromise Agreement

Issue	Alternatives	Candidate (points)	Recruiter (points)	
Salary	$90,000	6000	0	Value to
	$85,000	3000	3000	Candidate
	$80,000	0	6000	= 6,000
Bonus	10%	4000	0	Value to
	7.5%	2000	1000	Recruiter
	5%	0	2000	= 6,000
Vacation time	3 weeks/yr	2000	0	Total Value
	2 weeks/yr	1000	2000	= 12,000
	1 weeks/yr	0	4000	

multi-issue proposals of equal value to oneself. If a negotiation contains multiple issues, there are several ways that you can achieve desirable outcomes. Negotiators who make multiple equivalent offers enjoy more profitable negotiated outcomes and are evaluated more favorably by the other party.[35] Negotiators who present several options to the other party to choose among are viewed as more flexible by the other party, and they are more satisfied at the end of the negotiation. Multiple offers increase the discovery of integrative solutions.[36] Negotiators who make multiple, equivalent offers have an advantage in five critical aspects: They can (1) be more aggressive in terms of anchoring the negotiation more favorably; (2) gain better information about the other party; (3) be more persistent; (4) signal their priorities more effectively; and (5) overcome concession aversion on the part of the other side.[37]

Propose Contingency Contracts

Sometimes negotiators have fundamentally different beliefs about a product, event, service, or good that they cannot agree about. For example, a seller might argue that his product will dramatically improve the ROI (return on investment) on a potential client's firm; the client may have reason to be more skeptical, especially if previous products have not had such an impact. It may be impossible (even with facts) to persuade either party to alter their beliefs. The creative solution is to propose **contingent contracts**—in other words, propose if-then deals that pay high dividends for the negotiator whose view of the world is borne out.[38]

EXHIBIT 8.7f

Integrative Agreement

Issue	Alternatives	Candidate (points)	Recruiter (points)	
Salary	$90,000	6000	0	Value to
	$85,000	3000	3000	Candidate
	$80,000	0	6000	= 7,000
Bonus	10%	4000	0	Value to
	7.5%	2000	1000	Recruiter
	5%	0	2000	= 7,000
Vacation time	3 weeks/yr	2000	0	Total Value
	2 weeks/yr	1000	2000	= 14,000
	1 weeks/yr	0	4000	

EXHIBIT 8.7g

Another Example: Integrative Agreement

Issue	Alternatives	Candidate (points)	Recruiter (points)	
Salary	$90,000	6000	0	Value to Candidate
	$85,000	3000	3000	= 4,000
	$80,000	0	6000	(small pie slice)
Bonus	10%	4000	0	Value to Recruiter
	7.5%	2000	1000	= 10,000
	5%	0	2000	(big pie slice)
Vacation time	3 weeks/yr	2000	0	
	2 weeks/yr	1000	2000	Total Value
	1 weeks/yr	0	4000	= 14,000

Contingent contracts are effective in the following situations:

- When negotiators have different expectations about uncertain events
- When negotiators have different risk attitudes
- When negotiators have different time preferences

Contingent contracts allow negotiators to resolve conflicts without accusations of lying. However, to be effective, contingent contracts require that the interests of negotiators be sensibly aligned (i.e., negotiators should not create incentives for the other party to sabotage the success of a product, etc.), they must be enforceable, and the object in question must be clear and measurable. For example, when Royal Dutch Shell and the Total Group in Saudi Arabia signed a gas deal in 2003, it exemplified the contingency principle. Unlike previous agreements in which gas companies made enormous financial commitments in return for limited access to Saudi hydrocarbons, Shell and Total agreed to spend $200M over five years of exploration. If they found nothing, they could walk away. If they found oil, they could sell whatever gas they found and report the reserve on their books.[39]

Make Postsettlement Settlements

A **postsettlement settlement** is a technique whereby negotiators reach a mutually agreeable settlement and commit to it, as a first step, and, as a second step, attempt to improve upon it. That is, both negotiators attempt to find another settlement that each party would prefer more than the current settlement or, at the very least, that one party prefers and to which the other is indifferent. It is important to realize that a postsettlement settlement is not a renegotiation. Rather, it is a continuation of a negotiation.

EXHIBIT 8.8

Negotiation Outcomes

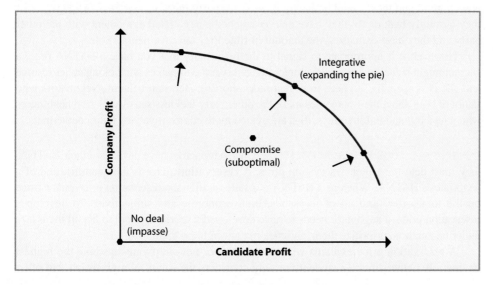

Claiming Value: Distributive Negotiation

Distributive negotiation is the study of how people allocate resources. We've talked in depth about expanding the pie; the next section takes up the topic of slicing the pie, or claiming value.

Know Your BATNA and Develop Your Reservation Price

The key question a negotiator needs to ask before sitting down at the bargaining table is: "What am I going to do if I don't take this agreement?" In other words, what are your alternatives to reaching a mutual agreement with this particular person today? The answer is determined by a negotiator's available alternatives. A negotiator's **BATNA** is the **B**est **A**lternative **T**o a **N**egotiated **A**greement.[40] The power to walk away and get a better deal is at the core of effective value claiming. A negotiator's BATNA is the ability to walk away from a given deal. As an example, think about a student who is just about to graduate and is actively looking for a job. Suppose that this student has one job offer from a large company that offers an annual salary of $60,000. Suppose that student is more interested in getting a job offer from a smaller, more exciting company. The smaller company initially offers a $55,000 salary. The student's BATNA is to simply take the first job.

YOUR BATNA IS NOT A PASSIVE CONCEPT BATNAs are constantly in a state of flux: they either improve (with effort) or deteriorate over time. Therefore, negotiators should not treat their BATNAs passively. Consider the case of a company considering a merger. The company could either wait patiently to see if some other company might also be interested in them; or they could aggressively seek suitors. Thus, a negotiator who regards her BATNA as a dynamic concept and keeps her BATNA alive is in a better position to demand more of the pie than is the negotiator whose BATNA is weak and underdeveloped.

SHOULD YOU REVEAL YOUR BATNA? No. Once negotiators embrace the BATNA concept and the idea of continual improvement of their BATNA, questions are often raised along the lines of, "Is it wise to exaggerate one's BATNA to the other party so as to improve one's own bargaining power?" First, let's distinguish between truthful revelation of one's BATNA, exaggeration (or lying), and signaling one's BATNA indirectly. Negotiators should never lie about their BATNA to the other party, no matter how poor or unattractive their actual BATNA might be. Why? First, lying about material facts (e.g., pretending to have an offer that does not actually exist) is punishable by law. Second, it could severely tarnish your reputation, making it much more difficult to reestablish it. Finally, lying about your BATNA reduces the probability that you will reach agreement, in situations where a positive bargaining zone exists.

We do not believe that negotiators should truthfully reveal their BATNA unless: (a) It is very good and they would be happy if the other party merely "matched" whatever offer they currently had; or (b) they have not yet reached a negotiated agreement with the other party and they have exhausted the amount of time they have for negotiation.

However, it is appropriate to signal to the other party that you have a BATNA (e.g., a student might signal to a potential employer that several companies are looking at her resume and she is "expecting" to hear from recruiters shortly). But, don't flaunt. Negotiators who flaunt or brag about their outcomes make the other party feel less satisfied.[41] And negotiators who gain a reputation for being selfish are treated more competitively by their counterparts.

DEVELOPING YOUR RESERVATION PRICE Once negotiators have developed their BATNA, they must determine their reservation price. A **reservation price** is the quantification of a negotiator's BATNA. Whereas a BATNA is a state of affairs, a reservation price puts a price on the total offer (and all of its issues, both economic and subjective). To develop a reservation price, a negotiator needs to have developed a scoring system to list all the issues under negotiation, prioritize them, and then put a weight on them.

A reservation price explains why a student does not simply always take the highest paying job. Quite simply, a student not only considers the salary of a given job, but other factors as well, such as chances for advancement, work hours, quality of life (as determined by how many days a week one must travel), travel distance from relatives and close friends, the employment location and opportunities for one's spouse, the availability and functional distance of schools for one's children, and so on. In this sense, anything that a person cares about—whether economic or social—needs to be factored in when determining your reservation price. Your reservation price for a job offer at company A represents an overall value of the offer to you on a scale that allows direct comparison with other offers.

Research the Other Party's BATNA and Assess Their Reservation Price

If you know the other party's BATNA, you can attempt to assess their reservation price. Whereas you can be somewhat certain of a person's BATNA, because it is a potentially observable state of affairs, you cannot be as certain of his or her reservation price because, as we noted above, reservation prices include subjective issues only the other negotiator may know. However, if you listen carefully to the other party when you are negotiating, you can learn what is important to them.

Anchoring

In any negotiation, people focus on focal points and tend to stay close to those points. This is known as the **anchoring effect** (which we also discussed in Chapter 7). The anchoring effect is the tendency for an initial offer or set of terms to strongly influence the final outcome of a negotiation. You can use the anchoring concept to your advantage if you can focus the other party on a particular number or set of terms. This might be the first offer on the table. If you are renegotiating a salary contract, a natural anchor would be your current salary.

REANCHORING   Once negotiators are anchored to a number, it is difficult to reanchor them. Thus, anchors are dropped early in the negotiation. If the other negotiator has opened aggressively, it is important to reanchor the negotiation by making an aggressive opening offer. Whereas anchors should be aggressive, they should not be insulting.

MAKE THE FIRST OFFER IF YOU ARE PREPARED   It is a reasonable derivation of the anchoring concept to infer that the first offers that each party makes act as anchors in the negotiation. For example, the first offers made by parties in a job employment negotiation predicted how well they would do in the negotiations. Moreover, the negotiator who makes the first offer has a distinct advantage in the negotiation because first offers act as powerful, psychological anchor points in the negotiation.[42]

DO NOT MAKE UNILATERAL CONCESSIONS   Monitor who is making concessions during the negotiation and the pattern of concessions by all the parties involved. Most important, do not make unilateral (one-sided) concessions. And watch the magnitude of your concessions.

Summary

We have carefully reviewed the best practices for integrative and distributive negotiation, based on theory and research. Exhibit 8.9 lists the six basic types of information in virtually any negotiation and how that information affects integrative and distributive negotiation. Notice that there are six different possible kinds of information that may "surface" in a negotiation. One type of information is BATNA information. Negotiators should not reveal their BATNA during a negotiation. Another type of information is a negotiator's position or their stated demand (e.g., "I want x"). This type of information is helpful, but too much of it can lead to a bargaining standoff. Probably the most important type of information concerns negotiators' underlying interests. Had the two sisters arguing over the orange shared this information, they might have avoided a suboptimal compromise. Another key type of information is information about negotiators' priorities. "Key facts" refers to information that relates to the quality and value of the issues. Finally, "substantiation" refers to the arguments that negotiators often make to buttress their positions.

EXHIBIT 8.9 **Types of Information in Negotiation and How Each Affects Distributive and Integrative Agreements**

Type of information	Definition (example)	Should you reveal this information?	How this information affects integrative negotiation
BATNA (and reservation price)	The alternatives a negotiator has outside of the current negotiation (e.g., "If I don't buy your car, I can buy my uncle's car for $2,000")	No; severely hurts ability to claim value	Revealing or obtaining this information does not affect ability to reach integrative agreements
Position (stated demand)	A negotiator's opening offer or optimal target point (e.g., "I will give you $1,500 for your car")	Opening up with an aggressive target point significantly increases the negotiator's gain (share of the bargaining zone)	Does not affect integrative agreements
Underlying interests	The underlying needs and reasons that a negotiator has for a particular issue or target (e.g., "I need a car because I need transportation to my job site, which is 15 miles away in a rural zone")	Revealing this information generally increases likelihood of obtaining favorable slice of pie because negotiators who can provide a rationale for their demands are more adept at realizing their targets	Very important for reaching win-win deals. By (truthfully) revealing underlying interests, negotiators can discover win-win agreements (e.g., one sister tells the other that she wants the orange because she needs to make juice and has no need for rind)
Priorities	A relative judgment about the importance of the issues to a negotiator (e.g., "I am more concerned about the down payment than I am about the financing for the car")	Increases a negotiator's slice of the pie indirectly, because if more value is created via sharing priorities, then the probability at that a negotiator will get larger slice of the pie increases	Vitally important for maximizing the pie (e.g., the sister who said she cared more about the rinds relative to the juice created potential for integrative agreement)
Key facts	Information that bears on the quality and the value of the to-be-negotiated issues (e.g., "The car has a rebuilt engine and has been involved in a major collision"; "the oranges are genetically modified")	This information can affect the slice of the pie the negotiator obtains in that facts either increase or decrease the value of the to-be-negotiated issues	Failure to reveal key information may lead a negotiator to over- or undervalue a particular resource (e.g., someone who sells "fresh organic orange juice" does not want to have genetically modified oranges as an ingredient)
Substantiation	Argument either made to support one's own position or to attack the other party's position (e.g., "You will get lots of dates if you buy my car because women like it")	Most dominant type of distributive tactic (24–27 percent of all statements); can increase a negotiator's slice of the pie because providing a rationale can often be effective in obtaining a demand	Does not increase win-win negotiation and may, in fact, reduce likelihood of win-win

Source: Thompson, L. (2005). *The mind and heart of the negotiator* (3rd ed.), p. 78. Upper Saddle River, NJ: Pearson Prentice Hall. Reprinted by permission of Pearson Education.

Improving Your Negotiation Skills

Everyone can certainly afford to constantly try to improve negotiation skills. What is the best way to do this?

Take Every Opportunity to Negotiate

Nothing can substitute for real negotiation experiences. So take every opportunity you can to negotiate. When you negotiate for your apartment, salary, job, graduation party, vacation plans, and so on, you not only have to concern yourself with economic issues, but you constantly have to monitor your reputation and your relationship with the other party.

Seek Feedback on Your Negotiation Skills

Professionals do this all the time. For example, car dealerships routinely mail surveys to their customers who have recently bought a car, asking about their experience. Why should you be any different? Seek feedback from friends, family, and co-workers about how you are doing in their eyes. One way of doing this professionally is to invite your co-workers, friends, and associates to evaluate you on an anonymous 360-degree Web survey.

Use Worksheets

They actually work. Negotiators who plan for their negotiations are better positioned to effectively expand the pie and claim resources.

Plan Your Approach

Don't ask anyone anything that you would not want to answer yourself. This, of course, rules out blatant questions about BATNAs.

Offer to Be a Negotiation Coach

Offer your coaching and consulting services to a friend who is in the middle of a negotiation. Pull out your preparation sheets. Help your friend plot the issues, develop a scoring system, and plan offers.

Don't Brag or Boast

Don't boast about your negotiation exploits. Negotiators who hear another party boasting ("I feel really good about the negotiation outcome!") feel less successful. Negotiators who earn a reputation for being good at negotiation often "pay" for it because others in the negotiation community begin to act tougher when negotiating with them.[43] Thus, it is best to keep a low profile about your negotiation exploits!

Third-Party Intervention

For many reasons, people may be unable or just plain unwilling to move toward agreement on their own accord. It is not a mark of failure of management to ask a third party for an impartial opinion or expertise on a complex conflict situation or negotiation. A **third party** is an individual (or collective) who is external to the conflict and tries to help the parties reach agreement. It is a good idea to decide what role this third party will play—informational only, exercising some **process control** (i.e., interviewing the parties involved), advisory (making recommendations), or exerting **outcome control** (having the power to impose binding agreements).

Ranges of Third-Party Roles

Third parties can be given a lot of power or very little power. The key choice that anyone makes when inviting a third party to intervene is whether the third party will have outcome control or only process control. A third party with process control can direct the flow of discussion and guide the interchange, but ultimately cannot impose a settlement. Mediators have process control. A stronger third-party function is outcome control, or the ability to impose a solution. This is the role of an arbitrator. Parties who have outcome control are **arbitrators;** people who have process control but no outcome control are **mediators.** Broadly speaking, there are two types of arbitration, traditional and final offer. In **traditional arbitration,** the arbiter hears both sides' positions and then imposes his or her own settlement. Because arbiters often opt for a compromise (halfway between the disputants' demands), each party may unrealistically exaggerate his or her demands. For this reason, a new method of arbitration was developed, known as **final offer arbitration,** in which the arbiter selects only one of the two demands submitted by the involved parties—thus incenting each party to be realistic and moderate in his or her final demand.[44]

Third parties can be formal, such as licensed and certified professionals, or informal, such as might occur in an organization in which disputants ask a colleague to intervene in a dispute. Third-party roles can be invited or uninvited. An invitation to intervene suggests that at least one of the parties is motivated to address the dispute. A third party can be uninvited, such as the case of a bystander attempting to intervene in a subway brawl. Third parties can be partial or impartial. Stated another way, some third parties may not have a stake in the outcome, while other third parties may hold a particular point of view. Third parties can intervene between two people, in an interpersonal dispute; or they may intervene between two groups, for instance, when two or more departments in an organization are in dispute.

Effective Third-Party Intervention

To be effective, third parties need to focus on three distinct sets of skills or spheres of influence: (1) the physical and social structure of the dispute or conflict, (2) the issue structure, and (3) the parties' motivations.[45]

PHYSICAL AND SOCIAL STRUCTURE OF THE DISPUTE Third parties can exert a great deal of influence on how and when disputing parties actually interact. Communication can be beneficial, but if conflict is escalating quickly and personal attacks are being issued, the third party should separate the disputants. It is often important to choose a neutral site so that there is not an inherent advantage for one of the parties. For example, when ex-president Jimmy Carter acted as a mediator in the Camp David negotiations, he chose a neutral site and blocked public access for the first 13 days.

ISSUE STRUCTURE Effective third parties can often modify the issue structure of the conflict by seeking to expand the issue mix, attempting to unearth parties' relative preferences, and crafting multi-issue proposals. Most important, mediators provide a face-saving mechanism for parties to reach agreement through a mediator, when they find it difficult to agree with what the other is saying.

MOTIVATION Effective mediators and arbitrators can use time pressure to gently motivate parties toward agreement. By allowing parties to find some points of agreement early on, mediators can create momentum in an otherwise deadlocked dispute resolution process.

Challenges Facing Third Parties

Third-party intervention is more difficult in many ways from negotiation. The third party should facilitate the process of reaching agreement and should increase the likelihood that parties reach agreement if a positive bargaining zone exists. Moreover, third parties should attempt to promote integrative, pie-expanding outcomes. In the case of arbitrators, third parties need to propose outcomes that are fair by objective standards. Effective third-party intervention should ideally involve a process that improves the relationship between parties and empowers parties in the process, rather than weakens them. Effective third parties must actively de-bias disputants and move them away from unrealistic positions. This is easier said than done, as most negotiators have an exaggerated perception of conflict. For example, opponents on either side of the Western canon debate (a conflict concerning which books should be on reading lists for introductory English courses) believe that they only have one book in common, when in fact traditionalists and revisionists share 6 (out of 10) books in common.[46] Another problem is the extreme overconfidence that negotiators have in their own positions. For example, most negotiators believe that an "unbiased" third-party judge would rule in their favor—obviously, that is not possible. As a further complication, third parties can have a biased view of disputants that can be magnified by the emotional tone that parties take. For example, observers' perceptions of conflict are influenced by the emotions of disputants. Observers are most likely to propose integrative, win-win agreements when observing negotiators who use a positive approach as opposed to a negative, angry approach.[47]

Conclusion

Conflict is a natural part of organizational life and an unavoidable aspect of human interaction. As pervasive as conflict is, most people have never had formal conflict resolution training. For this reason, many people are conflict avoidant. We've discussed the three main types of conflict: relationship, process, and task conflict. We've suggested that awareness of conflict is a first step in the effective management of conflict. We introduced negotiation as a managerial skill necessary any time one person cannot achieve his or her objectives without the cooperation of another party. We built our discussion of negotiation around three key skills: distributive skills, which focus on claiming resources; integrative skills, which focus on creating value; and building trust between negotiators. We then took up the role of third-party intervention as an option for disputants who are unable to reach agreement on their own. We distinguished mediation from arbitration in terms of process versus outcome control.

Notes

1. Blake, R. R., & Mouton, J. S. (1964). *The managerial grid.* Houston: Gulf.
2. Jehn, K. (1995). A multimethod examination of the benefits and detriments of intragroup conflict. *Administrative Science Quarterly, 40,* 256–282; Behfar, K. (2003). *The team exchange contract in autonomous work groups: Behaviors and work strategies for sustainable performance.* Doctoral dissertation, Cornell University.
3. De Dreu, C. K. W., & Weingart, L. R. (2003). Task versus relationship conflict, team performance and team member satisfaction: A meta-analysis. *Journal of Applied Psychology, 88,* 741–749; Jehn, "Multimethod examination," p. 133.
4. Guetzkow, H., & Gyr, J. (1954). An analysis of conflict in decision-making groups. *Human Relations, 7,* 367–381.
5. Peterson, R. S., & Behfar, K. J. (2003). The dynamic relationship between performance feedback, trust, and conflict in groups: A longitudinal study. *Organizational Behavior and Human Decision Processes, 92,* 102–112.
6. Behfar, K., Peterson, R., Mannix, E., & Trochim, W. (in press). The critical role of conflict resolution in teams: A close look at the links between conflict type, conflict management strategies, and team outcomes. *Journal of Applied Psychology.*
7. Kramer, R. M., & Brewer, M. B. (1984). Effects of group identity on resource use in a simulated commons dilemma. *Journal of Personality and Social Psychology, 46,* 1044–1057.
8. Sherif, M., Harvey, O., White, B., Hood, W., & Sherif, C. (1961). *Intergroup conflict and cooperation: The robbers' cave experiment.* Norman: Institute of Group Relations, University of Oklahoma.
9. Behfar, *The team exchange contract,* p. 133.
10. Drolet, A. L., & Morris, M.W. (2000). Rapport in conflict resolution: Accounting for how face-to-face contact fosters mutual cooperation in mixed-motive conflicts. *Journal of Experimental Social Psychology, 36,* 26–50.
11. Gardner, W. L., Gabriel, S., & Lee, A.Y. (1999). "I" value freedom, but "we" value relationships: Self-construal priming mirrors cultural differences in judgment. *Psychological Science, 4,* 321–326.
12. Lind, E. A., & Tyler, T. R. (1988). *The social psychology of procedural justice.* New York: Plenum Press.
13. Thompson, L., & Hrebec, D. (1996). Lose-lose agreements in interdependent decision making. *Psychological Bulletin, 120*(3), 396–409.
14. Thompson, L. (1990). Negotiation behavior and outcomes: Empirical evidence and theoretical issues. *Psychological Bulletin, 108,* 515–532.
15. Walton, R. E., & McKersie, R. B. (1965). *A behavioral theory of labor negotiation.* New York: McGraw-Hill.
16. Lax, D. A., & Sebenius, J. K. (1986). *The manager as a negotiator.* New York: The Free Press.
17. Bazerman, M. H., & Neale, M. A. (1982). Improving negotiation effectiveness under final offer arbitration: The role of selection and training. *Journal of Applied Psychology, 67,* 543–548.
18. Brett, J. M. (2007). *Negotiating globally: How to negotiate deals, resolve disputes, and make decisions across cultural boundaries* (2nd ed.). San Francisco: Jossey-Bass.

19. Babcock, L., Gelfand, M. J., Small, D. A., & Stayn, H. (2004). *Propensity to initiate negotiations: A new look at gender variation in negotiation behavior.* Unpublished manuscript, Carnegie Mellon University; Babcock, L., & Laschever, S. (2003). *Women don't ask: Negotiation and the gender divide.* Princeton: Princeton University Press.

20. Halpern, J. J., & McLean Parks, J. (1996).Vive la différence: Gender differences in process and outcomes in a low-conflict negotiation. *International Journal of Conflict Management, 7*(1), 45–70.

21. Barron, L. A. (2003). Gender differences in negotiators' beliefs. *Human Relations, 56,* 635–662.

22. Babcock & Laschever, *Women don't ask,* p.139.

23. Kray, L., Thompson, L., & Galinsky, A. (2001). Battle of the sexes: Gender stereotype confirmation and reactance in negotiations. *Journal of Personality and Social Psychology, 80*(6), 942–958.

24. Raiffa, H. (1982). *The art and science of negotiation.* Harvard University Press, Cambridge, MA.

25. Nadler, J., Thompson, L., & van Boven, L. (2003). Learning negotiation skills: Four models of knowledge creation and transfer. *Management Science, 49*(4), 529–540.

26. Fischer, R. (2001, September 1). Doctor YES—Roger Fisher interviewed. *CFO Magazine.*

27. Fisher, R., Ury, W. L., & Patton, B. (1991). *Getting to yes: Negotiating agreement without giving in* (2nd ed.). Boston: Houghton Mifflin.

28. Thompson, L., & Hastie, R. (1990). Social perception in negotiation. *Organizational Behavior & Human Decision Processes, 47,* 98–123.

29. Medvec, V., Leonardelli, G. J., Claussen-Schulz, A., & Galinsky, A. D. (2005). Navigating competition and cooperation: Multiple equivalent offers in deal-making. Rotman School of Management, University of Toronto, Ontario. *Manuscript in preparation.*

30. Froman, L., & Cohen, M. (1970). Compromise and logroll: comparing the efficiency of two bargaining processes. *Behavioral Science, 15,* 180–183.

31. Thompson, L. (1991). Information exchange in negotiation. *Journal of Experimental Social Psychology, 27,* 61–179.

32. Adair, W. L. (1999). Exploring the norm of reciprocity in the global market: U.S. and Japanese intra- and inter-cultural negotiations. In S. J. Havlovic (Ed.), *59th Annual Meeting of the Academy of Management Proceedings.*

33. Tiedens, L. Z. (1999). *Feeling low and feeling high: Associations between social status and emotions.* Unpublished dissertation, University of Michigan.

34. Rothbart, M., & Hallmark, W. (1988). In-group–out-group differences in the perceived efficacy of coercion and conciliation in resolving social conflict. *Journal of Personality and Social Psychology, 55,* 248–257.

35. Medvec, Leonardelli, Claussen-Schulz, & Galinsky, "Navigating competition and cooperation," p. 140.

36. Hyder, E. B., Prietula, M. J., & Weingart, L. R. (2000). Getting to best: Efficiency versus optimality in negotiation. *Cognitive Science, 24*(2), 169–204.

37. Medvec, V. H., & Galinsky, A. D. (2005). Putting more on the table: How making multiple offers can increase the final value of the deal. *Negotiation, 4.*

38. Bazerman, M. H., & Gillespie, J. J. (1999). Betting on the future: The virtues of contingent contracts. *Harvard Business Review, 77*(5), 155–160.

39. Reed, S. (2003, August 4). Suddenly, the Saudis want to close some deals. *BusinessWeek,* p. 51.

40. Fisher, Ury, & Patton, *Getting to yes,* p. 140.

41. Thompson, L., Valley, K., & Kramer, R. (1995). The bittersweet feeling of success: An examination of social perception in negotiation. *Journal of Experimental Social Psychology, 31,* 467–492.

42. Galinsky, A. D., & Mussweiler, T. (2001). First offers as anchors: The role of perspective-taking and negotiator focus. *Journal of Personality and Social Psychology, 81,* 657–669.

43. Tinsley, C. H., O'Connor, K. M., & Sullivan, B. A. (2002). Tough guys finish last: The perils of a distributive reputation. *Organizational Behavior and Human Decision Processes, 88,* 621–642.

44. Farber, H. S. (1981). Splitting-the-difference in interest arbitration. *Industrial and Labor Relations Review, 35*(1), 70–77; Farber, H., & Bazerman, M. S. (1986). The general basis of arbitrator behavior: An empirical analysis of conventional and final-offer arbitration. *Econometrica, 54,* 1503–1528.

45. Rubin, J. Z., Pruitt, D. G., & Kim, S. H. (1994). *Social conflict: Escalation, stalemate, and settlement* (2nd ed.). New York: McGraw-Hill.

46. Robinson, R. J., Keltner, D., Ward, A., & Ross, L. (1995). Actual versus assumed differences in construal: "Naive realism" in intergroup perception and conflict. *Journal of Personality and Social Psychology, 68,* 404–417.

47. Thompson, L., & Kim, P. (2000). How the quality of third parties' settlement solutions are affected by the relationship between negotiators. *Journal of Experimental Psychology: Applied, 6*(1), 1–16.

LEADING AND MANAGING TEAMS

Before reading this chapter, complete the brief teamwork analysis in Exercise 9.1. It asks you to analyze a team of which you are currently a member. In the analysis, you will consider several things, such as the goal of the team, the members of the team (and the roles they serve), and you will have an opportunity to evaluate the effectiveness of your team on several dimensions. By doing this exercise, you will have engaged in a "team performance evaluation" and you will develop a skill that is essential for the sustained performance of teams. Even the most high-performing teams can fail, and it is the analysis of team performance and the resulting changes that teams make that can put them back on the road of success.

EXHIBIT 9.1 Teamwork Quiz

Take 5–10 minutes to answer all questions. If possible, complete the quiz with other team members or classmates. You must choose only one answer; in cases where your team disagrees, you need to solve by consensus.

1. **When it comes to <u>conflict</u>, the highest-performing teams should:**
   a) Discourage it.
   b) Let members vent openly.
   c) Encourage conflict about attitudes; discourage conflict about behaviors.
   d) Encourage conflict about tasks; discourage conflict about personalities.

2. **When it comes to <u>making decisions</u>, teams are:**
   a) Superior to individuals
   b) Inferior to individuals
   c) Better than the average of its members, but not necessarily as good as the best performer

3. **When it comes to <u>creativity</u>, teams are:**
   a) Less creative than individuals
   b) More creative than individuals
   c) About equally creative

4. **The most commonly cited <u>problem</u> with regard to teamwork is:**
   a) Trusting one other
   b) Listening to one another
   c) Sustaining motivation

5. **When it comes to floor-time (talking) in a typical 8-person team meeting:**
   a) Every team member roughly contributes pretty much equally.

   b) 3 people do over 75% of the talking.
   c) 5 people do over 75% of the talking.

6. **The most important skills (competencies) that team members need to have are:**
   a) Task and people skills
   b) Speaking and listening skills
   c) Rationality and intuition skills

7. **All of the following can minimize the <u>"free rider"</u> problem in teams, except:**
   a) Develop a team contract—a written statement of team objectives and practices.
   b) Increase the size of the team.
   c) Performance reviews—periodically review and evaluate members.
   d) Increase each member's involvement and ownership.

8. **An <u>essential</u> condition for high-performance teamwork is:**
   a) Regular retreats
   b) Significant, meaningful performance incentives
   c) A shared goal
   d) Complementary skill sets

9. **The typical team is how old?**
   a) 0–6 months
   b) 6–12 months
   c) 12–24 months
   d) Over 2 years

Source: Thompson, L. (2007). *Leading high impact teams.* Kellogg Executive Program, Northwestern University.

It is nearly impossible to think of working in an organization without being part of a team. Teams and teamwork are the building blocks of organizations. Most of us, by the time we arrive at college, our MBA program, or our first job, have been a member of several teams. For this reason, most people think of themselves as highly expert when it comes to teams. (As a challenge, you can take the teamwork quiz in Exhibit 9.1 to test your knowledge about teams. Check your answers in Exhibit 9.14.)

A **team** is a group of interdependent people working toward a shared goal. "A **work team** is an interdependent collection of individuals who share responsibility for specific outcomes for their organizations."[1] Forty-three percent of managers report that their companies use teams "extensively."[2] There are two defining characteristics of teams: first and foremost is the presence of a *shared goal*. Second, team members are *interdependent*. Teams should not exist if the goal can be accomplished by a given individual working independently.

Despite the pervasiveness of teams in our schools, work, families, and communities, teamwork is not always easy. In fact, many people have never had a course of formal training in teamwork. The most commonly cited problem in teams is developing and sustaining motivation, mentioned by over half of managers who work in teams. A close second is coordination and communication problems (cited by 43 percent of managers who work in teams).

Types of Teams in Organizations

Organizations rely on teams to improve quality, productivity, customer service, and the experience of work for their employees. Yet not all teams are alike. Teams differ greatly in their degree of autonomy and control vis-à-vis the organization. Specifically, how is authority shared between the team and the organization? Who has responsibility for monitoring and managing group performance? Setting team goals? Consider four different types of teams in terms of the relative levels of responsibility and authority they have in the organization.[3] (See Exhibit 9.2.)

Manager-Led Teams

The most traditional type of team is the manager-led team. About 40 percent of all teams are manager-led. In the **manager-led team,** the manager acts as the team leader and is responsible for defining the goals, process, and functioning of the team. The team itself is responsible only for the actual execution of their assigned work. Upper management or a supervisor is responsible for monitoring and managing performance processes, overseeing design, selecting members, and interacting with the organization. Examples of manager-led work teams include automotive assembly teams, surgery teams, sports teams, and military teams. A manager-led team typically has a dedicated, full-time, higher-ranking supervisor, as in a coal-mining crew. Team members report to the manager on a regular basis.

Manager-led teams provide the greatest amount of control over team members and the work they perform; they allow the leader to have control over the process and products of the team. In addition, they can be efficient, in the sense that the manager does the work of setting the goals and outlining the work to be done. In manager-led teams, managers don't have to sit by and watch the team make the same mistakes they did. If the team is relatively low on the learning curve, the manager can provide guidance and direction and forestall problems. Manager-led teams require a great deal of supervision and hands-on management by the leader.

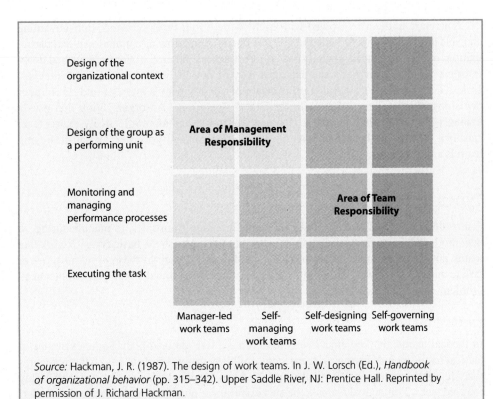

Source: Hackman, J. R. (1987). The design of work teams. In J. W. Lorsch (Ed.), *Handbook of organizational behavior* (pp. 315–342). Upper Saddle River, NJ: Prentice Hall. Reprinted by permission of J. Richard Hackman.

EXHIBIT 9.2

Four Types of High-Performance Teams

Self-Managing Teams

Self-managing or self-regulating teams monitor their own work and are responsible for creating their own performance conditions for achieving their goals. Self-managing teams require less supervision by the leader. Self-managing teams improve productivity, quality, and employee morale, as well as cut down absenteeism and turnover.[4] About 55 percent of all teams are self-managing. Self-managing teams build commitment, offer increased autonomy, and often enhance morale. One disadvantage is that the manager has much less control over the process and products, making it difficult to assess progress.

Self-Directing (or Self-Designing) Teams

Self-directing or self-designing teams determine their own objectives and the methods by which to achieve them. The self-directing team can determine who is on the team, as well. Self-directing teams enhance goal commitment, member motivation, and provide opportunity for organizational learning and change. However, they can be costly to build and maintain. Furthermore, because the manager has a "hands off" relationship with the team, it can be difficult to monitor the progress of the team. Self-directing teams are ideally suited for complex, ill-defined, or ambiguous problems and next-generation planning. They are well suited for managers who have several teams to manage.

Self-Governing Teams

Self-governing teams are responsible not only for execution, managing their own performance, and designing the group, but also for the organizational context itself. By *organizational context,* we mean the more overarching work and structure of the organization. For example, in many companies, the president or CEO has been replaced with an executive, self-governing team. Self-governing teams may be set up to act in an autonomous fashion, similar to the independent counsel's office; to investigate certain problems, such as in the Abu Ghraib prisoner abuse scandal; and for creative reasons, such as responding to new threats in the marketplace.

There are trade-offs involved with each of these four types of teams. Self-governing and self-directing teams provide the greatest potential in terms of commitment and participation, but are also at the greatest risk of misdirection. When decisions are pushed down in organizations, team goals and activities may be at odds with organizational interests. Unless everyone in the organization is aware of the company's interests and goals, poor decisions may be made, often with the best of intentions. An organization that uses a manager-led team is betting that a manager can run things more effectively than a team can. If it is believed that a team can do the job better, a self-governing or self-designing team is a better choice.

Types of Teamwork

Teams do many types of tasks in organizations, ranging from sales, to manufacturing, to new product development, and so on. It is useful to distinguish the basic types of work that teams do so that the optimal performance conditions for each of these different types of task teams can be created. Exhibit 9.3 describes three types of work that teams do: tactical, problem-solving, and creative.[5]

Tactical Teams

In tactical teams, the key objective is to execute a well-defined plan. Some examples of tactical teams include cardiac surgery teams, military teams, sports teams, and other teams that are tightly organized.[6] Tactical teams are ideal for directive, well-defined, and highly focused tasks. For tactical teams to be successful there must be a high degree of task clarity and unambiguous role definition. The biggest threats to effective tactical teamwork are role ambiguity, lack of training, and communication barriers.

EXHIBIT 9.3   Three Types of Work Teams Do

Tactical Teams

Tactical teams execute well-defined plans. Examples of tactical teams include: cardiac surgery teams, military teams, and sports teams. To be successful, tactical teams need to develop mental models pertaining to the operations that they perform. In addition, successful tactical teams have transactive memory systems that represent shared understanding of which team members know which knowledge. Tactical teams have a high need for role clarity.

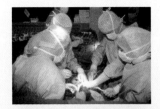

Problem-Solving Teams

Problem-solving teams resolve issues that are not initially understood. In this sense, problem-solving teams attempt to understand cause-and-effect relationships. For example, a problem-solving team might try to understand the causal determinants of a disease outbreak or the reasons why enrollment in a program may be declining. Examples of problem-solving teams include: Centers for Disease Control, Sandia Laboratories nuclear weapons team, FBI investigative teams, and many company task-forces. Problem-solving teams need to make decisions and collect data and, for this reason, they need to have a decision-making process that is error-free.

Creative Teams

Creative teams need to innovate products, services, and processes. Examples of creative teams include: Nissan Design International, IDEO design, and new product development teams. To be successful, creative teams need to have enough autonomy to depart from the traditional practices of the organization. Creative teams often use brain-storming techniques. However, creative teams are often not as innovative as individuals, especially when they do not follow the rules of brainstorming.

Source: Larson, C. E., & LaFasto, F. M. J. (1989). *Teamwork: What must go right/What can go wrong,* p. 43. Newbury Park, CA: Sage. Reprinted by permission of Sage Publications, Inc.

EXHIBIT 9.4   Lack of Shared Mental Models Leads to Team Tragedy

"On a beautiful night in October, 1978, in the Chesapeake Bay, two vessels sighted one another visually and on radar. On one of them, the Coast Guard cutter training vessel *Cuyahoga,* the captain (a chief warrant officer) saw the other ship up ahead as a small object on the radar, and visually he saw two lights, indicating that it was proceeding in the same direction as his own ship. He **thought** [emphasis added] it possibly was a fishing vessel. The first mate saw the lights, but saw three, and estimated (correctly) that it was a ship proceeding toward them. He had no responsibility to inform the captain, nor did he think he needed to. Since the two ships drew together so rapidly, the captain **decided** [emphasis added] that it must be a very slow fishing boat that he was about to overtake. This reinforced his incorrect interpretation. The lookout knew the captain was aware of the ship, so did not comment further as it got quite close and seemed to be nearly on a collision course. Since both ships were traveling full speed, the closing came fast. The other ship, a large cargo ship, did not establish any bridge-to-bridge communication, because the passing was routine. But at the last moment the captain of the *Cuyahoga* **realized** [emphasis added] that in overtaking the supposed fishing boat, which he assumed was on a near-parallel course, he would cut off that boat's ability to turn as both of them approached the Potomac River. So he ordered a turn to the port. This brought him directly in the path of the oncoming freighter, which hit the cutter. Eleven coastguardsmen perished."

Source: Perrow, C. (1984). *Normal accidents: Living with high-risk technologies.* New York: Basic Books. Copyright © 1999 Princeton University Press. Reprinted by permission of Princeton University Press.

SHARED MENTAL MODELS Tragic events, like the one in Chesapeake Bay described by Charles Perrow (see Exhibit 9.4), often stem from a lack of shared understanding among tactical team members.

If a mental model is a person's mental representation of the world that allows him or her to understand, predict, and solve problems in a given situation,[7] then a *shared* mental model or **team mental model** is the degree of correspondence between team members' mental models.[8] Based on their mental models, team members form expectations about not only what they should do in a given situation, but also about what they think other team members will do (or should do). Mental models are built naturally and without much cognitive awareness or deliberate thought—they form from our experiences and interactions with other people. There are two key considerations in terms of the effectiveness of team mental models: the accuracy of the model and the degree of correspondence (or noncorrespondence between members' mental models).

Accuracy If team members hold erroneous mental models about a task, either because they lack technical training or communicate poorly, their well-intentioned behaviors could produce disastrous results.

Correspondence Effective teams are able to adapt to external demands in a coordinated fashion and anticipate each other's information needs because they have shared mental models of a given problem or situation. For example, when novel or unexpected events arise, such as when an airplane enters another's airspace, team members base their decisions in part on what they believe others know or do not know. The greater the overlap or commonality among team members' mental models, the greater the likelihood that the team members will accurately predict the needs of the team and team members, adapt to changing demands, and coordinate activity with one another successfully.[9]

TRANSACTIVE MEMORY SYSTEMS A **transactive memory system** is a team-level information processing system that is an extension of the human information-processing system: a shared system for attending to, encoding, storing, processing, and retrieving information.[10] Think of a transactive memory system as the way in which team members can "read each other's minds." A transactive memory system is a combination of two things: (a) knowledge possessed by particular team members, and (b) the awareness of who knows what. In this way, transactive memory systems serve as an external storage device, such as a library or computer that can be visited to retrieve otherwise unavailable information. To study how transactive memory really works in teams, Argote and colleagues investigated the success with which doctors performed hip and knee replacement surgeries.[11] The doctors' number of years of expertise did not predict successful surgical outcomes. However, the number of times a given team of doctors had performed surgery together strongly predicted the success of surgeries. Another life-and-death example of the importance of transactive memory systems in teams comes from an analysis of coal-mining teams.[12] Goodman and Garber examined the consequences of team member absenteeism on production crews' accidents in five underground coal mines.[13] They reasoned that when team members are absent, the ability of teams to form transactive memory (or shared mental model) is impaired. The average accident rate was about 1 accident per 200 miner days worked. When teammates are "regulars" and highly familiar with each other, their accident rate is 0.251 less than the average rate. And lower levels of familiarity (working knowledge of one's job, co-workers, and work environment) mean lower productivity.[14]

Problem-Solving Teams

In **problem-solving teams,** teams attempt to get answers to vexing questions, see patterns in a myriad of data, and resolve issues that remain open. Often, this is an ongoing enterprise, such as the war against terrorism. Problem-solving teams are ideally suited to tasks that require a focus on data, information, tough issues, facts (not opinions), and the suspension of judgment. Some examples of problem-solving teams include the Mayo Clinic oncology group, the Centers for Disease Control, Sandia Laboratory's nuclear weapons team, and FBI investigative teams.[15] To be effective, each member of the problem-solving team must expect and believe that interactions among members will be truthful and of high integrity. Thus, a key feature of problem-solving teams is trust and respect. The biggest threats to effective problem solving are a failure to stick to the facts, fixation on solutions, succumbing to political pressures, and confirmatory information search.

INDIVIDUAL VERSUS TEAM DECISION MAKING   Is it better to relegate decision making to a team or to a given individual? In short, who is better at making decisions, teams or individuals? Teams are better at making decisions than are individuals.[16]

However, this raises the question of whether a team is superior to the performance of the "best individual" on the team, when it comes to making decisions. Many investigations clearly indicate that the best team member outperforms the team.[17] But, more realistic studies of actual work teams indicate that teams outperform their best teammate 97 percent of the time.[18] And team performance increases over that of an individual best team member as the demonstrability (concreteness) of the task increases. For example, teams perform at the level of the best team member on mathematical, insight, and information-rich problems. Teams perform at the level of the second-best team members on knowledge problems, such as vocabulary, analogies, and logic tasks. Teams perform at the level of the average group members on weakly demonstrable problems.[19] (A "demonstrable" problem is one that has a clear, best answer. Thus, a "weakly demonstrable" problem does not have clear, best answer.) Unfortunately, teams are much more confident—too confident—than is a given individual. For example, in one investigation, teams were asked to make stock price predictions.[20] The actual accuracy of the team was 47 percent, but their confidence level was 65 percent.

Next, we identify three of the most common problems in decision-making teams: groupthink, the Abilene paradox, and the common information effect. This list supplements the human biases and shortcomings identified in Chapter 7 ("Decision Making").

GROUPTHINK   When team members place consensus above all other priorities—including making good decisions—they have fallen victim to groupthink.[21] **Groupthink** involves a deterioration of cognitive vigilance, lack of reality testing, and failure of morality as a result of group pressures toward conformity of opinion. For examples of groupthink in the political and corporate world, see Exhibit 9.5. Symptoms of groupthink cannot be easily assessed by outside observers. Most groupthink symptoms represent private feelings or beliefs held by group members or behaviors performed in private. There are three tell-tale symptoms of groupthink that take root and blossom in groups that succumb to pressures of reaching unanimity:

- *Overestimation of the group:* Members of the group regard themselves as invulnerable and morally correct. They believe they are exempt from standards.
- *Close-mindedness:* Members of the group engage in collective rationalization of the problem.
- *Pressures toward uniformity:* There is a strong intolerance in a groupthink situation for diversity of opinion. Dissenters are subject to enormous social pressure. Group members often suppress their reservations and the group perceives themselves to be anonymous.

How to Avoid Groupthink   All teams are vulnerable to groupthink. Effective leaders know how to take preventive action so as to minimize the likelihood of groupthink occurring. The bigger the team, the more likely it is that groupthink could develop.[22] This is because people grow more intimidated and hesitant as team size increases.

Risk Technique   The **risk technique** is a structured discussion method that aims to reduce group members' fears about making decisions.[23] The discussion is structured so that team members talk about the dangers or risks involved in a decision and delay discussion of any potential benefits. Following this is a discussion of controls or mechanisms for dealing with risks and dangers. One method is to have a facilitator play the role of a devil's advocate for a particular decision.

EXHIBIT 9.5 **Instances of Groupthink in Politics and the Corporate World**

EXAMPLES FROM POLITICS	EXAMPLES FROM THE CORPORATE WORLD
• Neville Chamberlain's inner circle, whose members supported the policy of appeasement of Hitler during 1937 and 1938, despite repeated warnings and events that indicated it would have adverse consequences (Janis & Mann, 1977)	• Enron's board of directors was well-informed about (and could therefore have prevented) the risky accounting practices, conflicts of interest, and hiding of debt that led to the company's downfall; likewise, Arthur Andersen (Enron's accounting firm) did nothing to halt the company's high-risk practices (*BusinessWeek,* July 29, 2002; Aug. 12, 2002)
• President Truman's advisory group, whose members supported the decision to escalate the war in North Korea, despite firm warnings by the Chinese Communist government that U.S. entry into North Korea would be met with armed resistance from the Chinese (Janis & Mann, 1977)	• Grunenthal Chemie's decision to market the drug thalidomide (Raven & Rubin, 1976)
• President Kennedy's inner circle, whose members supported the decision to launch the Bay of Pigs invasion of Cuba, despite the availability of information indicating that it would be an unsuccessful venture and would damage U.S. relations with other countries (Janis & Mann, 1977)	• The price-fixing conspiracy involving the electrical manufacturing industry during the 1950s
	• The decision by Ford Motor Company to produce the Edsel (Huseman & Driver, 1979)
• President Johnson's close advisers, who supported the decision to escalate the war in Vietnam, despite intelligence reports and information indicating that this course of action would not defeat the Viet Cong or the North Vietnamese, and would generate unfavorable political consequences within the United States (Janis & Mann, 1977)	• The AMA's (American Medical Association's) decision to allow Sunbeam to use the AMA name as a product endorsement (*Chicago Sun-Times,* Nov. 11, 1998)
	• The selling of millions of jars of "phony" apple juice by Beech-Nut, the third largest baby food producer in the United States
• The decision of the Reagan administration to exchange arms for hostages with Iran and to continue commitment to the Nicaraguan Contras in the face of several congressional amendments limiting or banning aid	• The involvement of E. F. Hutton in "check kiting," wherein a money manager at a Hutton branch office would write a check on an account in Bank A for more money than Hutton had in the account. Because of the time lag in the check-collection system, these overdrafts sometimes went undetected, and Hutton could deposit funds to cover the overdraft in the following day. The deposited money would start earning interest immediately. The scheme allowed Hutton to earn a day's interest on Bank A's account without having to pay anything for it—resulting in $250 million in free loans every day (*ABA Banking Journal,* July 1, 1985; *New York Times,* June, 1988)
	• The illegal purchases by Salomon Brothers at U.S. Treasury auctions in the early 1990s (Sims, 1992)

Source: Thompson, L. (2004). *Making the team: A guide for managers* (2nd ed.). Upper Saddle River, NJ: Pearson Education, Inc. Reprinted by permission.

Invite Different Perspectives A key problem in decision-making groups is too much conformity or like-mindedness. For this reason, it is often desirable to consider as many and as different perspectives on a problem as possible. Team members may assume the perspective of other constituencies with a stake in the decision.[24] The absence of different perspectives has been identified as the root cause of several corporate, political, and managerial disasters that swept through Switzerland in 2001–2002, such as the grounding of Swissair in the fall of 2001; corporate governance battles at Zurich Financial Services Group and Credit Suisse Group; the July 11, 2002, arrest of the ambassador to Luxembourg on charges of money laundering; and the air traffic failures that contributed to the July 1, 2002, Uberlingen crash. The boards of most Swiss companies were often "little more than rubber stamps, made up for members of the country's small, conservative, smug establishment."[25] When it comes to different perspectives, those persons providing the counterpoint should prepare as they would if they were working on a court case—in other words, they should assemble data and evidence, as opposed to simply voicing a personal opinion.[26]

Appoint a Devil's Advocate By the time upper management is wedded to a particular plan, they are often impervious to evidence that may be contradictory. Moreover, subordinates don't want to challenge management's beliefs. This is why some teams institute a special "devil's advocate" responsibility to certain members of the team. For example, consider the case of Cisco Systems, which suffered a remarkable comedown in the spring of 2001, losing 88 percent of its value in one year. Cisco's upper management, enamored of their IT system, never modeled what would happen if a key assumption (namely, growth) disappeared from the equation.[27] In contrast, Winston Churchill knew how to combat groupthink and yes-men. Worried that his own larger-than-life image would deter subordinates from bringing him the truth, he instituted a unit outside his chain of command called the "statistical office" whose key job was to bring him the bleakest, most gut-wrenching facts. Similarly, Richard J. Schroth and A. Larry Elliott, authors of the book *How Companies Lie,* suggest that "counter-pointers" be appointed in teams, whose chief function is to ask the rudest possible questions.[28]

Whereas a devil's advocate procedure can be effective, it is contrived dissent, meaning that team members often pretend to disagree for the sake of argument. It is better for a team to have genuine dissent. Genuine dissent was more effective than contrived dissent in avoiding confirmatory decision making in investment decisions.[29]

Structured Discussion Principle The goal of the structured discussion principle is to delay solution selection and to increase the problem-solving phase. This prevents premature closure on a solution and extends problem analysis and evaluation. For example, teams may be given guidelines that emphasize continued solicitations of solutions, protect individuals from criticism, keep the discussion problem-centered, and list all solutions before evaluating them. Individual group members are discouraged from committing themselves to a position before the group has a chance to discuss the problem. The incidence of escalation was examined by comparing groupthink behavior in groups who made decisions after each person had staked an individual position versus that in groups who considered the project information as a group.[30] When individuals had each staked out their opinion before the group met, nonrational escalation was at its highest.

Establish Procedures for Protecting Alternative Viewpoints Few would disagree that alternative viewpoints are important to surface in any team. However, anyone who has ever been in a team has witnessed how people react to alternative viewpoints—usually with disdain. People who propose contrarian views are not well liked, and in fact, groups often vote those members out of the group! Latané examined how groups react to someone who proposes a point of view counter to that of the group.[31] The group inevitably follows a three-step cycle: (1) They first try to persuade that group member out of his or her views through gentle, but persistent persuasion and prodding (e.g., "Glen, we tried that two years ago and upper management did not think it would work"). (2) If persuasion does not work, then groups resort to simply ignoring the contrarian team member (e.g., Roger Boisjoly, the engineer who tried to halt the failed space shuttle Challenger flight in 1986 because he was aware of the likely trouble, said that when he tried to raise his objections in the mission management team meetings, "I received cold stares . . . with looks as if to say, 'go away and don't bother us with the facts.' No one in management wanted to discuss the facts; they just would not respond verbally . . . to me. I felt totally helpless and that further argument was fruitless, so I, too, stopped pressing my case."[32] (3) Finally, groups will outright reject someone who continues to disagree with the majority. However, this is one of the worst things groups can do, as it is the presence of a devil's advocate that can ward off disastrous decision making.

Second Solution This technique requires teams to identify a second solution or decision recommendation as an alternative to their first choice. This enhances the problem-solving and idea-generation phases, as well as performance quality.[33]

Beware of Time Pressure Time pressure has a negative effect on decision quality: The greater the time pressure, the worse the decision.[34] And people change their priorities depending on whether the decision they are making is in the distant future or immediately at hand: Moral principles are more likely to guide managers' decisions for the distant future than for the immediate future, whereas difficulty, cost, and situational pressures are more likely to be important in immediate decisions. In other words, people are more likely to compromise their principles in decisions regarding near future actions, as compared to distant future actions.[35]

ABILENE PARADOX The **Abilene paradox** refers to the "mismanagement of agreement."[36] The Abilene paradox was named as a result of a management scholar's experience in which his family (team) embarked on an ill-conceived course of action (driving to Abilene, Texas, for a miserable dinner). All family members expressed a desire to make the trip, but privately, nobody wanted to go. One obvious reason for this is the team's desire to avoid conflict and achieve consensus. To the extent that team members value consensus more than debate, and maintaining group solidarity more than making good decisions, they could fall prey to the Abilene paradox. When we suppress our concerns about a decision, this is known as **self-limiting behavior.** There are six key causes of self-limiting behavior in teams:[37]

- *The presence of someone with expertise:* When team members perceive that another member of the team has expertise or is highly qualified to make a decision, they will self-limit. Members' perception of other teammates' competence plays a key role, and these evaluations are formed quickly—often before a team meets for the first time.
- *The presentation of a compelling argument:* Frequently, the timing of a coherent argument influences decision making, such as when the decision is made after a lot of fruitless discussion.
- *A lack of confidence in one's ability to contribute:* If team members feel unsure about their ability to meaningfully contribute to the decision, they will be inclined to self-limit.
- *An unimportant or meaningless decision:* Unless the decision is seen as vital or important to the individual's well-being, there is a powerful tendency to adopt a "who cares" attitude.
- *Pressure from others to conform to the team's decision:* Roger Boisjoly, a lead engineer in the Challenger shuttle disaster in 1986, reported that he felt incredible pressures to conform exerted by the NASA management team.
- *A dysfunctional decision-making climate:* When team members believe that others are frustrated, indifferent, disorganized, or generally unwilling to commit themselves to making an effective decision, they are likely to self-limit. Such a climate can be created in the early stages of a decision by inadvertent remarks, such as, "This is a ridiculous assignment" or "Nothing is going to change, so why bother," and so on.

COMMON INFORMATION EFFECT The **common information effect** refers to the fact that when teams get together, they tend to discuss what they already have in common, to the detriment of discussing unique information that individual members may possess.[38] People feel compelled to discover what information they have in common with others, and commonly held information dominates the discussion. So far, this would seem to be fairly innocuous. However, if we consider the fact that most teams are composed precisely because they have complementary (rather than identical) skills and expertise, serious problems arise when they fail to enlighten each other (with each person's unique information). Christensen and his colleagues examined how teams of medical doctors made patient diagnoses and treatment plans.[39] They created three-person teams in which each member of the team (e.g., doctor, medical intern, etc.) was given a partial set of relevant facts regarding a given patient (e.g., is allergic to certain medications, has sun sensitivity, etc.). The doctors were told to meet and discuss the patient and then arrive at a diagnosis. When combined, the facts given to each member of the team lead to an obvious diagnosis. Thus, the teams had all the information they needed to properly diagnose the patient. The only obstacle was whether team members would share the facts and listen to one another. The discussions were videotaped and coded. Teams were most likely to discuss cues that all had in common (65 percent) rather than cues that one or two members had in common (42 percent). Second, when the critical information for a proper diagnosis was not shared fully among all three of the medical personnel, the accurate diagnosis rate plummeted from 100 percent to 70 percent.

One of the reasons why the common information effect is a problem is that there is often information that only one person is aware of. Surfacing such information is critical. Kathy Phillips and her collaborators suggest that the common information effect is magnified when the people who hold the same information are also part of the same social group.[40] People are more likely to discover critical hidden information if it is held by a "social outsider." Social "insiders" with unique information are less effective at sharing their information with their group.

Creative Teams

Creative teams attempt to develop new products, ideas, and services, and make the impossible happen. Some examples of creative teams include IDEO design teams, Hallmark's creative advisory group, and the teams responsible for HBO original programming. Creative teamwork is often taken for granted, when it should not be. We begin with a discussion of creativity and innovation. Then we discuss brainstorming.

CREATIVITY AND INNOVATION **Creativity** is the production of novel and useful ideas. It is also known as *ideation*. **Innovation** is the realization of actual ideas in the form of products, services, or whatever might be productive for an organization. Innovation is also known as *implementation*. Many organizations value innovation more than creativity: "We don't need any more bright ideas. In business, success is 5 percent strategy, 95 percent execution," said Percy Barnevik, chairman of ABB in 1997.[41] Similarly, the president of Sony, Masaru Ibuka, said, "If the weight of invention or discovery is 1, then the weight to bring it to actual development should be 10, and the weight to produce and market it should be 100."[42]

However, it would be foolish to dismiss the value of ideas. Linus Pauling admonishes, "The way to get good ideas is to get lots of ideas and throw the bad ones away. You aren't going to have good ideas unless you have lots of ideas and some sort of principle of selection."[43]

MEASURING CREATIVITY How might we measure the creativity of teams?

Guilford's Model A popular and important index is **Guilford's three-factor model of creativity,** which assesses creativity in terms of three dimensions: fluency, flexibility, and originality.[44] **Fluency** is a measure of quantity—it is generally assumed that more creative teams are ones that generate more ideas. **Flexibility** is a measure of how many different kinds of ideas a team generates. As a general principle, teams that can think of different kinds of ideas are more creative. Finally, **originality** is a measure of statistical rarity or novelty. Teams that are more creative can usually generate ideas that other teams don't even think of.

A common test of creativity is to ask teams (or individuals) to brainstorm as many different ideas for using a cardboard box as possible. Alternatively, teams can be asked to generate as many implications as possible of people having an extra thumb, and so on. Let's consider the "thumbs" task. Suppose that one team generates the following ideas: using the thumb to play the piano differently, using the thumb to play a flute with more range, and using the thumb to play a guitar with more chords. This team would be given a score of 3 for fluency because they have generated three ideas. But this team would be given a score of 1 for flexibility because all of the ideas pertain to the playing of musical instruments. Now, contrast that team to a team that suggests: using the extra thumb to pick crops with more efficiency, using the thumb to facilitate genetic experimentation, and using the thumb to design jewelry for that digit. This team would get a score of 3 for fluency because they have generated three ideas. However, this team would get a score of 3 for flexibility because they have generated ideas that span many different topics and industries—agriculture, medical genetics, and aesthetics and fashion. Flexibility is the driving force behind fluency. Moreover, flexibility is the driving force behind originality as well. If you are ever in need of creating a lot of ideas, the best approach is to increase the kinds of ideas—this can be done by assembling a diverse team (e.g., imagine the ideas that a team would produce if it contained a botanist, an artist, and an engineer).

EXHIBIT 9.6

Finke's Model of Evaluating the Usefulness of Creative Ideas

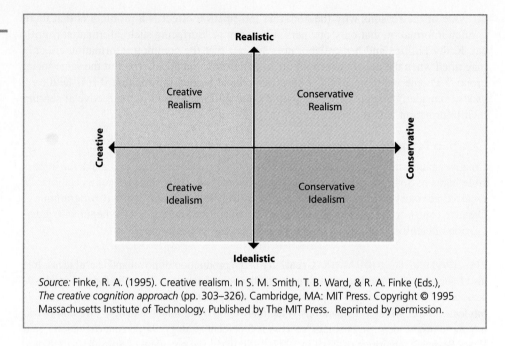

Source: Finke, R. A. (1995). Creative realism. In S. M. Smith, T. B. Ward, & R. A. Finke (Eds.), *The creative cognition approach* (pp. 303–326). Cambridge, MA: MIT Press. Copyright © 1995 Massachusetts Institute of Technology. Published by The MIT Press. Reprinted by permission.

Finke's Model **Finke** proposed a **model** for evaluating the usefulness of creative ideas as a function of two factors: their creativity (similar to Guilford's originality measure) and their realism (i.e., how useful the idea is in terms of working with existing products and services, etc.).[45] As can be seen in Exhibit 9.6, any idea that a team suggests might fall in one of four quadrants. Ideas that are typified by *conservative realism* are relatively commonplace (i.e., conservative) and realistic in terms of working within existing situations. For example, a group that suggests developing special mittens with extra thumbs illustrates a conservative and realistic idea. Some ideas are *conservative* and *idealistic,* such that they are not very original but also somewhat absurd, for example, if a team were to suggest that the base 10 numbering system should be changed to base 12 because so many people count on their hands. Still other ideas are *creative,* but *idealistic:* they are nontraditional and not very implementable. For example, a group might suggest that the extra thumb would be used by children sucking their thumbs to have more variety. Finally, some ideas are characterized by *creative realism.* In other words, the idea is very rare and creative, and will also prove useful, especially in terms of working with existing products. It is interesting that the "most innovative product" designs (as deemed by *BusinessWeek*) are for products that are creative and highly useful. Perhaps it is for this reason that most people believe that groups are more creative than individuals. For example, 80 percent of people in companies believe that groups are more creative than individuals.[46]

BRAINSTORMING   Alex Osborn, an executive at an advertising agency, was convinced that when it came to being creative, people could be much greater than the sum of their parts. So convinced was he that he developed a technique known as *brainstorming* to bring out the best in creative groups.[47] **Osborn's four rules** were simple and straightforward, and consistent with social psychological theory. (See Exhibit 9.7 for Osborn's rules for brainstorming.)

His first rule, expressiveness, was designed to encourage every member of the group to lower his or her inhibitions and not self-limit. This maxim is similar to groupthink prescriptions that encourage group members to voice their objections without the fear of social censure—here, group members are encouraged to voice their ideas. It is also similar to the key idea of self-limiting behavior in the Abilene paradox. Osborn's second rule, nonevaluation, provides a fail-safe of sorts for the first rule. In other words, Osborn recognized that even the most disinhibited of group members will self-censor if they faced the censure of their teammates. So, Osborn specifically cautioned group members not to evaluate any idea in any fashion. This applies to positive feedback as well. Osborn's third

EXHIBIT 9.7 **Osborn's Rules for Brainstorming**

Expressiveness	Group members should express any idea that comes to mind, no matter how strange, weird, or fanciful. Group members are encouraged not to be constrained nor timid. They should freewheel whenever possible.
Nonevaluation	Do not criticize ideas. Group members should not evaluate any of the ideas in any way during the generation phase; all ideas should be considered valuable.
Quantity	Group members should generate as many ideas as possible. Groups should strive for quantity, as the more ideas, the better. Quantity of ideas increases the probability of finding excellent solutions.
Building	Because all of the ideas belong to the group, members should try to modify and extend the ideas suggested by other members whenever possible.

Source: Adapted from Osborn, A. F. (1957). *Applied imagination* (revised edition). New York: Scribner.

rule is nothing more than Guilford's fluency maxim. Osborn correctly recognized that people might very well experience performance anxiety if they were limited to only high-quality suggestions. In contrast, anyone can rise to the challenge of quantity. And the probability of finding a really good idea is statistically much greater the more ideas that are generated. Osborn's last rule, building, represents the manner in which groups might be able to experience synergy—by combining, modifying, and integrating different ideas.

Most companies resonate to Osborn's rules. However, most companies severely violate the rules in actual practice—they repeatedly criticize team members, they are possessive with ideas, and they eschew quantity in favor of quality. Thus, Osborn's rules are rarely put into real practice without the help of a group facilitator.

Osborn's simple four rules launched the beginning of a new research era in group research. Hundreds of empirical investigations were conducted by scholars across the globe for the purpose of testing Osborn's theories. What did they find?

REAL GROUPS VERSUS NOMINAL GROUPS Virtually every research investigation ever done in comparing the creativity of groups with that of the same number of people working independently (known as a **nominal group**) reveals that nominal groups are more creative than real groups. For example, groups have lower quantity (fluency) and quality scores (the percentage of "good ideas" as judged by experts who did not know whose ideas they were evaluating) than do nominal groups.[48]

As you might imagine, these powerful findings contradict most people's intuition.[49] Not surprisingly, considerable attention has been directed to answering the critical question, Why is it that groups are distinctly inferior to individuals? The answer is determined by a confluence of several social, cognitive, and motivational factors that all thwart group effectiveness.[50]

Social Loafing **Social loafing** refers to the fact that people work less hard when they are part of a group than when they are working alone. Social loafing is evident in investigations of people performing physical tasks, such as clapping, pulling, or shouting, as well as cognitive-intellectual tasks, such as writing or generating ideas.[51] The tendency for people to work less hard when they are part of a group or team is not apparent to people. It is usually the case that they are blissfully unaware. And social loafing is more likely when people are not accountable for their behaviors or outcomes.[52]

Conformity Conformity occurs when people bring their behaviors in line with what they perceive to be what others are doing. People are most likely to conform when they desire acceptance in a group or team. Conformity is evidenced in many ways—from the way that group members tend to talk and walk in a similar fashion to the way they respond to events. Again, conformity works insidiously: Group members are not aware of how much they change their behavior to bring it in line with the group. For example, in one investigation, team members were given a word association test either in a group setting (with others physically present) or alone. Responses were more clichéd, safe, and traditional when team members were in a group setting than when alone.[53]

Production Blocking **Production blocking** refers to the fact that a person performing one task, say, writing or speaking, or even listening, cannot easily perform another task. Production blocking is similar to multitasking. In a brainstorming group, production blocking occurs when members cannot share all of their ideas at the same time because they have to take turns talking and listening; production blocking also occurs when members need to write their ideas (instead of listening to other's ideas or generating their own ideas).

The Illusion of Group Productivity Perhaps the biggest threat to group effectiveness is the group's own faulty confidence. Groups have a much greater sense of self-efficacy or self-confidence than is warranted by their actual productivity level. Why? People in a group affirm one another, and this can lead the group to have a false sense of the group's potency or true performance.[54] Indeed, people are more productive when they set higher goals[55] and when they feel that they have to work harder to achieve their goals.[56]

Together, social loafing, conformity pressures, production blocking, and the illusion of group productivity conspire to make groups less effective than they otherwise would be.

Paulus' Three New Rules

Paul Paulus developed and tested three new rules for brainstorming groups.[57] Paulus was not trying to replace Osborn's rules, but rather supplement Osborn's rules. **Paulus' new rules** include:

- ▪ *Stay focused on the task.* In particular, group members should not tell stories and should not explain their ideas.
- ▪ *Keep the brainstorming going.* There will be lulls in the ideation phase and during these times, group members should continue to brainstorm.
- ▪ *Return to previous categories.* Group members may have new ideas about a given topic or category later in the process, so they should cycle back to those ideas.

Paulus compared groups who follow Osborn's four rules to groups who follow the Osborn–Paulus list of seven rules. You can easily see how those groups perform dramatically better in terms of the number of ideas than groups that don't follow any rules (see Exhibit 9.8).

EXHIBIT 9.8 **Three Additional Brainstorming Rules**

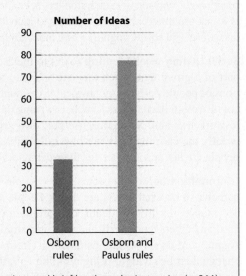

Source: Paulus, P. B., Nakui, T., Putman, V. L., & Brown, V. R. (2006). Effects of task instructions and brief breaks on brainstorming (p. 211). *Group Dynamics: Theory, Research, and Practice, 10*(3), pp. 206–219. Used with permission of American Psychological Association.

EXHIBIT 9.9

**Best Practices for
Improving Group
Creativity**

PRACTITIONER RECOMMENDATIONS	EMPIRICALLY BASED RECOMMENDATIONS
• Set goals*	• High group goals
• Trained facilitators*	• Individual accountability
• Following explicit set of rules*	• Brainwriting
• Diversity*	• Explicit set of rules
• Motivational techniques	• Trained facilitators
• Select "creative people"	• Intellectual diversity
• Directive cuing	• Reorganize individuals and teams
• Creative, relaxed context	• Brief breaks
• Fun	• One part of problem at a time
• Multisensing	• Positive mood

*empirical basis as well

Source: Adapted from Paulus, P., Nakui, T., & Putman, V. L. (2006). Group brainstorming and teamwork: Some rules for the road to innovation. In L. Thompson & H. S. Choi (Eds.), *Creativity and innovation in organizational teams.* Mahwah, NJ: Lawrence Erlbaum.

ENHANCING TEAM CREATIVITY What can teams do to enhance their creativity? Just because nominal groups are usually more creative than groups, this does not mean that organizations should abolish groups. Rather, the answer is to capitalize on what groups are best at (i.e., convergent thinking, getting corporate buy-in, networking, etc.) and capitalize on what individuals are best at (i.e., divergent thinking).

Exhibit 9.9 contains a list of creative practices divided into two columns. The left column is based on advice offered by practitioners who do not collect scientific data to back up their claims; nevertheless, they have the advantage of having often worked directly with real companies. The first four practitioner recommendations—setting high goals, adhering to Osborn's explicit rules, using trained facilitators (i.e., to enforce the rules), and using a diverse group that has several different viewpoints—are all prescriptions that have an empirical basis as well. However, we put them on the "practitioner" side because they are often not carried out as intended. Motivational techniques, such as giving people rewards (e.g., candy or gold coins, or conversely, punishing low performance or late arrivals) and multisensing (such as using paintings or music) are more questionable. The right-hand list is derived from controlled, scientific investigations, usually conducted in a laboratory setting.

Team Boundaries

Teams are not permanent entities. They come in and out of existence, change, reorganize, and eventually die. They recruit members, expel them, and mentor them; and sometimes, those members change the team. Such is the ebb and flow of the microcosm of the organization called the team.

Team Socialization and Norms Process

The process of becoming a full-fledged team member involves a series of distinct steps.[58] Some team members are "old-timers" with considerable longevity and seniority on a team, other members may exit the team, and still others may be in the process of joining. (See Exhibit 9.10 for a graph of Levine and Moreland's socialization process in teams.) As can be seen in Exhibit 9.10, in the first step of team socialization, the prospective member enters an "investigation" stage in which the group may attempt to "recruit" the new member and the new member may investigate the group. At the point of entry, the actual socialization process begins where the newcomer attempts to gain acceptance into the group. As a full member, people in groups effectively negotiate their roles (e.g., leader, nay-sayer, etc.). At some point, a member may separate him or herself from the group, perhaps

EXHIBIT 9.10

Role Transition in Groups

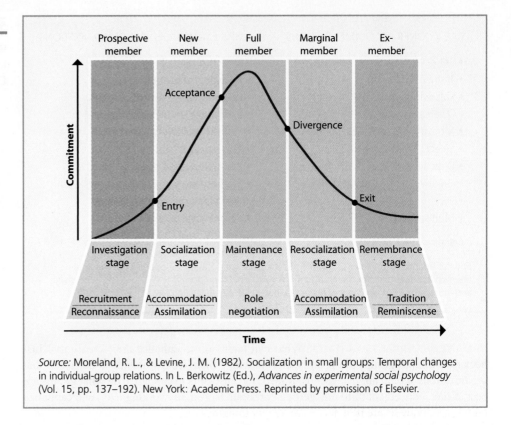

Source: Moreland, R. L., & Levine, J. M. (1982). Socialization in small groups: Temporal changes in individual-group relations. In L. Berkowitz (Ed.), *Advances in experimental social psychology* (Vol. 15, pp. 137–192). New York: Academic Press. Reprinted by permission of Elsevier.

because his or her interests begin to diverge. As members pass through groups, they may exit the group (such as the case in which someone is transferred to a new group).

Team Boundaries

Teams negotiate many things with other organizational groups. Negotiating their boundaries and what defines inclusion and exclusion is just one thing. Ancona's "Outward Bound" analysis makes a compelling and contrarian argument that the most effective teams are ones that reach up and across the organization in a fluid-type fashion.[59] Ancona takes this argument even further in her incisive analysis of the X-team in organizations. Ancona and Bresman build on their ground-breaking investigations of the dynamics of X-teams to build a theory of how innovative organizational actors beg, borrow, and steal outside the boundaries of their own team to import innovation.[60] They distinguish the process of creative idea generation from the organizational tightrope of winning support for ideas and ultimately receiving organizational buy-in. They argue that the most innovative teams have a marked disrespect for traditional team and even organizational boundaries, and that this fluidity drives the innovative process. They identify five key components of X-teams with respect to the innovative process: external activity, extensive (network) ties, expandable tiers (managing up and out), flexible membership, and coordination among ties.

BRIDGING AND BUILDING Innovation in teams is not about solitary genius.[61] Creative people, teams, and companies use old ideas as the raw materials for new ideas. This is known as the **knowledge-brokering process,** in which a team takes an idea that is commonplace in one area and moves it to a context where it isn't common at all. (See Exhibit 9.11 for a summary of Hargadon and Sutton's reciprocal knowledge-brokering cycle.) Through the process of building, rebuilding, and linking, Hargadon says, ideas take shape and breakthroughs happen. Hargadon argues that creativity involves two complementary but seemingly opposing processes: bridging and building. *Bridging,* according to Hargadon, requires that two previously distinct worlds or domains be brought together via pattern recognition or making a new connection. The *building* process

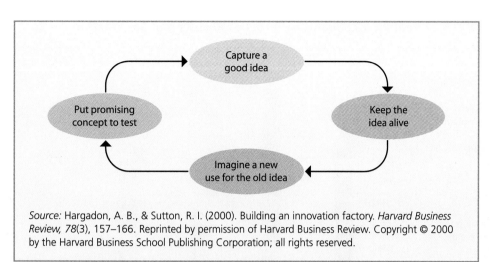

EXHIBIT 9.11

Knowledge-Brokering Cycle

Source: Hargadon, A. B., & Sutton, R. I. (2000). Building an innovation factory. *Harvard Business Review, 78*(3), 157–166. Reprinted by permission of Harvard Business Review. Copyright © 2000 by the Harvard Business School Publishing Corporation; all rights reserved.

requires that new patterns be built involving both understanding and action within those social groups that serve as the arbiters of the creative output.

Integrated Model of Successful Teamwork

We've discussed many aspects of teams and many types of teams in this chapter. Now, let's put all the pieces together. Exhibit 9.12 represents an integrated model of teamwork.

It is helpful to begin with the last step—team performance—when working through the integrated model. **Team performance** refers to all the different and important ways in which an organization might evaluate the performance of a team. Obviously, results would be very important (e.g., Is the team reaching its projected sales figures? Is the team making their deadlines?). Another, perhaps equally important criterion is the team's feeling of satisfaction or team spirit. If team members lack cohesion, then the forces working against the team will be stronger than the forces keeping it together. Behfar and her colleagues measured real project teams in terms of achieving results and their cohesiveness (see Exhibit 9.13).[62] The most commonly observed team had high results, low satisfaction. According to Behfar, it is only a matter of time before such teams become low results, low satisfaction.

The essential conditions for successful teamwork involve three key sets of skills: ability (i.e., knowledge and skill), motivation, and strategy (such as an effective

EXHIBIT 9.12   Integrated Model of Teamwork

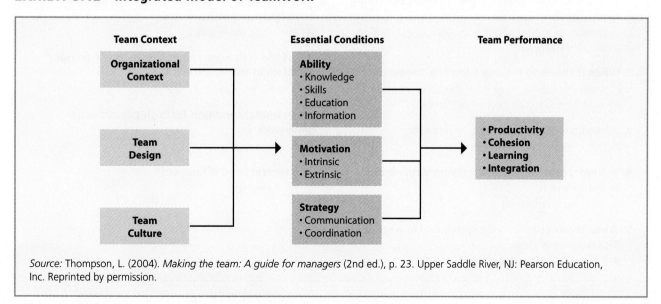

Source: Thompson, L. (2004). *Making the team: A guide for managers* (2nd ed.), p. 23. Upper Saddle River, NJ: Pearson Education, Inc. Reprinted by permission.

EXHIBIT 9.13 Behfar's Analysis of Real Project Teams in Terms of Results and Satisfaction

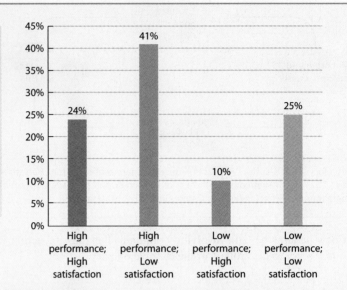

- Teams were measured in terms of meeting performance goals (results) and team member satisfaction
- The most common type of team had high performance, but low satisfaction
- This is usually because performance is emphasized (in short term)
- Over time, these teams become low-low

Source: Adapted from Behfar, K., Peterson, R., Mannix, E., & Trochim, W. (in press). The critical role of conflict resolution in teams: A close look at the links between conflict type, conflict management strategies, and team outcomes. *Journal of Applied Psychology.*

communication system). Suppose that the team task is organizing a successful dance marathon. Ability would include the organizing team's skill in advertising the marathon, developing and utilizing an effective recruitment system, and so on. Motivation would include the organizing team's willingness to put the necessary effort into meeting their objectives (e.g., if they are late to their organizing meetings or not carrying through with assigned tasks, the dance marathon will fail). Sustaining motivation is the most commonly cited problem that managers report about their teams. The strategy aspect includes the way in which members of the team communicate with one another. Suppose that some members of the committee do not know how to use e-mail, instant messaging, or voice mail. The success of their team would fall short even if they were highly skilled at marketing and had a lot of motivation.

EXHIBIT 9.14 Answers to Teamwork Quiz

1. When it comes to <u>conflict</u>, the highest-performing teams should:

D. Encourage conflict about tasks; discourage conflict about personalities.

2. When it comes to <u>making decisions</u>, teams are:

C. Better than the average of its members, but not necessarily as good as the best performer

3. When it comes to <u>creativity</u>, teams are:

A. Less creative than individuals

4. The most commonly cited <u>problem</u> with regard to teamwork is:

C. Sustaining motivation

5. When it comes to floor-time (talking) in a typical 8-person team meeting:

B. 3 people do over 75% of the talking.

6. The most important skills (competencies) that team members need to have are:

A. Task and people skills

7. All of the following can minimize the "free rider" problem in teams, except:

B. Increase the size of the team.

8. An <u>essential</u> condition for high-performance teamwork is:

C. A shared goal

9. The typical team is how old?

C. 12–24 months

The **team context** refers to the broad set of organizational factors that affect teamwork. Even if a team is high-functioning, it may not succeed if the organization does not support it. **Team design** refers to how the organizing team has been pulled together. If there are 20 people on the team, that might be too many; if there are only two members, that is probably not enough. Similarly, if the team is manager-led and there is no leader, that presents a problem. **Team culture** refers to the customs, culture, and spirit of the team.

Conclusion

We reviewed four major types of teams, distinguished in terms of their authority vis-à-vis the organizations: manager-led teams, self-managing teams, self-directing teams, and self-governing teams. We also considered the three major types of work that teams do: tactical, problem-solving, and creative. We delved into group decision making and group brainstorming and concluded that groups are superior to individuals when it comes to group decision making, but are inferior to individuals when it comes to idea generation. We put the team in the organizational context by analyzing team boundaries and considered how newcomers are not only socialized by their team, but influence their team as well.

Notes

1. Sundstrom, E. D., DeMeuse, K. P., & Futrell, D. (1990). Work teams: Applications and effectiveness. *American Psychologist, 45*(2), 120–133.
2. Thompson, L. (2007). *Leading high impact teams.* Kellogg Executive Program, Northwestern University.
3. Hackman, J. R. (1987). The design of work teams. In J. W. Lorsch (Ed.), *Handbook of organizational behavior.* Upper Saddle River, NJ: Prentice Hall.
4. Stewart, G. I., & Manz, C. C. (1995). Leadership and self-managing work teams: A typology and integrative model. *Human Relations, 48*(7), 747–770.
5. Larson, C. E., & LaFasto, F. M. J. (1989). *Teamwork: What must go right/what can go wrong* (2nd ed.). Newbury Park, CA: Sage.
6. LaFasto, F. M. J., & Larson, C. E. (2001). *When teams work best: 6,000 team members and leaders tell what it takes to succeed.* Newbury Park, CA: Sage.
7. Gentner, D., & Gentner, D. R. (1983). Flowing waters or teeming crowds: Mental models of electricity. In D. Gentner & A. Stevens (Eds.), *Mental models.* Mahwah, NJ: Lawrence Erlbaum.
8. Klimoski, R., & Mohammed, S. (1997). Team mental model: Construct or metaphor? *Journal of Management, 20*(2), 403–437.
9. Cannon-Bowers, J. A., Salas, E., & Converse, S. A. (1993). Shared mental models in expert team decision making. In D. Levine (Ed.), *Nebraska symposium on motivation* (pp. 283–311). Lincoln: University of Nebraska Press; Cannon-Bowers, J. A., Tannenbaum, S. I., Salas, E., & Converse, S. A. (1991). Toward an integration of training theory and technique. *Human Factors, 33*(3), 281–292.
10. Wegner, D. M. (1986). Transactive memory: A contemporary analysis of the group mind. In B. Mullen & G. Goethals (Eds.), *Theories of group behavior* (pp. 185–208). New York: Springer-Verlag; Wegner, D. M., Guiliano, T., &
    Hertel, P. (1995). Cognitive interdependence in close relationships. In W. J. Ickes (Ed.), *Compatible and incompatible relationships* (pp. 253–276). New York: Springer-Verlag.
11. Argote, L. (2002). *Organizational learning.* Presentation for the Kellogg School of Management/School of Education and Social Policy. Evanston, IL: Northwestern University.
12. Goodman, P. S., & Garber, S. (1988). Absenteeism and accidents in a dangerous environment: Empirical analysis of underground coal mines. *Journal of Applied Psychology, 73*(1), 81–86; Goodman, P. S., & Leyden, D. P. (1991). Familiarity and group productivity. *Journal of Applied Psychology, 76*(4), 578–586.
13. Goodman & Garber, "Absenteeism and accidents," p. 158.
14. Goodman & Leyden, "Familiarity and group productivity," p. 158.
15. LaFasto & Larson, *When teams work best,* p. 156.
16. Brown, R. (2000). *Group processes* (2nd ed.). Oxford, England: Blackwell; Stasser, G., & Dietz-Uhler, B. (2001). Collective choice, judgment and problem solving. In M. A. Hogg & S. Tindale (Eds.), *Blackwell handbook of social psychology: Group processes* (pp. 31–55). Oxford, England: Blackwell.
17. Hill, M. (1982). Group versus individual performance: are *n* + 1 heads better than one? *Psychological Bulletin, 91,* 517–539.
18. Michaelsen, L. K., Watson, W. E., & Black, R. H. (1989). A realistic test of individual versus group consensus decision making. *Journal of Applied Psychology, 74*(5), 834–839.
19. Laughlin, P. R., Bonner, B. L., & Miner, A. G. (2002). Groups perform better than the best individuals on letters-to-numbers problems. *Organizational Behavior and Human Decision Processes, 88,* 605–620.

20. Fischhoff, B., Slovic, P., & Lichtenstein, S. (1977). Knowing with certainty: The appropriateness of extreme confidence. *Journal of Experimental Psychology: Human Perception and Performance, 1,* 288–299.

21. Janis, I. L. (1972). *Victims of groupthink.* Boston: Houghton Mifflin and Janis, I. L. (1982). *Victims of groupthink* (2nd ed.). Boston: Houghton Mifflin.

22. McCauley, C. (1998). Groupthink dynamics in Janis's theory of groupthink: Backward and forward. *Organizational Behavior and Human Decision Processes, 73*(2–3), 142–162.

23. Maier, N. R. F. (1952). *Principles of human relations, applications to management.* New York: John Wiley & Sons.

24. Turner, M. E., & Pratkanis, A. R. (1998). A social identity maintenance model of groupthink. *Organizational Behavior and Human Decision Processes, 73*(2–3), 210–235.

25. Fairlamb, D. (2002, July 29). Switzerland: Trouble in paradise. *BusinessWeek,* pp. 72–74.

26. Kirsner, S. (2002, September 1). How to get bad news to the top. *Fast Company, 62,* p. 54.

27. Charan, R., & Useem, J. (2002, May 27). Why companies fail. *Fortune.*

28. Schroth, R. J., &Elliott, A. L. (2002). *How companies lie: Why Enron is just the tip of the iceberg.* New York: Crown Business.

29. Schulz-Hardt, S., Jochims, M., & Frey, D. (2002). Productive conflict in group decision making: Genuine and contrived dissent as strategies to counteract biased decision making. *Organizational Behavior and Human Decision Processes, 88,* 563–586.

30. Moon, H., Conlon, D. E., Humphrey, S. E., Quigley, N., Devers, C. E., & Nowakowski, J. M. (2003). Group structure and incrementalism in organizational decision-making. *Organizational Behavior and Human Decision Processes, 92,* 67–79.

31. Latané, B. 1981. The psychology of social impact. *American Psychologist, 36,* 343–356.

32. Boisjoly, R. M. (1987, December 13–18). *Ethical decisions—Morton Thiokol and the space shuttle Challenger disaster* (p. 7). Speech presented at the American Society of Mechanical Engineers, Winter Annual Meeting, Boston.

33. Hoffman, L. R., & Maier, N. R. F. (1966). An experimental reexamination of the similarity-attraction hypothesis. *Journal of Personality and Social Psychology, 3,* 145–152.

34. Morgan, B. B., & Bowers, C. A. (1995). Teamwork stress: Implications for team decision making. In R. A. Guzzo & E. Salas (Eds.), *Team effectiveness and decision making in organizations* (pp. 262–290). San Francisco: Jossey-Bass.

35. Liberman, N., & Trope, Y. (1998). The role of feasibility and desirability considerations in near and distant future decisions: A test of temporal construal theory. *Journal of Personality and Social Psychology, 75*(1), 5–18.

36. Harvey, J. (1974). The Abilene Paradox: The management of agreement. *Organizational Dynamics, 3*(1), 63–80. American Management Association International.

37. Mulvey, P. W., Veiga, J. F., & Elsass, P. M. (1996). When teammates raise a white flag. *Academy of Management Executive, 10*(1), 40–49.

38. Gigone, D., & Hastie, R. (1993). The common knowledge effect: Information sharing and group judgment. *Journal of Personality and Social Psychology, 65*(5), 959–974; Stasser, G., & Titus, W. (1985). Pooling of unshared information in group decision making: Biased information sampling during discussion. *Journal of Personality and Social Psychology, 48,* 1467–1478; Argote, L., Gruenfeld, D., & Naquin, C. (2000). Group learning in organizations. In M. Turner (Ed.), *Groups at work: Advances in theory and research.* Mahwah, NJ: Lawrence Erlbaum.

39. Christensen, C., Larson, J. R., Jr., Abbott, A., Ardolino, A., Franz, T., & Pfeiffer, C. (2000). Decision-making of clinical teams: Communication patterns and diagnostic error. *Medical Decision Making, 20,* 45–50.

40. Phillips, K., Mannix, E., Neale, M., & Gruenfeld, D. H. (2004). Diverse groups and information sharing: The effects of congruent ties. *Journal of Experimental Social Psychology 40,* 497–510.

41. Branegan, J. (1997, March 3). Percy Barnevik, chairman of ABB. *Time.*

42. Quoted in Barnett, C. (2002). *The verdict of peace.* London: Pan Books.

43. Shermer, M. (2003). What's the harm? *Scientific American, 289*(6), 2.

44. Guilford, J. P. (1959). *Personality.* New York: McGraw-Hill and Guilford, J. P. (1967). *The nature of human intelligence.* New York: McGraw-Hill.

45. Finke, R. A. (1995). Creative realism. In S. M. Smith, T. B. Ward, & R. A. Finke (Eds.), *The creative cognition approach* (pp. 303–326). Cambridge, MA: MIT Press.

46. Paulus, P. B. (2004). Making groups effective: Easier written than done. *American Psychological Association.*

47. Osborn, A. F. (1957). *Applied imagination* (rev. ed.). New York: Scribner.

48. Diehl, M., & Stroebe, W. (1987). Productivity loss in brainstorming groups: Toward a solution of a riddle. *Journal of Personality and Social Psychology, 53*(3), 497–509.

49. Sutton, R. I., & Hargadon, A. (1996). Brainstorming groups in context: Effectiveness in a product design firm. *Administrative Science Quarterly, 41,* 685–718.

50. Thompson, L. (2003). Improving the creativity of organizational work groups. *Academy of Management Executive, 17*(1), 96–109.

51. Ringelmann, M. (1913). Research on animate sources of power: The work of man. *Annales de l'Institut National Agronomique, 2e série-tome XII,* 1–40; Summarized in Kravitz, D. A., & Martin, B. (1986). Ringelmann rediscovered: The original article. *Journal of Personality and Social Psychology, 50*(5), 936–941.

52. Diehl & Stroebe, "Productivity loss in brainstorming groups," p. 165; Bouchard, T. J. (1972). Training, motivation, and personality as determinants of the effectiveness of brainstorming groups and individuals. *Journal of Applied Psychology, 56*(4), 324–331; Harkins, S. G., & Petty, R. E. (1982). Effects of task difficulty and task uniqueness on social loafing. *Journal of Personality and Social Psychology, 43*(6), 1214–1229; Shepperd, J. A. (1993). Productivity loss in performance groups: A motivation analysis. *Psychological Bulletin, 113,* 67–81.

53. Higgins, J. (1994). Creating creativity. *Training and Development, 48*(11), 11–15.

54. Stangor, C. (2004). *Research methods for the behavioral sciences* (2nd ed.). New York: Houghton Mifflin.

55. Paulus, P. B., & Dzindolet, M.T. (1993). Social influence processes in group brainstorming. *Journal of Personality and Social Psychology, 64,* 575–586; Paulus, P. B., Putman, V. L., Coskun, H., Leggett, K. L., & Roland, E. J. (1996). *Training groups for effective brainstorming.* Presented at the Fourth Annual Advanced Concepts Conference on Work Teams—Team Implementation Issues, Dallas, TX.

56. Shepherd, M. M., Briggs, R. O., Reinig, B. A., Yen, J., & Nunamaker, J. F., Jr. (1995–1996). Invoking social comparison to improve electronic brainstorming: Beyond anonymity. *Journal of Management Information Systems, 12,* 155–170.

57. Paulus, P. B., Nakui, T., Putman, V. L., & Brown, V. R. (2006). Effects of task instructions and brief breaks on brainstorming. *Group Dynamics: Theory, Research, and Practice, 10*(3), pp. 206–219.

58. Moreland, R. L., & Levine, J. M. (2000). Socialization in organizations and work groups. In M. Turner (Ed.), *Groups at work: Theory and research* (pp. 69–112). Mahwah, NJ: Erlbaum.

59. Ancona, D. G. (1990). Outward bound: Strategies for team survival in an organization. *Academy of Management Journal, 33*(2), 334–365.

60. Ancona, D., & Bresman, H. (2006). Begging, borrowing, and building on ideas from the outside to create pulsed innovation inside teams. In Thompson, L. & Choi, H-S., (Eds.). *Creativity and innovation in organizational teams* (pp. 87–108). Mahwah: NJ: Lawrence Erlbaum.

61. Hargadon, A. B. (2006). Bridging old worlds and building new ones: Towards a mircosociology of creativity. In L. Thompson & H. S. Choi (Eds.), *Creativity and innovation in organizational teams.* Mahwah, NJ: Lawrence Erlbaum.

62. Behfar, K., Peterson, R., Mannix, E., & Trochim, W. (in press). The critical role of conflict resolution in teams: A close look at the links between conflict type, conflict management strategies, and team outcomes. *Journal of Applied Psychology.*

Chapter | 10

LEADERSHIP

If you had to write your own leadership mission statement in one sentence, what would it be? Before you begin reading this chapter, complete Exercise 10.1 (the exercise asks you to evaluate statements made by famous leaders). In Exercise 10.1, some of the quotes were made by leaders whom we do not admire—at least in terms of their values. Whereas it is true that Hitler might have been effective in mobilizing people, certainly no one would want to emulate his leadership. Some leaders have used their capacity to influence people for the good of humankind (for pro-social purposes); others have used their leadership skills for self-interested purposes that often involve aggression toward others. Yet, we must admit that there is something in common among all 11 of the leaders mentioned in the opening paragraph. All were capable of mobilizing others around a goal. Thus, one of the key characteristics of leadership is the ability to mobilize and influence others.

In this chapter, we challenge you to articulate and develop your own theory of leadership and develop your own leadership approach. We distinguish leadership from management. We then raise the controversial question of whether leadership can be taught. We focus on leadership as a quality of a particular person (trait theories of leadership), as a behavior (behavioral theories of leadership), as a function of the particular context (situational theories of leadership), and as a complex interplay between people and situations (contingent theories of leadership).

Leadership in Organizations

More has been written about leadership than any other topic in all of organization science. Paradoxically, it is the least understood of management topics, if we are to judge by the degree of consensus in the field (see Chapter 1's discussion of paradigm development). It seems that there is a different brand of leadership published every day (for a humorous example of SpongeBob SquarePants' leadership style, see Exhibit 10.1).

Presidents, military heroes, revolutionaries, CEOs, consultants, statesmen, and stateswomen all have something to say about leadership. And most of us recognize that we have something to learn from the people doing the leading, not just the people studying the leaders.

Leadership versus Management

Leadership is the ability to influence people to achieve an organization's or group's goals. A leader is able to influence people to achieve a group's or organization's goals. Most people don't want to be managed, but they want to be led.[1] **Management** is a function that must be exercised in any business or team, whereas leadership is a *relationship* (between the leader and the team). For the differences between management and leadership see Exhibit 10.2.

EXHIBIT 10.1

SpongeBob SquarePants' Leadership Style

The folks at Fast Company extracted the 5 secrets to effective leadership in SpongeBob SquarePants cartoon episodes:

- **Resiliency is key**. When SpongeBob was marooned in an unfamiliar sea cave, he marshaled his resolve and found the resources to learn a new language, obtain food, and find his way back to his hometown, Bikini Bottom. (Episode: Rock Bottom)
- **Recruit the best**. Leadership experts know that leaders do not do it alone. On learning that superhero crime fighters Mermaidman and Barnacleboy live in a seniors' home, SpongeBob pulls them out of retirement to combat evil. (Episode: Mermaidman and Barnacleboy)
- **Don't rest on your laurels**. After SpongeBob wins employee of the month 26 times, SpongeBob is threatened by Squidward. So, SB rushes to outperform his previous record. (Episode: Employee of the Month)
- **Innovate, innovate, innovate**. When SpongeBob's suggestion for multicolored "pretty patties" is rejected by his company, he initiates his own start-up and is an overnight success, and then sells his product name at the height of its success. (Episode: Patty Hype)
- **Know your employees' limits**. SpongeBob's boss, Mr. Krab, is a tough old-school guy who docks workers' pay. When SpongeBob and Squidward protest, they are fired and then vow to dismantle the establishment. (Episode: Squid on Strike).

Source: Conley, L. (2004, September). Leadership secrets of SpongeBob SquarePants. *Fast Company, 86*, 45. Reprinted by permission of Mansueto Ventures LLC via Copyright Clearance Center.

EXHIBIT 10.2

Management versus Leadership

Management	Leadership
• A function	• A relationship
• Planning	• Selecting talent
• Budgeting	• Motivating
• Evaluating	• Coaching
• Facilitating	• Building trust

Source: Maccoby, M. (2000, January–February). Understanding the difference between management and leadership. *Research & Technology Management*, 57–59.

One characteristic of leadership is the point of view that person has. The leader of an organization has a point of view that allows him or her to: (1) see what needs to be done; (2) understand the underlying forces that are working in the organization; and (3) initiate action to make things better.[2] Exhibit 10.3 reveals that the leader's point of view is different from that of the followers' point of view and yet different from those who are "bureaucrats," administrators, and "contrarians" (critics of the organization).

What do we mean by *leadership is a relationship?* Fundamentally, the success of a leader is determined by his or her followers. The followers represent those—present, future, and past—that have been affected by the leader. Leadership is a relationship between those who aspire to lead and those who trust that person enough to follow. Kouzes and Posner have found that followers' responses to this question are remarkably consistent across time

EXHIBIT 10.3

The Leader's Point of View

Point of View	Examples of What This Person Would Say
Follower	"What do you want me to do?" "Will you give me more authority?" "I need you to clear the obstacles for me."
Bureaucrat	"That's not my job." "I'll pass that on to so-and-so." "Our procedures don't allow that." "We've never done it that way." "This hasn't been approved." "I can't do that without my supervisor's permission."
Administrator	"What did they do last time?" "We've never done it that way." "Let's see, what was the rule on that?"
Contrarian	"That will never work!" "We tried that before." "That's a terrible idea." "You won't be able to fund it." "You will never be able to do it on time."
Leader	"Do you see what needs to be done?" "Do you understand the underlying forces at play?" "Are you willing to initiate action to make things better?"

Source: Clawson, J. C. (2003). *Level 3 leadership: Getting below the surface* (2nd ed.). Upper Saddle River, NJ: Prentice Hall.

and different types of organizations.[3] They cite four key virtues of a leader that inspire followers to bestow trust:

■ *Honesty.* Honesty is named more than any other leadership characteristic. "If people are going to willingly follow someone, whether it is into battle or into the boardroom, they first want to assure themselves that the person is worthy of their trust."

■ *Forward-looking.* Leaders are expected to have a plan and to think about the future of their organizations. They should have lofty, yet attainable goals.

■ *Inspiring.* We expect leaders to be inspiring: "It is not enough for leaders to have dreams of the future. They must be able to communicate those dreams in ways that encourage us to sign on for the duration and to work hard for the goal."

■ *Competent.* Competency is a key way in which we evaluate anyone, particularly a leader. In short, we ask ourselves, "Can this person do the job?"

Highly Effective Leaders

According to Stephen Covey, effective leaders are effective people. The most effective people have mastered seven key habits or practices of living:[4]

■ *Be proactive:* Effective leaders are people who take responsibility for their own lives. Their behaviors are a function of their decisions, not their conditions. Highly proactive people do not make external attributions in the face of hardship and challenge. Covey distinguishes proactive leaders from those that are reactive. Reactive people are often affected by their physical environment (e.g., the weather is bad, so they feel bad). The proactive approach is spelled out in Exhibit 10.4.

■ *Begin with the end in mind:* Effective people start their journey toward any goal with a clear understanding of their desired destination. It is very easy to be caught up in the "activity trap," or the busyness of life and your schedule. People can be busy without being effective. To really find out what your core values are, imagine you are driving to your own funeral, three years from today. As you sit in the back of the funeral service, you will hear four people speak about you and your life. What would you want them to say? Another suggestion Covey makes is to scribe your own personal mission statement, which involves articulating all the things that you value and want to achieve in your life, both in the long- and short-term. Consider the 10 different

EXHIBIT 10.4

Proactive Leadership

Reactive Language	Proactive Language
There's nothing I can do	Let's look at our alternatives
That's just the way I am	I can choose a different approach
He makes me so mad	I control my own feelings
They won't allow that	I can create an effective presentation
I have to do that	I will choose an appropriate response
I can't	I choose
I must	I prefer
If only . . .	I will . . .

Source: Covey, S. R. (1989). *The seven habits of highly effective people: Powerful lessons in personal change* (1st. ed.), p. 78. New York: Free Press. Reprinted by permission of FranklinCovey Co.

EXHIBIT 10.5

Leadership Values

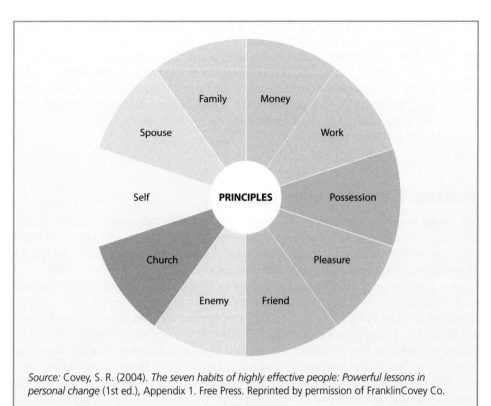

Source: Covey, S. R. (2004). *The seven habits of highly effective people: Powerful lessons in personal change* (1st ed.), Appendix 1. Free Press. Reprinted by permission of FranklinCovey Co.

values in Exhibit 10.5. Which are the most valued things to you, now, at this point in your life? What have you done today to move toward reaching those values?

■ *Put first things first:* What one thing could you do (that you are not doing now) that if you did on a regular basis, it would make a tremendous positive difference in your life? Habit 3, "put first things first," is about actually behaving in a way that realizes your own personal values.

■ *Think win-win:* Habit 4 reflects the key message of Chapter 8, which focuses on reaching your own goals and maximizing the goals of others. As we have seen in our discussion of negotiation (in Chapter 8), in order to reach mutually beneficial agreements, it is important to understand your own needs and priorities as well as those of others.

■ *Seek first to understand, then to be understood:* Habit 5 is the principle of empathic communication. Many leaders have a tendency to resolve problems in their organizations by applying solutions that they have mastered without taking the time to diagnose the situation or to deeply understand the problem. Think about the method of "active inquiry" introduced in Chapter 4 ("Communication"). Recall that in that model, before you attempt to help another who has a problem, you must first understand their problem. The best way of doing this is to ask questions that do not put the other person on the defensive.

■ *Synergize:* Habit 6 focuses on how the whole can often be greater than the sum of the parts. Covey argues that to experience synergy, people have to leave their comfort zones and be ready to respond to challenges as they unfold. One example that Covey shares occurred in his own classroom. For three weeks, the class followed a carefully planned structure. Then, one day something changed when one student related a powerful personal experience in class that was emotional and insightful. This led to others in the class putting aside their planned presentations for the day and, instead, sharing their own insights and experiences. As a result, the class abandoned the old syllabus and the presentation plans and set up new purposes and projects. Everyone became so excited that they wrote a collaborative book containing their learnings and insights. For several years after, alumni meetings were held among members of that class.

■ *Sharpen the saw:* Habit 7 is about personal renewal, focusing on four key aspects of your life: physical renewal (such as through exercise, nutrition, and stress management), social-emotional renewal, mental renewal (such as through reading, planning, and writing), and spiritual renewal (such as through value clarification). We will learn much more about renewal and energy in Chapter 15 ("Life, Learning, and Personal Development").

Systems View of Leadership

We cannot study leadership by isolating people and their behaviors from the social-organizational setting in which they act. As an example, consider how Bill Gates's leadership style was very effective in creating Microsoft, but a dismal failure when he applied the same idea to revamping a public school in Colorado.[5] Leadership is never the result of one person; it is the product of three main shaping forces: a set of social-organizational institutions, a message or idea (behavior), and the person himself or herself.[6] Thus, leaders are effective when three forces collide: the right person, with the right idea, in the right situation. For example, consider Martin Luther King, Jr., an extraordinarily gifted person and speaker. His leadership was situated in a social situation in which there was considerable, growing unrest concerning racist attitudes (the field). King's ideas about nonviolence and passive resistance (behaviors) were particularly effective in this era. The systems view of leadership also means that sometimes the best efforts of leaders may not be effective if the social-organizational support systems are lacking, such as in the case of the inability of FEMA (Federal Emergency Management Agency) during the Hurricane Katrina disaster of 2005.

Toxic Leaders

For every leader that is loved and respected, there are several who are bitterly despised. According to Roy Lubit, author of *Coping with Toxic Managers*, there are five types of "bad" leaders: narcissistic managers, unethical managers, aggressive managers, rigid managers, and impaired managers (see Exhibit 10.6). Lubit makes the point that anyone (not just leaders) can show some or some combinations of these character flaws.[7]

Narcissistic managers are preoccupied with themselves and concomitantly devalue others and have an inflated sense of entitlement. Lubit identifies three types of narcissistic managers: grandiose managers, control freaks, and paranoid managers.[7]

Unethical managers are either antisocial or unethical opportunists. Antisocial managers manipulate others and break rules partly because it provides a thrill as well as furthering self-gain. Antisocial managers lack a conscience and, therefore, are not constrained by normal inhibitions.

There are several types of **aggressive managers:** ruthless managers (calmly go after what they want without regard for others), volatile managers (who have a grandiose self-image and exploit others), bullying managers (seek to intimidate others for the pure excitement of it), homicidal managers (who are desperate, narcissistic, depressed, paranoid, or antisocial), frantic managers (generally agitated and pressured), sexual harassment managers (who lack appreciation of social and cultural norms or are narcissistic and angry), and chauvinists (narcissistic and angry).

Rigid managers include compulsive managers (who feel that there is only one right way), authoritarian managers (who will do what they are told by their boss), oppositional managers (who will reject your suggestions), passive-aggressive managers (who work behind the scenes to block your activities), control freaks (who feel that they know better than others), and dictatorial managers (obsessively task-focused).

EXHIBIT 10.6

Types of Dysfunctional Leaders

Major Type	Specific Type	Definition
Narcissistic Managers	Grandiose managers	Legend in their own mind
	Control freaks	You will do absolutely everything my way
	Paranoid managers	They're out to get me
Unethical Managers	Antisocial managers	Breaking rules is fun
	Unethical opportunists	I have to break this rule
Aggressive Managers	Ruthless managers	Cold, calculating, and cutthroat
	Bullying managers	Haze week never ends
	Homicidal managers	You won't get away with that
	Sexual harassment	I won't take "No" for an answer
	Chauvinists	I'm better than you
	Volatile managers	Everything upsets me
	Frantic colleagues	I can't stop racing around
Rigid Managers	Compulsive	Slaves to work and perfection
	Authoritarian	Bureaucratic monsters
	Dictatorial	I'm in charge
	Oppositional coworkers	Any way but your way
	Passive-aggressive managers	You can't make me
Impaired Managers	ADHD	Distracted, disorganized, and impulsive
	Anxiety	Nervous, frightened, worried, preoccupied
	Depression	Pessimistic, exhausted, irritable, unhappy
	Post-traumatic stress disorder	I can't believe this happened and I can't stop thinking about it
	Burned out	Used up
	Bipolar	Invincible to depressed and back
	Alcohol and drug addiction	Only the bottle takes away my stress

Source: Lubit, R. H. (2004). *Coping with toxic managers, subordinates and other difficult people: Using emotional intelligence to survive and prosper.* Upper Saddle River, NJ: Prentice Hall. Reproduced by permission of Pearson Education, Inc.

Finally, **impaired managers** include those with ADHD (attention deficit hyperactivity disorder), anxiety, depression, post-traumatic stress disorder, burnout, bipolar disorder, and/or alcohol/drug addiction.

Can Leadership Be Taught?

We've discussed characteristics of the worst types of leaders and the best types of leaders. A key question concerns whether leadership can be taught or whether it is simply a matter of fundamental personality traits. Recall the discussion in Chapter 2 ("Understanding People and Their Behavior") concerning internal versus external attributions. Probably no topic in organizational behavior raises the nature–nurture debate to the boiling point as much as leadership.[8] Trait theorists assert that leaders are born, not made; whereas behaviorists assert that leadership can be learned, much like any other skill. Strict proponents of leadership trait theory claim that people are either born leaders or born followers; they either have it or they don't. If they do have it, they dictate, command, and control. If they don't have it, they follow those who do have it. In this chapter, we view leadership from four distinctly different theoretical approaches, the first being *trait theories*, which have primarily focused on intelligence, temperament, personality, birth order, and gender. A second set of theories we review are *behavioral theories* of leadership, which essentially argue that people differ in their leadership styles, perhaps as a function of their personality or temperament; unlike strict trait theories, behavioral theories strongly suggest that people can change their style. A third set of theories are *situational theories* of leadership, which essentially argue that it is the situation that makes the leader, not the other way around. A fourth set of theories lies at the intersection of the person and the situation and are also known as *contingency theories* that involve interplays of personality and situational factors.

Leadership and Nature: Trait Theory

The **trait theory** approach to leadership seeks to identify personal characteristics that effective leaders possess. Recall from Chapter 2 that traits (or dispositions) are a person's particular tendencies to feel, think, and act in certain ways. The trait theory of leadership is sometimes referred to as the Great Man theory of leadership.[9] In fact, there is not just a single trait theory of leadership. There are several theories that all share the common belief that leadership is largely an inborn characteristic of a person and, therefore, is largely inflexible across time and place.

Leadership and Trait Intelligence

One trait theory of leadership considers intelligence: To be competent, leaders need to be intelligent. Many organizations (including the armed forces) for years have relied on selection of leaders based on intelligence: 91 percent of officers in the U.S. armed forces have a college degree;[10] a graduate degree is a requirement for promotion to the rank of major in the Air Force. The ASVAB test (Armed Services Vocational Aptitude Battery) is administered to all persons who wish to enlist in the U.S. military. It is a three-hour exam that tests word knowledge, paragraph comprehension, arithmetic reasoning, mathematics knowledge, general science, auto and shop information, mechanical comprehension, electronics information, numerical operations, and coding speed.

Leadership and Temperament

Temperament or personality is largely immutable, as our discussion of the "Big Five" personality traits in Chapter 2 suggests. If trait theory is true, then we should be able to identify personality traits that make someone a great leader, or at least characteristics that predict the emergence of leadership (see, for example, Exhibit 10.7 on Abraham Lincoln's temperament and leadership). Psychologists, political scientists, and historians have studied the personality of leaders in government, business, and education in an attempt to derive common traits. However, decades of research failed to yield an agreed-upon list of key traits shared by all leaders.[11] Simonton gathered information about 100 personal attributes of all U.S. presidents, such as their family backgrounds, educational experiences, and number of books published before taking office; then correlated it with how effective the presidents were in office;[12] results indicated that 97 characteristics, including personality traits, were not related to leadership effectiveness at all. By chance, 5 percent—5 out of 100—would be significant.

Birth Order and Leadership

One trait theory of leadership attempts to use birth order (e.g., firstborn, middle child, youngest child, etc.) to predict leadership. Underlying this theoretical perspective is the

EXHIBIT 10.7   Depression and Leadership?

President Abraham Lincoln, age 31

"I am now the most miserable man living. If what I feel were equally distributed to the whole human family, there would not be one cheerful face on the earth. Whether I shall ever be better I can not tell; I awfully forebode I shall not. To remain as I am is impossible; I must die or be better, it appears to me."

Source: Depressed? Read Abraham Lincoln's Words. (2002, November). Abraham Lincoln Research Website. Retrieved November 3, 2006, from http://home.att.net/~rjnorton/Lincoln84.html

Those who wonder how a person with Lincoln's mental instabilities and long history of failures could ever have led a deeply divided nation through its greatest challenge need only reflect on how disabilities, mental or physical, and personal setbacks can be enormous character builders. When Lincoln came to Washington, he was ready for the challenge. The unspeakable tragedy of the war, as distressing as it was to him, also imbued him with that elusive sense of purpose he had been seeking all his life, a commitment reinforced by his bold move to dismantle the institution of slavery.

Source: Lincoln and His Depressions. (2003, July). McMan's Depression and Bipolar Web. Retrieved January 3, 2005, from http://www.mcmanweb.com/index.htm.

belief that birth order is related to intelligence.[13] Cross-sectional data show some indication that firstborns may be more intelligent, but longitudinal data don't support this.[14]

Male and Female Differences and Leadership

There is much debate about whether differences in men and women exist when it comes to leadership style. The typical belief is that men are rational, independent, and assertive; whereas women are emotional, relationship-focused, and accommodating. Based on these stereotypes of men being assertive and women being passive, you might expect that gender would strongly influence a person's leadership style, such that female leaders might be more considerate and accommodating, whereas male leaders would be more decisive and task-oriented. Alice Eagly examined this very question using a meta-analysis (recall our discussion of meta-analysis as a research method in Chapter 1).[15] Contrary to stereotypical beliefs about male and female differences, men do not engage in more task-oriented behaviors nor do women behave in a more relational (considerate) fashion. Eagly and Johnson did find that women lead in a more democratic style and men used a more autocratic style.

The most important gender difference when it comes to leaders is not the leader's behavior; it is the behavior of the followers. Female leaders are judged more harshly than male leaders.[16] And people react differently to male and female leaders. As a case in point, women are regarded as less competent than men, and in group interactions people give men more opportunities to speak than women.[17]

People respond more favorably to men who are self-promoting than men who are modest; however, the exact opposite is true for women.[18] In fact, female leaders are devalued when they act in a masculine manner.[19] Overt displays of competence and confidence by women can result in rejection, especially from men.[20] In a simulated job interview and hiring task, both men and women prefer to hire a man over a woman if the two are equally qualified,[21] and men even prefer to hire a man, even if he is clearly less qualified.[22] A meta-analytic review of 75 studies of mixed-gender groups revealed that women are less likely to become leaders than men in laboratory and naturally occurring groups.[23]

Paradoxically, these attributions are misguided, as meta-analysis shows that women display more of the transformational leadership behaviors that are positively related to performance and effectiveness than do men.[24] Moreover, most people believe that gender equality exists, but it does not. To be sure, women's status has improved remarkably in the 20th and 21st centuries in many societies, but women continue to lack access to power and leadership compared with men. According to Rudman, the solution is to not coach women to act more like men.[25] Women experience a double-bind: They can either convey modesty and be liked and accepted by others, or they can self-promote and convey competence by risking rejection and harsh evaluation. Displays of competence, directness, and authority reduce women's influence (because it clashes with the traditional female stereotype), but these same behaviors usually enhance men's influence.[26]

Postscript on Trait Theories of Leadership

For all practical purposes, the evidence favoring trait theories of leadership is not empirically compelling. There is very little data linking any measurable trait to leadership. Further, there is little or no agreement on traits necessary for leadership. However, you might be thinking the following: If trait theories of leadership are flawed (or at least inconclusive), then why do so many companies spend so much money on selection? There are two reasons. One is that leadership is largely romanticized in our culture. That is, people have a strong desire to believe that leadership is rooted in traits.[27] Second, remember the fundamental attribution error we discussed in Chapter 2—the tendency to ascribe dispositional reasons to explain behavior is very powerful.

Behavioral Theories of Leadership

The behavioral approach to studying leadership assumes that the leader's behavior, rather than her or his personality (i.e., traits or intelligence), exerts the most effect on followers. Moreover, behavior, unlike traits, is something that can be learned. Thus, trait theories are based on stable characteristics of people that usually cannot be changed (i.e., we cannot change our birth order!), but we can change our behaviors. Put it this way: If leadership were entirely genetically determined, there would be no sense in offering leadership courses in business schools. **Behavioral theories** of leadership essentially argue that leadership, like so many other management competencies, is a skill.

Lewin, Lippit, and White's (1939) Studies of Reactions to Group Leadership Styles

The 1940s marked a shift in leadership from trait theories to behavioral styles. In one of the first empirical tests of the effectiveness of distinct leadership styles in an actual field study (using random assignment to conditions!), Lewin, Lippit, and White examined three types of leaders: autocratic leaders, democratic leaders, and laissez-faire leaders.[28] "Democratic" leadership was found to be more productive than the other two styles. This investigation nicely navigated some of the empirical concerns in examining leadership mentioned at the outset of this chapter; namely, there was random assignment to one of the three groups, and by examining three leadership styles, this allowed a comparative test. In this study, members were matched on other characteristics to rule out possible "third variable" effects—in short, they were matched on ability, popularity, energy, and so on (see Exhibit 10.8).

People versus Task (Managerial Grid)

One of the most time-tested distinctions of leadership style is that of people-focused leaders and task-focused leaders. **People-focused leaders** are highly considerate of others; **task-focused leaders** are more concerned with structure. In other words, some leaders place a premium on showing consideration for others (awareness of and sensitivity to subordinates' feelings, interest, and contributions); whereas other leaders focus on initiating structure (i.e., focusing attention on tasks and goals). Leaders high in consideration are typically friendly, prefer open communication, focus on teamwork, and are concerned with other people's welfare. Leaders high in structure focus on

	Autocratic	Democratic	Laissez-faire
Description	• Leader determined all policies for group members and detailed methods of goal attainment • Leader had overall view and shared method step by step as needed • Leader specified allowable actions and interactions • Leader provided praise and criticism	• Leader encouraged group to create policies • Leader gave overview of task and steps before work • Members chose actions and interactions that facilitate work • Feedback was factual and objective	• Complete freedom • Resources provided but leader gave information only when asked • No feedback unless asked
Findings	• Little discontent develops when the leader holds high standards • Much discontent develops when the leader enjoys dominance for its own sake • Production level remains high when group is satisfied with its efforts • Negative reaction develops when group is under constant pressure to produce • Leader's positive efforts make high productivity possible • Greater productivity provides personal satisfaction • Work effort tends to slack when leader is absent • Clearness of roles results in greater member satisfaction • Members satisfy their needs for order and absolutes in their world • Members satisfy their need for dependency • Aggressive status-seeking activities develop among members who have a need for status • Members may conceal the intensity of their anger and resentment • High demands for status develop, since members cannot obtain status satisfaction from the leader • Hero worship of the leader frequently immobilizes the group • Members accept the conditions of autocracy if they see it as the only alternative • Resignation to the inevitable may reduce tensions within the group	• Members gain satisfaction in making their own decisions • Individual self-confidence results from group achievement • Members grow in self-acceptance and confidence • Members become more willing to listen to the ideas of others and promote listening • Members are more willing to accept the ideas of others • Greater emphasis on "we" develops • Respect for the personalities of other members develops • Status-mindedness decreases amidst friendliness • Leaders and members function more as peers and colleagues • Good work becomes the criterion for gaining status within the group • Members begin to insist on equality of rights and opportunities for all • Groups develop greater sense of reality orientation and adjusting to it • Group pressures may result in over-conformity and groupthink	• Members have little sense of accomplishment • There is lack of clear goals • There is lack of clarity on how to achieve goals • Members do not understand what is expected of them • Little friendship for the leader develops • The group does not develop a sense of unity • Members tend toward idleness when direction from the leader is absent • Members do not develop self-confidence • Status-mindedness develops • Competitive hostility develops among the members • Members develop self-assertiveness without regard for the effect on others
Summary	• Members were increasingly more submissive and demanded the leader's attention and approval. Productivity was about the same as democratic, but required leader's presence	• Members showed less tension and hostility; more cohesion and cooperation. About as productive as autocratic, but also in leader's absence	• Overall, lower productivity, satisfaction, and cohesiveness

Source: Lewin, K., Lippitt, R., & White, R. K. (1939). Patterns of aggressive behavior in experimentally created social climates. *Journal of Social Psychology, 10*(2), 271–279. Reprinted with permission of the Helen Dwight Reid Educational Foundation. Published by Heldref Publications, 1319 Eighteenth St., NW, Washington, DC 20036-1802. Copyright 1939.

EXHIBIT 10.8

Lewin, Lippitt, and White's (1939) Study of the Effectiveness of Three Leadership Styles

EXHIBIT 10.9

Person–Task Managerial Grid

	Low Concern for Task	High Concern for Task
High Concern for People	**Country club management:** Thoughtful attention to the needs of people for satisfying relationships leads to a comfortable, friendly organization atmosphere and work tempo	**Team management:** Work accomplishment is from committed people; interdependent through a "common stake" in organization purpose leads to relationships of trust and respect
MID-MID	**Middle of the road management:** Adequate organization performance is possible through balancing the necessity to get out work with maintaining morale of people at a satisfactory level	
Low Concern for People	**Impoverished management:** Exertion of minimum effort to get required work done is appropriate to sustain organization membership	**Authority-compliance management:** Efficiency in operations results from arranging conditions of work in such a way that human elements interfere to a minimum degree

Source: Blake, R. R., & Mouton, J. S. (1964). *The leadership grid.* Houston, TX: Gulf. Reprinted by permission of Grid International, Inc.

achieving the task—sometimes at any cost. Most important, these two dimensions—consideration and task—are independent of each other, and thus, a leader may be high on both, low on both, or differ on each one.

One way of conceptualizing the person–task focus is via the managerial grid, developed by Blake and Mouton (see Exhibit 10.9).

Based on a person's location on the grid, Blake and Mouton identified five distinct management styles, with most managers falling at the midpoint on both scales. The ideal leadership style, argued Blake and Mouton, is a leader with a score of 9 and 9 (a team leader). However, there is little evidence to support their assertion.[29]

Leadership Styles and EQ Skills

Drawing from emotional intelligence research and theory, Daniel Goleman and the Hay McBer consulting group measured the leadership styles of 3,871 executives randomly selected from a database of 20,000 executives. They identified six different leadership styles that derive from different emotional intelligence skills. According to Goleman, the most effective leaders do not rely on only one leadership style; rather, they have mastered three or four different styles and use them in different situations. Goleman suggests, in true behaviorist fashion, that we think of leadership styles as the clubs in a golf bag. Over the course of a game, the pro picks and chooses clubs based on the demands of a shot, taking into account the various factors in the situation (see Exhibit 10.10).[30]

As indicated in Exhibit 10.10, coercive leaders demand immediate compliance. Authoritative leaders mobilize people toward a vision. Affiliative leaders create emotional bonds and harmony. Democratic leaders build consensus through participation. Pace-setting leaders expect excellence and self-direction from their followers. Finally, coaching leaders develop people for the future.

EXHIBIT 10.10   Goleman's Six Leadership Styles

	Coercive	Authoritative	Affiliative	Democratic	Pace-Setting	Coaching
Modus Operandi	Demands immediate compliance	Mobilizes people toward a vision	Creates harmony and builds bonds	Forges consensus through participation	Sets high standards for performance	Develops people for the future
Style, in a Phrase	"Do what I tell you"	"Come with me"	"People come first"	"What do you think?"	"Do as I do, now"	"Have you thought about this?"
When This Style Works Best	In a crisis; to kick-start a turn-around; or with problem team members	When changes require a new vision; or when clear direction is needed	Heal rifts in team; motivate people during stress	Build buy-in or consensus; get input from team	Get quick results from highly motivated and competent team	Help an employee improve performance or develop long-term strengths
Overall Impact	**Negative**	**Most strongly positive**	**Positive**	**Positive**	**Negative**	**Positive**

Source: Goleman, D. (2000). Leadership that gets results, *Harvard Business Review, 78*(2), 78–90. Reprinted by permission of Harvard Business Review. Copyright © 2000 by the Harvard Business School Publishing Corporation; all rights reserved.

Goleman and his team investigated how each leadership style affected six elements of climate, or organizational atmosphere. Exhibit 10.11 shows the correlation between each leadership style and each aspect of climate. Keep in mind that correlations show the extent to which two things co-vary, and can range between +1 and −1.

The data suggest that authoritative leadership style has the most positive effect on climate, but affiliative, democratic, and coaching styles also have largely positive correlations. Two styles, coercive and pace-setting, have a negative correlation with

EXHIBIT 10.11   Leadership Style and Effectiveness *(correlations)*

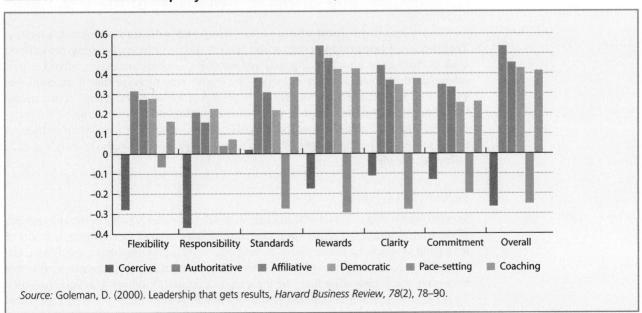

Source: Goleman, D. (2000). Leadership that gets results, *Harvard Business Review, 78*(2), 78–90.

climate. The six aspects of climate included: flexibility (how free employees feel to innovate, unencumbered by red tape); responsibility (how responsible employees feel for the organization); the level of standards that people set; the sense of accuracy about performance feedback and the aptness of rewards; the clarity people have about mission and values; and the level of commitment to a common purpose. In addition to looking at "soft" measures (such as climate) Goleman and his team looked at hard, economic measures as well, such as return on sales, revenue growth, efficiency, and profitability. They found correlations between climate and financial results. These data are correlations, not causal data. That means that there could be other factors that produced the more effective climates. Or the causality could simply work the other way around: The better climates led to a different leadership style.

Transactional versus Transformational Leadership

A fundamental distinction in leadership style is that between transactional leadership and transformational leadership.[31] Bass proposed a theory of "transformational" leadership that examines how leaders can sometimes have dramatic effects on their people and literally transform them. **Transformational leadership** relies on intrinsic motivation.[32] The transformational leader succeeds in gaining the support of followers, not on the basis of the promises he or she makes, but rather on the basis of helping the employee embrace the organization's goals.

Transformational leadership occurs when a leader changes his or her followers in three important ways: (1) increasing subordinates' awareness of their task and the importance of performing them well; (2) making subordinates aware of their needs for personal growth, development, and accomplishment; and (3) motivating subordinates to work for the good of the organization rather than exclusively for their own personal gain or benefit.

To examine the characteristics of transformational leadership, Avolio and team had 3,786 respondents in 14 independent samples in companies all over the globe complete the Multifactor Leadership Questionnaire, or MLQ, that asks respondents to describe their leader.[33] Results indicated that six key factors underlie transformational leadership: charisma and inspiration ("proud of him/her"; "has my respect"; "talks enthusiastically"), intellectual stimulation ("reexamines assumptions"; "suggests new ways"); individualized consideration ("focuses your strengths"; "differentiates among us"); contingent reward ("rewards your achievement"; "recognizes your achievement"), management by exception–active ("puts out fires"; "reacts to problems if serious"), and passive–avoidant (low scores in "delays responding"; "avoids deciding").

Transformational leadership is often compared with transactional leadership. **Transactional leadership** occurs when leaders motivate by exchanging rewards for high performance and noticing and reprimanding subordinates for mistakes and substandard performance. For example, the leader may promise that if an employee works very hard, the leader will give her a good performance evaluation. Transactional leadership is related in a large sense to the psychological contract concept we introduced in Chapter 2 and the concept of extrinsic motivation. The foundation of transactional leadership is that people perform rational cost-benefit analysis with regard to following a leader.

Servant Leadership

Servant leadership is a style of leadership in which the leader puts the needs and interests of the team ahead of his or her own. Greenleaf defined servant leadership as a model of leadership in which the leader places serving others, including employees, customers, and community, as the top priority.[34] A core idea of servant leadership is the assumption that by putting the organization first, the leader sets a model for others to behave similarly. Steven Covey's principle-centered leadership model is embodied by the servant leader model.[35] In Covey's model, leaders focus on changing themselves, and through their own change, they implicitly encourage and empower others to change.

Situational Theories of Leadership: How the Situation Shapes the Leader

If the trait approach to leadership is known as the "Great Man theory" of leadership, then the **situational approach** to leadership might very well be called the "great opportunity" theory of leadership. The systems view of leadership introduced at the beginning of this chapter is an example of situational leadership. Whereas traits are largely viewed to be invariant, situations are by definition controllable and variable.

How the Environment Shapes Leaders

Probably the most damning evidence of trait theories of leadership is studies of random selection of leaders. Organizations spend millions of dollars each year carefully selecting leaders, often using psychological tests to do so. However, selected leaders may actually hinder team performance. For example, in one investigation, teams with randomly selected leaders performed better on all organizational decision-making tasks than did teams whose leaders were systematically selected.[36] Moreover, teams with randomly selected leaders adhered more strongly to the team's decision. Apparently, systematically chosen leaders often undermine organizational goals because they assert their personal superiority at the expense of developing a shared sense of team identity. Consider another example: When a group sits at a table, the person at the head of the table has a greater probability of emerging as the leader, even when the seating is randomly determined.[37] And a leader is more likely to emerge when there are more "sightlines" to the leader. For example, when two people sit on one side of a table, and three on the other side, 70 percent of the leaders come from the two-person side; only 30 percent come from the three-person side. Why? Those seated on the two-person side could maintain easy eye contact with three of the group members and, consequently, influence more people than could the members of the three-person side. Another example of how the situation affects leadership concerns investigations of how the sociopolitical climate affects leadership choices. When organizations and teams have experienced a challenge or threat, they evaluate leaders as more effective than when they have not experienced a threat.[38]

Contingency Theories of Leadership

A final set of theories that we will examine are at the nexus between trait theories of leadership and purely situational theories of leadership. In short, they are **contingency theories,** which argue that leadership and leadership style depend on aspects of the people and the situation.

Situational Leadership®

It is not enough to simply attack trait theories of leadership and it is certainly not enough to demonstrate that seating arrangements affect leadership decisions. However powerful the studies might be, we need a situational theory of leadership. At its heart, a contingency theory of leadership is a model of leadership that tells a leader how and when to adjust his or her leadership style in accordance with the demands of the situation and the readiness of subordinates. Hershey and Blanchard developed a contingency model of leadership that they call Situational Leadership® (or SL) that has been used within many Fortune 500 companies.[39]

How does SL theory work? First, Hershey and Blanchard identify four specific behaviors, from highly directive to highly laissez-faire (see Exhibit 10.12).

If a follower is unable or unwilling to focus on a task, the leader needs to display a high task orientation to compensate for the follower's lack of ability and a high relationship

EXHIBIT 10.12

Situational Leadership® Model by Hershey and Blanchard

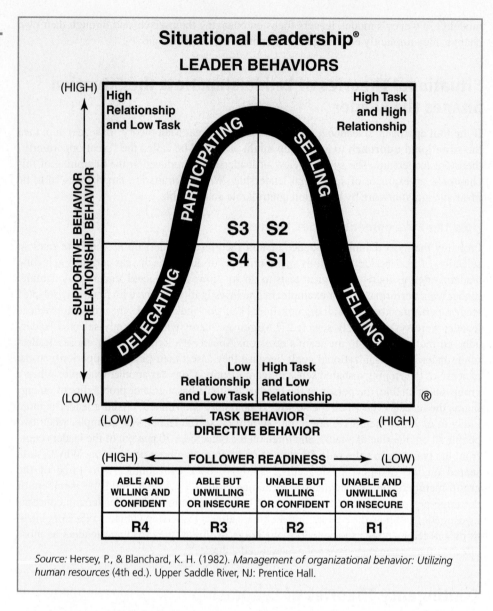

Source: Hersey, P., & Blanchard, K. H. (1982). *Management of organizational behavior: Utilizing human resources* (4th ed.). Upper Saddle River, NJ: Prentice Hall.

orientation to get the follower to buy into the organizational goals. At the other end of the continuum, if followers are able and willing, a leader can afford to be hands-off.

Path-Goal Theory of Leadership

The **path-goal theory** of leadership focuses on how leaders can best motivate their employees to achieve group and organizational goals. The path-goal theory is based on expectancy theory (discussed in Chapter 2), or the fundamental belief that certain behaviors will result in certain consequences. The path-goal theory of leadership is a prescriptive theory (see Chapter 1), which suggests the most effective approach leaders should use. In particular, three considerations are important: (1) Determine what outcomes subordinates are trying to obtain in the workplace; (2) reward subordinates for performing at a high level or achieving their work goals by giving them desired outcomes (e.g., similar to transactional leadership); and (3) make sure that subordinates believe that they can obtain their work goals and perform at a high level.

Moreover, attached to different consequences is the *valence* that a person attaches to it—the extent to which a given outcome is viewed as desirable. In particular, a leader must assess relevant factors in the organization, such as the control subordinates feel, their predictions of positive performance, members' tasks, and the authority system. Then a leader selects the best from one of four distinct approaches:

- *Directive leadership:* clearly spells out expectations for the group
- *Supportive leadership:* establishes an emotionally supportive work environment and develops mutually satisfying relations with the group
- *Achievement-oriented leadership:* continually pushes for work improvement
- *Participative leadership:* emphasizes consultation with group members and takes their suggestions seriously when making decisions

Normative Decision Model

Another situational theory of leadership behavior that is also prescriptive is Vroom and Yetton's decision-making model.[40] The model essentially argues that leaders have several different courses of action they might take when leading their subordinates, ranging from authoritative decision making with no input from the team to complete democracy. The model is considered a normative or prescriptive model because it provides a guideline for optimal leadership behavior based on different organizational conditions; it does not attempt to describe what leaders typically do.

The Vroom and Jago model identifies five styles along a continuum ranging from autocratic decision making to completely team-based decision making.[41] This model argues that the leader can best serve the organization by tuning her or his behavior in line with the demands of the situation. The model is presented in Exhibit 10.13.

Vroom and his colleague suggest that the leader ask him or herself the following eight questions as a guide for determining what decision-making style is ideal in a given situation (note that each question asks the leader to make a simple "yes" or "no" or "high" versus "low" decision).

1. Quality requirement (QR): How important is the technical quality of the decision? (high or low)
2. Commitment requirement (CR): How important is subordinate commitment to the decision? (high or low)
3. Leader's information (LI): Do you (the leader) have sufficient information to make a high-quality decision on your own?
4. Problem structure (ST): Is the problem well structured (e.g., defined, clear, and time-limited)?
5. Commitment probability (CP): If you were to make the decision by yourself, is it reasonably certain that your subordinates would be committed to the decision?
6. Goal congruence (CG): Do subordinates share the organizational goals to be attained in solving the problem?
7. Subordinate conflict (CO): Is conflict among subordinates over preferred solutions likely?
8. Subordinate information (SI): Do subordinates have sufficient information to make a high-quality decision?

After working through each of these binary questions, the model indicates the decision-making style that is best to follow. Note that the model outlines five possible decision-making styles (with some branches of the decision tree indicating more than one acceptable style). The autocratic decision style (AI) is when the leader makes the decision with little or no involvement among the team members. The inquiry model (AII) involves the leader asking for information from the team, but ultimately making the decision independently. The consultative approach (CI) involves different degrees of consultation with team members; however, the leader is still the final decision maker. The consensus model (CII) involves extensive consultation and consensus building with the team. Thus, the leader shares the problem with the team as a whole and together, they try to reach a consensus. The leader is essentially another member of the team and has no more nor less influence than any other member. The final

EXHIBIT 10.13

Decision Analysis Model

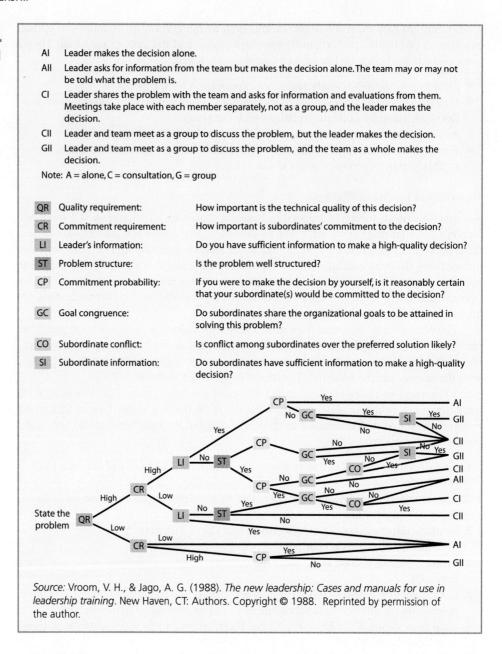

AI   Leader makes the decision alone.

AII   Leader asks for information from the team but makes the decision alone. The team may or may not be told what the problem is.

CI   Leader shares the problem with the team and asks for information and evaluations from them. Meetings take place with each member separately, not as a group, and the leader makes the decision.

CII   Leader and team meet as a group to discuss the problem, but the leader makes the decision.

GII   Leader and team meet as a group to discuss the problem, and the team as a whole makes the decision.

Note: A = alone, C = consultation, G = group

QR	Quality requirement:	How important is the technical quality of this decision?
CR	Commitment requirement:	How important is subordinates' commitment to the decision?
LI	Leader's information:	Do you have sufficient information to make a high-quality decision?
ST	Problem structure:	Is the problem well structured?
CP	Commitment probability:	If you were to make the decision by yourself, is it reasonably certain that your subordinate(s) would be committed to the decision?
GC	Goal congruence:	Do subordinates share the organizational goals to be attained in solving this problem?
CO	Subordinate conflict:	Is conflict among subordinates over the preferred solution likely?
SI	Subordinate information:	Do subordinates have sufficient information to make a high-quality decision?

Source: Vroom, V. H., & Jago, A. G. (1988). *The new leadership: Cases and manuals for use in leadership training*. New Haven, CT: Authors. Copyright © 1988. Reprinted by permission of the author.

method, delegation (GI), involves total delegation of decision making to the team. The team makes decisions without the leader. The leader gives the problem to the team and allows the team to take whatever action they deem necessary.

Many investigations have compared the effects of decisions made according to the model's prescriptions with effects of decisions made in a way inconsistent with the model.[42] In general, the results support the model. For example, Vroom and Jago computed the success rate across five investigations and found that for decisions made in accordance with the model, the mean success rate was 63 percent, versus 37 percent for decisions made using a decision procedure not suggested by the model.[43] Leaders who adapt their style of decision making to existing conditions are generally more successful than those who are either uniformly autocratic or participative in style.[44] However, most team members prefer a participative approach by their leader, even under conditions where the decision model recommends an autocratic style.[45] Thus, the leader's perceived effectiveness of her decisions may differ from that of the team.[46]

Fiedler's Contingency Theory of Leadership Effectiveness

Fiedler passionately believes that leadership effectiveness depends on a critical interplay between the leader's style and the demands of the situation. This means that a given leader may be effective in one situation, but not in another. Fiedler firmly believed that leadership style was a fixed trait. To assess a leader's style, Fiedler used the Least Preferred Coworker scale (or LPC). The LPC asks a leader to think of all the people with whom he or she has ever worked and then describe the person that he worked the least well with (this person could be someone from the past or present). From a scale of 1 to 8, the leader then describes this person in terms of: friendly, cooperative, supportive, and open. The responses to the scale are summed and averaged. A high LPC score suggests that the leader has a people, or human relations, orientation; a low LPC score suggests the leader has a strong task orientation. Presumably, everyone has had roughly equal unpleasant people to work with; so the key difference is how people perceive these annoying people. Leaders who enjoy people are going to find positive virtues in even the least favorable of their followers (see Exhibit 10.14).

A second major factor in Fiedler's theory is *situational favorableness*, which refers to the degree to which a situation enables a leader to exert influence over a group. There are three key situational factors, including leader–member relations (the degree of mutual trust, respect, and confidence between the leader and subordinates), task structure (the degree to which the task is low in multiplicity and high in verifiability, specificity, and clarity), and position power (the power inherent in the leader's position).

EXHIBIT 10.14   **Fiedler's Leadership Contingency Theory; Fielder's Model: Relationship between LPC and Group Performance**

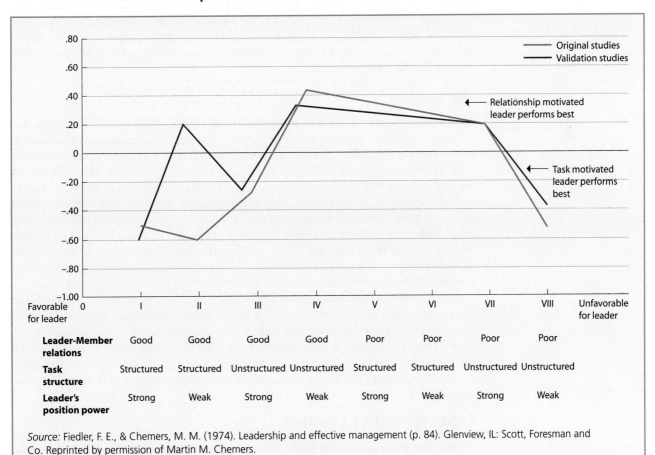

Source: Fiedler, F. E., & Chemers, M. M. (1974). Leadership and effective management (p. 84). Glenview, IL: Scott, Foresman and Co. Reprinted by permission of Martin M. Chemers.

EXHIBIT 10.15

Fiedler's Contingency Theory of Leadership

Leader–Member Relations (Does group accept leader?)	Task Structure	Leader's Position Power (Strong or weak?)	Most Effective Leadership Style
Yes	Structured	Strong	Task orientation
Yes	Structured	Weak	Task orientation
Yes	Unstructured	Strong	Task orientation
Yes	Unstructured	Weak	Relationship orientation
No	Structured	Strong	Relationship orientation
No	Structured	Weak	Relationship orientation
No	Unstructured	Strong	Task orientation
No	Unstructured	Weak	Task orientation

Source: Fiedler, F. E., & Chemers, M. M. (1974). *Leadership and effective management* (p. 70). Glenview, IL: Scott, Foresman and Co. Reprinted by permission of Martin M. Chemers.

By classifying a group according to these three considerations, it is possible to identify eight different group "conditions" (i.e., $2 \times 2 \times 2 = 8$); Fiedler then prescribes which type of leadership is best in each of the eight conditions (see Exhibit 10.15).

A "match" exists between a task-motivated leader and either a very favorable or unfavorable situation. A relationship-motivated leader, on the other hand, matches an intermediate favorable situation.

LMX Theory

The **Leader–Member Exchange model** (LMX) operates on the premise that leaders give different employees (subordinates) differential amounts of attention and treatment.[47] Leaders do not treat all of their subordinates in the same way and may develop different types of relationships with different people. Leader–member exchange theory focuses on the relationships that develop between leaders and their subordinates and what leaders and subordinates offer and receive in such relationships. When the leader spends a lot of time with a particular subordinate and the subordinate is given special privileges, that subordinate may perform very well. This may create an "in-group" among those with whom the leader invests. In other words, people will come to view the leader and that particular subordinate as a team or coalition. Other subordinates might not have such a close, trusting relationship with the leader. The leader may treat certain subordinates in a more distant, impersonal fashion and consequently, the subordinate is not as involved in his or her job and might not perform as well. A leader makes some initial decisions early on about whether a given employee will be part of an in-group. Leaders who are treated in a close, connected fashion to their superiors often develop close relationships with their subordinates. Some of the key determinants of which people are accorded in-group status include their similarity to the leader, demonstrated competence, and greater extraversion.

Expectations of Leaders

People who are dependent on leaders not only tend to evaluate and judge leaders quite often, but also they have particular expectations of leaders, or **implicit leadership theories (ILTs)** about whether a **leader is worthy of influence (LWI).** (For an inside look at how

EXHIBIT 10.16

Criteria That the World Economic Forum Uses to Select Leaders

The World Economic Forum released the names of 200 exceptional individuals selected for the Young Global Leaders (YGL) program in 2006. The YGL program is newly formed with a "2020 Initiative" to provide a framework for understanding the social and industrial problems and risks we face in the coming decades. The YGL community represents the new generation of global leaders, comprising nearly 1,111 business, political, public interest, media, art, and science leaders. Each year, the members, constituents, collaborators, and associates of the World Economic Forum nominate new YGLs.

The criteria for selection include requirements that candidates:

- are under 40 years old
- have substantial leadership experience
- have already clearly demonstrated a commitment to serving society
- are willing to devote their energy and expertise to tackle the most critical issues facing the world

Source: World Economic Forum, Young Global Leaders. (2006). *New class of young global leaders announced.* Retrieved May 30, 2006, from http://www.younggloballeaders.org/Newsroom/Press_releases/New_Class_of_Young_Global_Leaders_Announced.html

the World Economic Forum selects leaders, see Exhibit 10.16.)[48] ILTs are preconceived ideas that specify what teams expect of their leaders.[49] If a leader is judged to be LWI, teams are more willing to be influenced by that leader. Thus, the LWI accorded by teams to their leaders in large part determines the effectiveness of the leader. Given that ILTs drive LWI, it behooves leaders to understand the ILTs that teams hold of them.

An examination of the behaviors that people expect of leaders (the ILTs that drive LWIs) are somewhat different for appointed versus elected leaders.[50] For appointed leaders, being sympathetic (i.e., humorous, caring, interested, truthful, and open to ideas) and taking charge (i.e., responsible, active, determined, influential, aggressive, and in command) are key. For elected leaders, being well dressed (i.e., clean-cut), kind, and authoritative are most important (for a specific list of the characteristics, see Exhibit 10.17).

EXHIBIT 10.17

Leader Behaviors That Determine Whether People Accord Influence to a Leader

Appointed leaders are expected to have these characteristics and skills:		Elected leaders are expected to have these characteristics and skills:	
Caring	Determined	Tall	Independent
Interested	Influential	Clean-cut	Influential
Sense of humor	Aggressive	Open to others' ideas	Determined
Truthful	In command	Respect for team	Risk-taker
Open to others' ideas		Friendly	Aggressive
Imaginative		Caring	In command
Knowledgeable		Honest	Speak well
Responsible		Enthusiastic	Responsible
Speak well		Sense of humor	Popular
Active		Knowledgeable	

Source: Kenney, R. A., Schwartz-Kenney, B. M., & Blascovich, J. (1996). Implicit leadership theories: Defining leaders described as worthy of influence, *Personality and Social Psychology Bulletin, 22* (11), 1128–1143. Reprinted by permission of Sage Publications, Inc.

Does Leadership Matter?

Is there any conclusive evidence that leadership makes a difference in organizations? In general, leaders do make a difference and affect people and their organizations.[51] However, this is not always true: Some leaders have little effect on people's attitudes and behaviors.[52] In other words, no matter what some leaders do, some people are dissatisfied with their jobs and perform at a low level. Similarly, some people are consistently highly motivated and always perform well, no matter who is "in charge." Kerr and Jermier identified two forces that might limit how much influence leaders actually have (good or bad) in an organization.[53] They call these two forces leadership substitutes and leadership neutralizers. **Leadership substitutes** are anything that acts in place of a formal leader, and would include a variety of the "situational" factors that we discussed at the beginning of this chapter. For example, one substitute for leadership is intrinsic interest. A **leadership neutralizer** is something that prevents a leader from having influence and negates the leader's efforts. For example, if a leader is not physically present to influence his or her team (and merely communicates through e-mail), his or her influence will be dampened (or neutralized). In general, substitutes for leadership help people and organizations because they allow leaders to focus on several other initiatives. Conversely, leadership neutralizers are dysfunctional because people lack direction.

Conclusion

We distinguished leadership from management. Whereas management encompasses a variety of functions and behaviors, leadership is a relationship. We raised thorny issue of whether leadership can be taught and used that discussion to identify four classes of leadership theories: great person theories, behavioral-style theories, situational theories, and contingency theories. We found the least support for great person theories, which indirectly suggests that leadership can be taught. Leadership is very difficult to study as laboratory investigations do not allow the act of leadership to be meaningfully contextualized, and field studies are often post-hoc in nature and do not allow causal inference.

Notes

1. Maccoby, M. (2000, January–February). Understanding the difference between management and leadership. *Research & Technology Management*, pp. 57–59.
2. Clawson, J. C. (2003). *Level 3 leadership: Getting below the surface* (2nd ed.). Upper Saddle River, NJ: Prentice Hall.
3. Posner, B. (2004). Leadership is a relationship. *National Associates Committee Quarterly Journal*. Retrieved December 15, 2004, from http://www.aia.org/ nwsltr_nacq.cfm?pagename=nacq_a_0402_leadership.
4. Covey, S. R. (1992). *Principle-centered leadership*. New York: Simon & Schuster.
5. Greene, J., & Symonds, W. C. (2006, June 26). Bill Gates gets schooled. *BusinessWeek*.
6. Csikszentmihalyi, M. (1988). Society, culture, and person: A systems view of creativity. In R. J. Sternberg (Ed.), *The nature of creativity* (pp. 325–339). New York: Cambridge University Press.
7. Lubit, R. H. (2004). *Coping with toxic managers, subordinates and other difficult people: Using emotional intelligence to survive and prosper*. Upper Saddle River, NJ: Prentice-Hall.
8. Doh, J. P. (2003). Can leadership be taught? *Academy of Management Learning and Education, 2*(1), 54–67.
9. Bass, B. M. (1990). *Bass & Stogdill's handbook of leadership* (3rd ed.). New York: Free Press.
10. *Education profile of active duty force.* (1994). [Data file]. Arlington, VA: Department of Defense, Defense Manpower Data Center.
11. Yukl, G. (1981). *Leadership in organizations*. Englewood Cliffs, NJ: Prentice-Hall.
12. Simonton, D. K. (2001). Talent development as a multidimensional, multiplicative, and dynamic process. *Current Directions in Psychological Science, 10*(2), 39.
13. Plucker, J. (2003). *Does birth order affect intelligence?* Retrieved April 19, 2006, from http://www.indiana.edu/ ~intell/birthOrder.shtml.
14. Andeweg, R. B., & Van Den Berg, S. B. (2003). Linking birth order to political leadership: The impact of parents on sibling interaction. *Political Psychology, 24*, 605–623.
15. Eagly, A. H., & Johnson, B. T. (1990). Gender and leadership style: A meta-analysis. *Psychological Bulletin, 108*, 233–256.
16. Eagly, A., Makhijani, M., & Klonsky, B. (1992). Gender and the evaluation of leaders: A meta-analysis. *Psychological Bulletin, 111*, 3–22.
17. Berger, J., Fisek, M. H., Norman, R. Z., & Zelditch, M. (1977). *Status characteristics and social interaction: An expectation states approach*. New York: Elsevier.
18. Giacolone, C. M., & Riordan, C. A. (1990). Effect of self-presentation on perceptions and recognition in an organization. *Journal of Psychology, 124*, 25–38.

19. See note 16.
20. Rudman, L. A. (1998). Self-promotion as a risk factor for women: The costs and benefits of counter-stereotypical impression management. *Journal of Personality and Social Psychology, 74*, 629–645.
21. Foschi, M., Lai, L., & Sigerson, K. (1994). Gender and double standards in the assessment of job applicants. *Social Psychology Quarterly, 57*, 326–339.
22. Foschi, M., Sigerson, K., & Lembesis, M. (1995). Assessing job applicants: The relative effects of gender, academic record, and decision type. *Small Group Research, 26*, 328–352.
23. Eagly, A. H., & Karau, S. J. (1991). Gender and leadership style: A meta-analysis. *Journal of Personality and Social Psychology, 60*, 685–710.
24. Eagly, A. H., Johannesen-Schmidt, M. C., & van Engen, M. L. (2003). Transformational, transactional and laissez-faire leadership styles: A meta-analysis comparing women and men. *Psychological Bulletin, 29*(4), 569–591.
25. See note 20.
26. Ibid.
27. Meindl, J. R., Ehrlich, S. B., & Dukerich, J. M. (1985). The romance of leadership. *Administrative Science Quarterly, 30*, 78–102.
28. Lewin, K., Lippit, R., & White, R. (1939). Patterns of aggressive behavior in experimentally created social climates. *Journal of Social Psychology, 10*, 271–299.
29. Blake, R. R., & Mouton, J. S. (1964). *The leadership grid.* Houston, TX: Gulf.
30. Goleman, D. (2000). Leadership that gets results. *Harvard Business Review, 78*(2), 78–90.
31. Burns, J. M. (1978). *Leadership.* New York: Harper & Row; Bass, B. (1985). *Leadership and performance beyond expectations.* New York: Free Press; Bass, B. M., & Avolio, B. (1993). Transformational leadership: A response to critiques. In M. M. Chemers & R. Ayman (Eds.), *Leadership theory and research: Perspectives and directions* (pp. 49–80). New York: Academic Press.
32. Bass, *Leadership and performance*, p. 188.
33. Avolio, B. J., Bass, B. M., & Jung, D. (1999). Reexamining the components of transformational and transactional leadership using the Multifactor Leadership Questionnaire. *Journal of Occupational and Organizational Psychology, 7*, 441–462.
34. Greenleaf, R. K. (1977). *Servant leadership: A journey into the nature of legitimate power and greatness.* New York: Paulist Press.
35. See note 4.
36. Haslam, S. A., McGarty, C., Brown, P. M., Eggins, R. A., Morrison, B. E., & Reynolds, K. J. (1998). Inspecting the emperor's clothes: Evidence that random selection of leaders can enhance group performance. *Group Dynamics: Theory, Research and Practice, 2*, 168–184.
37. Nemeth, C., & Wachtler, J. (1974). Creating perceptions of consistency and confidence: A necessary condition for minority influence. *Sociometry, 37*, 529–540.
38. Emrich, C. G. (1999). Context effects in leadership perception. *Personality and Social Psychology Bulletin, 25*(8), 991–1006.
39. Hershey, P., & Blanchard, K. H. (1982). *Management of organizational behavior: Utilizing human resources* (4th ed.). Upper Saddle River, NJ: Prentice Hall.
40. Vroom, V. H., & Yetton, P. H. (1973). *Leadership and decision making.* Pittsburgh: University of Pittsburgh Press; Vroom, V. H., & Jago, A. G. (1988). *The new leadership: Managing participation in organizations.* Englewood Cliffs, NJ: Prentice Hall.
41. Vroom, V. H., & Jago, A. G. (1987). *The new leadership: Cases and manuals for use in leadership training.* New Haven, CT: Authors.
42. Yukl, G. (2002). *Leadership in organizations* (5th ed.). Upper Saddle River, NJ: Prentice Hall.
43. See note 41.
44. Vroom, V. H., & Jago, A. G. (1978). On the validity of the Vroom–Yetton model. *Journal of Applied Psychology, 63*, 151–62.
45. Heilman, M., Homstein, H., Cage, J., & Herschlag, J. (1984). Reactions to prescribed leader behavior as a function of role perspective: The case of the Vroom-Yetton model. *Journal of Applied Psychology, 69*, 560.
46. Field, R. H., & House, R. J. (1990). A test of the Vroom-Yetton model using manager and subordinate reports. *Journal of Applied Psychology, 75*, 362–366.
47. Graen, G. B. (1976). Role making processes within complex organizations. In M. D. Dunnette (Ed.), *Handbook of industrial and organizational psychology* (pp. 1201–1245). Chicago: Rand McNally.
48. Kenney, R. A., Schwartz-Kenney, B. M., & Blascovich, J. (1996). Implicit leadership theories: Defining leaders described as worthy of influence. *Personality and Social Psychology Bulletin, 22*(11), 1128–1143.
49. Lord, R. G., & Maher, K. J. (1993). *Leadership and information processing.* London: Routledge.
50. See note 48.
51. Podsakoff, P. M., Niehoff, B. P., MacKenzie, S. B., & Williams, M. L. (1993). Do substitutes for leadership really substitute for leadership? An empirical examination of Kerr and Jermier's situational leadership model. *Organizational Behavior and Human Decision Processes, 54*, 1–44.
52. Meindl, J. R. (1990). On leadership: An alternative to the conventional wisdom. In B. A. Staw (Ed.), *Research in organizational behavior* (Vol. 12, pp. 159–203). New York: JAI Press.
53. Kerr, S., & Jermier, J. (1978). Substitutes for leadership: Their meaning and measurement. *Organizational Behavior and Human Performance, 22*, 374–403.

ORGANIZATIONAL CHANGE

Before reading this chapter, think about a change you want to make in an organization in which you are a member. Be clear about what change you want to make and why. Then complete Exercise 11.1 on the Web site for this chapter. We will refer to your "change effort" throughout this chapter.

Change can occur at each of the four levels we have talked about throughout this book: the individual level, the interpersonal level, the group level, and at the level of the organization. In this chapter, we briefly review individual, interpersonal, and group change. We spend the majority of the chapter focusing on organizational change. Organizational theorists agree that broad-level change in organizations is only possible if leaders have an understanding of persuasion and behavioral change at the individual level. We provide a context for the discussion of change by reviewing the life cycle and stages of organizational development. We then introduce several prescriptive models of organizational change.

Individual Change

The primary way that individual change has been studied is via studies of attitude and behavioral change. Attitude change occurs when a person changes his or her cognitions and attitudes. Behavior change occurs when a person behaves differently.

Cognitive dissonance is a classic model of attitude change. According to **cognitive dissonance theory,** people desire their behaviors to be consistent, or congruent with their attitudes.[1] If people sense an inconsistency or incongruence between their beliefs and behaviors, they are driven to reduce this incongruence. Dissonance is an aversive motivational state that results when our behaviors are inconsistent with our attitudes. Dissonance is most likely to occur when the attitudes and behaviors are important to us.[2] One action that almost always arouses dissonance is decision making. When we must decide between two or more job offers, for example, the final choice is usually inconsistent with at least some of our beliefs.

Another example of cognitive dissonance theory is smoking. Most people know that smoking is dangerous for one's health (attitude). Further, most people want to engage in healthy behaviors so as to maximize their quality of life (attitude). However, smoking (behavior) is incongruent with their attitudes. According to cognitive dissonance theory, there are several ways to reduce dissonance, including: (1) changing one's behavior (i.e., stop smoking), (2) changing one's attitudes, such as through rationalization (i.e., question the validity of the medical reports produced by the Surgeon General), or (3) minimizing the importance of the dissonant beliefs.[3]

Self-perception theory offers an alternative prediction to why people change their attitudes and behaviors.[4] In contrast to dissonance theory, **self-perception theory** argues that people do not spend a lot of time attempting to align their behaviors and attitudes.[5] In fact, people's attitudes are not necessarily even apparent to them. Rather, people *infer* their attitudes by looking at their behaviors. For example, people may not know what kind of music they like, but if they find themselves attending hard rock concerts and listening to hard rock on the radio, they will then infer that they enjoy hard rock. Thus, according to self-perception theory, attitudes follow behaviors, not vice versa. Moreover, consistency may be an important value only in certain cultures (e.g., in the United States) but not others. For example, Japanese people may express very different attitudes in their social interactions depending on the situation because they believe it is appropriate to express agreement with others to ensure social harmony, rather than threaten social accord through disagreement.

Interpersonal Change

Interpersonal change, or situations in which one person attempts to persuade another, is at the core of much organizational interaction. Exhibit 11.1 is a basic model of the persuasion process. The model is an example of a linear process in which external stimuli directly affect the target, and the ultimate reaction of the target is either to change or possibly to resist change through various mechanisms. You are a "target" when you receive a call from a telemarketer, for example. As can be seen in Exhibit 11.1, there are three key external factors that can influence someone (referred to in the model as the persuasion target): the

EXHIBIT 11.1 Model of the Persuasion Process

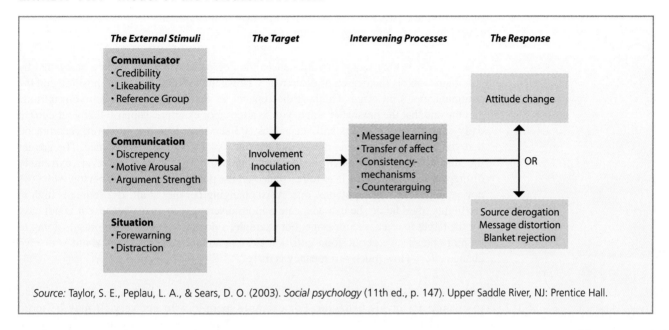

Source: Taylor, S. E., Peplau, L. A., & Sears, D. O. (2003). *Social psychology* (11th ed., p. 147). Upper Saddle River, NJ: Prentice Hall.

characteristics of the communicator (i.e., influence agent), the communication (i.e., the message itself), and the surrounding situation (i.e., the context). (It is worthwhile noting the stage similarity between the basic model of persuasion presented in this chapter and the basic model of communication presented in Chapter 4.) We review all three factors.

Communicator Characteristics

The *communicator,* also known as the *source or influence agent,* is a powerful aspect of influence. Probably the most important determinant of how much influence the communicator has over the target is the degree to which the source holds the communicator in high regard. In other words, if the target values and admires the source, the target is more likely to change his or her behavior and attitudes. Think about your own change effort. What communicator characteristics do you possess?

CREDIBILITY As might be expected, people are more influenced by credible communicators than by people with low credibility. For example, business people might be much more persuaded to follow the advice of a *Harvard Business Review* article than by an article posted on a low-credibility blog. Two factors combine to determine whether someone is regarded as credible: expertise and trustworthiness. People are more influenced by those who are regarded as established experts in their field. (This is why business consultants are often successful in their change efforts.) Regardless of expertise, a communicator must be viewed as trustworthy. One way that people can encourage others to trust them is to argue for positions that are contrary to their own self-interest. In other words, people who appear to have little to gain if others adopt their suggestions are viewed as particularly trustworthy.

LIKING In addition to credibility, the extent to which change agents are liked is directly correlated with their effectiveness. For example, students who are rated by other students as physically attractive are more persuasive.[6]

REFERENCE GROUP A **reference group** is a group that is important and meaningful to a person. For many students, sororities and fraternities are powerful reference groups. A person is more likely to be persuaded by a member of his or her own reference group. This means that a student is more likely to be persuaded by a respected member of his own fraternity or social club than by a member of another fraternity or club.

The Communication

In addition to characteristics of the communicator, the communication (or message itself) is very important for change to occur.

DISCREPANCY One factor that influences the degree to which people are persuaded by communication is the degree of discrepancy between the source's current position and the communicator's message. Think of discrepancy as the difference between your attitude and the one that the persuader wants you to adopt. For example, suppose that your current daily consumption of fruits and vegetables is 3 servings. Doctors, however, recommend that you eat 9 servings. This means that the discrepancy is 6 in this instance. The greater the discrepancy, the greater the potential pressure to change. However, extremely discrepant messages often lead to resistance on the part of the target.[7] A person who does not eat any fruits and vegetables may resist changing her diet at all. If a source is high in credibility, then he or she can advocate a more discrepant message because it is not easy for the target to reject the message. For example, a doctor or sports nutritionist is going to be more persuasive about good nutrition than an auto mechanic. Think about your own change effort. How much discrepancy is there?

MOTIVE AROUSAL **Motive arousal** refers to the extent to which a target is motivated to change her or his behavior. For example, people who get very ill may be more motivated to change their eating behavior than those who are not currently ill. Similarly, a person who wants to go to graduate school may be more motivated to change her or his study behaviors than someone who does not have postgraduate plans that require strong grades for admission. Many advertisers attempt to arouse people's motives for change via the use of threatening or upsetting persuasive messages. For example, someone may not be particularly motivated to make changes in their personal hygiene until they witness an advertisement in which a person is unable to get a date because of bad breath. The advertisement might motivate people to be concerned about their own hygiene. What is the motivational level of the individuals in your own organization?

ARGUMENT STRENGTH Argument strength refers to how powerful the persuasive message is. Some messages are very subtle; other messages are very direct.

The Situation

So far, we have considered characteristics of the communicator and the message and how they affect attitude change. The model in Exhibit 11.1 also indicates that certain aspects of the situation are important to consider.

FOREWARNING Forewarning refers to whether a target is alerted to the fact that he or she is going to be subjected to a persuasive message. People who are given a forewarning (e.g., that their organization is going to be subjected to a change management program) immediately begin to marshal counterarguments and anticipate what the change agent will say.[8] If organizational members are distracted (by an impending budget deadline or a conference), their ability to counterargue is severely hampered.[9] Again, think about your own change effort. How much forewarning did you give the organization?

DISTRACTION It is not always the case that people are fully tuned in to a persuasive message. In fact, people are often distracted or not engaged when a source attempts to persuade them. At first glance, you might think that a persuader might be more effective when the target is fully engaged—that is, not distracted. However, this is not always the case. In some situations, targets are more persuadable when they are distracted. For example, a target who is distracted cannot effectively marshal counterarguments to a persuasive message. In your own change effort, do you think that distraction would increase your effectiveness or weaken it?

The Target

Target people—those people who are the focus of a change agent's communication—must be understood in order for change to be effective. Some targets might be predisposed to agree with a message or to actively resist it or reject it outright. Here, we consider ego involvement and fear.

EGO INVOLVEMENT To the extent that a target's current attitudes and behavior are highly self-relevant, their attitudes and behavior will be very resistant to change. In short, some people feel great commitment to their current attitudes and behaviors. Such people are much more likely to outright reject change efforts by others.

INOCULATION **Inoculation** refers to the ability of a target to protect him- or herself against a persuasive argument. Think of a persuasive communication like a virus or bacteria that could infect you. If you knew in advance that someone was going to try to persuade you to change your mind or your behavior, there might be steps you could take to inoculate yourself against the persuasive message. For example, you might be able to plan some counterarguments or even do some of your own research. Or, you might simply plan to "tune out" the message. To the extent that people are forewarned about a persuasion attempt, they can often inoculate themselves.

FEAR AND ANXIETY As we will see below, several organizational change models rely on the arousal of fear or negative consequences to evoke change. However, fear- or anxiety-arousing messages will be successful only if the change agent offers fear-reducing recommendations. Moreover, if the change agent arouses too much fear and anxiety, organizational actors may not be able to effectively process the details of the message and the type of change requested by the organization.

INTERVENING PROCESSES AND RESPONSE According to the model, there are several intervening processes that might occur on the part of the target. Persuasion can often occur via different routes or paths, including message learning, transfer of affect, consistency mechanisms, and counterarguing.

Message learning refers to the degree to which the target comprehends the message itself. For example, consider your classes in school as a persuasive message; the exams in your classes are a direct test of the extent to which you have understood and learned the message of the classes. The extent to which targets understand the persuasive messages is related to how much they are changed. This is why some companies attempt to educate customers and clients about a particular issue; they are relying on the fact that someone who understands and learns a message are more likely to be persuaded and stay persuaded. Think about your own attempt to persuade others that you wrote about in the opening exercise for this chapter. Did you attempt to educate others?

Transfer of affect is a different idea. It refers to the fact that people often have strong emotional reactions to different things and that sometimes, persuasion occurs because people simply transfer the emotions they have for one thing to another thing. For this reason, advertisers often have beautiful models selling personal products and luxury items. In their 2006 advertisements, Jaguar, the maker of luxury sports cars, launched an advertising campaign on TV in which beautiful models drove the cars. The only word used in the advertisements was "gorgeous"; the idea was that most people would find the models gorgeous and would simply transfer their desire to associate with these gorgeous people to the cars.

Consistency mechanisms refer to the principles of cognitive dissonance discussed earlier. People are often persuaded to change when they realize that their attitudes and behaviors are inconsistent.

Counterarguing refers to the natural tendency for targets of persuasive messages to argue against your persuasive message. Counterarguing is a form of resistance. People with greater knowledge, expertise, and time to prepare are more effective at counterarguing.

The "response" in the persuasion model refers to how the target of persuasion is ultimately affected. As can be seen in Exhibit 11.1, targets may be persuaded (i.e., change their attitude) or they may simply derogate the source, distort what the source was saying, or outright reject the message itself. Think about your own persuasion attempt that you wrote about in the opening exercise. What was the reaction to your persuasion attempt?

Elaboration Likelihood Model

Petty and Cacioppo's elaboration likelihood model challenges the traditional view of persuasion in which organizational actors are highly rational, attentive, and thoughtful.[10] According to the **elaboration likelihood model** of persuasion, people are motivated to engage in thoughtful consideration of the pros and cons of an argument under some circumstances, but under other conditions, they simply use peripheral cues that have nothing to do with the merits of an argument. In this regard, Petty and Cacioppo draw a distinction between central routes to persuasion and peripheral routes to persuasion.[11] The **central persuasion route** is the most deliberate and rational: People who process information via the central persuasion route do so with great care and consideration, carefully weighing and reviewing each fact. In contrast, the **peripheral route of persuasion** is based on more automatic processing. As might be expected, when people are more involved in a particular issue, are concerned about being accurate, and recognize that others are attempting to change their attitudes, they are more likely to use the central route.[12] When the source of the persuasive message is highly physically attractive, likeable, and appears to possess expertise, people use peripheral processing. Think about your own change effort. Did you rely on rational processing or emotional images?

Group Change

We introduced social impact theory in Chapter 5 ("Power and Influence in Organizations"). Here we apply social impact theory to organizational change. **Social impact theory** addresses how much influence a group has on a person.[13] According to social impact theory, the total impact that others have on a person depends on three characteristics of observers (source of influence): the *size* of the group (i.e., how many people are in the group), their *strength* (i.e., how important they are to you), and their *immediacy* (i.e., how close in space and time they are to you during the influence attempt).

In terms of group size, as the size of the group gets larger, they have more impact on a person. However, each additional person has a relatively smaller impact on us. In other words, the difference between a 3-person group and a 4-person group is larger than is the difference between a 50-person unit and a 51-person unit. In fact, conformity does not increase very much after the group size reaches about 4 or 5 people.[14]

In terms of how influential the group is, to the extent that the social group is high in status and organizational importance, their impact increases.[15] Pressures for change are much greater when we respect and value a team or group, because we realize that there is a possibility of losing the affection that this group bestows on us.

In terms of immediacy, or the extent that the social group is highly present (i.e., they are physically present as opposed to simply interacting via e-mail or the telephone), their impact increases. Indeed, the impact of one's manager being in the same room as oneself has much greater impact than if our supervisor is located in another room and communicating with us on a video monitor.

Organizational Development

Organizational development focuses on how organizations naturally evolve and grow, as well as how change theories can intervene in the natural process of development. We first discuss the organizational life cycle and theories focusing on stages of group development.

Organizational Life Cycle

Relevant to the topic of change is organizational development. Organizations experience a predictable sequence of stages of growth and change, known as the **organizational life cycle** (Exhibit 11.2). The four key stages of the organizational life cycle include birth, growth, decline, and death. Organizations move through these stages at different rates and some do not experience every stage. And some organizations never experience growth before they die.

As an example of the organizational life cycle, consider Microsoft Corporation. In the 1990s, Microsoft's revenues soared an average of 36 percent, but in 2005, it experienced single-digit growth. During its early years, there was an explosion of major product updates, yet a newer one, Longhorn, has taken over five years, and there are very few new markets. Microsoft's share price in 2005 was the same as it was in mid 1998. In 2004, some business scholars commented that Microsoft was experiencing a "midlife crisis" and looked like "a star athlete who's past his prime."[16] There is speculation that Microsoft is becoming what IBM was in the 1980s—a profitable but lumbering giant. Companies often have an explosive early period of growth, followed by a tapering-off period.

Type of Change

When organizational theorists talk about organizational change, they often draw a distinction between **evolutionary change** on the one hand and **revolutionary change** on the other.[17] Evolutionary change, also known as incremental change, is carried out in a slow, methodical, step-by-step fashion and is very focused, whereas revolutionary change, also known as *radical change,* is carried out in an explosive, all-or-nothing fashion and is organizationwide. Moreover, organizational theories suggest that change may be carried out in different ways in different parts of the organization. For example, the program of change carried out at the British company, Cadbury (which makes candies and chocolates), was incremental in some parts of the organization, but radical in other parts.[18]

A powerful example of radical, revolutionary change is Gersick's **punctuated equilibrium model** of change.[19] Gersick suggests that organizations (and teams) often do not follow a smooth, linear pattern of change; rather, change often emerges in the later stages of an organization or group's life.[20] According to Gersick, "fundamental change cannot be accomplished piecemeal, slowly, gradually, or comfortably."[21]

EXHIBIT 11.2

The Organizational Life Cycle

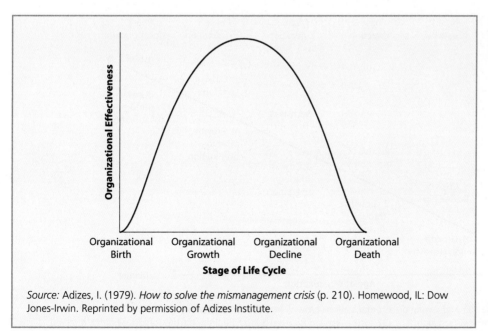

Source: Adizes, I. (1979). *How to solve the mismanagement crisis* (p. 210). Homewood, IL: Dow Jones-Irwin. Reprinted by permission of Adizes Institute.

Greiner's Five Phases of Growth

Greiner uses both revolutionary and evolutionary change principles in his model of organizational development.[22] He argues that the future of an organization may be less determined by outside forces than by their own history.[23] Specifically, as an organization passes through developmental phases, each evolutionary period creates its own revolution. Greiner considers four key dimensions in his analysis of organizational development: (1) the age of the organization; (2) the size of the organization; (3) its stage of evolution; and (4) the growth rate of the industry.[24]

Greiner argues that there are five specific phases of evolution and revolution that organizations experience (see Exhibit 11.3).[25]

As organizations pass through each phase, the evolutionary period is characterized by a dominant management style used to achieve growth, and the revolutionary period is characterized by a dominant management problem that must be solved before growth can continue. Whereas all organizations experience each of these five stages, high-growth companies experience all five phases more rapidly; those in slower growth industries encounter only two or three phases over many years. The critical task for management in each revolutionary period is to find a new set of organizational practices that will become the basis of evolutionary growth. In this sense, each phase is both an outcome of the previous phase and a cause for the following phase. For example, the evolutionary management style in phase 3 is "delegation" which grows out of and becomes the solution to "demands for greater autonomy" in the preceding phase 2 revolution. However, the delegative style used in phase 3 eventually provokes a revolutionary crisis that is characterized by attempts to regain control over the diversity created through delegation.

In terms of the phases that organizations pass through, it is useful to consider Exhibit 11.4, which identifies the five key phases of growth and considers the management focus, organizational structure, top management style, control system, and management reward emphasis at each stage.

In phase 1 (*creativity*), the emphasis is on creating a product and a market. Consequently, "make and sell" is the dominant management focus. During this period of time, the organizational structure is loose and informal, and managers are highly

EXHIBIT 11.3   Five Phases of Growth: Evolutionary Management Challenges and Revolutionary Crises

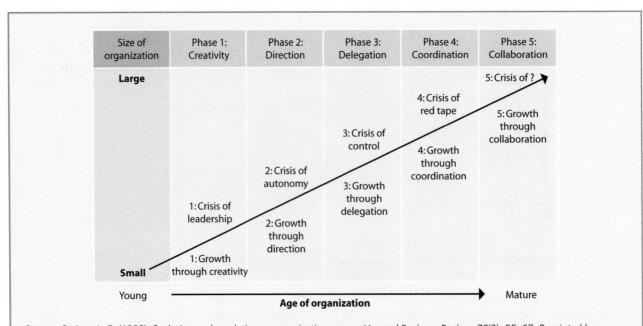

Source: Greiner, L. E. (1998). Evolution and revolution as organizations grow. *Harvard Business Review, 76*(3), 55–67. Reprinted by permission of Harvard Business Review. Copyright © 1998 by the Harvard Business School Publishing Corporation; all rights reserved.

EXHIBIT 11.4 Five Phases of Organizational Development

Category	Phase 1 Creativity	Phase 2 Direction	Phase 3 Delegation	Phase 4 Coordination	Phase 5 Collaboration
Management Focus	Make and Sell	Efficiency of Operation	Expansion of Market	Consolidation of Organization	Problem Solving & Integration
Organization Structure	Informal	Centralized & Functional	Decentralized & Geographical	Line-Staff & Production Groups	Matrix of Teams
Top Management Style	Individualist and Entrepreneurial	Directive	Delegative	Watchdog	Participative
Control System	Market Results	Standards & Cost Centers	Reports & Profit Centers	Plans & Investment Centers	Mutual Goal Setting
Management Reward Emphasis	Ownership	Salary & Merit Increases	Individual Bonus	Profit Sharing & Stock Options	Team Bonus

Source: Greiner, L. E. (1998). Evolution and revolution as organizations grow. *Harvard Business Review, 76*(3), 55–67. Reprinted by permission of Harvard Business Review. Copyright © 1998 by the Harvard Business School Publishing Corporation; all rights reserved.

entrepreneurial and individualistic. Long hours of hard work are rewarded with the promise of (stock) ownership. Greiner argues that in this first phase, the *leadership crisis* (see Exhibit 11.3) rears its head: As the company grows larger, someone needs to consider the efficiencies of manufacturing, and increasing numbers of employees cannot be managed with informal (water-cooler) communication. The founders must locate a strong business manager who can streamline the make and sell process.

The second phase, *direction,* occurs after companies have dealt with the leadership crisis by appointing a business manager to continue to embark on a process of sustained growth. Thus, the focus is on efficiency; and most often a functional organizational structure is introduced. Incentives, budgets, and performance standards are introduced. The crisis in this stage is the *autonomy crisis:* Lower-level employees begin to demand more autonomy, and the company is pressured to move to greater delegation.

In the third phase, *delegation,* much greater responsibilities are given to the managers of markets and areas. Profit centers and bonuses may be used to stimulate motivation. The company is decentralized and geographical; management successfully delegates. Communication by top management is infrequent and conducted from afar (in Latane's social impact theory model, the communication would not be as "immediate" as in earlier phases). The serious problem that rears its head, however, is that as delegation works, silos emerge: Autonomous field managers prefer to run their own fiefdoms without coordinating with the others in the organization.

In phase 4, *coordination,* the successful organization will have introduced and deployed formal systems for achieving greater coordination, such as the development of product groups and practice areas that cut across geographies and sometimes, functional groups. Certain technical functions, such as sales data, inventory, orders, and so on are centralized, whereas day to day operating decisions are decentralized. The crisis that emerges here is that of "red tape": A lack of confidence and trust emerges between headquarters and the field. The proliferation of systems and programs begins to feel cumbersome, field managers become resentful, and there is much criticism of the bureaucratic system.

Phase 5, *collaboration,* involves a focus on problem solving and innovation and the use of matrix models. Phase 5 encourages greater spontaneity in management action through teams and participative management. In short, the new system is more flexible than the old by solving problems quickly, and managers increase the frequency and volume of their interaction in the field.

Greiner concludes his developmental model by offering three guiding principles for managers, leaders, and change agents:[26]

1. Know where you are in the developmental sequence (awareness of the stages and the crises that will emerge is the best defense). Effective leaders work with the natural stages of organizations rather than try to deny or fight them.
2. Recognize that there are a limited range of solutions. If you have accurately identified the stage and the consequent crisis, this will lead to particular solutions. Often, it is tempting to keep reapplying a given solution, but this would not be effective.
3. Understand that solutions will always breed new problems. As the model indicates, companies never reach homeostasis; there is always a crisis in the works. Many leaders judge company health by the absence of a crisis, but this is misleading.

Theories of Change

Organizational change is the process by which organizations move from their present state to some desired future state to increase their effectiveness.[27] Several theories of change at the organizational level have been introduced by theorists.

Lewin's Unfreezing-Change-Refreezing Model

Kurt Lewin, a social psychologist, theorized that for people to change, they need to "unfreeze" their old habits and ways and then adopt new behaviors. Further, new behaviors will only be effective if the individual refreezes them (i.e., practices the new behavior). **Lewin's theory of change** is based on a force-field theory in which two sets of opposing forces within an organization (forces for change and forces for resistance) determine how and whether change will take place. When the forces for change are perfectly balanced by resistance, the organization is in a state of inertia and does not change. To get an organization to change, management must find a way to increase the forces for change or decrease the resistance to change, or do both simultaneously. (As an exercise, consider the change that the U.S. intelligence community has experienced since 9/11; see Exhibit 11.5.)

Sociotechnical Systems Theory

Sociotechnical systems theory[28] focuses on how organizations can change roles, tasks, and technical relationships to increase organizational effectiveness. The first application of sociotechnical systems theory occurred in British coal mines.[29] Traditional coal mining, termed the "hand got method," was a small-batch process in which teams of miners dug coal from the coal face underground and then transported the coal to the surface. The team

EXHIBIT 11.5 Change in the U.S. Intelligence Community

Over the past 50 years, 40 studies have noted the lack of focus, organization, and cooperation among the autonomous intelligence branches [of the United States]. Since 9/11, there have been strong demands from the public, the Senate, and other Washington leaders for massive reorganization of how intelligence is collected, shared, stored, and acted upon. One of the things that intelligence agencies need to learn to do is to share information that once they protected. A stumbling block in this massive reorganization effort is the Cold War culture. For example, the (old) FBI culture was focused on reacting to crime and incarcering criminals. The new culture is focused on prevention. Another stumbling block is the Internet. "If the intelligence community is to make the best effort to protect the nation, fiefdoms must be dismantled, data shared, and institutional egos put aside."

Source: Adapted from Magnusson, P. (2004, June 28). The smart way to fix intelligence. *BusinessWeek,* p. 81.

worked in a small space and cooperated closely. To increase efficiency, managers began using the "long wall method," in which a mechanized, mass-production technology was introduced. Coal was cut by miners using power drills and transported to the surface via conveyor belts. Tasks became more routine. However, despite the changes, absenteeism increased dramatically, and thus, production did not improve. Closer inspection revealed that the new technology changed the task and role relationships among miners such that it destroyed informal norms and social support. The key to improving productivity was to link the new technology with the traditional social system, by respecting the tasks and roles that had emerged in these close groups.

Thus, sociotechnical systems theory argues that mangers need to fit technology to people, not vice versa. A poor fit between technology and people leads to failure, but a close fit leads to success. Sociotechnical systems argue for gradual change, allowing the fit between technology and social systems to be optimized.

Total Quality Management

Total Quality Management (TQM) is an ongoing and constant effort by all of an organization's functions to find new ways to improve the quality of an organization's products and services.[30] Like sociotechnical systems theory, TQM is based on slow, incremental change, rather than abrupt, revolutionary change. TQM was developed by U.S. managers, but first adopted by Japanese companies. For example, in Japan, shop-floor employees were traditionally organized into **quality circles,** or groups of employees who met regularly to discuss the way work was performed to find new ways to increase performance. For example, quality circles might involve people who have different, but related functions to work together to reduce the number of errors or points of failure.

Successfully implementing a TQM program is difficult because it requires managers and employees to continuously focus on how they can improve their own role. Moreover, some managers are unwilling to relinquish their decision control and empower workers. In short, TQM is rooted in giving employees a great deal of control and autonomy in terms of restructuring their jobs and roles. To be effective, all employees must embrace the TQM approach, meaning that they need to care enough to attempt to improve their roles.

Reengineering

Reengineering is the process by which managers redesign how tasks are bundled into roles and functions to improve organizational effectiveness.[31] Unlike sociotechnical systems theory and TQM, reengineering is more radical and therefore, more revolutionary than evolutionary. Reengineering requires managers to painstakingly break down every task in the production of goods and services into their most basic parts and then identify a better way to coordinate and integrate the activities. Reengineering focuses on process, not functions. Business processes cut across functions. Simply put, companies don't reengineer sales or manufacturing, they reengineer the process by which their products or services are produced and sold. Managers committed to reengineering need to completely rethink how they do their business. The reengineering process begins with the end-user (i.e., the customer or client) and works backward from there. Three guidelines characterize effective reengineering:[32]

- Organize around outcomes, not tasks. Work should be organized so that one person or one function can perform all the activities necessary to complete the process, thus avoiding the need for integration between functions.
- Have those who use the output of the process perform the process. The people who use the outcome care the most and understand best what they want.
- Decentralize decision making to the point where the decision is made.

Restructuring

Restructuring or reorganization is the process by which managers change task and authority relationships and redesign organizational structure and culture to improve organizational effectiveness.[33] As might be expected, restructuring and reengineering are closely linked. One type of common restructuring is the move from a functional (e.g., sales, marketing, manufacturing) structure to a divisional structure. Probably the most feared type of restructuring is **downsizing,** the process by which a company streamlines the organizational hierarchy and consequently lays off managers and employees to reduce costs.

It is easy to see how reengineering and restructuring are often met with considerable concern, anxiety, and resistance by managers and employees. This often creates a wall of active resistance that can severely challenge the change process.

Prescriptive Models of Change

Recall the distinction between descriptive models and prescriptive models introduced in Chapter 7. Descriptive models explain how organizations actually change; prescriptive models outline the steps an organization should follow to achieve change. Prescriptive models specify best practices for organizational actors attempting to introduce a change initiative in their organization. Departmental and organizational level change is often offered in the form of prescriptive models. Moreover, these prescriptive models typically have a number of steps. A common theme concerns how to overcome resistance from people who are averse to change or threatened by change.

Kotter's Eight Steps

Based on extensive research from over 100 organizations in the profit and nonprofit sectors, Kotter introduced eight sequential steps that significantly increase the likelihood of leading a major change effort in an organization. In his original formulation, Kotter presented the eight steps as errors that a well-meaning leader could make.[34] The steps are depicted in Exhibit 11.6.

Kotter argues that the most critical success factor in terms of producing effective change is effective leadership, rather than effective management.[35] According to Kotter, leadership is a "set of processes that creates organizations and adapts them to significantly changing circumstances."[36] In contrast, management is a "set of processes that can keep a complicated system of people and technology running smoothly." According to Kotter, successful transformation is 70–90 percent leadership and only 10–30 percent management.[37]

Kotter was careful to present his model as a specific sequence of steps that should be followed in order; he cautioned that "skipping steps creates only the illusion of speed and never produces a satisfying result."[38] He further cautioned that mistakes are cumulative, such that a mistake in a previous phase can have a devasting impact on the success of future steps.

The first step in Kotter's model is establishing a sense of urgency. In this step, the change agent examines the market and competitive realities. In addition, the change agent identifies and discusses crises, potential crises, and major opportunities. Kotter implicitly recognizes people's tendency toward risk aversion in the first step.[39] In other words, most managers view the current set of circumstances as the status quo and are reluctant to take risks. Accordingly, Kotter suggests that leaders may need to engage in dramatic reframing, so as to position the status quo as an aversive state.[40] Kotter describes how one chief executive officer deliberately engineered the largest accounting losses in the history of the company so as to make the status quo seem unacceptable to others.[41]

In step 2, the change agent assembles a group with enough power to lead the change effort and encourages the group to work together as a team. (An understanding of the concepts in Chapter 9, "Leading and Managing Teams," is essential.) Whereas top leadership is essential for successful change, it is not sufficient; top management needs an additional 5–50 people to work together in a committed fashion.

In step 3, the change agent creates a vision to help direct the change effort and develops strategies for achieving that vision. In step 4, the change agent communicates the vision, using every vehicle possible to communicate the new vision and strategies.

EXHIBIT 11.6

Kotter's Eight-Step Change Model

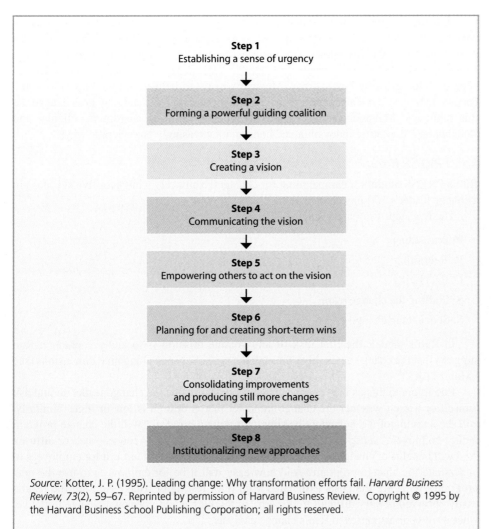

Step 1
Establishing a sense of urgency

Step 2
Forming a powerful guiding coalition

Step 3
Creating a vision

Step 4
Communicating the vision

Step 5
Empowering others to act on the vision

Step 6
Planning for and creating short-term wins

Step 7
Consolidating improvements
and producing still more changes

Step 8
Institutionalizing new approaches

Source: Kotter, J. P. (1995). Leading change: Why transformation efforts fail. *Harvard Business Review, 73*(2), 59–67. Reprinted by permission of Harvard Business Review. Copyright © 1995 by the Harvard Business School Publishing Corporation; all rights reserved.

The change agent also models the new behaviors via the example set by the guiding coalition.

In step 5, the change agent attempts to neutralize or eliminate obstacles to change. This often means changing systems or structures that can possibly undermine the new vision and also encouraging risk taking and nontraditional ideas, activities, and actions.

In step 6, the change agent plans for visible performance improvements and attempts to create those improvements. Employees and organizational members involved in the improvements are recognized and rewarded.

In step 7, the change agent leverages the increased credibility to change the systems, structures, and policies that don't fit the vision. This means hiring, promoting, and developing employees who can implement the vision and reinvigorate the process with new products, themes, and change agents. Finally, in step 8, the change agent must institutionalize the new approaches. This means articulating the connections between the new behaviors and corporate success and developing the means to ensure leadership development and succession.

In sum, successful change programs are multistep processes that mobilize sufficient power and motivation to overcome the forces of inertia.[42] (In this sense, Kotter's model is reminiscent of Lewin's force field theory.) Kotter also uses Lewin's unfreezing metaphor to provide a theoretical foundation for the first four steps of the model: "The four steps in the transformation process help defrost a hardened status quo."[43] Steps 5–7 introduce new practices (the "change" aspect of Lewin's model). Finally, the last stage is analogous to Lewin's refreezing, in which the changes are reflected in the corporate culture. Kotter reflects that leaders often try to bypass the first four steps and jump straight to steps 5–7), which Kotter argues is never successful.[44] Kotter's dominant, prescriptive message concerns the importance of leadership (versus management).[45] To this end, Kotter paints a dismal picture of the "over-managed, under-led corporate culture."[46] In such a culture, a company experiences early success and then hires and promotes managers (not leaders) to cope with the growing bureaucracy. Managers begin to believe in their superiority and become more and more arrogant; top management does not react and may even exaggerate this tendency. Managers fail to acknowledge the value of customers, clients, and stockholders; they stifle innovation and behave in increasingly bureaucratic ways.

Rao's PRESS Model

Rao's PRESS model for campaigning for change (Exhibit 11.7) involves five key steps in a change leader's 100-day change plan.

The five steps form an acronym, PRESS:

P: Persuading

R: Recruiting

E: Energizing

S: Staffing the change team

S: Sequencing change

In Rao's model, the first task of any change mission is to analyze change. Rao suggests that the change agent think through the type of change along nine dimensions (see Exhibit 11.8).[47]

Rao refers to this as the "change analysis." Specifically, the change leader should ask himself or herself whether the change mind-set that is desired is low or high. Similarly, will the learning of old behaviors be simple or quite a big deal? Will the change program reduce employees' sense of control? Will the costs of change be concentrated or diffuse? And will benefits of change be concentrated or diffuse? How difficult is it for employees to understand the change program? And how easy will it be for employees to use the new program? What are the costs associated with pilot testing or trials? And are the results easily observed or very difficult to discern? In thinking about your own change initiative, what were your responses to Rao's change analysis?

EXHIBIT 11.7

Rao's PRESS Model of Change

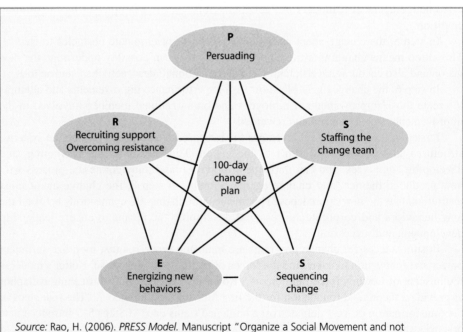

Source: Rao, H. (2006). *PRESS Model.* Manuscript "Organize a Social Movement and not a Roadshow: Leading Change in Organizations" in progress, Stanford University. Reprinted by permission of Hayagreeva Rao.

EXHIBIT 11.8   Change Analysis

Issues	Scale
Mind-set change	*Low* ·· *High*
Unlearning of old behaviors	*Small potatoes* ····················· *Big deal*
Extent to which change reduces sense of control of employees	*Low* ·· *High*
Distribution of costs of change	*Concentrated* ························ *Diffuse*
Distribution of benefits from change	*Concentrated* ························ *Diffuse*
Complexity: Understanding	*Easy to understand* ······· *Difficult to understand*
Complexity: Usage	*Easy to use* ····························· *Hard to use*
Triability	*Easy to experiment* ············ *Hard to experiment*
Observability of results	*Easily observable* ············· *Difficult to observe*

Source: Rao, H. (2006). *PRESS Model.* Manuscript "Organize a Social Movement and not a Roadshow: Leading Change in Organizations" in progress, Stanford University. Reprinted by permission of Hayagreeva Rao.

PERSUADING In the first step of the change process, persuading, Rao uses Bruch and Ghoshal's analysis of energy zones in organizations (Exhibit 11.9).[48]

As can be seen in Exhibit 11.9, the model considers the nature of the emotions people in the organization have concerning the change program (generally positive versus negative) and the strength of the emotions (strong versus weak). Bruch and Ghoshal's analysis of emotions has its roots in the classic model of persuasion in which the source of the persuasive message needs to accurately assess the target's characteristics.[49] When emotions are strongly negative, this creates the "aggression zone." Strong, positive emotions create the "passion zone." Weakly negative emotions create the "resignation zone," and weakly positive emotions create the "comfort zone." Part of the persuasion process then depends on the ability of the change agent to develop a story around the emotions. In particular, Bruch and Ghoshal propose that the change agent create a concrete, vivid threat when confronted with the aggression zone.[50] When the change agent assesses the workplace to be in the passion zone, the leader should create a simple, convincing vision that inspires confidence and relies on tight execution. Rao notes that in the case of real threats to the organization, positive emotion is not realistic and thus, "killing the dragon" may be the only option.[51]

EXHIBIT 11.9

Energy Zones in Organizations

	Negative Emotions	Positive Emotions
Strong Emotions	Aggression zone (fear, anger)	Passion zone (enthusiasm, excitement)
Weak Emotions	Resignation zone (disappointment, frustration)	Comfort zone (contentment)

Source: Bruch, H., & Ghoshal, S. (2003). Unleashing organizational energy. *MIT Sloan Management Review, 45*(1), 45–51. Reprinted by permission of Massachusetts Institute of Technology, Sloan School of Management.

The persuasion tactics available to the change agent involve presentation moves (packaging ideas to make the case for change), involvement moves (engaging employees), and modeling moves (changing one's own behaviors).[52] In terms of presentation moves, Rao notes that labeling the change is critical and influences compatibility; receiver-oriented names rather than provider-oriented names are important. Moreover, the more visceral and immediate the story can be, the better. In terms of involvement moves, Rao argues that change agents need to be both actors and observers (something Rao terms "being on the dance floor" and on "the balcony"). Modeling moves are most effective when the behavior is simple and depicts positive qualities.

RECRUITMENT According to Rao, persuasion tactics set the stage for commitment, but are not sufficient. Rao identifies "hard core resisters" and "minority influence." Rao suggests the following four-pronged solution to deal with resisters: (1) encirclement (locate "hubs," put them in committees, and create dissonance, a la Festinger); (2) isolation (physically relocate resisters to move them away from one another); (3) sideline the resisters through structural change (e.g., isolating key resisters through reorganization or redistricting); (4) fire them.

ENERGIZING Rao relies on the critical attitude-behavioral linkage in terms of energizing behavior. In short, behavior sometimes, but not always follows changes in beliefs, and vice versa. Rao suggests increasing behavioral change by rewarding behavior, empowering people, and sending strong messages.

STAFFING THE CHANGE TEAM Rao provides several prescriptions for staffing the change team, and many of these principles derive from the classic attitude change model in Exhibit 11.1.[53] Credibility is a key aspect (it is essential that the change team be viewed as trustworthy and competent). Commitment by the members of the change team is essential—do they want to be there (or are they grudgingly there)? For change agents to be effective, they must use their social networks; boundary spanners and change agents are high in social capital. Finally, it is important for the change team to have its own governance and structure.

SEQUENCING CHANGE Rao advocates a 100-day plan for effective change.[54] This 100-day plan is further segmented into day 1, day 10, day 50, and day 100 milestones. Rao cautions that the most common mistakes made by change agents include inadequately modeling behavior (i.e., they fail to behaviorally demonstrate the action they advocate); overlooking symbols and messages in the environment; offering rewards before people have the relevant behavioral skills in their repertory; and failing to deal with hard-core resisters.[55]

Garvin and Roberto's Change Through Persuasion

At the heart of Garvin and Roberto's model of change is persuasion.[56] They liken a change program in an organization to a political campaign. The successful "turnaround leader" relies on a four-part communication strategy: (1) setting the stage for acceptance; (2) creating the frame through which information and messages are interpreted; (3) managing the mood so that employees' emotional states support implementation and follow-through; and (4) at critical intervals, reinforcing behaviors to ensure that desired changes are "refrozen." (Again, note the similarity of these subprocesses to the basic attitude-change model depicted in Exhibit 11.1).

SETTING THE STAGE In terms of "setting the stage," the change leader needs to accurately identify all of the involved parties that the change effort will affect. Garvin and Roberto suggest that the most effective stage-setters are leaders who have face-to-face interaction with their organizational members (as opposed to electronic or paper memos); leaders who create opportunities for informal dialogue, such as in the hallways (rather than planned, canned speeches); and leaders who have several, successive meetings (as opposed to one-shot meetings).[57]

CREATING THE FRAME Once the stage has been set for acceptance, leaders need to help organizational members interpret proposals for change. Again, much of this involves perception and framing (see Chapter 7, "Decision Making").

MANAGING THE MOOD As noted earlier, restructuring and downsizing are often met with anxiety. Relationships are torn apart, and people must reconstruct their social lives. In such situations, managing the mood of the organization is essential for effective change. This step requires high emotional intelligence.

REINFORCING GOOD HABITS As foreshadowed by Lewin's model, the refreezing aspect of change is the most difficult. Organizations are subject to "drift" in which the cultural forces of inertia exert a pull back to the old routines. Garvin and Roberto also consider several "dysfunctional routines" (analogous to the negative forces in Lewin's force-field theory):[58] (1) a culture of "no" (some organizations are composed of cynics and critics who've made a career of pointing out problems); (2) the dog and pony show must go on (some organizations put so much weight on the process that they confuse the means and the ends); (3) the grass is always greener (to avoid facing challenges in their core business, managers often look to new products and services rather than addressing the heart of the issue); (4) after the meeting ends, debate begins (cordial, apparently cooperative meetings are followed by resistance, making meetings an empty ritual); (5) ready, aim, aim (the organization fails to settle on a definitive course of action; organizational members generate a continual stream of proposals and reports and fine-tune each one ad infinitum); and (6) "this too shall pass" (in organizations in which employees have been subjected to too many failed change efforts, they often develop a heads-down, bunker mentality and believe that the wisest course of action is to ignore the new initiatives, work around them, or wait things out).

Organizational actors need support to maintain new behaviors; this involves practice, feedback, and reinforcement. Many managers react punitively when they see evidence of an old, undesired behavior, but they fail to reinforce new, effective behaviors. Change leaders must also serve as role models.

Beer and Nohria: Theory E versus Theory O Change

Beer and Nohria's descriptive-prescriptive model of change is based on their dismal observation that 70 percent of all change initiatives fail.[59] The "code of change" model advanced by Beer and Nohria identifies two dominant mental models of change held by senior managers: Theory E and Theory O.[60] **Theory E** is change based on economic value. **Theory O** is change based on organizational capability (see Exhibit 11.10).

Beer and Nohria argue that both Theory E and Theory O are valid models of change, but that to be most effective, change leaders need to employ both models.[61]

Theory E change strategies are the ones that represent the traditional, hard approach to change in which shareholder value is viewed as the single, most important (and legitimate) measure of corporate success. In this sense, change usually involves extensive application of economic incentives, large-scale layoffs and downsizing, and extensive restructuring and reorganization.

In contrast, Theory O managers believe that you cannot just look at the price of stock to know if a company is in good health or not. Theory O managers are often characterized as "softies." Theory O managers desire to develop corporate culture and human capability through learning, feedback, and involvement.

Beer and Nohria acknowledge that companies often do use a mix of Theory E and Theory O change processes, but they fail to deal with the tensions between the two approaches.[62] Beer and Nohria argue that the heart of successful change is the ability to balance these two mental models or approaches.[63] For example, in terms of the goals of change, Beer and Nohria caution that change leaders must explicitly embrace the paradox between economic value (theory E) and organizational capability (theory O).[64] In terms of leadership, Beer and Nohria suggest that leaders need to set direction, but then actively engage people from lower levels of the organization.

EXHIBIT 11.10 **Dimensions of Change**

	Theory E	Theory O	Theories E and O Combined
Goals	maximize shareholder value	develop organizational capabilities	explicitly embrace the paradox between economic value and organizational capability
Leadership	manage change from the top down	encourage participation from the bottom up	set direction from the top and engage the people below
Focus	emphasize structure and systems	build up corporate culture: employees' behavior and attitudes	focus simultaneously on the hard (structures and systems) and the soft (corporate culture)
Process	plan and establish programs	experiment and evolve	plan for spontaneity
Reward System	motivate through financial incentives	motivate through commitment—use pay as fair exchange	use incentives to reinforce change but not to drive it
Use of Consultants	consultants analyze problems and shape solutions	consultants support management in shaping their own solutions	consultants are expert resources who empower employees

Source: Adapted from Beer, M., & Nohria, N. (2000). Resolving the tension between theories E and O of change. In M. Beer & N. Nohria (Eds.), *Breaking the code of change* (pp. 1–34). Boston: Harvard Business School.

Conclusion

We reviewed attitude and behavior change at each of the four levels that have guided this book: the individual level, the interpersonal (one-on-one) level, the team level, and finally, the level of the organization. We began our analysis of organizational change by focusing on the developmental stages of organizations. In particular, we focused on Greiner's five phases of organizational growth and the particular crises that confront organizations at each stage of development. We distinguished evolutionary change from revolutionary change. We reviewed theoretical models of organizational change, including Lewin's unfreezing-change-refreezing model, sociotechnical systems theory, total quality management, reengineering and restructuring. We then focused on prescriptive models of change, including Kotter's eight steps. Rao's PRESS model, Garvin and Roberto's change through persuasion model, and Beer and Nohria's Theory E versus Theory O change model. If you had to choose one model to guide your change effort, what would it be and why?

Notes

1. Festinger, L. (1957). *A theory of cognitive dissonance.* Stanford, CA: Stanford University Press.

2. Aronson, E. (1968). Dissonance theory: Progress and problems. In E. A. R. Abelson, W. McGuire, T. Newcomb, M. Rosenberg, & P. Tannenbaum (Eds.), *Theories of cognitive consistency: A sourcebook.* Chicago: Rand McNally; Stone, J., & Cooper, J. (2001). A self-standards model of cognitive dissonance. *Journal of Experimental Social Psychology, 37,* 228–243.

3. See note 1.

4. Bem, D. J. (1967). Self-perception: An alternative interpretation of the cognitive dissonance phenomena. *Psychological Review, 74,* 183–200.

5. Ibid.

6. Chaiken, S. (1979). Communicator: Physical attractiveness and persuasion. *Journal of Personality and Social Psychology, 37,* 1387–1397.

7. Eagly, A. H., & Telaak, K. (1972). Width of the latitude of acceptance as a determinant of attitude change.

Journal of Personality and Social Psychology, 23, 388–397.

8. Petty, R. E., & Cacioppo, J. T. (1977). Forewarning, cognitive responding and resistance to persuasion. *Journal of Personality and Social Psychology, 35,* 645–655.

9. Petty, R. E., & Brock, T. C. (1981). Thought disruption and persuasion: Assessing the validity of attitude change experiments. In R. E. Petty, T. M. Ostrom, & T. C. Brock (Eds.), *Cognitive responses in persuasion.* Hillsdale, NJ: Erlbaum.

10. Petty, R. E., & Cacioppo, J. T. (1986). *Communication and persuasion: Central and peripheral routes to attitude change.* New York: Springer-Verlag.

11. Ibid.

12. Nienhuis, A., Manstead, A., & Spears, R. (2001). Multiple motives and persuasive communication: Creative elaboration as a result of impression motivation and accuracy motivation. *Personality and Social Psychology Bulletin, 27*(1), 118–132.

13. Latane, B. (1981). The psychology of social impact. *American Psychologist, 36,* 343–365.

14. Campbell, J. D., & Fairey, P. J. (1989). Informational and normative routes to conformity: The effect of faction size as a function of norm extremity and attention to the stimulus. *Journal of Personality and Social Psychology, 57,* 457–468.

15. Guimond, S. (1999). Attitude change during college: Normative or informational social influence? *Social Psychology of Education, 2,* 237–261.

16. Greene, J. (2004, April 19). Microsoft's midlife crisis. *BusinessWeek,* p. 88.

17. Miller, D. (1982). Evolution and revolution: A quantum view of structural change in organizations. *Journal of Management Studies, 19,* 11–151.

18. Child, J., & Smith, C. (1987). The context and process of organizational transformation: Cadbury Ltd. in its sector. *Journal of Management Studies, 12,* 12–27.

19. Gersick, C. (1991). Evolutionary change theories: A multi-level exploration of the punctuated equilibrium paradigm. *Academy of Management Review, 16,* 10–36.

20. Ibid.

21. Ibid., p. 34.

22. Greiner, L. E. (1998). Evolution and revolution as organizations grow. *Harvard Business Review, 76*(3), 55–59.

23. Ibid.

24. Ibid.

25. Ibid.

26. Ibid.

27. Jones, G. (2004). *Organizational theory, design, and change* (4th ed.). Upper Saddle River, NJ: Pearson, Prentice Hall.

28. Trist, E. L., Higgin, G. W., Murray, H., & Pollock, A. B. (1963). *Organization choice: Capabilities of groups at the coal face under changing technologies; the loss,* *rediscovery and transformation of a work tradition.* London: Tavistock.

29. Trist, E., & Bamforth, K. (1951). Some social and psychological consequences of the longwall method of coal-getting. *Human Relations, 1,* 3–38.

30. Deming, W. E. (1982). *Out of the crisis.* Cambridge: Center for Advanced Engineering Study, Massachusetts Institute of Technology.

31. See note 27.

32. Hammer, M. (1990). Reengineering work: Don't automate, obliterate. *Harvard Business Review, 68*(4), 104–111.

33. See note 27.

34. Kotter, J. P. (1995). Leading change: Why transformation efforts fail. *Harvard Business Review, 73*(2), 59–67.

35. Kotter, J. P. (1996). *Leading change.* Harvard Business School Press: Boston, MA.

36. Ibid.

37. See note 34.

38. See note 34.

39. See note 34.

40. See note 34.

41. See note 34.

42. Kotter, "Leading change," p. 210; Kotter, *Leading change,* p. 210.

43. See note 35.

44. See note 35.

45. See note 35.

46. See note 35.

47. Rao, H. (2006). Organize a social movement and not a roadshow: Leading change in organizations. Manuscript in progress, Stanford University.

48. Bruch, H., & Ghoshal, S. (2003). Unleashing organizational energy. *MIT Sloan Management Review, 45*(1), 45–51.

49. Ibid.

50. Ibid.

51. See note 47.

52. See note 47.

53. See note 47.

54. See note 47.

55. See note 47.

56. Garvin, D. A., & Roberto, M. A. (2005). Change through persuasion. *Harvard Business Review, 83*(2), 104–112, 149.

57. Ibid.

58. Ibid.

59. Beer, M., & Nohria, N. (2000). Resolving the tension between theories E and O of change. In M. Beer & N. Nohria (Eds.), *Breaking the code of change* (pp. 1–34). Boston: Harvard Business School Press.

60. Ibid.

61. Ibid.

62. Ibid.

63. Ibid.

64. Ibid.

Chapter | 12

FAIRNESS AND JUSTICE

Think about the most recent experience you have had in which you felt unfairly treated (e.g., you learned that someone was paid more than you for identical work; a sales clerk helped someone else when you had been waiting in line longer; your phone company billed you for "hidden charges" after verbally promising there would be no such charges). What was your reaction to the unfair situation? Did you feel anger? Or resentment? Did you attempt to educate someone about the unfair practice or did you simply attempt to "get even"? Would your reaction have been different if the situation had involved a friend? Or a superior? In this chapter, we examine mental models of fairness in organizations and people's reactions to breaches of justice.

Nothing is more important to employees than being treated fairly and justly. Fairness and justice don't just pertain to compensation and rewards. Considerations such as work allocation, staffing, and respect are all factored into most people's perceptions of justice.

Distributive and Procedural Justice

There are two key ways of thinking about justice: *distributive justice* and *procedural justice*.[1] These two major branches of justice theory don't just reflect how scholars study justice, but also how organizations design justice systems and how people voice their concerns. **Distributive justice** is the science of how people allocate resources.[2] **Procedural justice** is the science of how people enact justice.[3] Thus, distributive justice answers the question of "how much I get"; procedural justice deals with the question of the process by which justice is doled out.

Distributive Justice

Distributive justice is the science of how people allocate resources.[4] Virtually all remuneration and pay systems in organizations are derivatives of a distributive justice scheme. Similarly, nonfinancial rewards, such as recognition, are also examples of distributive justice. Whereas people are highly concerned with money and pay, they also care about other things. For example, as we saw in Chapter 6 ("Relationships and Social Networks"), the resources that people care about can be concrete and tangible or highly abstract and very particular. Moreover, who is providing the resource can make a difference. For example, consider the simple act of praise. Whereas praise from a co-worker or subordinate is much appreciated, praise from a supervisor is even more appreciated.

REMUNERATION AND PAY Organizations struggle with the development of pay and incentive systems. The challenge is how to provide a clear link between merit (as based on achievement and effort) and reward. Rewarding the individual sometimes leads to competition within the team. As one person at a Fortune 100 company put it, "My company rewards the individual but relies on the team. As a consequence, people are at each others' throats."[5] This employee has correctly recognized that pay is the ultimate reinforcement mechanism. If a certain behavior is rewarded in an organization, it reinforces that behavior. Many companies are surprised at how their incentive systems backfire. According to Steve Kerr, companies often erroneously reward a given behavior *A,* while hoping to increase another behavior *B.* According to Kerr, many companies create incentive plans that backfire for fairly predictable reasons. One of those reasons is that organizations are often fascinated with "objective" criteria that can be easily measured and place too much emphasis on highly visible behaviors.[6]

There has been much concern about pay in organizations.[7] Business publications regularly create lists of CEOs who make the highest salaries. In 2006, Steven Jobs, CEO of Apple, made $646.6 million in total pay. (To see the top-paid CEOs in 2006, look at Exhibit 12.1.)

To put the pay of CEOs in perspective, the top 25 highest-paid CEOs' average pay came to $125.14 million in 2006. That is more than 8 times the average pay for all the CEOs in *Forbe*'s Executive Pay Scoreboard for the same period and more than 3,300 times the annual salary of the average U.S. worker.

There is growing concern that the amounts business leaders are paid are not justifiable. Proactive boards of directors are taking a direct hand in determining executive pay.[8] One of the most common benchmarks in compensation practice has been the competitive survey, which provides statistics on what several hundred companies pay executives. Based on the data, a median pay level for each position can be determined. However, because most companies want to pay above the median, this leads to salary inflation—without a commensurate increase in actual performance. As one director recently stated in a compensation decision, "If you want us to pay the executives at the 63rd percentile, then the company has to perform at the 63rd percentile."[9]

EXHIBIT 12.1 **The 25 Most Highly Paid Chief Executive Officers**

RANK	NAME	ORGANIZATION	PAY
1	**Jobs, Steven**	Apple	$646,600,000
2	**Irani, Ray**	Occidental Petroleum	$321,640,000
3	**Diller, Barry**	IAC/InterActiveCorp.	$295,140,000
4	**Foley, William**	Fidelity National Finl.	$179,560,000
5	**Semel, Terry**	Yahoo	$174,200,000
6	**Dell, Michael**	Dell	$153,230,000
7	**Mozilo, Angelo**	Countrywide Financial	$141,980,000
8	**Jeffries, Michael**	Abercrombie & Fitch	$114,640,000
9	**Lewis, Kenneth**	Bank of America	$99,800,000
10	**Duques, Henry**	First Data	$98,210,000
11	**Messmer, Harold Jr.**	Robert Half Intl.	$74,250,000
12	**Ellison, Lawrence**	Oracle	$72,420,000
13	**Simpson, Bob**	XTO Energy	$72,270,000
14	**Kovacevich, Richard**	Wells Fargo	$72,040,000
15	**Chambers, John**	Cisco Systems	$71,330,000
16	**Engles, Gregg**	Dean Foods	$66,080,000
17	**Frankfort, Lew**	Coach	$65,860,000
18	**Moglia, Joseph**	TD Ameritrade Holding	$62,240,000
19	**Dimon, James**	JPMorgan Chase	$57,170,000
20	**Berkley, William**	WR Berkley	$54,600,000
21	**Fuld, Richard Jr.**	Lehman Bros. Holdings	$51,650,000
22	**Whitacre, Edward Jr.**	AT&T	$49,010,000
23	**Ulrich, Robert**	Target	$48,090,000
24	**Hassey, L. Patrick**	Allegheny Technologies	$44,240,000
25	**Linde, Edward**	Boston Properties	$42,250,000

Source: Adapted from DeCarlo, S. (2007, May 21). Big paychecks. *Forbes, 179*(11), 112–116. Copyright © 2007 Forbes Media LLC. Reprinted by permission.

REWARDS AND RECOGNITION Base pay and base salary are one aspect of distributive justice; but in addition to base pay, there are other ways to reward and recognize organizational actors. Recognition is a powerful way to build employee loyalty and motivation. In addition to base pay, we consider five additional ways to reward employees: incentive pay, profit sharing, gain sharing, spot rewards, and recognition (see Exhibit 12.2).

Incentive pay, profit sharing, gain sharing, spot rewards, and recognition are all designed to increase employees' motivation to achieve organizational goals. In terms of salary, a person's base pay is how companies determine an individual's base salary. Such considerations are based on internal equity (based on job evaluation) and external equity (i.e., market data). The second issue in pay is variable pay. One type of variable pay is **incentive pay,** in which extra pay is tied to performance. (A critical issue concerns whether to reward effort or results.

EXHIBIT 12.2 **Methods of Rewarding Employees in Addition to Base Pay**

Type	Description/Example	Advantages	Disadvantages
Incentive Pay	Employee receives money based on increased performance against predetermined targets	Employee has a clear line of sight to goals that he/she can realistically affect and achieve	Is short-term in nature
Profit Sharing	A share of corporate profits are distributed in cash to all employees (driven by financial factors)	• Mobilizes all employees toward common goal • Informs and educates employees about financial well-being of organization (gives employees broader perspective)	Too far removed from any given employee's direct control (e.g., how can average employee increase stock price?)
Gain Sharing	A percentage of the value of increased productivity is given to workers under pre-arranged formula (driven by operational factors, such as quality, productivity, customer satisfaction, etc.)	• Similar advantages to profitsharing • Ideally suited to production-oriented employees	Too far removed from a given employee's direct control
Spot Rewards	One-time cash reward for employee (or team) who achieves major goal or performing beyond expectations	• Easy to implement (i.e., does not require layers of approval) • Generally inexpensive	Often rewards achievements instead of effort; this may lead employees to abandon important, but risky projects
Recognition	Usually noncash; special attention, honoring of employee	Touches employee at emotional level; serves as organizational culture-building device	If employees expect that everyone will eventually be recognized (e.g., employee of month, or birthday), then recognition is less distinctive and loses its value

Source: Thompson, L. (2004). *Making the team: A guide for managers* (2nd ed.), p. 44. Upper Saddle River, NJ: Prentice Hall. Reprinted by permission.

Obviously, results are most highly valued, but if everyone simply strives for positive results, there will be no tolerance for error, and it is through error and experimentation that some of the most important organizational breakthroughs are achieved.)

Profit sharing is a system in which a portion of the bottom-line economic profits that a company makes are given to employees. These profits may be distributed equally or based on seniority, performance, and so forth. Profit-sharing plans attempt to directly link employee pay with organizational economic health. In this way, they inform and educate employees about the importance of the financial health of the organization.

Gain sharing is similar in spirit to profit sharing, but involves a precise measure of productivity. In this sense, employees are offered a share of any increases in total organizational productivity against a specified benchmark. The organization establishes a historical base period of performance and uses this to determine whether gains in performance have occurred. Thus, the organization's performance is always compared with the time period before it started the gain-sharing plan.

Recognition is usually nonmonetary or noncash, but is often more meaningful to the employee. For example, Bank of America's recognition program uses a Customer Experience Leadership Award (CELA) plaque to recognize exceptional performance.[10] For example, if a customer writes a positive letter about an associate, the associate's manager might present him or her with a CELA in recognition. Also, in some cases, the accumulation of recognition is tied to a reward: An elite group of Bank of America employees is rewarded with a trip to New Orleans and Las Vegas after accumulating a number of CELAs.

THE BIG THREE DISTRIBUTIVE JUSTICE SYSTEMS There are several types of distributive justice systems. As we noted in Chapter 6, most people use one of three highly common justice principles when allocating resources: equality, equity, and need.[11]

Equality rule, or blind justice, is the simplest of the distributive justice principles. It simply prescribes equal shares for everyone concerned. Outcomes are distributed in an organization (or within a team) without regard to who has contributed what; consequently, everyone benefits (or suffers) equally. Some organizational systems, such as the educational system and the legal system in the United States, are examples of equality justice. In these systems, everyone receives equal entitlement. In a company, all employees have equal entitlement to sick days and internal review and grievance systems. The equality rule is one of the first rules that people learn; children are more likely to use equality than are adults.

Equity rule, or proportionality of contributions principle, is considerably more complex because it bases rewards and outcomes on what people have contributed. Equity rule is based on the idea that people who contribute more to an organization should be rewarded with more. The free market system in the United States is an example of the equity principle. Job titles and job pay are equity systems in most companies. People who bring more value and more human capital (e.g., experience and training) are rewarded with greater influence and rewards.

Needs-based rule, or welfare-based allocation, states that benefits should be proportional to need. The social welfare system in the United States is based on need. Also, within an organization, access to such benefits as child care and family medical leave is presumably based on need.

Most for-profit companies use an equity-based rule. However, at a deeper level, many organizations (even for-profit ones) brand themselves to their employees using different values, reflecting the different justice systems.[12] For example, Google and Intel have created an image (internally and externally) of being a challenging, cutting-edge place to work. Their value proposition appeals to employees who want to work for a top industry leader in a unique corporate culture. Thus, Google and Intel are examples of the equity rule: Do your best, and surround yourself with others who are doing the same, and you will be rewarded. In contrast, at Federal Express, employees are ingrained with the equality principle. There is no executive dining room, executive offices are modest, no one has a company car, and no one has an assigned parking spot.

SITUATION-SPECIFIC RULES OF FAIRNESS We have described equality, equity, and need as three distinct distributive justice systems that would appear to operate independently. However, in any organization each of these principles is operating in a different context at any given time. Thus, distributive justice rules are very situation-specific. As an example, consider the simple act of getting a cup of coffee. Each person buying a coffee is charged the same amount, no matter who they are. Thus, purchasing the coffee is an equality-based system. (Note that the same is true for traffic violations in the United States. Everyone found guilty of a traffic violation pays the same fine; however, in an equity-based system, such as Finland, fines for traffic violations are based on income—an equity-based system—so that one man who was speeding was charged $103,000!)[13] Suppose that, on the way into the coffee shop, you had trouble parking because there were no open parking spaces, except those reserved for handicapped persons displaying an appropriate sticker or label (needs-based system). Finally, while in the coffee shop, you worked on your term paper for your Business Strategy class, which will receive a grade based on merit (equity-based system).

You can imagine that within an organization, people might very well find themselves in conflict about which distributive justice system to use. Even if they could agree on that, they might disagree on what should be measured (e.g., in an equity-based system, do we base it on the amount of work accomplished or the hours it took to do the work?). Thus, different fairness rules apply in different situations.[14]

Often, people's goals determine their preferred method of distributive justice. For example, if the goal is to minimize waste, then a needs-based or social welfare policy is most appropriate.[15] If the organizational goal is to maintain or enhance harmony and group solidarity, equality-based rules are most effective.[16] If the organization's goal is to enhance productivity and performance, equity-based allocation is most effective. Consider the dilemma facing a student who is asked to allocate 100 points to her project team based on their perceived contributions. A student wishing to maximize harmony in the group would simply give each member of the four-person team 25 points. However, if the student anticipates working with the same project group in the next academic term, she might allocate based on perceived contributions.

Our relationships also influence our choice of fairness rules. When we share similar attitudes and beliefs with others, are physically close to one another, or anticipate future interaction, people often prefer equality rule. Moreover, when the allocation is public (i.e., others know what choices are made), organizational actors often prefer equality; in contrast, when the allocation is anonymous, equity is preferred. Friends tend to use equality; business partners use equity.[17] The choice of fairness rules also depends on whether people are dealing with rewards versus costs: Equality is often used to allocate benefits, but equity is more commonly used to allocate burdens.[18]

Equity Theory

Because issues of fairness are so key in all of our relationships, scholars developed equity theory to explain how people evaluate equity in relationships.[19] At first, the theory was applied to personal relationships, such as marriage and friendship; then, it was applied to organizational settings. At its core, equity theory assumes that:

▉ People are highly concerned with fairness in their relationships, so much so that when they perceive inequity, they become distressed. Equity theory places so much emphasis on fairness that it predicts people in relationships will feel distressed even if they are being paid too much.

▉ When people perceive inequity, they attempt to restore it, using whatever mechanism is easiest.

According to **equity theory,** people judge an outcome as "fair" when the ratio of their own inputs and outputs equals the ratio of the inputs and outputs of others. Equity theory argues that people make judgments about what is fair based on what they are investing in a relationship and what they are getting out of that relationship. Investments in a relationship (inputs) usually entail costs. For example, the person who produces a report and creates a presentation for a sales team incurs time and energy costs. The other members of the sales team who do not have to create the presentation or do the research, but perhaps just make the presentation, still enjoy the benefits of winning a contract. The outputs or outcomes that actors receive in an organization may be positive or negative. In short, outcomes such as praise, recognition, good grades, or a sales contract are positive. In many cases, A's input is B's outcome, and B's input is A's outcome. For example, a company pays (input) an employee (outcome) who gives time and expertise (input) to further the company's goals (outcome). Interestingly, many companies plot the "crossover" point at which the investments they had made in a given employee (in terms of remuneration, training, mentoring, etc.) lead to gains.

Measuring Equity

Equity exists in a relationship if each person's outcomes are proportional to his or her inputs. Equity, therefore, refers to the equivalence of the outcome/input *ratio* of the people in a relationship. Inequity exists when the ratio of outcomes to inputs is unequal. Equity exists when the profits (rewards minus costs) of two actors are equal.[20]

The advantage of equity theory is that it can mathematically measure equity in a relationship. Equity exists when a person perceives equality between the ratio of his or her own outcomes (O) to inputs (I) and the ratio of the other person's outcomes to inputs, where a and b represent two people.[21]

$$\frac{O_a}{I_a} = \frac{O_b}{I_b}$$

For example, suppose that two students are sharing a two-bedroom apartment. One of the bedrooms is 50 percent larger than the other, has a nice lake view, and is very quiet. The other bedroom is smaller, with no window, and is noisy. They agree that the student in the large bedroom should pay two thirds of the rent and the other student would pay one third. Although there is nothing special about two thirds or one third (it could easily be three quarters and one quarter), the students feel that the arrangement is equitable because the student paying more money (input) is enjoying a more desirable resource.

The above equity formula, while it is clear, is less applicable to situations in which inputs and outputs might be either positive or negative. To deal with this, the basic equity formula may be reconstructed as follows:

$$\frac{O_a - I_a}{|I_a|^{ka}} = \frac{O_b - I_b}{|I_b|^{kb}}$$

This formula proposes that equity prevails when the disparity between person a's outcomes and inputs and person b's outcomes and inputs are equivalently proportional to the absolute value of each of their inputs. The numerator is "profit" and the denominator adjusts for positive or negative signs of input. Each k takes on the value of either $+1$ or -1 depending on the value of participants' inputs and gains (outcomes minus inputs).

However, complications arise if two people have different views of what constitutes a valued investment, cost, or reward, and how they rank each one. For example, consider the salaries paid to basketball players in the NBA. With the starting players taking the greatest salaries (capped at a fixed amount), little is left over to pay the last three or four players on a 12-person team roster. The minimum salary of $427,163 might seem extraordinarily high to the average person, but in the context of the team, with an average salary of $5.2 million and a star salary of $23.75 million per year to the Boston Celtics' Kevin Garnett in 2007–2008 season, it reflects a sizeable disparity.[22]

Reactions to Inequity

What do organizational actors do when they "calculate" an inequity in their relationship? People who perceive themselves in an inequitable relationship feel distressed. As a case in point, consider what happened when two vice presidents of a major Fortune 100 company were promoted to senior vice president at about the same time.[23] Both of them moved into new offices, but one of them suspected his office was smaller. He pulled out blueprints and measured the square footage of each office and, sure enough, the other guy's office was a few feet larger. A former employee said, "He blew a gasket." Walls were moved and his office was reconfigured to make it as large as the other guy's.

In the same way, consider a situation in which one person, Tom, believes that he is contributing more than his business partner, Roy. Tom's own assessment is that he (Tom) is working longer days, forgoing dinner with his family for the sake of the business, and so on. Tom believes Roy is working shorter days, taking family vacations, and never working weekends. Yet they are both benefiting equally. Tom has at least six courses of action to restore equity:[24]

- *Alter the inputs.* (Tom could work less, by shortening his own hours.)
- *Alter the outcomes.* (Tom could suggest that he be given more remuneration than Roy.)
- *Cognitively distort inputs or outcomes.* (Tom could try to convince himself that although he works longer, he is learning a lot from putting in all those hours and building important social networks that will help him in the future.)
- *Leave the situation.* (Tom could dissolve the partnership or simply leave.)
- *Cognitively distort the inputs or outcomes of the other person.* (Tom could try to tell himself that although he works hard, Roy is the brilliant one.)
- *Change the object of comparison.* (Tom may stop comparing himself to Roy and focus on how much better his entire company is than that of his neighbor, Pete.)

The course of action that Tom takes depends on what is easiest for him to do and what will bring him the most desirable outcomes. Sometimes, it is easier to rationalize a situation than to address it. When you think about your own relationships, do you see a pattern in terms of how you attempt to restore equity?

It is almost impossible to overstate what people will do when they sense an inequity in a valued relationship. As a case in point, Greenberg examined the conditions under which employees would actually steal from their organizations as a way of balancing a perceived inequity.[25] In a laboratory investigation, an organization was created in which students performed a clerical task in which they were either equitably paid or markedly underpaid. Students were told to take their own pay in a situation in which they were led to believe that the supervisor would not be able to determine how much they took. Equitably paid people took precisely the amount they were supposed to take; in contrast, underpaid people took more than they were permitted to (i.e., they "stole").

Procedural Justice: The Science of How People Enact Justice

People in organizations not only evaluate the fairness of the outcomes they receive, but also the fairness of the procedures by which those outcomes are determined.[26] People's reactions to a variety of organizational outcomes are affected by their perceptions of the process.

The distinction between procedural and distributive justice is not merely conceptual, it arises naturally in people's cognitions about justice. For example, experiments manipulate procedures while holding outcomes constant and find that changes in procedure strongly affect perceptions of fairness.[27] People care just as much (and often more) about procedural justice than they do about distributive justice. People want to feel that they have been fairly *treated.*[28] In one of the most notable examinations of the pervasive effects of procedural justice, Tyler examined people's experiences with the police and courts.[29] To the extent that citizens believed that the police and/or court authority considered the person's own views of the situation, they were more likely to interpret a negative outcome (i.e., having to pay a traffic ticket) in a way that was sympathetic to the authorities.

People's evaluations of the fairness of procedures in their organization determine their satisfaction and willingness to comply with outcomes. For example, managers who educate their employees (e.g., explain to them why change is occurring, such as in the case of a merger) increase employee commitment to change.[30] In an investigation of 183 employees of seven private-sector organizations that had each just completed a relocation, perceived fairness was higher when justification was provided in the case of unfavorable change.[31]

There are several concepts that are central to the study of procedural justice, with the most important being that of voice.

Voice

Voice is, quite simply, letting people speak their mind and be heard. The important aspects of voice are that people feel that they have had a chance to explain why they did or did not do something. When people are given the opportunity to present information relevant to a decision, they believe that the process is fairer. The finding that voice greatly enhances perceptions of fairness is known as the process control effect[32] or the voice effect.[33] Even when it is made perfectly clear to people that voicing their concerns will have no effect on the decision itself, giving people voice still enhances their feelings that justice has been served.[34] A key question, however, is whether voice works because people believe that it will serve instrumental goals (i.e., a more favorable outcome) or whether voice matters for noninstrumental reasons. To test this idea directly, Lind, Kanfer, and Early examined whether procedural justice judgments were enhanced by an opportunity to voice one's views after a decision had been made.[35] Such "postdecision" voice could in no way affect an outcome, because the decision had already been made. Moreover, giving people voice after the fact could lead people to feel very frustrated.[36] Giving people voice either before or after a decision had been made enhanced feelings of fairness compared to situations in which people had no voice at all.[37] Further, predecision voice led to greater fairness judgments than did postdecision voice. Thus, people care about voice, especially when it has a chance to affect their outcomes.

There are several models that fall under the procedural justice umbrella, including Thibaut and Walker's original version, the group value model, the relational model of authority, and fairness heuristic theory.[38]

Thibaut and Walker's Model of Procedural Justice

Thibaut and Walker's model of procedural justice flows directly out of social exchange theory (see Chapter 6, "Relationships and Social Networks").[39] Thibaut and Walker argue that people are motivated to maximize their personal gains in their interactions with others and that people seek to control procedures so that they can indirectly control outcomes.[40]

Much of Thibaut and Walker's theoretical model focused on the conditions under which organizational actors involve third parties in dispute resolution.[41] In one investigation, organizational actors' preferences for particular kinds of dispute resolution were examined as a consequence of three factors—the need to resolve a dispute quickly, the degree of outcome correspondence, and the extent to which a clear standard exists for resolving disputes.[42] The different types of dispute resolution included **mediation** (third party suggests resolution, but does not impose it), **moot** (both disputants and third party must agree on resolution), **arbitration** (third party makes binding judgment), and **adjudication** (third party imposes resolution without input from the parties). Overall, organizational actors preferred arbitration most, followed by moot, mediation, no intervention, and finally, autocratic adjudication. Moreover, under severe time pressure, the presence of a standard, or severe noncorrespondence of outcomes, more third-party control was desired.

Group Value Model

The group value model has roots in Thibaut and Walker's model of procedural justice, but represents a dramatic departure from the underlying principle of self-interest.[43] If the heart of Thibaut and Walker's model[44] is self-interest and outcome maximization, the heart of Lind and Tyler's group value model is group identity.[45] That is, the **group value model** assumes that people are concerned about their long-term social relationship with the leaders or organizations responsible for justice systems. Most people in organizations view their relationships with the company with a long-term (as opposed to one-shot) perspective. The group value model is based on a group identification model, in which people, in a sense, define themselves in terms of their organizations.[46] People identify with social and organizational groups, so much so that these relationships are a critical part of their self-concept, and they seek to build long-term bonds with valued organizational members. People in organizations and teams are more likely to put aside their own self-interest and act in a way that helps all group members, if they trust that the person leading the group will act in a fair and responsible fashion. In particular, to the extent that the group believes that the decision-making procedure is neutral, that the decision makers are trustworthy, and that the organizational authorities will provide honest information about the group's social standing, then organizational members believe that the organization is acting fairly. Tyler tested the group value model by surveying a large random sample in Chicago with respect to their legal experiences, including appearances in court, calls to the police for help, and being stopped by the police.[47] Belief that authority figures are neutral and trustworthy was a more important predictor of people's feelings of fair treatment than was the actual outcome the people received in a given situation.

RELATIONAL MODEL OF AUTHORITY   The **relational model of authority** focuses on the conditions under which an authority is perceived to be a legitimate decision maker and is given discretionary power to make decisions for a committee.[48] According to Tyler and Lind, several aspects of legitimacy are important, with respect to legitimacy of the leader: (1) feelings of trust in the authority, (2) willingness to accept decisions, and (3) feelings of obligation to follow the rules authorities implement. Exhibit 12.3 illustrates two key dimensions that affect legitimacy: fairness and a focus on either outcomes or procedures. Tyler and Lind argue that the key to authoritativeness and legitimacy for leaders is not so much dependent on the decisions they make, but rather, on how their followers regard the procedures, process, and quality of interaction they have with their leader. Unlike outcomes, which change across circumstance and time, procedures are repeated across situations and across time. Because most people approach authorities with ambivalence, it is paramount for leaders to develop fair and consistent procedures.[49]

FAIRNESS HEURISTIC THEORY   **Fairness heuristic theory** is based on the group value model of procedural justice and the relational model of authority.[50] The theory assumes that, because ceding authority to another person provides an opportunity for exploitation and exclusion, people feel uncertain and uncomfortable about their relationships with an authority figure. Therefore, people ask themselves whether the authority can be trusted not to exploit them or threaten their identity.[51] The most common approach is to establish a fairness judgment, which then serves as a fairness heuristic that guides the interpretation of subsequent events.

EXHIBIT 12.3

Potential Determinants of Legitimacy

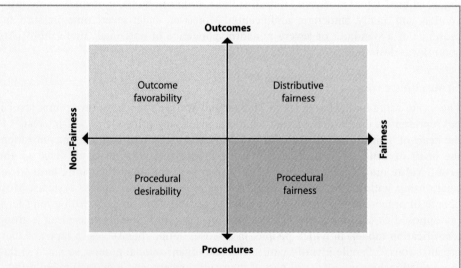

Source: Tyler, T. R., & Lind, A. (1992). A relational model of authority in groups. In M. Zanna (Ed.), *Advances in experimental social psychology* (Vol. 25, pp. 115–191), p. 124. San Diego, CA: Academic Press. Reprinted by permission of Elsevier.

Retributive Justice

Retributive justice is the science of how people "get even" and "retaliate a wrongdoing." For example, consider the Martha Stewart case in which the CEO was accused of lying about insider trading. There was much questioning about what her sentence should be if she were found guilty. Some believed that she was being made an example and that she could be of greater use to society by doing other things; still others believed it was important for her to serve actual time behind bars so as to set an example for other CEOs and famous folk.

In their treatment of retributive justice, Bies and Tripp give the following examples:[52]

- A boss takes credit for a subordinate's ideas and the subordinate responds by "bad-mouthing" the boss behind his back.
- A graduate student in the engineering department at a prestigious university murders a member of his dissertation committee because he believes that the committee is intentionally blocking his dissertation completion.[53]

In each of these examples, people are motivated by revenge, or the desire to get even. Moreover, most of these people believe that such revenge is justified—hence the term **retributive justice.** Bies and Tripp surveyed MBA students and asked them to give a personal account of an experience on the job in which they wanted to "get even."[54] The students' responses indicated that revenge could be best understood in terms of (1) the specific actions that violate trust; (2) the attributions and cognitions in response to the trust violation; and (3) the responses to the trust violation.

Evaluating Organizational Employees

When it comes to organizational rewards, it is assumed that people will be appropriately evaluated by their organizations. There are at least three types of evaluations: (1) supervisor evaluations; (2) peer evaluations; and (3) 360-degree evaluations. Stated another way, most employees routinely undergo a performance evaluation conducted by their immediate supervisors.

An increasingly popular form of evaluation is peer evaluation. If an employee's job responsibilities involve him or her working in a team with others, then those relevant others should have a chance to weigh in on how the employee performs as a team member. For peer evaluations to be effective, they should be conducted with reasonable anonymity; even under these conditions, the system is subject to contamination, such as in the case where employees mutually agree to rate one another highly so as to get raises, recognition, and the like. Another solution is not to tie pay to peer evaluations, but rather use them solely as a source of self-development.

For this reason, 360-degree evaluations have become increasingly popular, with the idea that a given employee has subordinates provide feedback, superiors provide feedback, and teammates provide feedback along with suppliers and customers. In short, the idea is to gain information about an employee from as many perspectives as possible.

Social Comparison

It is not just organizations that measure and evaluate their employees. People are constantly sizing themselves up against others. In fact, people have an irrepressible need to compare themselves to others. **Social comparison** is the act of comparing ourselves to others. In organizations, social comparison is rampant. Organizational members constantly compare the rewards and resources they hold with those held by others—office size, salary (of course), staffing, and so on. Organizational resources are constant remainders of how others compare to us. Given the powerful forces of social comparison, it is not surprising that, when it comes to pay and compensation, people are more concerned about how much they are paid relative to other people they consider to be peers than about the absolute level of their pay.

In organizations, people have essentially three choices that guide whom they compare themselves to:

Upward comparison occurs when people compare themselves to someone who is superior to them in terms of status or rank, or who is, simply, more accomplished. The young entrepreneur starting her own software company may compare herself to Sergey Brin of Google. Oftentimes, people compare upward for inspiration and motivation.

Downward comparison occurs when people compare themselves to someone who is less fortunate, of lower rank, less able, or lower in status. For example, when a young manager's marketing campaign proves to be a complete flop, she may compare herself to a colleague whose decisions led to the loss of hundreds of thousands of dollars. People engage in downward comparison to boost their self-esteem.[55]

Comparison with similar others occurs when people choose someone of similar background, skill, and ability with whom to compare. For example, students may compare themselves to other first-year students in their MBA program when assessing the quality of their summer internships. People engage in comparison with similar others when they desire to have accurate appraisals of their abilities.

When does the performance of another person in our organization enhance our self-concept, and when does it threaten our self-worth? According to Tesser's self-evaluation maintenance model, whether we feel threatened or prideful as a result of social comparison depends on our relationship to that person and how important that skill is to our self-worth (see Exhibit 12.4).[56]

When we observe someone close to us performing extremely well in an area that we highly identify with, our self-evaluation is threatened. Such "upward" comparison can lead to envy, competition, frustration, anger, and even sabotage. For example, upon hearing that a member of their college graduating class made an extremely timely investment in a company and is now a multimillionaire, finance majors probably feel threatened. The fact that our colleague excels in an area that we pride ourselves on rubs salt in the wounds of our psyche. Conversely, when another person outperforms us on a behavior that is irrelevant to our self-definition, the better their performance and the closer our relationship, the more we gain in self-evaluation. We take pride in their success.

Justice Systems

According to Messick all good justice (and incentive) systems in organizations share certain guiding principles: consistency, simplicity, effectiveness, and justifiability.[57] We supplement Messick's list with Levine and Thompson's list: consensus, generalizability, and satisfaction.[58]

EXHIBIT 12.4   **Tesser's Self-Evaluation Maintenance Model**

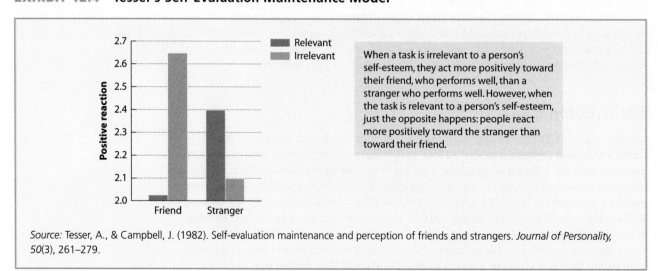

When a task is irrelevant to a person's self-esteem, they act more positively toward their friend, who performs well, than a stranger who performs well. However, when the task is relevant to a person's self-esteem, just the opposite happens: people react more positively toward the stranger than toward their friend.

Source: Tesser, A., & Campbell, J. (1982). Self-evaluation maintenance and perception of friends and strangers. *Journal of Personality, 50*(3), 261–279.

Consistency

A hallmark of an effective justice and incentive system is consistency or invariance across settings, time, and people. In short, the system should not adopt different standards for different people.

Simplicity

If people understand the system, it is more likely to work. Systems that are overly complex or confusing generate uncertainty, in some cases anxiety, and are more likely to backfire. In contrast, simple systems are most effective.

Effectiveness

Simply put, the justice system should be able to not only articulate standards and benchmarks; it should be able to produce or emit decisions.

Justifiability

The system should be justifiable to others. A justice system might be consistent, simple, and effective, but it may not be justifiable. For example, suppose that in one company, raises are based on physical attractiveness: Attractive people get big raises, others don't. This policy is consistent, simple, and effective, but hardly justifiable.

Consensus

Organizational members should agree on the justice system. Effective justice and incentive systems are internalized by organizational members, and norms act as strong guidelines for behavior and decision making in groups. Moreover, justice systems often outlive the particular members who are part of the system, and new members are indoctrinated with procedures that have been part of the organization.[59]

Generalizability

The justice system should be applicable to the organization at large.

Satisfaction

The justice system should be one in which organizational members feel satisfied.

Conclusion

Fairness and justice are top of mind for most people in any relationship. And, when it comes to their jobs, nothing stirs up more emotion, ignites, or extinguishes motivation as much as does the feeling of being treated fairly or not. We distinguish two major branches of justice theory: distributive justice (which focuses on the allocation of outcomes, both good and bad), and procedural justice, which focuses on the methods and procedures that authorities and organizations use to enact justice. We discussed the ultimate type of distributive justice in organizations: pay. And we noted that in addition to base pay, there are a variety of compensation-incentive systems, such as incentive-based pay, profit sharing, gain sharing, and recognition. None are perfect. We introduced equity theory as the leading theory of how people react when they perceive an injustice, and we noted that contrary to popular thought, people do not want to blindly take advantage whenever and wherever they can. Instead, people want rewards to be distributed equitably. We also discussed evaluation systems, such as peer feedback and 360-degree evaluations.

Notes

1. Thibaut, J. W., & Walker, L. (1975). *Procedural justice: A psychological analysis.* Hillsdale, NJ: Erlbaum.
2. Deutsch, M. (1985). *Distributive justice.* New Haven, CT: Yale University Press.
3. See note 1.
4. See note 2.
5. Personal communication, July 30, 2004.
6. Kerr, J. (1985). Diversification strategies and managerial rewards: An empirical study. *Academy of Management Journal, 28,* 155–179.
7. How much pay. . . . (2004, July/August). *Across the Board,* pp. 14–18.
8. Ibid.
9. Ibid.
10. Abrams, M. N. (2004, July/August). Employee retention strategies: Lessons from the best. *Healthcare Executive, 19*(4), 18.
11. See note 2.
12. See note 10.
13. Huuhtanen, M. (2002, April 15). Finnish man gets six-figure speeding ticket. *Associated Press.* Retrieved from http://www.freerepublic.com/focus/f-news/666155/posts on 9 September 2005.
14. Schwinger, T. (1980). Just allocation of goods: Decisions among three principles. In G. Mikula (Ed.), *Justice and social interaction.* New York: Springer-Verlag.
15. Berkowitz, L. (1972). Social norms, feelings and other factors affecting helping and altruism. In *Advances in experimental social psychology* (Vol. 6, pp. 63–108). New York: Academic.
16. Leventhal, G. S. (1976). Fairness in social relationships. In J. W. Thibaut, J. T. Spencer, & R. C. Carson (Eds.), *Contemporary topics in social psychology.* Morristown, NJ: General Learning Press.
17. Austin, W. (1980). Friendship and fairness: Effects of type of relationship and task performance on choice of distribution rules. *Personality and Social Psychology Bulletin, 6,* 402–408.
18. Sondak, H., Neale, M. A., & Pinkley, R. (1995). The negotiated allocation of benefits and burdens: The impact of outcome valence, contribution, and relationship. *Organizational Behavior and Human Decision Processes, 64,* 249–260.
19. Adams, J. S. (1965). Inequity in social exchange. In L. Berkowitz (Ed.), *Advances in experimental social psychology* (Vol. 2). New York: Academic Press; Walster, E., Berscheid, E., & Walster, G. W. (1973). New directions in equity research. *Journal of Personality and Social Psychology, 25,* 151–176; Walster, E., Walster, G. W., & Berscheid, E. (1978). *Equity: Theory & research.* Boston: Allyn & Bacon.
20. Homans, G. C. (1961). *Social behavior: Its elementary forms.* New York: Harcourt, Brace & World.
21. Adams, "Inequity in social exchange," p. 224.
22. HoopsHype.com. Retrieved on August 14, 2006, from http://www.hoopshype.com/salaries.htm.
23. Joyce, A. (2003, June 15). Bad news, good practices; prompt, thorough answers key to maintaining employee morale in crisis. *Washington Post.*
24. See note 21.
25. Greenberg, J. (1993). Stealing in the name of justice: Informational and interpersonal moderators of theft reactions to underpayment inequity. *Organizational Behavior and Human Decision Processes, 54,* 81–103.
26. Thibaut & Walker, *Procedural justice,* p. 220; Thibaut, J., & Walker, J. (1978). A theory of procedure. *California Law Review, 66,* 541–566; Lind, E. A., & Tyler, T. R. (1988). *The social psychology of procedural justice.* New York: Plenum Press; Tyler, T. R., & Lind, E. A. (1992). A relational model of authority in groups. In M. Zanna (Ed.), *Advances in experimental social psychology* (Vol. 25, pp. 115–191), p. 124. New York: Academic Press.
27. Thibaut, J., Friedland, N., & Walker, L. (1974). Compliance with rules: Some social determinants. *Journal of Personality and Social Psychology, 30,* 782–801.
28. Thibaut & Walker, "Theory of procedure," p. 226.
29. Tyler, T. R. (1987). Procedural justice research, *Social Justice Research, 1*(1), 41–65.
30. Kotter, J. P., & Schlesinger, L. A. (1979, March–April). Choosing strategies for change. *Harvard Business Review,* 4–11.
31. Daly, J. P., & Geyer, P. D. (1994). The role of fairness in implementing large-scale change: Employee evaluations of process and outcome in seven facility relocations. *Journal of Organizational Behavior, 15,* 623–638.
32. See note 28.
33. Folger, R. (1977). Distributive and procedural justice: Combined impact of "voice" and improvement on experienced inequity. *Journal of Personality and Social Psychology, 35,* 108–119.
34. Kanfer, R., Sawyer, J., Earley, P. C., & Lind, E. A. (1987). Participation in task evaluation procedures: The effects of influential opinion expression and knowledge of evaluative criteria on attitudes and performance. *Social Justice Research, 1,* 235–249; Folger, "Distributive and procedural justice," p. 227; Lind, E. A., Kurtz, S., Musante, L., Walker, L., & Thibaut, J. W. (1980). Procedure and outcome effects on reactions to adjudicated resolution of conflicts of interest. *Journal of Personality and Social Psychology, 39,* 643–653.
35. Lind, E. A., Kanfer, R., & Early, P. (1990). Voice, control, and procedural justice: Instrumental and non-instrumental concerns in fairness judgments. *Journal of Personality and Social Psychology, 59,* 952–959.
36. See note 33.
37. See note 35.
38. See note 3.
39. See note 3.
40. See note 3.
41. See note 3.
42. Thibaut & Walker, *Procedural justice,* p. 220; LaTour, S., Houlden, P., Walker, L., & Thibaut, J. (1976). Procedure: Transnational perspectives and preferences. *Yale Law Journal, 86,* 258–290.
43. Tyler & Lind, "Relational model," p. 226.
44. See note 1.
45. See note 43.
46. Tajfel, H. (1978). *Differentiation between social groups.* London: Academic Press.

47. Tyler, T. R. (1989). The psychology of procedural justice: A test of the group-value model. *Journal of Personality and Social Psychology, 57,* 830–838.

48. See note 43.

49. Ibid.

50. Ibid.

51. Lind & Tyler, *Social psychology of procedural justice,* p. 226; Tyler & Lind, "Relational model of authority in groups," p. 226; Huo, Y. J., Smith, H. J., Tyler, T. R., & Lind, E. A. (1996). Superordinate identification, subgroup identification, and justice concerns: Is separatism the problem, is assimilation the answer. *Psychological Science, 7,* 40–45.

52. Bies, R. J., & Tripp, T. (1995). Beyond distrust: "Getting even and the need for revenge." In R. Kramer & T. R. Tyler (Eds.), *Trust in organizations* (pp. 246–260), p. 246. Newbury Park, CA: Sage.

53. Zeman, D., Walsh-Sarnecki, P. & Helms, M. (1998, December 12). Grad student faces charges in slaying of WSU professor. *Detroit Free Press.* Retrieved January 10, 2005, from www.freep.com/news/locway/qwsu12.htm.

54. See note 52.

55. See note 47.

56. Tesser, A., & Campbell, J. (1982). Self-evaluation maintenance and perception of friends and strangers. *Journal of Personality, 59*(3), 261–279.

57. Messick, S. (1993). Validity. In R. L. Linn (Ed), *Educational measurement* (2nd ed., pp. 13–104). Phoenix: American Council on Education and Oryx Press.

58. Levine, J. M., & Thompson, L. (1996). Conflict in groups. In E. T. Higgins & A. W. Kruzlanski (Eds.), *Social psychology: Handbook of basic principles* (pp. 745–776). New York: Guilford.

59. Bettenhausen, K., & Murnighan, J. K. (1985). The emergence of norms in competitive decision-making groups. *Administrative Science Quarterly, 30,* 350–372; Levine, J. M., & Moreland, R. L. 1994. Group socialization: Theory and research. In W. Stroebe & M. Hewstone (Eds.), *European review of social psychology* (pp. 305–336). Chichester, England: Wiley.

Chapter 13

DIVERSITY AND CULTURE

Think of a group, team, or organization of which you are a member and that you highly value. Think about the people in the group. Now, think about what makes you a particularly distinctive member of this group. List all the ways you are different from the other members of your group. Put a star next to the most critical differences. How would an outside observer recognize you, if he or she were to observe the group? What would be the key way in which you would distinguish yourself from the group?

Looking back at how you described yourself as different from your group, what type of characteristic did you focus on? Your appearance? Your gender? Your personality traits? There are a potentially infinite number of dimensions by which we can distinguish ourselves from others. Some of these dimensions seem superficial, such as age, gender, or hair color. Other dimensions are not as obvious, such as intelligence or political attitude. Is the dimension that you mention important in terms of the type of work that the group does? Some distinctions might seem, in certain contexts, to be inappropriate to mention, such as race and ethnicity.

In this exercise, you have engaged in a type of diversity awareness. You have observed yourself as an individual and you have attempted to focus on how you are unique and distinct from your group. In this chapter, we will focus on diversity and what makes it important for organizational effectiveness.

The exhibit that outlines FBI recruiting criteria (Exhibit 13.1) indicates several things relevant to diversity. First, most people often hold faulty stereotypes. Second, many organizations can profit by hiring a less traditional (i.e., more diverse) workforce. And third, education is key in managing diversity. However, let's be honest. When most people think of diversity, they think of corporate rules and regulations. As one colleague put it on his first day on the job, he received a 300-page manual on sexual harassment. Yet, it is an empirical fact that the workforce is increasingly diverse, not only with respect to demography (e.g., race, gender, national origin), but also with respect to work styles, intellectual training, and so on.

In this chapter, we define diversity. We raise the question of what diversity achieves for the organization, and then make a business case for diversity. We point to four serious problems that need to be addressed in organizations, which represent the biggest threats to diversity. We then deal with the issues of gender diversity and cultural diversity.

Diversity Defined

One way of thinking about diversity is in terms of four distinct layers (see Exhibit 13.2).

The most basic type of diversity is that based on **personality.** As we saw in Chapter 2, there are fundamental aspects of human personality that differ from person to person. In this sense, everyone (even identical twins) has a different personality from anyone else. One level up from personality diversity is what Gardenswartz and Rowe refer to as **internal aspects,** which are less visible than external aspects, and include age, race, ethnicity, physical ability, sexual orientation, and gender. One level up from internal dimensions is **external aspects,** which are, by definition, more visible and include geographic location, income, personal habits, recreational habits, religion, educational background, work experience, appearance, parental status, and marital status. Finally, the

EXHIBIT 13.1   FBI Recruiting Criteria

The FBI wants you, especially if you are a female, according to the Applicant Coordinator for the FBI. Historically, the FBI has found it difficult to attract qualified women to apply for the position of Special Agent. Of the 11,649 Special Agents in the force, only 2,105 (18 percent) are women. The question is why. The stereotype of the typical FBI agent is totally masculine—a door-busting, gun-toting, tough guy. This stereotype just does not fit with how most women view themselves. Consequently, most women say "I'm not qualified"; "you would not want me"; "I can't shoot a gun"; "I can't knock down a door," etc. However, FBI recruiters want to regenerate the FBI stereotype. The skills that make for an effective FBI agent, especially in the post-9/11 world, involve the ability to recognize patterns, pick up on innuendo, and defuse hostility. And forget the college major in law enforcement; a degree in computer science or engineering is much more desirable. As for why females are so attractive as Special Agents—they can detect subtle changes in facial expression— immensely useful in investigatory interviews. Their verbal skills and tendency to rely on landmarks (rather than maps) make them better at discerning patterns. As it turns out, a key skill is "linkage," the ability to establish commonalities or links between such things as victims' occupations and ages. Women's interpersonal skills make them better able to engender trust and defuse violent situations. Such abilities result in fewer lawsuits. In short, physical prowess is less key than mental and emotional prowess.

Source: Adapted from Knights, J. J. (2004, July 1).What makes a woman valuable as an FBI special agent? *Women Police.*

EXHIBIT 13.2 **Four Layers of Diversity**

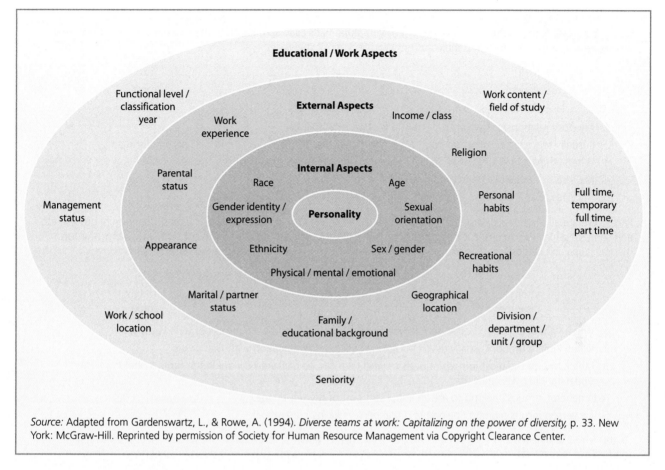

Source: Adapted from Gardenswartz, L., & Rowe, A. (1994). *Diverse teams at work: Capitalizing on the power of diversity,* p. 33. New York: McGraw-Hill. Reprinted by permission of Society for Human Resource Management via Copyright Clearance Center.

broadest level is **organizational aspects,** which include functional level or classification, work content or field of expertise, division, unit or group, seniority, work location, union affiliation, and management status.[1]

Individual, Relational, and Collective Selves

People's self-concept consists of three fundamental self-representations: the individual self, the relational self, and the collective self. People define themselves in terms of their unique traits (individual self), in terms of their dyadic relationships (relational self), and in terms of their group memberships (collective self).[2]

The **individual self** is realized by differentiating ourselves from others and relies on interpersonal comparison processes; it is associated with the motive of protecting or enhancing the person psychologically.[3] The **relational self** is achieved by assimilating with significant others (i.e., relationship partners, such as parents, friends, siblings, etc.) and is based on personalized bonds of attachment. Such bonds include parent-child relationships, friendships, romantic relationships, specific teacher-student, boss-subordinate, or client-provider relationships. The **collective self** is achieved by inclusion in large social groups and by contrasting the group to which one belongs with relevant out-groups. The collective self contains those aspects of the self-concept that differentiate the in-group members from members of relevant out-groups (e.g., rivalries between dorms, rivalries between different sporting groups, such as the Cubs and the White Sox, or rivalries between different brands, such as PC and Mac users, and so on).

These three self-representations coexist within the same person. However, at any given time, one or more of these different self-identities may seem relevant. (See Exhibit 13.3 to assess your chronic relational versus collective identity.) Your score on Part 1 reflects your relational identity. Your score on Part 2 reflects your collective identity. It is possible that both are high or low.

EXHIBIT 13.3 **Relational and Collective Identity**

Part 1: Your task is to indicate the extent to which you agree with each statement. In the space next to each statement, please, write the number that best indicates how you feel about the statement.

1	2	3	4	5	6	7
strongly disagree						strongly agree

1. My close relationships are an important reflection of who I am.___
2. I usually feel a strong sense of pride when someone close to me has an important accomplishment.___
3. When I think of myself, I often think of my close friends or family as well.___
4. My sense of pride comes from knowing I have close friends.___
5. My close relationships are important to my sense of what kind of person I am.___

Part 2: We are all members of different groups some of which we choose (such as sports teams, community groups, etc.) and some of which we do not (such as racial or religious groups). We would like you to consider your various group memberships and respond to the following questions with them in mind. Please, use the same scale as above.

1	2	3	4	5	6	7
strongly disagree						strongly agree

1. When I am in a group, it often feels to me like that group is an important part of who I am.___
2. When I join a group, I usually develop a strong sense of identification with that group.___
3. I think one of the most important parts of who I am can be captured by looking at groups I belong to and understanding who they are.___
4. In general, groups I belong to are an important part of my self-image.___
5. If a person insults a group I belong to, I feel personally insulted myself.___

Source: Table 2 (adapted) from page 795 from Cross, S. E., Bacon, P. L., & Morris, M. L. (2000). The relational-interdependent self-construal and relationships. *Journal of Personality and Social Psychology, 78*(4), pp. 791–808. Reprinted by permission of American Psychological Association.

Optimal Distinctiveness Theory

The theory of optimal distinctiveness[4] is a theory of collective social identity. The theory was developed to explain why people seek and maintain conceptualizations of the self that extend to the collective level.[5] **Optimal distinctiveness theory** argues that a person's collective identity derives from the interplay of two opposing social motives: inclusion and differentiation. On the one hand, people desire to be included in larger social collectives, such as organizations and groups. However, people also want to feel distinct or different from others. The two different motives act as opposing drives and hold a person in check. For example, as a person becomes immersed in larger and more inclusive social units (e.g., classmates, dorm, university, etc.), the need for inclusion is decreased, but the motive to differentiate himself or herself increases. Conversely, as a person moves toward disconnection from large social collectives (such as might a person who works from a home office), the need for inclusion increases. The optimal collective social identity meets a person's need for inclusion by assimilating with groups and organizations and serves a need for differentiation by distinguishing oneself from others. Think about a group of which you are a part. When have you desired more differentiation? When did you desire greater inclusion? What did you do?

The Business Case for Organizational Diversity

How does diversity affect the organizational actor and the organization? Once again, it is useful to consider the impact of diversity on each of the four key levels of analysis in this book.

Individual Level

At an individual level, diversity can have positive effects.[6] It is useful to examine how diversity affects a person's **commitment** to her or his organization and group. Members of different demographic groups respond differently to being the "token" (dissimilar) member of their work group. For example, when men are the numerical minority in their work groups, they are absent more often, less committed, and more likely to leave.[7] People who are more dissimilar to a group are more likely to express lower commitment and reduced affect, and more likely to leave.[8] Chatman and O'Reilly examined 178 professional men and women in a clothing retailing organization and found that women were more likely to want to leave homogenous groups than were men, even though they expressed greater commitment, positive affect, and cooperation in their all-female groups.[9]

Interpersonal Level

Diversity affects our choices for friendship and information. Diversity affects how people build their social networks. Ibarra distinguished motivations for homophily (seeking out similar others and high-status others) as explanations for how men and women build their social networks.[10] Women are more likely to differentiate their networks: They choose women as friends but choose men to gain access to organizational rewards. Men, in contrast, prefer relationships with men for both instrumental and social support needs.

Teams and Groups

Diverse groups are likely to contain at least two types of diversity: social-cultural diversity (i.e., race, gender, etc.) and intellectual diversity (e.g., functional expertise).[11] Not surprisingly, the impact of diversity on the performance of small groups and teams is more mixed.[12] Phillips, Mannix, Neale, and Gruenfeld used Heider's balance theory to argue that information sharing in diverse groups depends on the match between intellectual diversity (what people know) and gender and racial diversity.[13] In theory, diverse teams have access to more points of view and perspectives on a problem. Phillips et al. constructed groups that either had congruent ties (groups of friends that also share the same intellectual knowledge) or incongruent ties (group members who are socially tied but possess different information; and group members who are socially tied but are more intellectually similar to a stranger). A three-person group with congruent social and knowledge ties utilized information more effectively, reported a more effective group process, and actually made better and more accurate group decisions than groups with incongruent ties.[14]

Organizational Level

One theory of diversity is Blau's theory of heterogeneity, which considers organizations low, moderate, and high in cultural diversity.[15] Blau proposes a curvilinear relationship between diversity and organizational performance, such that very low and very high levels of diversity result in better outcomes than do moderate levels of diversity. Within culturally homogeneous groups, people communicate more often, presumably because they hold shared perceptions.[16] As cultural diversity increases, however, social comparison and social categorization problems occur and an us-versus-them mentality is created. This results in similar-gender or similar-race based groups, group conformity, and negative attitudes toward out-groups. This adds up to negative performance outcomes for organizations.[17] The very factors that lead to negative performance with moderate levels of diversity could actually conspire to produce positive outcomes when diversity is very high.[18] Because group members will be more evenly diffused over various categories of cultural diversity, in-groups and out-groups will not be as visible.[19] The very fact that there is less in common for subgroup formation (e.g., gender, race) makes it more likely that people will base their friendship and communication not on superficial categories, but on other factors. The effects of diversity were examined in 700 banks with $100 million or less in total assets.[20] In banking firms with highly innovative strategic postures, both low and high management group diversity were associated with higher productivity than moderate levels of diversity.

What is the optimal level of diversity? Either a very low or very high amount of diversity might be ideal. However, the nature of the diversity—intellectual, cultural, gender, and so on—is yet another consideration.[21]

Barriers to Diversity

The above analysis of the effects of diversity implicates a number of social-cognitive phenomena that occur in organizations. If diversity is such a good idea for organizations and their people, what is to prevent people from adopting it? There are four powerful psychological principles that erect barriers to diversity: stereotyping, the homogeneity principle, in-group bias, and privilege systems.

Stereotyping

Many people are under the mistaken impression that discrimination and prejudice are a thing of the past; however, prejudiced attitudes and racial bias are still commonplace.[22] This faulty belief creates a serious problem: Only the victims (and likely targets) of prejudice are apt to perceive stereotyping. Others will defensively claim that it is not there because they cannot perceive it. For example, women are more likely than men to perceive sexism and racism.[23] Similarly, African Americans are more likely than Caucasian Americans to perceive racism. This denial—the belief that "I have not seen it"—is an act of discrimination itself.

Stereotyping is the tendency to make judgments of others based on their membership in certain groups, not based on knowledge of that person himself or herself. In fact, within microseconds of meeting people we "categorize" or "stereotype" a person according to gender, race, and age. Even when people are given an opportunity to consider stereotypical and nonstereotypical information about someone, they preferentially attend to stereotype-confirming rather than disconfirming information. When given an opportunity to interview another person, most people seek to confirm their stereotypical beliefs about him or her. For example, when people interview someone who they are led to believe is an extrovert, they ask the person more questions that would lead to answers consistent with an extrovert.[24] Similarly, when people believe that someone is an introvert, they ask questions that yield answers consistent with introversion.

If stereotyping is the cognitive aspect of prejudice, then racism is its emotional aspect and racial discrimination its behavioral aspect. To investigate the extent of race-based discrimination in hiring, the Urban Institute in Washington, D.C., selected and trained minority and majority group testers. Testers were matched on age, gender, physical strength and size, appearance, education, experience, demeanor, openness, observed energy level, and articulateness—in short, all possible characteristics relevant to hiring, except for race.[25] Then, the testers applied for the same advertised low-skill, entry-level job; 476 audits conducted by 10 pairs of tests (one African American and one Caucasian American male) revealed clear differences in treatment of minority and majority job seekers. In 20 percent of the audits, Caucasians progressed further in the hiring process than their equally qualified African American testing partners; in 15 percent of the audits, the Caucasian received a job offer but his African American counterpart did not. These findings suggest that Caucasian males continue to receive favorable treatment in the hiring process three times more frequently than their equally qualified African American counterparts.[26] Moreover, government data agree with these field results: In 2006, the Office of Federal Contract Compliance Programs obtained settlements worth $51,525,235 for 15,273 minority and female workers who were victims of discrimination.[27] Full-time working women in the United States earn 77 percent of full-time working men, and the earnings of African American households were 61 percent of Caucasian households.[28] These statistics clearly suggest that gender and racial discrimination are hardly a thing of the past.

is a member of that social group to perform less well. Steele further conjectured that in the situations where the stereotype is triggered, it is more "on the brain" than it is for other groups.[51] Consequently, he created a situation in which he asked test-takers to complete words when given only a few letters. Specifically, the stereotype-activation measure asked participants to complete 80 word fragments, 10 of which Steele knew from pretesting could be completed with words symbolic of African American stereotypes (e.g., _ce [race], la_ [lazy], or p_r [poor]) and 5 of which could be completed with, among other words, words signifying self-doubts (e.g., lo__ [loser], du_ [dumb], or sha_ [shame]). And, in line with Steele's theory, African American participants who were "primed" with test-taking were more likely to complete the words consistent with the African American stereotype and the self-doubt related words.[52]

Privilege Systems

According to Rosette, the historically dominant perspective that drives diversity issues in organizations views inequality as the result of mistreatment perpetrated against the disadvantaged party.[53] This perspective holds the advantaged group as the normative group and views the disadvantaged group as different. A different perspective holds that inequity is the result of the privileged treatment received by advantaged groups. In many organizational settings, status hierarchies result in the conferral of privileges that are based on achievement. However, in the same settings, status may result in the bestowal of privileges that are unearned. Rosette argues that these unearned privileges are often awarded based on *ascribed* characteristics, but are perceived to be *achieved*.[54] Achieved statuses are those that require special qualities and are left open to be filled through competition and individual effort (e.g., income, occupation, education). Where ascribed status is predominant, people are respected because of the family that they are born into, because of their affiliations and group membership, and, later in life, because of their age and seniority. People are accorded status through inheritance, or as a result of characteristics such as social class, gender, or race. In organizational settings, high status may result in the conferral of privileges that are often not merit-based and therefore unearned. The unearned nature of the privilege, however, is often not acknowledged by the organizational actor and others in the organization and may even be perceived as being earned.[55] Rosette and Tost surveyed more than 500 employees who worked in organizations where the majority of the employees were White. White employees agreed that they could engage in activities such as excelling in challenging situation at work without being called a "credit to their race"; they could also arrive late to a meeting without having tardiness reflect negatively on their racial group. However, Black, Hispanic, and Asian employees reported that such activities were less available to them in the work place.[56] Rosette created group situations in which some groups clearly had an unearned privilege, whereas others did not.[57] In her investigation, groups had to create mobiles (decorative elements that hang overhead). Some groups were given much better raw materials (e.g., colored paper, streamers, etc.) than others. Even though "privileged" groups saw that other groups had impoverished materials, the privileged groups did not admit they had an advantage. They simply took more credit. Those that had unearned privilege were not aware that they were benefiting by factors that were not available to other groups.

Creating and Sustaining Diversity

Suppose that your organization has decided to diversify on one of the dimensions discussed earlier. What is the best method or practice to ensure the success of the diversity program? There are three major approaches to diversity: affirmative action, valuing diversity, and managing diversity.[58] (See Exhibit 13.4.)

Affirmative Action

Affirmative action is designed to correct inequities and inequalities in the workforce. As such, it provides special consideration for people whose social groups have suffered discrimination in the past. In this sense, affirmative action is a remedial measure whose purpose is to right a past wrong. Examples of affirmative action include quotas (i.e., providing a guaranteed number of slots, spaces, or positions for people representing a certain targeted group) or "race-conscious remedies."[59] The goal of the affirmative action

EXHIBIT 13.4

Three Approaches for Dealing with Diversity

Approach	Focus	Initiating Force	Benefits
Affirmative Action (Remedial)	Equality of opportunity	Laws	Targeted groups
Valuing Diversity (Idealistic)	Appreciation of differences	Ethics	All employees
Managing Diversity (Realistic)	Leveraging talents and skills	Corporate strategy	The organization and the employees

Adapted from: Gardenswartz, L., & Rowe, A. (1994). *Diverse teams at work: Capitalizing on the power of diversity.* New York: McGraw-Hill.

approach is to give people who have been previously disadvantaged an opportunity to assimilate. Affirmative action allows groups that have been historically disadvantaged an opportunity to catch up with those who have been historically privileged. The biggest roadblock to affirmative action is that those who enjoy privilege do not realize it.

Valuing Diversity

Valuing diversity is an idealistic approach that seeks to celebrate and approach differences. The policies dictated by such an approach might vary from allowing employees to wear the dress and observe the customs of their country of birth while at work to having a multicultural company potluck dinner. The valuing diversity approach is focused on educating others about the cultures of other groups, particularly groups with which they may not be familiar. The focus in valuing diversity is the celebration of differences and the respect of different categories. Whereas the affirmative action model focuses on assimilation, the valuing diversity approach focuses on maintaining unique differences with deeper appreciation and respect.

Managing Diversity

The managing diversity approach focuses on how to leverage differences among people in such a way that people complement one another and on how to best utilize the talents within the organization. Thus, the focus of managing diversity is skill building across the organization. The synergy model argues that the whole or best combination of parts is greater than their mere sum. There are several different methods by which organizations can manage diversity, including the contact hypothesis.

CONTACT HYPOTHESIS According to the contact hypothesis, people who are diverse may be able to negotiate their coexistence and profit from mutual exchange by merely coming into contact with one another. The contact hypothesis has been tested and confirmed, so perhaps it should be called the *contact effect*. The **contact hypothesis** is based on the principle that greater contact among members of different groups increases cooperation and trust between group members. However, contact in and of itself does not lead to better intergroup relations, and in some cases may even exacerbate negative relations between groups. For example, contact between African Americans and Caucasian Americans in desegregated schools does not reduce racial prejudice;[60] and there is little relationship between interdepartmental contact in organizations and conflict in organizations.[61] Also, college students studying in foreign countries become increasingly negative toward their host countries the longer they remain in them.[62]

Several conditions need to be met before contact can have its desired effects on reducing prejudice:

- *Social and institutional support:* For contact to work, there should be a framework of social and institutional support. That is, people in positions of authority should be unambiguous in their endorsement of the integration policies' goals. This fosters the development of a new social climate in which more tolerant norms can emerge.

■ *Acquaintance potential:* There should be sufficient frequency, duration, and close-ness between people to permit the development of meaningful relationships between members of the groups. Infrequent, short, and casual interaction will not foster more favorable attitudes and may even make them worse.[63] One key to successful contact is self-disclosure, or the revealing of personal information about oneself.[64]

■ *Equal status:* A key aspect of successful contact is that group members need to have equal status. If contact involves unequal-status relationships, with some people in the subordinate role, stereotypes are likely to be reinforced rather than weakened.[65]

■ *Shared goal:* Another key aspect for successful contact is that members of diverse groups must work toward a shared goal. Ideally, they should be dependent on each other for the achievement of the goal. In other words, if a minority of individuals in the group can achieve the goal without the cooperation and input of others, then contact is not likely to work.

The contact hypothesis has received support in groups ranging from students at a multiethnic high school to banking executives involved in corporate mergers.[66]

CROSS-CUT ROLE ASSIGNMENTS **Cross-cut role assignments** are situations in which people are simultaneously members of more than one task group or team. Cross-cut role assignments decrease in-group bias of both minority and majority groups.[67] In one example, employees "shadow" other employees for a full day. Each week, one employee observes and develops a relationship with a fellow employee in an unfamiliar department. The program at Anthro Technology Furniture, for example, assigns members of the manufacturing department to join the accounting team for a day; warehouse employees get involved in marketing, and so on. The cofounder and vice president of marketing and sales, Cathy Filgas, says, "You simply cannot spend an entire day with a person, eat lunch with them, and walk away with a sense of animosity."[68]

Educate Members on the Reasons Underlying the Plan

Rather than simply stating the advantages of diversity, organizational leaders should explain it in hard numbers. Instead of preaching to the team (e.g., "you should diversify because it is the law"), managers should explain why diversity is in organizational members' best interests.

Gender Diversity

Gender diversity in organizations is an ongoing debate. Anyone who thinks that the days of gender inequity are a thing of the past is seriously misinformed. The pay gap is real. The glass ceiling is real and the double standard is real.

Gender Pay Gap: The Evidence

A male–female earnings gap has persisted for over 50 years. Furthermore, there is no evidence to suggest that it is narrowing.[69] Media reports sometimes suggest that the gender pay gap is disappearing or narrowing.[70] Contrary to this optimistic belief, data released by the U.S. Census Bureau, the U.S. General Accounting Office, and the Internal Revenue Service (IRS) suggest a significant chasm between men's and women's pay. Women's pay is nearly 76 percent of what men's compensation is.[71] The ratio of men to women in particular salary brackets is highest at the highest income levels. For example, for salaries of $1 million or more, the ratio of men to women is 13:1, and it is necessary to drop down to the $25,000 to $30,000 range before the numbers of men and women in an income category start to look equal.

However, over her career, a woman makes only 44 percent of what the average man makes.[72] Rose and Hartmann studied the average earnings of men and women between the prime working ages of 26 and 59 for a 15-year period from 1983 to 1998.[73] First, most women worked most of their adult lives—kids or not—clocking an average of 12 out of 15 years. More than half of the women spent at least a year out of the labor force, which ended up hurting their earnings severely. The women who "dropped out" for a time earned an average of $21,363 *over the years they actually worked* compared to nearly $30,000 for women who worked all 15 years. Dropping out for a time may seriously derail one's career and permanently slash one's pay. Taking one year off results in a 32 percent pay reduction, two years off reduces pay by 46 percent, and three years slices pay by 56 percent. Yet, there is a strange equality: The same negative pay effects happen to men if they take the same time off. However, fewer than 8 percent of men take time off.[74]

Glass Ceiling: The Evidence

A small, but highly visible subset of women has made great strides in traditionally male-dominated jobs: Carly Fiorina as CEO of Hewlett-Packard; Madeline Albright's reign as Secretary of State; and the smattering of female celebrities (Oprah Winfrey) and law, business, and financial pundits (e.g., Suze Orman). It may be that because such famous names are so easily called to mind, we gain a false sense that everything is OK concerning gender equality, when it is not.

Just 15 percent of women work in jobs that are typically held by men, such as engineer, stockbroker, and judge, while fewer than 8 percent of men hold female-typed jobs, such as nurse, teacher, or sales clerk. Overall, women earn less than men with the same education at all levels: Male dropouts earned an average of $36,000 per year between 1983 and 1998, after inflation adjustments, but women with a bachelor's degree made $35,000. Women with a graduate degree (e.g., MBA, PhD, etc.) earned $42,000, but men got nearly $77,000.[75]

Double Standards: The Evidence

Considerable research has focused on how perceived sex differences (e.g., in intelligence, competence, assertiveness, etc.) prevent women from being selected as leaders.[76] One prescription, therefore, is to "coach" women to behave more like men. However, this may not work and perhaps even can backfire.

According to Rudman and Glick, women in organizations face a Catch-22.[77] If they behave in *agentic* ways (i.e., goal-directed and assertive, necessary to attain leadership roles), they achieve competence ratings equal to those for agentic men.[78] However, they suffer on evaluations of interpersonal skills. Specifically, these agentic women are viewed as socially deviant, compared to identically qualified men, which may result in hiring discrimination.[79] Thus, women who strive for leadership positions are in a double bind. They can act "communal" (i.e., with people-friendly behaviors) and be liked, but not respected; or they can engage in agentic behaviors and be respected, but not liked. Obviously, in both cases, they may fall short on leadership selection criteria.

The fallout that happens as a result of women engaging in counter-stereotypical behavior (such as taking a leadership role in an organization) has been termed the *backlash effect*.[80] The backlash can be particularly severe for people who step outside gender bounds—also known as *gender deviants*.[81] For example, female leaders who exhibit a directive style receive more negative evaluations than those who have a participatory style;[82] likewise, female speakers are less persuasive when their style is "task-oriented" rather than "people-oriented."[83] Assertiveness is viewed negatively in women;[84] if females succeed, their co-workers, both male and female, may view them as unsociable and difficult to work with.[85] In one investigation, a competition between organizational actors was set up so that people lost to either a stereotypical man or woman, or a nonstereotypical man or woman.[86] Both men and women were more likely to sabotage "deviants"—i.e., nonstereotypical people. Furthermore, when people engaged in sabotage, they had a rush of self-esteem, suggesting that backlash is psychologically rewarding. The organizational members who were the deviants apparently were aware of the tendency for sabotage because they resorted to strategies designed to avoid it, such as hiding, deception, and trying to conform to stereotypical gender behavior.

Cultural Diversity

The rise of globalization has created the seamless organization that attempts to know no borders. Cultural diversity is even more pronounced than gender diversity. But first, a word about cultural diversity. There is an important distinction between stereotypes and prototypes.

Stereotypes versus Prototypes

Jeanne Brett distinguishes stereotypes from prototypes (see Exhibit 13.5).[87] **Prototypes** are *central tendencies,* which recognize that substantial variation is likely even within a given culture. In contrast, stereotypes do not recognize variation within a culture. Prototypes acknowledge natural variation within a culture; stereotypes naively assume that everyone from a given culture behaves and thinks in a similar fashion. Acknowledging prototypes means that a person from culture *A* might think and act more like a person from culture *B*.

Culture as an Iceberg

Culture does not just pertain to geographical country of origin. As can be seen in Exhibit 13.6, **culture** is the unique character of a social group: the values and norms shared by its members that set it apart from other social groups.[88] Culture encompasses economic, social, political, and religious institutions. Culture influences people's mental models of how things work, their behavior, and their cause-and-effect relationships.

Schneider modeled culture as an iceberg, in which only about one-ninth of culture is visible to the naked eye.[89] The rest is submerged. As Exhibit 13.6 indicates, the top (visible) part of the cultural iceberg is the behaviors, artifacts, and institutions that characterize a culture. This portion includes things such as traditions, customs, habits, and so on. Obviously, these visible signs are expressions of deeper-held values, beliefs, and norms. Driving these values and norms, at the base of the cultural iceberg, are the fundamental assumptions about the world and humanity. The artifacts and customs that characterize a culture are not arbitrary; rather, they are manifestations about fundamental values and beliefs about the world.

Cultural Values

There are many ways that cultures can differ. We focus on the "big three" cultural differences[90] (see Exhibit 13.7):

- Individualism versus collectivism
- Egalitarianism versus hierarchy
- Direct versus indirect communication

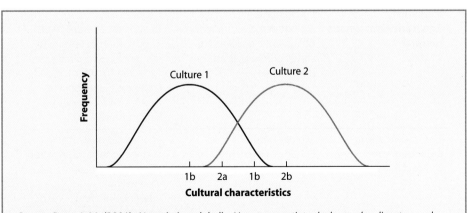

Source: Brett, J. M. (2001). *Negotiating globally: How to negotiate deals, resolve disputes, and make decisions across cultural boundaries,* p. 10. San Francisco: Jossey-Bass. Reprinted by permission of John Wiley & Sons.

EXHIBIT 13.5

Cultural Stereotypes versus Cultural Prototypes

EXHIBIT 13.6

Culture as an Iceberg

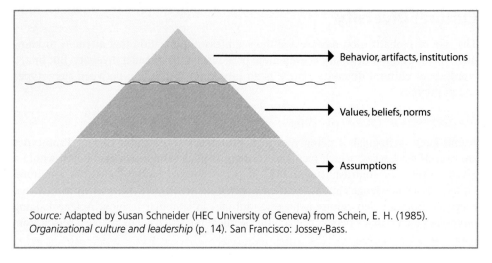

Source: Adapted by Susan Schneider (HEC University of Geneva) from Schein, E. H. (1985). *Organizational culture and leadership* (p. 14). San Francisco: Jossey-Bass.

INDIVIDUALISM VERSUS COLLECTIVISM In individualistic cultures, the pursuit of happiness and regard for personal welfare is paramount. The focus is on the individual as a distinctive level of analysis. In collectivist cultures, the focus is on the social group or unit. The fundamental unit of analysis is not the individual, in possession of his or her unalienable rights; rather, the focus is on the social group. People in individualistic cultures are more apt to use the words "I," "me," and "mine"; people from collectivistic cultures are more apt to use plural pronouns "we," "us," and "ours." Most modern Western and democratic societies and their organizations place ultimate value on the individual person; as such, this creates an intrinsic and inherently irresolvable tension between the individual and the group and the individual and the organization.[91] In contrast, Eastern and Asian societies have a synergistic view of the person and the group.

EXHIBIT 13.7

Dimensions of Culture

Cultural Dimension		
Goal: **Individual versus collective orientation**	*Individualists/Competitors:* Key goal is to maximize self-interest; source of identity is the self; people regard themselves as free agents and independent actors.	*Collectivists/Cooperators:* Key goal is to maximize the welfare of the group or collective; source of identity is the group; individuals regard themselves as group members; focus is on social interaction.
Influence: **Egalitarianism versus hierarchy**	*Egalitarians:* Do not perceive many social obligations; believe that status differences are permeable.	*Hierarchists:* Regard social order to be important in determining influence; subordinates are expected to defer to superiors; superiors are expected to look out for subordinates.
Communication: **Direct versus indirect**	*Direct Communicators:* Engage in explicit, direct information exchange; ask direct questions.	*Indirect Communicators:* Engage in tacit information exchange such as storytelling, inference-making; situational norms.

Source: Adapted from Brett, J. M. (2007). *Negotiating globally: How to negotiate deals, resolve disputes, and make decisions across cultural boundaries* (2nd ed.). San Francisco: Jossey-Bass.

EGALITARIANISM VERSUS HIERARCHY Egalitarianism versus hierarchy refers to how the different status layers in a society or organization relate to one another. In egalitarian cultures, members of high and low status groups communicate frequently and do not go to great lengths to perpetuate differences. Further, the status levels in egalitarian cultures are inherently permeable—meaning that if a person works hard enough, he or she can advance in an organization. In hierarchical cultures and organizations, status differences are not easily permeated. As a consequence, members of different classes or status levels do not communicate frequently, and there is a deep sense of obligation among those at the highest levels to provide for and protect those at the lowest status levels who, in turn, put their trust in the high-status members of their organization.

DIRECT VERSUS INDIRECT COMMUNICATION A final, key difference among cultures is in terms of how people communicate. Some cultures are characterized by direct communication between organizational actors. In other cultures, communication, particularly that between members of different status levels, is indirect and highly nuanced.

Models of Social Relationships

There are four broad models of relationships that not only apply to all kinds of relationships (both with family and friends, as well as bosses), but also account for virtually any culture.[92] With knowledge of these four models, a person traveling to any organization in any culture might see any given model in action.

- *Communal sharing (immediate family):* Communal sharing characterizes relationships in which people are highly responsive to the needs of the others involved. In communal relationships, people do not differentiate who brings what to the relationship. They simply provide for the people involved. In this sense, communal sharing is similar to the needs-based justice principle discussed in Chapter 12.
- *Authority ranking (subjects and monarch):* In authority-ranking relationships (similar to hierarchical relationships), people have asymmetric positions in a linear hierarchy, within an organization in which subordinates defer to, respect, and follow the directives of superiors. Superiors are responsible for subordinates. For example, military organizations and law enforcement agencies with strict command-and-control structures are authority-ranking relationships.
- *Equality matching (casual friends):* In equality matching (very similar to the exchange concept discussed in Chapter 6), people keep track of the balance or difference between the organizational actors. Common examples include turn-taking, voting, equal distribution, and quid-pro-quo relationships.
- *Market pricing (buyers and sellers):* In market-pricing relationships, people are highly sensitive to market worth. It is important to note that market-pricing relationships do not necessarily imply ruthless competition, but rather that people engage in cost-benefit analysis. For example, a couple that determines that one member has greater market worth and should therefore be the breadwinner for the family, whereas the other member brings greater value by taking the role of a full-time parent, has engaged in market pricing.

Predictors of Success in Intercultural Interactions

Cultural intelligence is "an outsider's seemingly natural ability to interpret someone's unfamiliar and ambiguous gestures the way that person's compatriots would."[93] (See Earley and Mosakowski's Cultural Intelligence test in Exhibit 13.8.) Personality tests are not good predictors of who is successful at bridging cultural divides.

The following characteristics have some value in predicting success:[94]

- Conceptual complexity: People who think in terms of shades of gray rather than black and white show less social distance to different others.[95]
- Broad categorization: People who use broad categories adjust to new environments better than do narrow categorizers.[96]

EXHIBIT 13.8   Testing Your Cultural Intelligence

*Rate the extent to which you agree with each statement, using the scale: **1 = strongly disagree, 2 = disagree, 3 = neutral, 4 = agree, 5 = strongly agree.***

___ Before I interact with people from a new culture, I ask myself what I hope to achieve.

___ If I encounter something unexpected while working in a new culture, I use this experience to figure out new ways to approach other cultures in the future.

___ I plan how I'm going to relate to people from a different culture before I meet them.

___ When I come into a new cultural situation, I can immediately sense whether something is going well or something is wrong.

Total ___ ÷ 4 =   Cognitive CQ

___ It's easy for me to change my body language (for example, eye contact or posture) to suit people from a different culture.

___ I can alter my expression when a cultural encounter requires it.

___ I modify my speech style (for example, accent or tone) to suit people from a different culture.

___ I easily change the way I act when a cross-cultural encounter seems to require it.

Total ___ ÷ 4 =   Physical CQ

___ I have confidence that I can deal well with people from a different culture.

___ I am certain that I can befriend people whose cultural backgrounds are different from mine.

___ I can adapt to the lifestyle of a different culture with relative ease.

___ I am confident that I can deal with a cultural situation that's unfamiliar.

Total ___ ÷ 4 =   Emotional/motivational CQ

Source: Earley, C., & Mosakowski, E. (2004). Cultural intelligence. *Harvard Business Review, 82*(10), 139–146. Reprinted by permission of Harvard Business Review. Copyright © 2004 by the Harvard Business School Publishing Corporation; all rights reserved.

- Empathy
- Sociability
- Critical acceptance of stereotypes (i.e., healthy skepticism)
- Openness to different points of view
- Interest in the host culture
- Task orientation
- Cultural flexibility (the ability to substitute activities in the host culture for own culturally valued activities)
- Social orientation (the ability to establish new intercultural relationships)
- Willingness to communicate (e.g., use the host language without fear of making mistakes)
- Patience (suspend judgment)
- Intercultural sensitivity
- Tolerance for differences among people
- Sense of humor
- Skills in collaborative conflict resolution

Options for Change

A useful model for considering how two (or more) cultures may work with one another is Berry's acculturation model (see Exhibit 13.9).[97] The acculturation model raises two key questions: (1) Is it considered to be of value to maintain your cultural identity and characteristics? And, (2) is it considered to be of value to maintain relationships with other cultural groups? If a person desires only to maintain her or his own culture and not maintain relationships with other groups, this leads to separation. If a person does not desire to maintain her or his own culture, but desires to maintain relationships with other groups, this leads to assimilation. If a person has a low desire to maintain her or his own group and little desire to build relationships with other groups, this leads to marginalization.

EXHIBIT 13.9

**Acculturation
Framework**

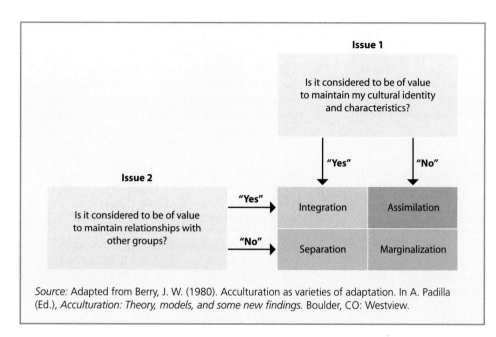

Source: Adapted from Berry, J. W. (1980). Acculturation as varieties of adaptation. In A. Padilla (Ed.), *Acculturation: Theory, models, and some new findings.* Boulder, CO: Westview.

Finally, if a person desires to maintain strong ties to her or his own culture and build ties to another culture, this leads to integration.

Conclusion

Diversity is multidimensional. It would be impossible (and undesirable) to diversify on every conceivable dimension. We used Gardenswartz and Rowe's four-dimensional model of diversity, which moves from a microfocus on personality diversity to internal diversity to external diversity to, finally, organizational diversity. A strong business case for diversity can be made using the four levels of analysis that are the foundation of this book: individual, dyad, team, and organizational. We identified the major barriers to diversity, which are primarily biased mind-sets, such as stereotyping, in-group favoritism, and organizational privilege systems. We discussed several ways to create and sustain diversity, including affirmative action, valuing diversity, managing diversity, and education. We focused on gender diversity in the workplace and noted the pay gap between men and women. We documented the glass ceiling and the double standards that often impede women's advancement in the organization. Finally, we raised the issue of cultural diversity and outlined three key cultural differences that may profitably help employees better understanding cultural values and behaviors: individualism-collectivism; egalitarianism-hierarchy; and direct-indirect communication.

Notes

1. Gardenswartz, L., & Rowe, A. (1994). *Diverse teams at work: Capitalizing on the power of diversity.* New York: McGraw-Hill.

2. Brewer, M. B., & Gardner, W. (1996). Who is this "we"? Levels of collective identity and self representations. *Journal of Personality and Social Psychology, 71,* 83–93.

3. Brewer & Gardner, "Who is this 'we'," p. 237; Markus, H. (1977). Self-schemata and processing information about the self. *Journal of Personality and Social Psychology, 35,* 63–78.

4. Brewer, M. (1991). The social self: On being the same and different at the same time. *Personality and Social Psychology Bulletin, 17,* 475–482; Brewer, M. (1993). The role of distinctiveness in social identity and group behavior. In M. Hogg & D. Abrams (Eds.), *Group motivation: Social psychological perspectives* (pp. 1–16). London: Harvester Wheatsheaf.

5. Turner, J. C., Hogg, M., Oakes, P., Reicher, S., & Wetherell, M. (1987). *Rediscovering the social group: A self-categorization theory.* Oxford, England: Basil Blackwell; Brewer, M., & Roccas, S. (2001). Individual values, social identity, and optimal distinctiveness. In C. Sedekides & M. B. Brewer (Eds.), *Individual self,-relational self and collective self* (pp. 219–240). Ann Arbor: Psychology Press.

6. Cox, T. H., Lobel, S. A., & McLeod, P. L. (1991). Effects of ethnic group cultural differences on cooperative and competitive behavior on a group task. *Academy of Management Journal, 34,* 827–847; Watson, W. E., Kumar, K., & Michaelson, L. K. (1993). Cultural diversity's impact on interaction process and performance: Comparing homogeneous and diverse task groups. *Academy of Management Journal, 36,* 590–602.

7. Tsui, A. S., Terri, E. D., & O'Reilly, C. A. (1992). Being different: Relational demography and organizational attachment. *Administrative Science Quarterly, 37,* 549–579.

8. Williams, K. Y., & O'Reilly, C. A. (1998). Demography and diversity in organizations: A review of 40 years of research. In B. Staw & R. Sutton (Eds.), *Research in organizational behavior* (Vol. 20, pp. 77–140). Greenwich, CT: JAI Press.

9. Chatman, J. A., & O'Reilly, C. A. (2004). Asymmetric reactions to work group sex diversity among men and women. *Academy of Management Journal, 47*(2), 193–208.

10. Ibid.

11. Granovetter, M. (1973). The strength of weak ties. *American Journal of Sociology, 78,* 1360–1380.

12. Pelled, L., Eisenhardt, K., & Xin, K. 1999. Exploring the black box: An analysis of work group diversity, conflict and performance. *Administrative Science Quarterly, 44,* 1–28; Tsui, Terri, & O'Reilly, "Being different," p. 239; Gruenfeld, D. H., Mannix, E. A., Williams, K. Y., & Neale, M. A. (1996). Group composition and decision making: How member familiarity and information distribution affect process and performance. *Organizational Behavior and Human Decision Processes, 67,* 1–15.

13. Phillips, K., Mannix, E., Neale, M., & Gruenfeld, D. H. (2004). Diverse groups and information sharing: The effects of congruent ties. *Journal of Experimental Social Psychology, 40,* 497–510; Heider, F. (1958). *The psychology of interpersonal relations.* New York: John Wiley & Sons.

14. Phillips, Mannix, Neale, & Gruenfeld, "Diverse groups and information sharing," p. 239.

15. Blau, P. M. (1977). *Inequality and heterogeneity: A primitive theory of social structure.* New York: Free Press.

16. Earley, P. C., & Mosakowski, E. (2000). Creating hybrid team cultures: An empirical test of transnational team functioning. *Academy of Management Journal, 43,* 26–49.

17. Ibid.

18. See note 15.

19. Alexander, J., Nuchols, B., Bloom, J., & Lee, S. (1995). Organizational demography and turnover: An examination of multiform and nonlinear heterogeneity. *Human Relations, 48,* 1455–1480.

20. Richard, O., Barnett, T., Dwyer, S., & Chadwick, K. (2004). Cultural diversity in management, firm performance, and the moderating role of entrepreneurial orientation dimensions. *Academy of Management Journal, 47,* 255–266.

21. See note 15.

22. Crosby, F., Bromley, S., & Saxe, L. (1980). Recent unobtrusive studies of black and white discrimination and prejudice: A literature review. *Psychological Bulletin, 87,* 546–563.

23. Inman, M. L., & Baron, R. S. (1996). The influence of prototypes on perceptions of prejudice. *Journal of Personality and Social Psychology, 70*(4), 727–739.

24. Snyder, M. (1984). When belief creates reality. In M. P. Zanna (Ed.), *Advances in experimental social psychology* (Vol. 18, pp. 247–305). Orlando, FL: Academic Press.

25. Turner, M. A., Fix, M., & Struyk, R. (1991). *Opportunities denied, opportunities diminished: Racial discrimination in hiring.* Washington, D.C.: The Urban Institute Press.

26. Ibid.

27. Improvements at OFCCP produce record financial recoveries for record number of american workers in FY 06. U.S. Department of Labor, Employment Standards Administration. Retrieved August 14, 2007 from http://www.dol.gov/esa/ofccp/enforc06.pdf

28. DeNavas-Walt, C., Proctor, B. D., Lee, C. H. (2006, August). *Income, poverty, and health insurance coverage in the United States: 2005.* Current population reports, U.S. Census Bureau.

29. Linville, P., Fischer, G., & Salovey, P. (1989). Perceived distributions of the characteristics of in-group and out-group members: Empirical evidence and a computer simulation. *Journal of Personality and Social Psychology, 57,* 165–188.

30. Judd, L. M., & Park, B. (1988). Out-group homogeneity: Judgments of variability at the individual and group level. *Journal of Personality & Social Psychology, 54,* 778–788.

31. Knight-Ridder News. (1991, February 2). AWOL Marine in Indiana admits seven racial killings, sources say. *Miami Herald.*

32. Hinds, P. J., Carley, K. M., Krackhardt, D., & Wholey, D. (2000). Choosing work group members: Balancing similarity, competence, and familiarity. *Organizational Behavior and Human Decision Processes, 81*(2), 226–251.

33. Ibid.

34. Byrne, D. (1971). *The attraction paradigm.* New York: Academic Press.

35. Condon, J. W., & Crano, W. D. (1988). Inferred evaluation and the relation between attitude similarity and interpersonal attraction. *Journal of Personality and Social Psychology, 54,* 789–797.

36. Pfeffer, J. (1983). Organizational demography. In L. L. Cummings and B. M. Staw (Eds.), *Research in organizational behavior* (Vol. 5, pp. 299–357). Greenwich, CT: JAI Press; Tsui, A. S., & O'Reilly III, C. A. (1989). Beyond simple demographic effects: The importance of relational demography in superior-subordinate dyads. *Academy of Management Journal, 32*(2), 402–423.

37. Zenger, T. R., & Lawrence, B. S. (1989). Organizational demography: The differential effects of age and tenure distributions on technical communication. *Academy of Management Journal, 32,* 353–376.

38. O'Reilly, C. A., Caldwell, D., & Barnett, W. (1989). Work group demography, social integration, and turnover. *Administrative Science Quarterly, 34,* 21–37.

39. Chatman, J., Polzer, J., Barsade, S., & Neale, M. (1998). Being different yet feeling similar: The influence of demographic composition and organizational culture on work processes and outcomes. *Administrative Science Quarterly, 43*(4), 749–780; Jehn, K., Northcraft, G., &

Neale, M. (1999). Why differences make a difference: A field study of diversity, conflict and performance in workgroups. *Administrative Science Quarterly, 44,* 741–763.

40. Riordan, C., & Shore, C. (1997). Demographic diversity and employee attitudes: An empirical examination of relational demography within work units. *Journal of Applied Psychology, 82,* 342–358.

41. Jackson, S. E., Brett, J. F., Sessa, V. I., Cooper, D. M., Julin, J. A. & Peyronnin, K. (1991). Some differences make a difference: Individual dissimilarity and group heterogeneity as correlates of recruitment, promotion and turnover. *Journal of Applied Psychology, 79*(5), 675–689.

42. Tajfel, H., & Turner, J. C. (1986). An integrative theory of intergroup conflict. In S. Worchel & W. Austin (Eds.), *Psychology of intergroup relations* (pp. 2–24). Chicago: Nelson-Hall.

43. Meindl, J. R., & Lerner, M. J. (1984). Exacerbation of extreme responses to an out-group. *Journal of Personality and Social Psychology, 47,* 71–84.

44. Moreland, R. L., & McMinn, J. G. (1999). Gone, but not forgotten: Loyalty and betrayal among ex-members of small groups. *Personality and Social Psychology Bulletin, 25,* 1476–1486.

45. Klar, B. (2002). A treatment of multivariate skewness, kurtosis and related statistics. *Journal of Multivariate Analysis, 83,* 141–165.

46. Duck, J. M., & Fielding, K. S. (1999). Leaders and subgroups: One of us or one of them? *Group Processes and Intergroup Relations, 2,* 203–230.

47. Banaji, M. R., & Greenwald, A. G. (1995). Implicit gender stereotyping in judgments of fame. *Journal of Personality and Social Psychology, 68,* 181–198.

48. Steele, C. M., & Aronson, J. (1995). Stereotype threat and the intellectual test performance of African-Americans. *Journal of Personality and Social Psychology, 69,* 797–811.

49. Spencer, S. J., & Steele, C. M. (1994). *Under suspicion of inability: Stereotype vulnerability and women's math performance.* Unpublished manuscript. SUNY Buffalo and Stanford University.

50. Kray, L. J., Thompson, L., & Galinsky, A. (2001). Battle of the sexes: Gender stereotype confirmation and reactance in negotiations. *Journal of Personality and Social Psychology, 80,* 942–958; Kray, L. J., Galinsky, A., & Thompson, L. (2002). Reversing the gender gap in negotiations: An exploration of stereotype regeneration. *Organizational Behavior and Human Decision Processes, 87*(2), 386–409.

51. Steele, C. M. (1997). A threat in the air. *American Psychologist, 52*(6), 613–629.

52. Ibid.

53. Rosette, A. S. (2006). Unearned privilege: Race, gender, and social inequality in U.S. organizations. In M. Karsten (Ed.), *Gender, ethnicity, and race in the workplace* (pp. 253–268). Westport, CT: Praeger.

54. Rosette, A. S., & Thompson, L. (2005). The camouflage effect: Separating achieved status and unearned privilege in organizations. In M. Neale, E. Mannix, & M. Thomas-Hunt (Eds.), *Research on managing teams and groups* (Vol. 7, pp. 259–281). San Diego, CA: Elsevier.

55. Wildman, S. M. (1996). *Privilege revealed: How invisible preference undermines America.* New York: New York University Press.

56. Rosette, A. S., & Tost, L. P. (2006). *Intersecting unrecognized advantage with experienced disadvantage: The revelation of White privilege in organizations.* Duke University working paper.

57. Rosette, A. S. (2004). Unacknowledged privilege: Setting the stage for discrimination in organizational settings. *Academy of Management Proceedings.*

58. See note 1.

59. Prince, R. (2003, April 2). Reporters of color rise to occasion on U-Mich. *Richard Prince's Journal-isms.* Retrieved February 1, 2004, from http://www.maynardije.org/columns/dickprince/030402_prince.

60. Schofield, J. W. (1986). Black-white contact in desegregated schools. In M. Hewstone & R. Brown (Eds.), *Contact and conflict in intergroup encounters* (pp. 79–92). Oxford: Basil Blackwell; Gerard, H. (1983). School desegregation: The social science role. *American Psychologist, 38,* 869–877.

61. Brown, R. J., Condor, F., Mathew, A., Wade, G., & Williams, J. A. (1986). Explaining intergroup differentiation in an industrial organization. *Journal of Occupational Psychology, 59,* 273–286.

62. Stroebe, W., Lenkert, A., & Jonas, K. (1988). Familiarity may breed contempt: The impact of student exchange on national stereotypes and attitudes. In W. Stroebe, D. Bar-Tal, & M. Hewstone (Eds.), *The social psychology of intergroup relations* (pp. 167–187). New York: Springer.

63. Brewer, M. B., & Brown, R. J. (1998). Intergroup relations. In D. T. Gilbert, S. T. Fiske, & G. Lindzey (Eds.), *The handbook of social psychology* (pp. 554–594). New York: McGraw-Hill.

64. Ensari, N., & Miller, N. (2002). The outgroup must not be so bad after all: The effect of disclosure, typicality and salience on intergroup bias. *Journal of Personality and Social Psychology, 83,* 313–329.

65. Bradford, D. L., & Cohen, A. R. (1984). *Managing for excellence: The guide to developing high performance in contemporary organizations.* New York: John Wiley and Sons.

66. Gaertner, S. L., Dovidio, J. F., & Bachman, B. A. (1996). Revisiting the contact hypothesis: The induction of a common ingroup identity. *International Journal of Intercultural Relations, 20,* 271–290.

67. Bettencourt, B. A., & Dorr, N. (1998). Cooperative interaction and intergroup bias: Effects of representation and cross-cut role assignment. *Personality and Social Psychology Bulletin, 24,* 1270–1287.

68. Layne, A. (2000, September 1). Walk a mile in my shadow. *Fast Company,* p. 38.

69. Lips, H. M. (2003). The gender pay gap: Concrete indicator of women's progress toward equality. *Analyses of Social Issues and Public Policy, 3*(1), 87–109.

70. Bernstein, A. (2004, June 14). Women's pay: Why the gap remains a chasm. *BusinessWeek.*

71. *2003 median annual earnings by race and sex.* Retrieved July 9, 2007 from http://www.infoplease.com/ipa/A0197814.html.

72. See note 70.

73. Rose, S. J., & Hartmann, H. I. (2004). *Still a man's labor market: The long-term earnings gap.* Washington, DC: Institute for Women's Policy Research.

74. Ibid.

75. Ibid.

76. Cejka, M. A., & Eagly, A. H. (1999). Gender-stereotypic images of occupations correspond to the sex segregation of employment. *Personality and Social Psychology Bulletin, 25,* 413–423; Glick, P., Wilk, K., & Perreault, M. (1995). Images of occupations: Components of gender and status in occupational stereotypes. *Sex Roles, 32,* 565–582.

77. Rudman, L. A., & Glick, P. (2001). Prescriptive gender stereotypes and backlash toward agentic women. *Journal of Social Issues, 57,* 743–762.

78. Glick, P., Zion, C., & Nelson, C. (1988). What mediates sex discrimination in hiring decisions? *Journal of Personality and Social Psychology, 55,* 178–186; Rudman, M. (1998). A volume-tracking method for incompressible multifluid flows with large density variations. *International Journal for Numerical Methods in Fluids, 28,* 357–378.

79. Glick, Zion, & Nelson, "What mediates sex discrimination," p. 246; Rudman, L. A., & Glick, P. (1999). Feminized management and backlash toward agentic women: The hidden costs to women of a kinder, gentler image of middle-managers. *Journal of Personality and Social Psychology, 77,* 1004–1010.

80. Rudman, "Volume-tracking method," p. 246.

81. Bartol, K. M., & Butterfield, D. A. (1976). Sex effects in evaluating leaders. *Journal of Applied Psychology, 67,* 446–454.

82. Eagly, A. H., Makhijani, M. G., & Klonsky, B. G. (1992). Gender and the evaluation of leaders: A meta-analysis. *Psychological Bulletin, 111,* 3–22.

83. Carli, L. L., LaFleur, S. J., & Loeber, C. C. (1995). Nonverbal behavior, gender, and influence. *Journal of Personality and Social Psychology, 68,* 1030–1041.

84. Powers, T. A., & Zuroff, D. C. (1988). Interpersonal consequences of overt self-criticism: A comparison of neutral and self-enhancing presentations of self. *Journal of Personality and Social Psychology, 54*(6), 1054–1062.

85. Heilman, M. E., Wallen, A. S., Fuchs, D., & Tamkins, M. M. (2004). Penalties for success: Reactions to women who succeed at male gender-typed tasks. *Journal of Applied Psychology, 89,* 416–427.

86. Rudman, L. A., & Fairchild, K. (2004). Reactions to counterstereotypic behavior: The role of backlash in cultural stereotype maintenance. *Journal of Personality and Social Psychology, 87,* 157–176.

87. Brett, J. M. (2007). *Negotiating globally: How to negotiate deals, resolve disputes, and make decisions, across cultural boundaries* (2nd ed.). San Francisco: Jossey-Bass.

88. Lytle, A. L., Brett, J. M., & Shapiro, D. L. (1999). The strategic use of interests, rights, and power to resolve disputes. *Negotiation Journal, 10,* 31–49.

89. Schneider, S. C. (1997). *Managing across cultures.* Upper Saddle River, NJ: Prentice Hall.

90. Brett, *Negotiating globally,* p. 247; Triandis, H. C. (1994). *Culture and social behavior.* New York: McGraw Hill.

91. Drechsler, W. (1995). Collectivism. In H. Drechsler, W. Hillinge, & F. Neumann (Eds.), *Society and state: The lexicon of politics* (9th ed., pp. 458–459). Munich, Germany: Franz Vahlen.

92. Fiske, A. P. (1991). *Structures of social life: The four elementary forms of human relations.* New York: Free Press (Macmillan).

93. Earley, C., & Mosakowski, E. (2004, October). Cultural intelligence. *Harvard Business Review,* p. 140.

94. Triandis, H. C. (1994). *Culture and social behavior.* New York: McGraw-Hill.

95. Gardiner, G. S. (1972). Complexity training and prejudice reduction. *Journal of Applied Social Psychology, 2*(4), 326–342.

96. Detweiler, R. (1980). Intercultural interaction and the categorization process: A conceptual analysis and behavioral outcome. *International Journal of Intercultural Relations, 4,* 275–293.

97. Berry, J. W. (1980). Acculturation as varieties of adaptation. In A. Padilla (Ed.), *Acculturation: Theory, models, and some new findings.* Boulder, CO: Westview.

Chapter | 14

THE VIRTUAL WORKPLACE

Before reading this chapter, complete Exercise 14.1 on the Web site for this chapter. The exercise asks you about how much time you spent yesterday communicating via e-mail, BlackBerry, and cell phone as compared to face-to-face interaction. One of the things that people find is that they often spend more time engaged in virtual interaction (e.g., e-mail, phone, and BlackBerry) than in real interaction. Virtual communication changes the way we behave and the way we do our work. Sometimes we get more work done, but it can come at a cost to ourselves, others, and our organizations.

There is no escaping the fact that information technology is woven into the fabric of our personal lives, as well as our business transactions. One of the most significant organizational changes that was never discussed as a strategic decision was the introduction of information technology, in particular, the Internet and its applications, including e-mail and Web browsing. Over 50 percent of U.S. households have access to the Internet[1] and 90 percent of employees in companies believe that e-mail has made them more efficient.[2] The average employee spends 25 percent (2 hours) of each workday using e-mail, and the number of e-mail messages received each day can be well over 150. Many people believe that doing without e-mail for more than one week would cause them more trauma than a divorce.[3] Surveillance of e-mail in companies is at an all-time high, with 52 percent of large companies in the United States monitoring their employees' use of e-mail, compared with only 15 percent in 1997.[4] Technology affects how we work, how we feel, and even with whom we interact.

In this chapter, we introduce the place-time model of social interaction and discuss the impact of information technology on human behavior. We also discuss the advantages and disadvantages of distance teamwork.

Place-Time Model of Social Interaction

The **place-time model of social interaction** considers two key dimensions (see Exhibit 14.1). The first dimension focuses on whether organizational actors are located in the same physical space. The other dimension focuses on whether organizational actors are communicating at the same time. The four quadrants of the model focus on all possible combinations of place and time communication.

Same-Time, Same-Place Communication

Same-time, same-place communication is commonly known as face-to-face communication. Until recently, most businesspeople would never have dreamed of conducting

EXHIBIT 14.1

Place-Time Model of Social Interaction

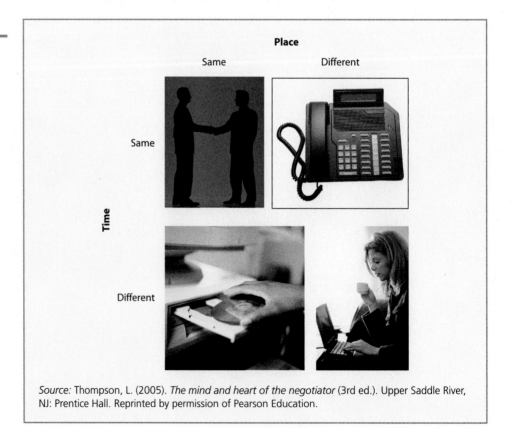

Source: Thompson, L. (2005). *The mind and heart of the negotiator* (3rd ed.). Upper Saddle River, NJ: Prentice Hall. Reprinted by permission of Pearson Education.

EXHIBIT 14.2 **Wireless Man and Wireless Woman**

Not so long ago, it used to be that teenagers were the only part of the social strata we might see who would choose wires and headsets in favor of actual human contact as they paraded through public places. Not anymore. David Brooks argues that the wireless men and women of the modern corporation are what drive the U.S. economy. However, they often seem to be talking about things other than business; much of the time, they narrate their own lives, "Yeah, I'm boarding a plane to Atlanta. Hold on, I'm just putting my stuff in the overhead rack" (p. 25). Brooks affectionately refers to these creatures as infoholics—who struggle with a moral quandary at the landing of every flight: They are tempted to turn on their phones, but the pilot has not yet given the go-ahead. Brooks describes the wireless company worker as a master of the digital road: "[He] has his seven frequent-flier numbers memorized. . . . He is insanely impressed by his own ability to almost never set off the metal detectors [in airports], and he knows which shoes will keep his winning streak going. . . . If Wireless man had an orgasm every time he was reminded that the luggage may have shifted in the overhead bins during flight, he would be the happiest man on the face of the earth. . . . He knows that in the world of the travel lords, you never say you are flying 'first class.' You say you are flying 'up front.' He knows that when he settles into his wide seat, 2C, he should never make eye contact with the proles trudging back to 17F. He knows the ultimate secret of the frequent [wireless] traveler, which is that all the luxuries and amenities going to the top rung of the corporate fliers—the airport clubs, the first-class cabins, the express security lanes—are actually shabby and disappointing, but you must never let the folks back in the cabin suspect this. All that matters is that you have access—testimony to the vital role you play in the turbo of American Capitalism—and others do not" (pp. 27–28).

Source: Brooks, D. (2004, July/August). Wireless men and women. *Across the Board,* pp. 25–28.

everything from high-level mergers and acquisition deals to business meetings in any format other than face-to-face. However, it is now quite commonplace for people to opt out of face-to-face interaction for the convenience of cell phones. Popular TV ads show information workers headed for the beach with kids and dog in tow and with their cell phones at the ready (see Exhibit 14.2 for a humorous account of the wireless worker).

Many businesspeople, though, are still old-fashioned; whereas they might chat through e-mail and the phone, they would never sign a deal anywhere but face-to-face. Their intuitions about the value of face-to-face interaction are supported by empirical research. As compared to other types of interaction, face-to-face interaction has three key advantages, in that it: (1) is easier (once you are there), (2) allows for multiple channels of information (and is therefore high in "richness"), and (3) allows for immediate clarification and is ultimately the most flexible (e.g., a communicator may cut short an interaction if it becomes clear that the other person is really not interested in hearing what you have to say, is taking yet another call, or reading her own e-mail).

Same-Time, Different-Place Communication

Same-time, different-place communication is rapidly replacing face-to-face communication as the most common form of interaction among organizational members. The most prototypical same-time, different-place communication is the telephone. However, it does not have to be. CEO Henning Kagermann of SAP, the world's second-largest computer firm, predicts that people will soon run all their business in real time, by remote control.[5] He predicts that factories and plants will be without people, but the plants will still react in real time. Exhibit 14.3 graphs how our face-to-face and telephone sociability differ between family and friends through our life cycle.

People's communication style and ethical standards change when they communicate on the telephone. People lie more often over the telephone than in any other form of communication.[6] Exhibit 14.4 indicates the percentage of time that students reported lying within the course of a week.[7] According to Hancock et al., it is easier to lie over the telephone because the other person cannot see our expressions.[8] On the flip side, e-mail leaves a paper trail.

Instant messaging is another form of same-time, different-place communication. Instant messaging would seem to be an advantage in that it takes the frustration out of waiting for a response from the other party. Nevertheless, sometimes it is that buffer of

EXHIBIT 14.3   Face-to-Face and Telephone Sociability Through the Life Cycle

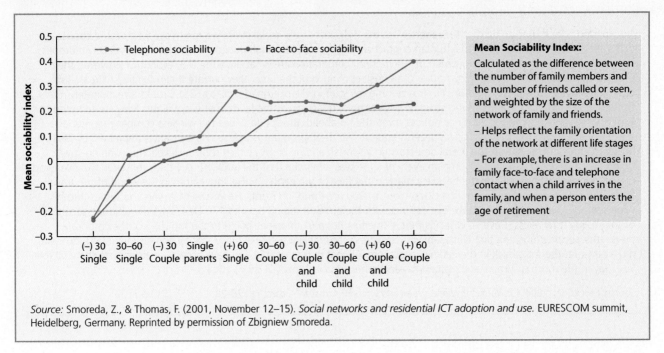

Source: Smoreda, Z., & Thomas, F. (2001, November 12–15). *Social networks and residential ICT adoption and use.* EURESCOM summit, Heidelberg, Germany. Reprinted by permission of Zbigniew Smoreda.

time that allows people to best strategize their response, especially in a competitive situation. In one investigation, negotiations that took place either via instant messaging or via e-mail were examined.[9] In some situations, the seller had a good bargaining position (e.g., strong arguments) or a weak bargaining position (weak arguments). It was hypothesized that if negotiators with strong positions negotiated via instant messaging, they would perform much better than when communicating via e-mail, precisely because they would take their target off-guard. In short, when facing a tough, prepared negotiator, you might want to hide behind an e-mail exchange so that you can take time to strategize,

EXHIBIT 14.4

Incidence of Lying as a Function of Different Communication Modes

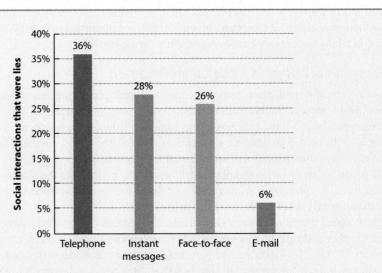

Source: Hancock, J. T., Thom-Santelli, J., & Ritchie, T. (2004). Deception and design: The impact of communication technology on lying behavior. *Proceedings of the SGICHI Conference on Human Factors in Computing Systems* (pp. 129–134). Vienna, Austria. Reprinted by permission of Jenn Thom-Santelli.

EXHIBIT 14.5   Instant Messaging and Competitive Advantage

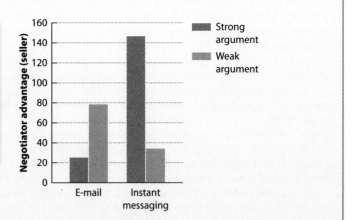

- If you have a **strong** bargaining position, "enriched" communication – FtF or IM/Conference call allows your advantage to be amplified because other team cannot "counter" in real time
- If you have a **weak** bargaining position, you can better defend yourself if you have media buffer (e.g., e-mail/speakerphone) because you can take "timeouts" to strategize

Source: Chakravarti, A., Loewenstein, J., Morris, M., Thompson, L., & Kopelman, S. (2005). At a loss for words: Negotiators disadvantaged in technical knowledge are vulnerable to verbal domination and economic losses as a function of communication media tempo. *Organizational Behavior and Human Decision Processes, 98*(1), 28–38. Reprinted by permission of Elsevier.

muster your confidence, think about how to make your arguments, and prevent yourself from saying *yes* too quickly. As can be seen in Exhibit 14.5, this is exactly what happened: The stronger negotiators did better when in instant message mode; the weak negotiators did better via e-mail.

Different-Time, Same-Place Communication

Different-time, same-place communication is best exemplified by shift work, or job sharing, such as when two or more people share a workstation or computer, but use it at different times. Different-time, same-place communicators must "hand off" information to each other.

The characteristics of the environment strongly affect how people react to such spaces and how well they perform. According to psychologists and interior environmental design experts Susan Painter and Constance Forrest, people's response to their physical environments is linked to their evolutionary history and taps into two key needs—taking refuge and prospecting.[10] Our early ancestors needed both a refuge—a safe place to eat, sleep, and take care of young—and a prospect—a perch or view out over a long distance to see predators and prey. (This is the reason why everyone wants an office with a window.)

Different-Time, Different-Place Communication

Different-time, different-place communication is best exemplified by e-mail. E-mail was originally developed to allow academics to send files and data to one another. Collaborating scholars were often working at different universities and needed a mechanism to transfer their ideas and data. The developer of e-mail never imagined that the business world would quickly become enamored of e-mail.

The purpose of e-mail can range from strictly task-based or work-based to strictly personal (not work-based). Moreover, e-mail can be solicited (desired) or unsolicited (not desired). Undesired e-mail is known as spam. A survey of 1,100 U.S. companies in May 2003 revealed that spam reaches over 90 percent of employees in the workplace.[11] Half or more of incoming e-mail for a substantial proportion of the private sector comes in the form of spam. If we consider that the daily volume of e-mail in the United States is 20 billion messages, the time and energy involved in detecting spam and then disposing of it constitutes an enormous burden on the productivity of businesses and the entire economy. One company president calculated that if one person in the organization were to dispatch an "all staff" e-mail message to the 300 employees of the organization, in which each recipient spent only 1 minute reading, 5 hours of staff time would be lost.

EXHIBIT 14.6 **An Online Alibi and Excuse Club**

A 20-year-old college student in Denver, Colorado, used his cell phone to send a text message to hundreds of other cell phone users—all of whom were members of an "alibi and excuse club"—a virtual network of 3,400 perfect strangers who help each other break dates and otherwise cut corners at work and in their personal lives. The members use cell phones to stay in contact with each other. The Internet allows people to find conspirators quickly and for a one-shot situation. When a willing helper responds to someone's request for help in a lie, the request sender and the helper devise a lie and the helper then calls the victim with the excuse (e.g., "he's had an accident"). Moreover, audio recordings of background sounds (like dentists' drills, auto traffic, and even a rasp of a hacking cough) add realism to the lie. How did it all start? Michelle Logan, a 26-year-old employee at an airline company, imported the idea from Europe to the United States. Her first mission? To help herself get out of a blind date. After she sent out a help call, a member of the network from San Jose, California, called the blind date himself, pretended to be Logan's boss, and explained that she had to go to Europe for a training seminar.

Source: Adapted from Richtel, M. (2004, June 26). For liars and loafers, cellphones offer an alibi. *New York Times.*

Another type of different-time, different-place communication is the Web. People surf the Web with increasing frequency. Web sites are identity claims for companies as well as people themselves. Companies use Web sites to communicate their values and sell products; people use the Web sites of others to learn about someone they might not know, a behavior that has been deemed ethical by the *New York Times* ethics columnist, Randy Cohen.[12] Personal Web sites provide people with an outlet for presenting information about themselves to anyone who cares to investigate them.[13] In one investigation, 11 observers surfed 89 personal Web sites and then rated the authors' personalities (in terms of the Big Five; see Chapter 2). The ratings that the surfers made were compared with an accuracy criterion (self and informant reports) and with the authors' ideal self-ratings. There was a high level of consensus between what the observers saw and what the authors intended.[14]

What about ethics and e-mail? Interestingly, people are more likely to tell the truth—the blunt truth—in e-mail than when they are face-to-face, over the phone, or through instant messaging.[15] However, people sometimes use e-mail and the Web for unethical behavior. There are even Web sites for liars (see Exhibit 14.6).

See Exhibit 14.7 for tips on using e-mail as efficiently, productively, and safely as possible.

Psychological Distancing Model: Media Richness

One of the advantages of face-to-face communication is that communicators have more channels of information available to them when interacting face-to-face (consider Exhibit 14.8). Face-to-face communication is considered the "richest" form of social interaction because it provides no fewer than four channels of cues for the social actor, including kinetic cues (moving closer, patting someone on the shoulder, etc.), visual cues (dilated pupils, blinking, smiling, etc.), paralinguistic cues (such as high pitch, disfluency, laughter, etc.) and linguistic cues (the content of what is said). By moving to two-way, same-time, different-place communication, such as videoconferencing, the kinetic channel is lost (we can't shake hands, pat the other person on the shoulder, or move closer). When

EXHIBIT 14.7   Tips for Using E-Mail Efficiently, Productively, and Safely in Business

- Adopt clear policies concerning appropriateness, retention, and deletion of e-mail messages. Five Wall Street firms were fined $8.3 million in 2002 for failing to properly archive significant e-mail records. In 2002, only one third of U.S. employers distributed written policies concerning e-mail. Even a sketchy set of rules can help business leaders and employees steer clear of costly and career-damaging faux pas.
- Use e-mail only for positive communication. It takes only a few seconds to congratulate or praise someone. Negative or punitive communication should be delivered face-to-face.
- Err on the side of parsimony. Otherwise, there is misunderstanding and frustration.
- Save graphic creativity and witticisms for other media. They are distracting in e-mail.
- When e-mails are really short (less than 15 words), use the subject line only and write EOM (end of message) afterwards. Each minute saved is much appreciated.

Source: Venditti, P. (2004, March 1). E-mail is a great communicator but also a time waster. *Everett Business Journal,* p. B5. Reprinted by permission of Phil Venditti.

we move to the cell phone (without visual), we are down to two channels only, the paralinguistic and linguistic; and in e-mail (the most impoverished channel) we can only rely on linguistic cues.

Electronic Brainstorming

The typical perception is that teams that interact with less richness will suffer relative to teams that have more rich media available to them. Thus, it is surprising when we observe situations in which impoverished media enhances organizational performance. Such is the case with electronic brainstorming. In electronic brainstorming, teams do not have the luxury of interacting in a face-to-face format. Moreover, people consider face-to-face interaction to be superior to non-face-to-face interaction. Electronic brainstorming is a technique in which team members brainstorm (in the fashion described in Chapter 9), but do this via information technology. For example, in the University of Arizona's Artificial Intelligence Lab, companies bring in their teams for a half day or full day of brainstorming. Although the team members are all physically present, they do not interact in a typical face-to-face format. Rather, each team member is positioned in front of a computer terminal and, therefore, can submit ideas and suggestions at any time. Moreover, team members stay

EXHIBIT 14.8   Psychological Distancing Model

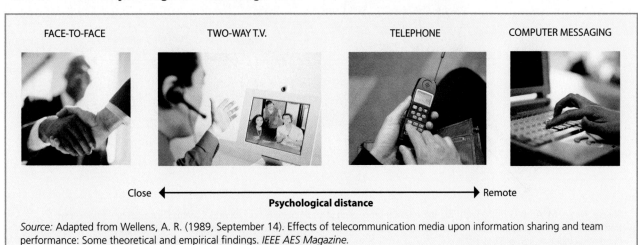

Source: Adapted from Wellens, A. R. (1989, September 14). Effects of telecommunication media upon information sharing and team performance: Some theoretical and empirical findings. *IEEE AES Magazine.*

informed of the ideas generated by others—not by hearing them (as in the case of face-to-face-brainstorming), but rather by simply glancing up at a screen.

People who interact in a non-face-to-face fashion are more likely to get down to business. In short, the normal, seemingly required pleasantries that characterize face-to-face meetings (greetings, how are you's, etc.) are not usually present in e-mail.

Virtual Teams

Virtual teams are increasingly common in organizations. Neale and Griffith provide a multidimensional framework for understanding the range of "virtualness" (see Exhibit 14.9).[16] One dimension is physical distance (close to far); another dimension is the level of tech support (low to high); and finally, the percentage of time that group members are apart on the task (0–100 percent). Teams that are physically close, have low tech support (and needs), and spend no time apart are "traditional" (i.e., face-to-face) teams. Another type of team is the "virtual" team, which is defined as a team that spends the majority of its time apart when completing tasks, but varies in terms of its tech support and the physical distance actually separating members. A final type of team is the "hybrid" team, which represents the greatest majority of teams (in Exhibit 14.9, the large box at the intersection of all three dimensions). How do hybrid teams stack up against nonhybrid teams (i.e., either traditional or purely virtual teams)? To tackle this question, Neale and Griffith examined the degree of conflict in each type of team. They found that in terms of task conflict and relationship conflict, low and high hybrid teams were virtually indistinguishable. However, hybrid teams reported considerably greater procedural conflict than did low hybrid teams.[17]

EXHIBIT 14.9 Traditional, Hybrid, and Virtual Teams

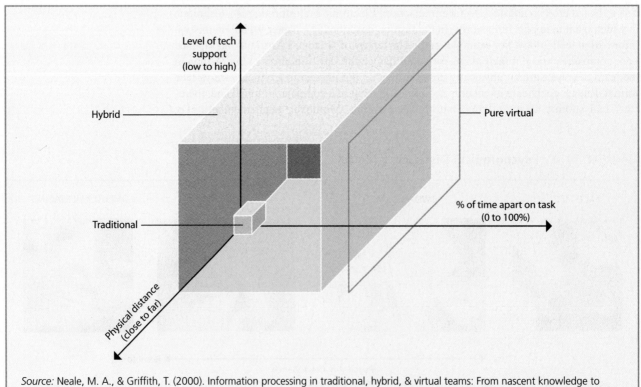

Source: Neale, M. A., & Griffith, T. (2000). Information processing in traditional, hybrid, & virtual teams: From nascent knowledge to transactive memory. In B. Staw & R. Sutton (Eds.), *Research in organizational behavior* (Vol. 23, pp. 379–421). Greenwich, CT: JAI Press. Reprinted by permission of Elsevier.

Information Technology and Its Effects on Social and Organizational Behavior

How does information technology, particularly e-mail and video conferencing, affect organizational behavior? There are advantages and disadvantages (see Exhibit 14.10).

Disadvantages

GREATER MISUNDERSTANDING In terms of disadvantages, distance work leads to more misunderstandings, primarily because people separated by distance ask each other fewer questions and fail to check and recheck their assumptions. Consider, for example, the miscommunication that occurred with the Mars Climate Orbiter in September 1999 (see Exhibit 14.11).

LESS RAPPORT People working across distance also feel less rapport, less trust, and less cohesion with members of the distance team. This is because people who communicate face to face follow politeness rituals.[18] Politeness rituals involve the exchange of greetings, pleasantries, compliments, and smiles. Keisler and Sproull suggest that people interacting via information technology do not feel bound by the same social norms that guide face-to-face encounters.[19] Geographically separated teams report lower trust and lower cohesion. The members feel less attracted to their teams. Rapport is built most effectively through face-to-face communication.

LESS EFFICIENCY Distance teamwork is often less efficient. In particular, people working across distance take more time to make decisions (than do face-to-face groups), but at the same time, this does not lead to a greater volume of information exchange. Thus, the increased time to make decisions does not mean that more information is unearthed.

RISKY DECISION MAKING Members of distance groups also tend to make more risky decisions. In Chapter 7, we noted that people are risk-averse for gains and risk-seeking for losses. However, when making decisions via e-mail, people tend to show more risk-seeking behavior. Computer-mediated groups make riskier decisions and exhibit greater polarization of judgment than do face-to-face groups.[20] As a case in point, group members' decision recommendations in face-to-face groups tend to conform to the recommendations of other group members, but not so in computer-mediated groups.[21] Whereas most people are risk-averse for gains and risk-seeking for losses (see Chapter 7),

Disadvantages	Advantages
• More misunderstandings	• Greater task focus (less joking around)
• Less rapport (lower trust and cohesion)	• Reduced status differences ("weak-get-strong" effect)
• Less efficient	• Equalization of team members' participation
• More "risky" decision making	• Less inhibition; potentially more healthy task conflict
• Less inhibition; more interpersonal conflict	• Less conformity
• Greater temptation and abuse of multitasking	• Greater likelihood of "fierce conversations"
	• Potential for rise of diverse communities

EXHIBIT 14.10

Distance Teamwork

EXHIBIT 14.11   Mars Climate Orbiter Failure

On September 23, 1999, the Mars Climate Orbiter fired its main engine to go into orbit around the planet. The spacecraft was over 56 miles off course and was ultimately lost in space—an avoidable human error costing hundreds of millions of dollars.

The key problem concerned a "Failed translation of English units into metric units"—One team used English units (e.g., inches, feet, and pounds); the other used metric units for a key spacecraft operation.

The failure investigation board concluded the following:

- Inconsistent communications
- Operational navigation team not fully informed of details
- Communication channels too informal
- Verification and validation process inadequate

Source: NASA: NSSDC Master Catalog: Spacecraft.1998. Mars Climate Orbiter. Retrieved November 22, 2004, from http://nssdc.gsfc.nasa.gov/database/MasterCatalog?sc=1998–073A.

groups that make decisions via computer mediation are risk-seeking for both gains and losses.[22]

LESS INHIBITION Members of distance groups are less inhibited, and the personal system of checks and balances may lead to more risky decisions. The lower a person's inhibitions, the more likely it is that he or she may engage in confrontational conflict, which increases interpersonal conflict. People are more likely to communicate bluntly and without pretense when interacting via e-mail as compared to face-to-face. Most of the time, face-to-face interactions encourage people to behave more cooperatively. They often exchange pleasantries, deliver feedback more gently, and smile quite often. However, the same person delivering the same message via e-mail may be blunt to the point of insulting. Lack of inhibition can eventually threaten team performance if conflicts are not properly addressed or if conflict becomes unhealthy.

MULTITASKING Because members of distance teams do not share a physical presence with one another, they often do not fully involve themselves with the team. Consequently, they are more likely to multitask. For example, during a conference call, they might check e-mail or even have someone else in their office for a different purpose.

Advantages

GREATER TASK FOCUS One advantage of virtual teamwork is that members have a greater task focus. They get down to business and spend less time socializing.

REDUCED STATUS DIFFERENCES Another advantage is that the cues that signal status differences among team members are not as salient, and therefore low-status people have more influence in virtual teams. Who are the people in a group or organization that are likely to be the most talkative in a typical face-to-face interaction? Power and influence in groups derives from real status cues as well as superficial (secondary) status cues. People defer to those whom they expect to be the leaders of a group and, in so doing, pay attention to a variety of cues or signals that provide clues about a person's status in an organization. Real status cues include job title, rank, and tenure in an organization. Not surprisingly, people of higher organizational rank and authority are more likely to be given the floor and to usurp the floor than are people of lower rank in the organization. In addition, people with more experience or tenure are more likely to be given the floor as well. In the absence of real status cues, people often look for other cues to signal a person's importance. These are often superficial aspects of a person that are highly visible, but of questionable validity. The three most commonly used cues that people use to determine whom they will give influence to in a group are age (up to a point), gender (males are accorded more status than females, holding constant their actual rank in an organization), and dress (people who look more influential, such as someone wearing a "power suit," are often assumed to be more influential).

However, status cues are more difficult to discern when people interact via information technology. Real status cues are often missing; job title and rank may be apparent on a Web page, but not so much in an e-mail signature. Similarly, superficial cues are missing as well; e-mail addresses mask a person's age, gender, and dress.

Not surprisingly, this constellation of factors effectively levels the technology-mediated playing field. Thus, people who might be otherwise ignored in a face-to-face meeting have more impact through e-mail. In one investigation of mixed-gender business groups, men were five times more likely than women to make the first decision proposal.[23] When the same groups met via computer, women made the first proposal just as often as the men did.

EQUALIZATION OF TEAM MEMBERS' PARTICIPATION Team members who interact virtually participate more equally in group discussions and group decisions. As we noted in Chapter 4, face-to-face groups are anything but a democracy, at least when it comes to actual input and voice. The most talkative member in a six-person group consumes over 37 percent of the available airtime. The second most talkative member consumes 18 percent of the available airtime. The least talkative members are relegated to only 45 percent of the available time. However, the tables turn when information technology is involved. There is greater equalization of team members' participation. This occurs for two primary reasons: First and foremost, less assertive team members no longer have to "compete" for the floor in face-to-face interaction. Competition for the floor involves a complex choreography of making eye contact, making verbal utterances that are not actually speech, and in some cases, fidgeting in one's chair. People who are uncomfortable in the spotlight can seek solace in e-communication because they can control their entry into the conversation. Second, e-mail moves the focus from who is saying what to the content of what is said.

LESS CONFORMITY Conformity occurs when people bring their behavior and attitudes into alignment with a group or organization's expectations and beliefs. Conformity pressures can be quite strong in face-to-face groups of four or more people, so much so that people often engage in behaviors or agree with statements that they privately know are wrong.[24] Conformity in groups tends to be highest when people admire and value their team. People interacting virtually are less likely to conform as compared to people interacting in a face-to-face situation.[25]

LESS INHIBITION: POTENTIALLY HEALTHIER TASK CONFLICT Because people are less inhibited when they interact virtually and less likely to conform to the beliefs of others, there is greater potential for healthy task conflict in virtual teams. However, too much task conflict can be disruptive for groups; and if trust in the group is low, then task conflict might also accompany unhealthy relationship conflict.[26]

POTENTIAL FOR DIVERSE COMMUNITIES Many people use the Internet to be "connected" to others. But sometimes, people prefer e-interaction to real, face-to-face communication (for an example, see Exhibit 14.12). The power of community on the Internet is so strong that people show signs of real depression when they are excluded or ostracized, even by someone that they know isn't a human.[27] For example, Williams and Zadro created a computer game that consisted largely of a laboratory-based ball-tossing game in which participants engaged spontaneously with two other (confederate) participants.[28] At a key point, the two confederates started tossing the ball just between themselves, effectively ostracizing one person. The ostracized participants slumped in their chairs and showed signs of depression after only four minutes. Studies of long-term ostracism report incidences of suicide and depression[29] and even mass shootings.[30]

EXHIBIT 14.12 **Preferring E-Mail to Real Social Interaction?**

One executive wrote to *Fast Company* editors, "I think I am truly addicted [to e-mail]. Wireless e-mail pushed me over the edge. My wife gets upset when I check my BlackBerry over dinner and has threatened to toss out my device. I know she's right, but I can't help myself." The *Fast Company* corporate shrink, Dr. Kerry J. Sulkowicz, writes back, "I feel sorry for your wife. You are avoiding your wife and others, and throwing away your device won't fix that. Talking to them and listening would make a difference."

Source: Sulkowicz, K. J. (2004, July 1). The corporate shrink. *Fast Company,* p. 42.

Going the Distance: Making the Best of Virtual Teams

Virtual teams are groups of employees with unique skills, situated in distant locations, whose members must collaborate using technology across space and time to accomplish important organizational tasks.[31] Distance teamwork is often not a choice for companies; it is a necessary aspect of the global era. And the use of virtual teams is expanding exponentially.[32] Therefore, it makes sense for most companies to try to optimize the effectiveness of teams and organizations that must interact in a non-face-to-face fashion.

It is unwise to assume that the factors that influence collocated teams are valid for virtual teams.[33] In practice, virtual teams vary on the amount of face-to-face interaction they have, which can range from no physical interaction to monthly, face-to-face team meetings.[34] Organizations that accurately know the challenges of virtual teamwork are better positioned to effectively deal with the challenges that face them. What are some specific recommendations on how to best address the threats of virtual teamwork? (See Mittleman for an extensive treatment of this subject.)[35] We consider two types of solutions for virtual teamwork: structural solutions and process solutions (see Exhibit 14.13). Structural solutions are ones that involve significant infrastructure and support and, therefore, represent a greater expenditure. Process solutions are not nearly as expensive and are more psychological in nature.

Structural Solutions

As noted above, structural solutions are ones that involve a significant investment in the form of organizational resources and support.

CHALLENGING TASK THAT REQUIRES INTERDEPENDENCE Don't expect teams to surmount an electronic obstacle course unless it is clear to them why it is important to do so. The best way of bringing people together across distance is to put them in a position where

EXHIBIT 14.13

Optimizing Distance Teamwork

Structural Solutions	Process Solutions
• Challenging task that requires interdependence	• Role clarity
• Team empowerment	• Revisit collective assumptions regularly
• Initial face-to-face experience	• Perspective-taking
• Temporary engagement	• Boundary-spanning
• One-day video conference	• Team contract
	• Structured task conflict

they need each other (i.e., they are interdependent) and the goal is abundantly clear. It is for this reason that we hear about virtual teamwork, not simply distance-organizations or distance-groups. People who are bridging distances are doing so to achieve a collective goal.

TEAM EMPOWERMENT   Team empowerment is defined as increased task motivation that is due to team members' collective, positive assessments of their own organizational tasks.[36] Teams experience empowerment on four dimensions, including:[37]

- **Potency:** the collective belief of a team that it can be effective
- **Meaningfulness:** the extent to which team members feel an intrinsic dedication to their task
- **Autonomy:** the degree to which team members believe that they have freedom to make decisions
- **Impact:** the extent to which team members feel that their tasks make significant organizational contributions

In an investigation of 35 virtual sales and service teams in a high-technology organization, team empowerment proved to be positively related to process improvement and customer satisfaction.[38] And the less often team members met face-to-face, the more important empowerment was in predicting their success. Stated another way, for teams that have the luxury of meeting face-to-face more often, empowerment is less important in ensuring their success than for teams that are more virtual.

INITIAL FACE-TO-FACE EXPERIENCE   Within the first few moments of meeting someone, we form impressions about that person and, perhaps even more significantly, quickly develop a rhythm or cadence of interaction with that person. It affects a complex system of verbal and nonverbal behavior. In short, we "negotiate" how far apart we stand, the rate of speech, the amount of eye contact, the choice of words, and so forth. The purpose of this communication dance is to optimize understanding and rapport. Without our ability to socialize and be socialized, human interaction would be very difficult. Not surprisingly, people who already have formed a relationship on the basis of face-to-face interaction are better communicators when they are separated electronically. In one investigation, some people were allowed to "schmooze" with each other before negotiating a business deal via e-mail. Other people were not given this opportunity. People who had a chance to schmooze with each other were more likely to reach deals;[39] and when they did carve out a deal, it was more likely to be win-win. Thus, when teams are given an early opportunity to sync with one another, presumably they are not only more committed to the success of their team, but they have already laid a complex groundwork of communication.

TEMPORARY ENGAGEMENT   A temporary engagement takes the idea of an initial face-to-face experience one step further: Teams are brought together for a fixed amount of time to work together. For example, more and more universities are offering degrees that do not require students to be physically present. For example, in Duke University's Global Executive MBA program, students spend approximately two weeks in residency—building working relationships and laying a groundwork with other members with whom they will work collaboratively over long distance. Black compared traditional, online, and hybrid methods of course delivery in business classes.[40] In terms of student-rated satisfaction, students preferred hybrid courses (involving some face-to-face interaction time and some Internet time) to either online-only or classroom-only courses. Moreover, as students grew to be more computer expert, their level of satisfaction with the Internet-only and hybrid modes of course delivery increased.

ONE-DAY VIDEO CONFERENCE   A one-day video conference can improve the richness of communication and establish a rapport that may not be achieved in more impoverished communications.

Process Solutions

Process solutions are cost-effective because they don't involve lots of investment, but they can be very powerful. They are best practices that over a short amount of time serve as group norms.

ROLE CLARITY   All virtual team members need to not only know their own role, but also understand the roles that others play. If it is not clear what roles others play, people on virtual teams will not be able to tap into one another's expertise at the time it is most needed.

REVISIT COLLECTIVE ASSUMPTIONS REGULARLY   Group reflexivity is the ability of a group to analyze how it does work.[41] In short, group reflexivity is the ability of a group to step back and look at how they do things. Groups that exhibit reflexivity are more effective performance-wise than are groups who do not look at themselves. And group reflexivity improves creative performance.[42]

PERSPECTIVE-TAKING   Perspective-taking is the ability to take another person's point of view. As straightforward as this sounds, most people do not engage in perspective-taking unless they are specifically instructed or coached to do so.

BOUNDARY-SPANNING   As we noted in Chapter 6, boundary-spanning is a key organizational activity. Effective boundary-spanning is essential for distance teamwork.

TEAM CONTRACT   A team contract is a more elaborate version of the psychological contract we discussed in Chapter 2. A team contract is a living document that team members write jointly that focuses on their shared expectations and how they will do their work. It is not a strategic plan per se, but rather, it outlines the process by which they intend to achieve their goals and the expectations they hold of themselves and of others. The team contract, because it is a living document, should be revisited every three to four months. At that time, team members should candidly discuss what is working well and what is not working well vis-à-vis their teamwork. What norms are being flagrantly ignored? What expectations are unrealistic? What expectations have proved essential for the success of the team?

STRUCTURED TASK CONFLICT   Conflict can be the silent killer of effective distance teamwork. We noted that conflict is present in all aspects of organizational life. Distance teams are no exception. Because of the distance between them, team members may attempt to suppress conflict, ignore it, or rechannel it. We suggest that team members engage in structured task conflict at planned times. This ensures that conflicts have a chance to emerge. Team leaders can be instructed how to express conflict in either task or process terms, rather than in relational terms.

Conclusion

We introduced the place-time model of social interaction and examined how the incidence of non-face-to-face communication has increased rapidly in the business world. We focused in particular on virtual teams and distinguished them from traditional teams and hybrid teams in terms of three key underlying dimensions: the extent of time they all work on the same task, the amount and quality of technical support, and how physically close or far they are from one another. Hybrid teams compose the largest proportion of teams. We discussed how information technology affects organizational behavior. Some positive effects include the equalization of group members' participation, greater task focus, less conformity, and lowered inhibitions. The disadvantages include greater misunderstanding, lower rapport, increased risky decision making, and less focus (i.e., more multitasking). We discussed two sets of solutions or best practices when it comes to virtual teamwork. One set of solutions is structural and involves investment in technology or human resources. The other type of solution is process oriented and involves changing norms, such as the use of a team contract.

Notes

1. In a statement by Martin N. Baily, Chairman, Council of Economic Advisers. Retrieved from http://www.ntia.doc.gov/ntiahome/press/2000/all3g101300.htm.
2. Venditti, P. (2004, March 1). E-mail a great communicator but also a time waster. (Tool box for business). *Everett Business Journal.*
3. Ibid.
4. Hammonds, K. (2004, July 1). We, incorporated. *Fast Company,* p. 67.
5. Battelle, J. (2004, August). Titans of tech. *Business 2.0,* p. 93.
6. Hancock, J. T., Thom-Santelli, J., & Ritchie, T. (2004). Deception and design: The impact of communication technology on lying behavior. *Proceedings of the SGICHI Conference on Human Factors in Computing Systems, 6*(1), 129–134.
7. Ibid.
8. Ibid.
9. Loewenstein, J., Morris, M., Chakravarti, A., Thompson, L., & Kopelman, S. (2005). At a loss for words: Dominating the conversation and the outcome in negotiation as a function of intricate arguments and communication media. *Organizational Behavior and Human Decision Processes, 98*(1), 28–38.
10. Winerman, L. (2004, July 1). Designing psychologists. *APA Monitor,* p. 30.
11. See note 2.
12. Cohen, R. (2002). *The good, the bad, and the difference: How to tell right from wrong in everyday situations.* New York: Doubleday.
13. Vazire, S., & Gosling, S. D. (2004). e-Perceptions: Personality impressions based on personal websites. *Journal of Personality and Social Psychology, 87,* 123–132.
14. Ibid.
15. Sproull, L., & Keisler, S. (1991). *Connections: New ways of working in the networked organization.* Cambridge, MA: MIT Press.
16. Neale, M. A., & Griffith, T. (2000). Information processing in traditional, hybrid, & virtual teams: From nascent knowledge to transactive memory. In B. Staw & R. Sutton (Eds.), *Research in organizational behavior* (Vol. 23, pp. 379–421). Greenwich, CT: JAI Press.
17. Ibid.
18. Morris, M. W., Nadler, J., Kurtzberg, T., & Thompson, L. (2002). Schmooze or lose: Social fiction and lubrication in e-mail negotiations. *Group Dynamics: Theory, Research, and Practice, 6*(1), 89–100.
19. Keisler, S., & Sproull, L. (1992). Group decision making and communication technology. *Organizational Behavior and Human Decision Processes, 52,* 96–123.
20. McGuire, T., Keisler, S., & Siegel, J. (1987). Group and computer-mediated discussion effect in risk decision-making. *Journal of Personality and Social Psychology, 52*(5), 917–930; Siegel, J., Dubrovsky, V., Keisler, S., & McGuire, T. (1986). Group processes in computer-mediated communication. *Organizational Behavior, 37,* 157–187; Weisband, S. P. (1992). Group discussion and first advocacy effects in computer-mediated and face-to-face decision-making groups. *Organizational Behavior and Human Decision Processes, 53,* 352–380.
21. Weisband, "Group discussion," p. 263.
22. McGuire, Keisler, & Siegel, "Group and computer-mediated discussion," p. 263.
23. Ibid.
24. Asch, S. E. (1956). Studies of independence and conformity: A minority of one against a unanimous majority. *Psychological Monographs, 70* (Whole no. 416).
25. Schmidt, J., Montoya-Weiss, M., & Massey, A. (2001). New product development decision-making effectiveness: Comparing individuals, face-to-face teams, and virtual teams. *Decision Sciences, 32*(4), 8–10.
26. Peterson, R. S., & Behfar, K. J. (2003). The dynamic relationship between performance feedback, trust, and conflict in groups: A longitudinal study. *Organizational Behavior and Human Decision Processes, 92,* 102–112.
27. Zadro, L., Williams, K. D., & Richardson, R. (2004). How low can you go? Ostracism by a computer is sufficient to lower self-reported levels of belonging, control, self-esteem, and meaningful existence. *Journal of Experimental Social Psychology, 40,* 560–567.
28. Williams, K. D., & Zadro, L. (2001). Ostracism: On being ignored, excluded and rejected. In M. R. Leary (Ed.), *Interpersonal rejection* (pp. 21–53). New York: Oxford University Press.
29. Ibid.
30. Leary, M. R., Kowalski, R. M., Smith, L., & Phillips, S. (2003). Teasing, rejection, and violence: Case studies of the school shootings. *Aggressive Behavior, 29,* 202–214.
31. Lipnack, J., & Stamps, J. (2000). *Virtual teams: People working across boundaries with technology* (2nd ed.). New York: John Wiley & Sons.
32. Kirkman, B. L., Rosen, B., Gibson, C. B., Tesluk, P. E., & McPherson, S. O. (2002). Five challenges to virtual team success: Lessons from Sabre, Inc. *Academy of Management Executive, 16*(3), 67–79.
33. Potter, R. E., & Balthazard, P. A. (2002). Understanding human interaction and performance in the virtual team. *Journal of Information Technology Theory and Application, 4*(1), 1–23.
34. Lipnack & Stamps, *Virtual teams,* p. 266; Townsend, A. M., DeMarie, S. M., & Hendrickson, A. R. (1998). Virtual teams: Technology and the workplace of the future. *Academy of Management Executive, 12*(3), 17–29.
35. Mittleman, D., & Briggs, R. (1999). Communication technology for teams: Electronic collaboration. In E. Sundstrom (Ed.), *Supporting work team effectiveness: Creating contexts for high performance.* San Francisco: Jossey-Bass.
36. Kirkman, B. L., & Rosen, B. (2000). Powering up teams. *Organizational Dynamics, 28*(3), 48–66.

37. Kirkman, B., Rosen, B., Tesluk, P., & Gibson, C. (2004). The impact of team empowerment on virtual team performance: The moderating role of face-to-face interaction. *Academy of Management Journal, 47,* 175–192; Kirkman, B. L., & Rosen, B. (1997). A model of work team empowerment. In R. W. Woodman & W. A. Pasmore (Eds.), *Research in organizational change and development* (Vol. 10, pp. 131–167). Greenwich, CT: JAI Press.

38. Kirkman, Rosen, Tesluk, & Gibson, "Impact of team empowerment," p. 267.

39. Moore, D., Kurtzberg, T., Thompson, L., & Morris, M. (1999). Long and short routes to success in electronically mediated negotiations: Group affiliations and good vibrations. *Organization Behavior & Human Decision Processes, 77*(1), 22–43.

40. Black, G. (2001). A student assessment of virtual teams in an online management course. Paper submitted to the *AABSS Journal/Perspectives* for publication.

41. West, M., Sacramento, C., & Fay, D. (2006). Creativity and innovation implementation in work groups: The paradoxical role of demands. In L. Thompson & H. Choi (Eds.), *Creativity and innovation in organizational teams.* Mahwah, NJ: Lawrence Erlbaum.

42. Ibid.

LIFE, LEARNING, AND PERSONAL DEVELOPMENT

Imagine that you are 90 years old. You are in reasonably good health and you are writing a letter to your 20-year-old self. If you could give yourself only one piece of advice, what would you say? Mark Twain said it this way:[1]

> *Dance like nobody's watching;*
> *Love like you've never been hurt.*
> *Sing like nobody's listening,*
> *Live like it's heaven on earth.*

Are you living the way you want to live, right now? Or are you waiting to be happy? This chapter focuses on the happiness of work and the work of happiness.

Life Maxims versus Practical Advice

The message of this chapter is going to be this: Don't look for your work to sustain you, and don't hope that if you are fascinated by your organization you will be a fascinating person. Rather, the message of this chapter is going to be about life in the broadest context, and that going to work and doing work is part of life. Thus, if we live well, we work well, not the other way around.

We hear lots of advice as we grow up, such as, "Live each day as if it were your last"; "Don't sweat the small things"; and "No one ever regretted spending more time with their kids." Most of us would heartily agree with these maxims. Yet sometimes we wonder, if we did follow all of this advice, how would we ever get our work done? If this were our last day to live, no one would opt to complete a tax return or a monthly budget statement, or even write a newspaper column to be read by millions. But, if we never did this, we'd be in trouble. So the advice that is offered to us touches our heart and soul but, when looked at critically, is not very practical. This chapter focuses on practical advice for the long-term of organizational life.

Critical Choice Points

We began this book by making the point that the typical person will spend more time working than doing anything else in life. The other thing to keep in mind is that the best predictor of the future quality of your life is the current quality of your life. Are you making the most of it? Or are you in a self-perpetuating holding pattern? Seasoned businesspeople and executives will tell you that the hardest part is not landing the job or making the big money; rather, sustaining yourself is the key to organizational and life success. It is imperative to make the experience of being part of an organization as enjoyable and as rewarding as possible. All of the following are options:

- *Complaining:* The complainer is never happy with his or her lot; something is always wrong. The complainer is passive and occasionally passive-aggressive. Things will never be right, so the complainer would prefer to talk about what is wrong rather than do something about it. How many times have you complained today?
- *Opting out:* People who opt out simply decide they've had enough. They've run out of steam or energy. Also known as dropouts, these folks are characterized by moving away from situations, rather than being drawn toward their goals.
- *Controlling:* Controllers fight every step of the way. They attempt to control their lives and the people with whom they work.
- *Engaging:* Engaged people see how they matter to their organizations and they feel a personal sense of accountability. They immerse themselves in their missions, recognize when they are off course, and examine what it will take to get back on course. However, less than 30 percent of U.S. workers are fully engaged at work, according to Gallup Organization data.[2] A full 55 percent are not engaged, and 19 percent are actively disengaged, meaning that they are not just unhappy; they are disgruntled and complaining.

100-Day Plan? What Are You Going to Do?

Research indicates that the first 90 to 100 days (three or so months) of an endeavor—whether it is a marriage, friendship, business deal, or new job—is a critical period. Not only are norms being set by the involved parties, but psychological contracts are being constructed, and people's views of themselves are being shaped. Michael Watkins, author of *The First 90 Days,* starkly states, "The actions you take during your first three months in a new job will largely determine whether you succeed or fail."[3] The first three months are critical because employees and companies are essentially in an imprinting period. They are making judgments about each other and forming patterns that will last for decades, on the basis of very little information. For this reason, successfully building credibility early on can propel a manager on the high course. According to Watkins, the most common mistake people make is not paying attention during this acculturation process. This advice cuts both ways; companies need to adequately socialize their new hires—no matter at what level—and the new hires need to monitor their environment.[4]

Transition Acceleration and the Breakeven Point

Watkins introduces two key concepts relevant for the first 90 days: transition acceleration and the breakeven point. **Transition acceleration** refers to the ability of new hires to move quickly from the transition of being hired into their new job and being on top of their job, regardless of their level in the organization. Managers who succeed in transitioning from the new guy on the block to the essential manager are then able to exploit opportunities. Transition acceleration helps new managers quickly reach the breakeven point. The **breakeven point** is the point at which new leaders have contributed as much value to their new organizations as they have consumed from it. As shown in Exhibit 15.1, new leaders are net consumers of value early on (e.g., training costs, using people's time, acquiring hardware and software, etc.). As they learn and begin to take action, they begin to create value for the organization. Watkins asked 210 company CEOs and presidents to estimate the time it took a typical mid-level manager in their organization to reach the breakeven point, and the average response was 6.2 months.[5]

Each year over 500,000 people enter new positions in Fortune 500 companies and nearly 250,000 managers in these Fortune 500 companies change jobs.[6] This means that managers spend an average of four years in a given job. The "eras" of higher-level managers are even shorter, according to Watkins—about 2.5 years. Thus, transitions are happening constantly. What can companies and leaders do to accelerate the transition of new hires? According to Watkins, it is as simple as giving time to them. If you don't spend time with new hires, this can be deadly. Get these new hires into your office and see where they are struggling. Ask how things are going. What's more, the size of the company is critical: "A bad hire can be an inconvenience for a large organization. For a small business that doesn't have the same margin for error, a new hire in the wrong role at the wrong time—that can be near-death experience."[7]

What about the advice on the other side of the coin? What should you, as a new manager, be doing in that first 90 days? Watkins advises that people do the following: promote

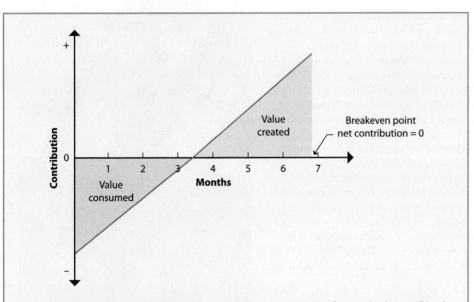

EXHIBIT 15.1

The Breakeven Point

Source: Watkins, M. (2003). *The first 90 days: Critical success strategies for new leaders at all levels* (p. 3). Boston: Harvard Business School Press. Reprinted by permission of Harvard Business Review. Copyright © 2003 by the Harvard Business School Publishing Corporation; all rights reserved.

themselves (which includes assessing their own vulnerabilities), accelerate their own learning through structured methods, secure early wins by quickly iterating, negotiate effective working relationships that include the ability to talk about the relationship, build their teams, and create coalitions.

The Self-Sustaining Person

We all know people who seem to be perpetually upbeat, excited about what they are doing, and forward-thinking. They are not simply lucky. They really shine under pressure. When these people suffer a setback, they move through it and transform it into a learning opportunity. They are not necessarily charismatic, but they seem to have that special something that sustains them across all of their life and organizational pursuits. We call this person the *self-sustaining person.* And this person is in a slim statistical minority. After six months on the job, only 38 percent of employees remain engaged and excited by what they are doing. And, after three years, this plummets to 22 percent. How engaged are you right now? Reading this book? And in your classes?

In the following paragraphs, we introduce a variety of models of the self-sustaining person. These are not competing models. Each works for certain people. We strongly urge you to pick the model (or combination of models) that works for you.

The Corporate Athlete

Did you know that insomnia (a symptom of depression and other psychological aliments) is wreaking havoc on our health and taxing businesses?[8] More than half of all Americans report insomnia at least a few nights a week.[9] Lack of sleep is associated with a number of health problems, including coronary heart disease. Sleep disorders cost companies $18 billion in productivity per year.[10] (See Exhibit 15.2.) Another debilitator is depression. The incidence of depression and anxiety has increased tenfold in the last 50 years.[11] Each

EXHIBIT 15.2   Strengthen Your Brain While Resting It

The data are in. Dr. James B. Mass has devoted his life to sleep—or studying it—and the lack of it on human performance. Mass is not overstating the case when he says, "We have a crisis in America. If we treated machines like we treat the human body, we would be accused of reckless endangerment. Most adults are moderately to severely sleep deprived and it affects their productivity, their work, and their relationships." A whopping 60 percent of Americans sleep less than 7 hours per night on average and 60 percent have problems sleeping a few nights each week. Good sleep is the best predictor of life span or quality of life. Sleeping is the key to learning. Mass uses golf as an example. If you take lessons on Wednesday to improve your swing before your Saturday game, but you sleep only 6 hours each night for the rest of the week, your performance will be worse than if you had not taken the lessons at all. Why? Sleep spindles that occur during REM sleep are only fully operative between the 6th to 8th hours of sleep. Sleep spindles transfer short-term information in the motor cortex to the temporal lobe to become long-term knowledge. The science of sleep is so advanced that, in one study, rats' brain patterns during sleep were observed and found to be nearly identical to the patterns they exhibited while running a maze the previous day. The patterns were so similar that the researchers could tell what part of the maze the rat was dreaming about!

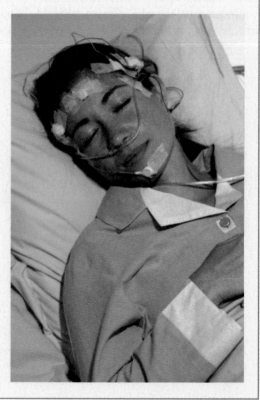

Source: Adapted from Greer, M. (2004, July 1). Strengthen your brain by resting it. *APA Monitor on Psychology,* p. 60.

EXHIBIT 15.3 The High Performance Pyramid

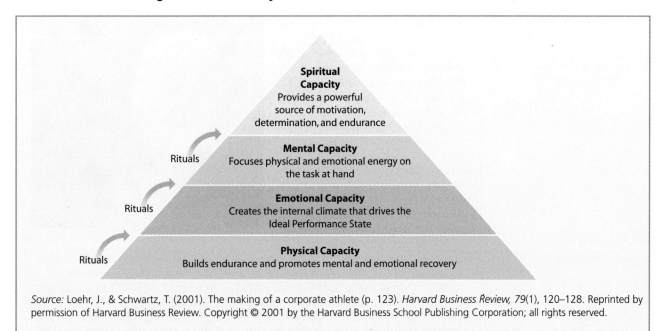

Source: Loehr, J., & Schwartz, T. (2001). The making of a corporate athlete (p. 123). *Harvard Business Review, 79*(1), 120–128. Reprinted by permission of Harvard Business Review. Copyright © 2001 by the Harvard Business School Publishing Corporation; all rights reserved.

generation of adults has a higher rate of depression than their parents.[12] Murray and Lopez estimate that by 2020 depression will be the second leading cause of disability-adjusted life years (i.e., the loss of ability to do everyday, normal tasks).[13]

The link between physical health and mental health is overpowering. For this reason it is not surprising that books like *The Corporate Athlete,* by Jack Groppel and Bob Andelman, are taking the idea that a healthy body and strict training regimen can improve the bottom line as well as the waistline.[14] In his foreword to *The Corporate Athlete,* Jim Loehr argues that successful corporate executives are in effect "corporate athletes"—they perform at a high level and train in the same systematic, multilevel way that world class athletes do. Loehr and Schwartz posit the "high performance pyramid" (see Exhibit 15.3). The managers who have not learned to manage their energy say, "We return home from long days at work feeling exhausted and often experience our families not as a source of joy and renewal, but as one more demand in an already overburdened life."[15]

There are at least two other reasons to learn how to marshal your energy: First, you are going to need it to manage your family life. Most people in college are accountable for themselves and they don't have family responsibilities as yet. Marriage, and especially children, represents a major commitment of time and energy. In her book, *The Time Bind: When Work Becomes Home and Home Becomes Work,* Arlie Russell Hochschild argues that it is more than a wake-up call when we start looking forward to work, but dread coming home.[16]

The other thing to keep in mind is that none of us are getting younger. Whereas you are probably not experiencing any signs of the aging process yet, you will, according to cognitive aging experts such as Timothy Salthouse. Salthouse examined five cognitive skills: vocabulary, reasoning, spatial visualization, episodic memory, and speed. Every single skill weakened with age except vocabulary.[17] Thus, age-related declines in cognitive function are relatively large, begin early (not late) in adulthood, and are clearly apparent before age 50. Other key skills, such as motivation, persistence, and positive outlook, are all essential and are either not related to age or follow a different trajectory. (See Exhibit 15.4 for an example of an active hundred-plus-year-old person.)

IDEAL PERFORMANCE STATE The **ideal performance state, or IPS,** according to Groppel and Andelman in *The Corporate Athlete,* is a condition in which people can bring their talents and skills to full ignition and sustain high performance over time. The capacity

EXHIBIT 15.4

The Active Centenarian

Ray Crist began his organizational life at the age of 4 when he went to Little Grantham School. After graduating from college, Crist earned his Ph.D. in chemistry and was a member of the Manhattan Project crew. He was a professor at Columbia University and had a stint as a director of research for Union Carbide. Crist retired from his job at Dickinson College at age 70. After that he began another job at Messiah College that lasted 34 years. He drew an annual salary of $1 and in exchange he taught classes on environmental science, published papers, and made speeches. In 2002, at 102 years of age, Ray was the oldest worker in America. Crist loves to work. After 34 years at Messiah College, at the ripe old age of 104, Ray Crist retired—for the third time. He had plans to write his autobiography, as well as another book. He has loved every job he ever held and brought great value to the organizations he worked for. Messiah College president Rodney Sawatsky said, "You [Crist] helped put this little college on the map." What was Crist's secret for such incredible energy and dedication? Quite simply, Crist was fascinated with life. Said Crist, "I never thought of work as just a job." Crist believed that "working maintains a person as an integral part of the living process." That philosophy served him well for the 100 years he has been an organizational man.

Source: Adapted from Linecker, A. C. (2004, May 13). Never stop learning, a 104-year-old student. *Investor's Business Daily,* p. A03.

to mobilize energy on demand is the foundation of IPS. According to Loehr and Schwartz, who've worked with and trained hundreds of professional athletes, there are two key elements that help us manage the energy people need to achieve IPS: energy expenditure (stress) and energy renewal (recovery). In fact, it is not stress that befalls most managers; it is the lack of recovery. Chronic stress without recovery depletes energy, leads to burnout, and undermines performance. Oscillation is the process of going from stress to recovery. Effective corporate athletes ritualize this process of recovery. Loehr and Schwartz encourage us to think of it this way: The average professional athlete spends most of her or his time practicing and only a small percentage actually competing. In contrast, the typical manager devotes almost no time to training and has to perform on demand 10 or 14 hours a day. Moreover, athletes enjoy several months off-season but managers are lucky to get 3 weeks of vacation per year. The topper? The career of the average professional athlete lasts 7 years; the career of an executive can last 40 to 50 years.

Loehr and Schwartz anoint leaders as the "stewards of organizational energy." They ask each manager, "If you could wake up tomorrow with significantly more positive, focused energy to invest at work and with your family, how significantly would that change your life for the better?"[18]

RITUALS AND RECOVERY For this reason, Loehr and Schwartz encourage managers to take tips from athletes who have ritualized their recovery. Recovery rituals can be phenomenally short—lasting only 15 to 20 seconds—but the trained athlete knows how to make the most of the recovery. Chronobiologists argue that the human body and mind need recovery every 90 to 120 minutes. Loehr and Schwartz offer practical strategies for renewing energy at the physical level:

- *Actually do all those healthy things you know you ought to do,* such as eat five to six small meals per day (as opposed to two to three larger meals). Always eat breakfast;

drink several glasses of water; and above all, get cardiovascular exercise.

Dr. Kathy Bogacz recommends that you don't need to go to a fancy gym and have all the fancy gear. But you do need 30 minutes at least three times per week. As a start, she advises, go out and start walking for 15 minutes in one direction and then walk back.[19]

■ *Go to bed early and wake up early; maintain a consistent bedtime and wake-up time.* People who stay up late have a more difficult time dealing with the demands of the business world. Ideally, most adults should sleep seven to eight hours a day. Your body works best when it has consistent rituals; in this way, you can tune your own biological clock.

■ *Seek recovery every 90 to 120 minutes.* Hormones, glucose levels, and blood pressure drop every 90 minutes. The trained manager seeks recovery not by reaching for a donut, but rather by eating something healthy, drinking water, and moving physically (e.g., taking the stairs rather than the elevator). It takes about two weeks for new behavior to become a habit.

■ *Do at least two weight training workouts a week.* No form of exercise turns back the aging clock more than does weight training. It increases strength, retards osteoporosis, speeds up metabolism, enhances mobility, improves posture, and dramatically increases energy.

■ *Set boundaries between work and home.* The effective corporate athlete will transition between work and home. Frustrations at work should not be brought to bear in one's home life.

■ *Focus on your energy, not your technical or tactical skills.* Loehr and Schwartz have worked with 80 of the most elite athletes in their laboratory, including Pete Sampras, Jim Courier, Gabriela Sabatini, and Monica Seles. Once in the laboratory, no time is spent focusing on technical or tactical skills (e.g., serving techniques); rather, the focus is on energy.

Mental Exercise

Davidson starkly asserts that people are very involved and committed to their physical fitness, but they don't pay attention to their minds.[20] According to Davidson, people's minds are as plastic as their bodies. In particular, Davidson recommends meditation. And he is not alone. Several respectable health care organizations, such as the National Institute of Health and the Mind/Body Medical Institute at Harvard University, are documenting how meditation enhances the ability of managers on the job. In particular, the ability to focus, deal with stress, and approach problems markedly change with mediation. In short, meditation alters the biochemistry of the brain. As a case in point, the brains of two groups—monks (who meditate regularly) and regular people (who don't mediate regularly)—were compared using MRI technology. The monks' left prefrontal cortexes (they are associated with positive emotion) were more active as compared to the nonmeditators (see Exhibit 15.5 for examples of companies that have embraced mediation in the C-suite and beyond).

Psychological Flow

Mihaly Csikszentmihalyi believes that people should live their lives as a work of art, rather than as a chaotic response to external events.[21] His work started with artists, who often

---

EXHIBIT 15.5

Meditation and the Art of Business

AOL, Raytheon, Nortel Networks, Medtronics, and Aetna all offer meditation classes for their employees.

Bill George, former CEO of Medtronics, has meditated twice a day for 20 minutes for 30 years and says, "Out of anything, it has had the greatest impact on my career."

Michael Stephen, former chairman of Aetna, claims that meditating helped transform him from an impatient, demanding, arrogant leader into a transformational leader.

Source: Conlin, M. (2004, August 30). Meditation and the art of business. *BusinessWeek,* p. 136.

described themselves as being in ecstatic states or feeling that they were outside of themselves. Then he examined people in several different professions, including athletes. In all these cases, the major constraint on enjoyment is when people are conscious of how they appear to others and concerned about their performance. To attempt to document flow experiences, Csikszentmihalyi armed people with watches that would beep randomly during the day, and participants completed a survey. Most people were generally unhappy when they did nothing and happy when they did something, but often did not know what made them happy. Csikszentmihalyi coined the term **flow** to refer to situations in which people are completely involved in what they are doing, to the extent that they lose themselves in the activity. Flow is characterized by:

- Complete involvement in an activity.
- Sense of ecstasy or excitement.
- Great inner clarity: Knowing what needs to be done and how well it is going.
- Confidence: Knowing the task is achievable.
- Serenity: Little or no concerns about the self or ego.
- Focus on the present: Engagement in the here and now rather than being preoccupied with the past or future.
- Intrinsic motivation: The activity itself is the ultimate reward.

Consider Exhibit 15.6, "The Flow Experience." In this exhibit, we see that the experience of flow is a precise combination of a person's skills and the challenge that is presented. If a person is tasked with a job that exceeds his capacities, he will experience anxiety. If that same person is underchallenged with a low-level skill, that person will experience boredom. A less skilled person who is not challenged will experience apathy. A person who is highly challenged and has the skills to perform the task is in a state of flow. Exhibit 15.7 represents an even more detailed view of the relationship between a person's skills and the challenge he or she faces.

Happiness Is a Skill

"How can I be happy?" is a question that nearly everybody asks themselves at some point in their life. People often puzzle to their friends and coworkers that they simply have no clue as to how to be happy. We take the radical point of view that happiness is not a state that one "falls" into; happiness is a skill. And truly happy people are experts at the skill of staying happy. (See Exhibit 15.8, which tells how one psychologist realized that helping

EXHIBIT 15.6

The Flow Experience

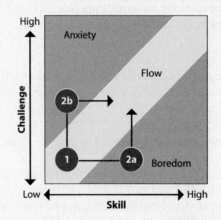

A person (1) will move out of flow and become bored, as her skills for a specific task increase (2a), unless the challenge to succeed also increases. Likewise, a person (1) will move out of flow if the demand on her is too great (2b). To stay in flow, she must increase her level of skill.

Source: Based on Csikszentmihalyi, M. (1990). *Flow: The psychology of optimal experience* (p. 74). New York: HarperCollins.

EXHIBIT 15.7

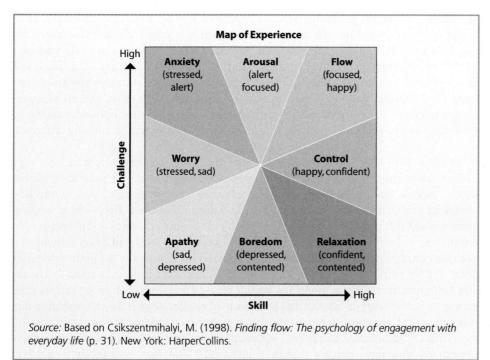

Map of Experience

Source: Based on Csikszentmihalyi, M. (1998). *Finding flow: The psychology of engagement with everyday life* (p. 31). New York: HarperCollins.

people improve their happiness is just as important as avoiding negative emotions, such as depression.)

According to Seligman, happiness is nothing more than a chronic personality trait—that can be honed and learned. In their book, *Character Strengths and Virtues,* Peterson and Seligman classify and describe 24 separate human strengths, including authenticity,

EXHIBIT 15.8   From Depression to Ultimate Happiness

Marty Seligman had a decorated research career as a clinical psychologist. He published several books on depression and other emotional disorders. Seligman spent decades studying depression and anxiety. It wasn't until his patients posed the question to him, "How can I be happy?" that it dawned on him that positive emotions like happiness, elation, and pride were understudied. Somehow, psychologists had missed the boat and spent their time warding off the negative and never focused on how to accentuate the positive. So Seligman began his foray into mirth. In his book, titled *Authentic Happiness,* Seligman takes up the fundamental question of why evolution has endowed us with positive feeling. What are the functions and consequences of positive emotions? Peterson and Seligman outline six virtues that can sustain people and make them happy: wisdom, courage, humanity, justice, temperance, and transcendence.

Sources: Seligman, M. E. P. (2002). *Authentic Happiness.* New York: Free Press. Peterson, C., & Seligman, M. E. P. (2004). *Character strengths and virtues: A handbook and classification.* Oxford University Press & American Psychological Association.

persistence, kindness, gratitude, hope, and sense of humor, which fall into basic categories of virtues: wisdom, courage, humanity, justice, temperance, and transcendence (see Exhibit 15.9).[22] In terms of how to nurture these virtues, Peterson and Seligman suggest complementary paths: (1) Construct families and workplaces that encourage and foster gratitude in their members, as a way of training people to routinely experience gratitude. (2) Encourage marital partners to express gratitude to each other; expressed appreciation is one of the cornerstones of healthy relationships. (3) Incorporate training on expressing and inspirational gratitude into leadership and management training programs.

HAPPINESS AND MONEY A common belief is that money can buy happiness. To a very limited extent this is true. If people are so poor that they are unable to meet basic human needs, such as having shelter, food, immunization against disease, and so on, then obviously having money can bring greater well-being or happiness. People from wealthy countries and rich people are happier than people from poor countries and poorer people within one country, but only up to a point.[23] According to David Myers, there is a positive correlation between wealth and happiness, but only up to a point; above this point, further increases in wealth do not increase happiness. And, according to Diener and Seligman, increases in monetary wealth create escalating desires, so that as time passes, the same level of income that once seemed satisfactory results in frustration and discontent.[24] Happiness depends on the gap between one's income and material aspirations.[25] "Frustrated achievers" are people who become less happy because their aspirations grow more quickly than their incomes.[26] This may even create a negative, self-fulfilling prophecy, as people who are unhappy often focus on material wealth. Thus, for most people in Western culture and developed societies, basic needs are not the problem. And most people rank happiness and life satisfaction ahead of money as a life goal.[27]

Interestingly, happy people earn more money. For example, happiness expressed by people in their first year of college correlated with yearly income 20 years later (when these people were in their late 30s).[28] Several longitudinal findings indicate that there is a positive relationship between happiness and income.[29]

HAPPINESS AND WORK PERFORMANCE Are happy workers more productive workers? People who are high in subjective well-being perform better at work than people who are low in subjective well-being.[30] Happy employees are better organizational citizens, meaning that they help other people at work in ways they are not directly obligated to do. And happy people have better social relationships, such that they are more likely to get married, stay married, and have rewarding marriages. Happy people are more "engaged" in their work and in their personal lives, and it is this social engagement with friends, family, co-workers, and community that has dramatic positive benefits for the person, group, and

EXHIBIT 15.9

Human Virtues

Virtue	Description
Wisdom & knowledge	Creativity, curiosity, open-mindedness, love of learning, and ability to put things in perspective
Courage	Bravery, persistence, integrity, and vitality
Humanity	Love, kindness, and social intelligence
Justice	Citizenship, fairness, and leadership
Temperance	Forgiveness, humility, prudence, and self-regulation
Transcendence	Appreciation of beauty and excellence, gratitude, hope, humor, and spirituality

Source: Kersting, K. (2004, July 1). Accentuating the positive. *APA Monitor on Psychology,* p. 65. Derived from Peterson, C., & Seligman, M. E. P. (2004). *Character strengths and virtues: A handbook and classification.* New York: Oxford University Press.

organization. People are just happier when they are with others than when they are alone (this is even true for introverts).[31]

A positive mood at work helps the organization; the costs of unhappy managers to organizational productivity are enormous. Unhappy workers are absent more often, change jobs more often, are less cooperative and helpful to others, and perform worse than happy managers and workers.[32] Moreover, the happiness of managers and workers affects the loyalty of customers and clients.[33] The statistical correlation between job satisfaction and job performance is about 0.3.[34] If we then factor in the effects of happiness on health, the argument for a happiness premium gets even stronger. Happy people are less likely to get sick and suffer from debilitating diseases.[35]

THE EVIDENCE FOR HAPPINESS AND LONGEVITY Happiness has a direct link to health and longevity. In a powerful longitudinal investigation of the relationship between happiness and longevity, the autobiographical statements written by nuns were examined for evidence of positivity (i.e., references to happiness and joy).[36] In the study, 180 Catholic nuns wrote autobiographies when they were 22 years old that were analyzed by "blind" observers for emotional content and then used to "predict" their health and longevity from ages 75 to 95. Because nuns have a controlled lifestyle, there is no reason to believe that the happy nuns differed from the sad nuns in terms of recreational activities and diet. A strong correlation was found between positive emotional content in these writings and risk of mortality: 90 percent of the nuns who expressed the most positive emotions were still alive at age 85 versus only 34 percent of the least positive; 54 percent of the most cheerful nuns were alive at age 94, as opposed to only 11 percent of the least cheerful nuns.

In another investigation, the emotional expression of college yearbook photos of 141 women from the 1960 yearbook of Mills College were rated.[37] All the women but three were smiling, but only about 50 percent of the smilers expressed Duchenne smiles. A Duchenne smile, named after its discoverer, Guillaume Duchenne, is a genuine smile in which the corners of a person's mouth turn up and the skin around their eyes crinkles into crow's feet. The muscles that do this are very difficult to control voluntarily. The other smile—the fake one, also known as the Pan American smile after the flight attendants in TV ads for the now-defunct airline—is nonauthentic, with none of the Duchenne features. Trained psychologists can at a glance separate Duchenne from Pan American smilers. The yearbook women were contacted at ages 27, 43, and 52, and asked about their marriages and life satisfaction. Duchenne smilers were more likely to be married, stay married, and to experience personal well-being over the next 30 years of their lives. The results were not just about physical attractiveness. Trained investigators independently rated how attractive the women were and attractiveness had nothing to do with good marriages or life satisfaction. This means that getting plastic surgery, for example, will not make us happier. With regard to the "big five" aspects of personality (neuroticism, extraversion, openness, agreeableness, conscientiousness), extraversion and neuroticism are the strongest predictors of life satisfaction.[38] Cheerfulness and the absence of depression are the best predictors of life satisfaction.

PLEASURE VERSUS PHILANTHROPY So, what will give us those real Duchenne smiles and make us happy? Before you start using this research as a license to go and live it up, think twice. The road to happiness is not paved with partying and self-indulgence. Seligman vehemently argues against basic hedonism. Hedonism, or simple pleasure-seeking, is not the way to a better life or to build a better company. To examine this, the students in Seligman's class were assigned a simple homework assignment: to engage in one pleasurable activity and one philanthropic activity and to write about both. The results were life-changing for the students and Professor Seligman. The afterglow of "pleasurable" activities (such as shopping, drinking, watching a movie, or eating a hot fudge sundae) paled in comparison with the effects that kind action (e.g., coaching a friend through a tough course assignment) has on the human psyche. The best possible combination? Philanthropic acts that are spontaneous and call on our personal strengths. The exercise of kindness consists of total engagement and the loss of self-consciousness. Time stops. One business student in the course wrote that he had elected to come to the

EXHIBIT 15.10 **Intrinsic Goals versus Extrinsic Goals and Learning and Performance**

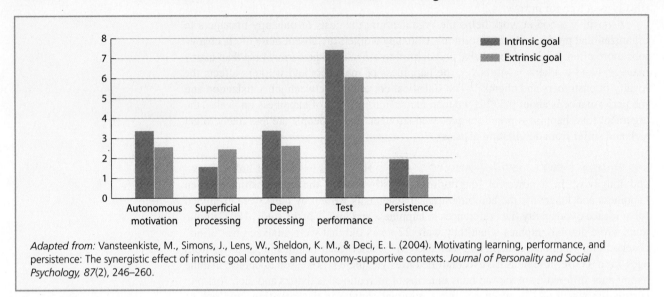

Adapted from: Vansteenkiste, M., Simons, J., Lens, W., Sheldon, K. M., & Deci, E. L. (2004). Motivating learning, performance, and persistence: The synergistic effect of intrinsic goal contents and autonomy-supportive contexts. *Journal of Personality and Social Psychology, 87*(2), 246–260.

University of Pennsylvania to learn how to make money, but he was floored to find that he liked helping people more than spending his money shopping (his pleasurable activity).

In another scientific investigation, students who pursued either intrinsic goals (community, personal growth, and health) or extrinsic goals (wealth, image, and fame) were examined.[39] The intrinsically motivated students learned more, performed better, and persisted longer in a testing situation. As can be seen in Exhibit 15.10, intrinsically motivated students were more likely than extrinsically motivated students to be self-motivated, to process information at a deeper (meaningful) level, perform better on tests, and persist longer in the face of challenge; extrinsically motivated students processed information more superficially. Pursuing extrinsic goals is associated with poorer mental health than pursuing intrinsic goals.[40] People who focus on extrinsic goals engage in excessive social comparisons with others and have unstable self-esteem.

ENGAGING OUR STRENGTHS AND VIRTUES According to Seligman, "when well-being comes from engaging our strengths and virtues, our lives are imbued with authenticity."[41] The trait of optimism is the cornerstone of happiness. To see if trait optimism predicts longevity, scientists at the Mayo Clinic in Rochester, Minnesota, selected 839 patients who had referred themselves for medical care 40 years prior (Mayo Clinic patients take a battery of tests, one of which measures trait optimism). Of these patients, 200 had died by the year 2000; the optimists had 19 percent greater longevity in terms of their expected lifespan compared to the pessimists. Grant and Higgins examined optimism and two types of pride—promotion pride and prevention pride—as predictors of quality of life.[42] **Promotion pride** refers to the sense of achievement people feel when they use eagerness to attain a goal (e.g., "how often have you accomplished things that got you 'psyched' to work even harder?"). In contrast, **prevention pride** refers to the sense of achievement people feel when they use vigilance to achieve a goal (e.g., preventing negative outcomes, such as obeying rules and regulations). Only promotion pride predicted a sense of purpose in life and goal directness. However, both prevention pride and promotion pride predicted adaptive coping.

THREE TYPES OF HAPPINESS Seligman warns, "The 'pleasant life' might be had by drinking champagne and driving a Porsche, but not the good life. Rather, the good life is using your signature strengths every day to produce authentic happiness and abundant gratification. This is something you can learn to do in each of the main realms of your life: work, love, and raising children." Material goods (like cars or new clothes) are stimuli that give people a short-lived boost in mood. Even winning the lottery does not buy long-term happiness.[43] Seligman identifies three categories of happy people:

■ *The good life:* Some happy people are low on pleasure but high on absorption and immersion, meaning that they take great pleasure in the things that they do. These people may be hobbyists who become immersed in their work.
■ *The pleasant life:* These happy people laugh a lot and thrive on pleasures, such as eating good food. They seem surrounded by contentment, pleasure and hope.
■ *The meaningful life:* These people apply their highest strengths and virtues to the greater good, such as through charities and volunteer work, or even politics. For example, Albert Lexie shines shoes for a living and lives on $10,000 a year; the rest of his money, he gives to hospitals. In 2004, his donations totaled over $90,000. Albert Lexie views his giving as creating a meaningful life. (See Exhibit 15.11 to read about the most generous wealthy philanthropists.)

Inspiration

Inspiration refers to the process of breathing in or inhaling. In a more figurative sense, it refers to the infusion of some idea, purpose, or meaning into the mind. Inspiration can come from within or outside of oneself. Thrash and Elliot examined inspiration and argued that it is both a trait and a state.[44] They identified three core ideas: evocation, motivation, and transcendence. *Evocation* means that a person does not will himself to be inspired; rather, it just happens. *Motivation* means that a person who is inspired is moved to take action. *Transcendence* means that a person focuses on goals that are outside of herself. In

EXHIBIT 15.11

Not Waiting Until They Are Dead to Give

It used to be that the wealthiest people in the world would bestow their fortunes on charities and organizations posthumously. The newest trend among the most wealthy, such as Bill Gates (upper right) and Michael Dell (lower right), is to give it away now. This act of generosity may lead such business greats to experience the greatest happiness imaginable.

The top givers, according to *BusinessWeek,* are Bill and Melinda Gates, Gordon and Betty Moore (Intel), Warren Buffet, George Soros, James and Virginia Stowers (American Century), Eli and Edythe Broad (SunAmerica), Michael and Susan Dell, Alfred Mann, Paul Allen, and the Walton family (Wal-Mart).

These billionaires have certainly enjoyed the "good life" of exotic cars and Italian tile, but seem to have realized early on that the half-life of a luxury good is not nearly as long as giving to those who really need it.

For this reason, Dell and cohorts are happier than their predecessors.

Source: Conlin, M., Gard, L., & Hempel, J. (2004, November 29). The top givers. *BusinessWeek,* pp. 87–94.

one of their investigations, Thrash and Elliott correlated inspiration with the holding of U.S. patents. Patent holders were found to experience considerably more inspiration than a control group sample, and the frequency of their inspiration predicted the number of patents they held.

Threat and Hardship: The Ultimate Test

Happiness is a skill that has real payoffs in terms of health and longevity. The road to happiness is not about indulgence and rampant hedonism. Being happy does not mean that you won't experience disappointment or even severe setbacks. You can't control what happens to you (e.g., layoffs, crime, terminal disease), but you can control how you choose to respond. This is where the power of the human spirit really makes a difference.

None of us seek out hardship, but it inevitably will find us. Pulley and Gurvis warn, "If you haven't already experienced a professional or personal setback, you will—inevitably. How you deal with it will determine whether you reach your full potential or will derail while reaching a plateau, getting demoted, or losing your job."[45] Most often, hardship strikes when we are least expecting it. Consider the following examples:

- Two business partners have a terrible falling-out, resulting in public humiliation; one ultimately leaves the company.
- A person loses his/her job and has to inform his/her spouse that he/she will be the single wage earner for the family.
- The birth of one's first child reveals a serious learning disability that requires full-time care.
- A routine surgical procedure leads to serious complications that leave you partially paralyzed.
- A spouse unexpectedly files for divorce.

Common to all of these hardships is the experience of loss. The loss can be of one's credibility, control, self-efficacy, or identity. People who are able to learn from and recover from hardships (sometimes stronger than they were before) share four characteristics:

- A sense of purpose and meaning.
- Social support: People with better social networks are less likely to succumb to disease and, overall, are happier and healthier.[46]
- Positive cognitive strategies.
- Flexibility.

Forgiveness

Organizations are systems of relationships. In those relationships, people are going to fail one another from time to time. Sometimes, this will be deliberate, such as when a colleague attempts to get someone else's job. More often, the failure will be a complex assortment of confused communications and misread intentions, where no one is really at fault. In such situations, people can either harbor a grudge or grant forgiveness. How we choose to respond has ramifications for our emotional and physical well-being and health. Witvliet, Ludwig, & Vander Laan examined the effects that occurred when people nursed grudges (i.e., were unforgiving) or engaged in forgiveness for a wrong-doing that occurred in their lives.[47] Those who held grudges experienced greater negative emotions and had much greater and negative physiological reactions, such as increased heart rate and blood pressure. Moreover, these negative effects persisted over time. In contrast, those who forgave the other party experienced a greater sense of control and lower physiological stress.

Executive Coaching

Sometimes people turn to an executive coach when going through a transition or when facing a hardship (see Exhibit 15.12). Perhaps no other job title has proliferated at a faster rate

EXHIBIT 15.12

Executive Coaching

T. J. Skelly, a high-level manager, believes in coaching. "Being coached made me a more interesting person. I could die tomorrow, and know that I loved my life."

Coaches are not therapists and not mentors, but they are personal trainers for one's life. They can cost anywhere in the $1,000 to $1,200 range per month, which usually entails 3–4 45-minute sessions either in person, over the phone, or through e-mail correspondence.

To be a coach, you need a two-year training course and 250 hours logged with clients to receive an associate coaching certificate from the ICE, the credentialing association, composed of 6,000 members.

Source: Clifford, S. (2004, February). The well-balanced life. Got game? *Inc. Magazine*, pp. 71–73.

since year 2000 than that of executive coach. An executive coach is not a therapist. Nor is a coach a mentor. Coaching is direct interaction with a person that is intended to help him or her acquire, develop, and use his or her talents (including knowledge, skills, ability, and passion) more effectively to accomplish the goals of the organization.[48] Coaching is not therapy. Unlike therapy, coaching does not purport to diagnose psychological states or problems. Coaching operates within the parameters of the business environment (versus in different life domains), and unlike therapy, where the patient is not "accountable" for producing "results," coaches are accountable.[49] Coaching is not mentoring; mentoring is more informal and open-ended. Mentoring is more generic show-and-tell; coaching is highly focused on the person.

THREE LEVELS OF COACHING Coaching is usually viewed as leader behavior, but subordinates have opportunities to coach leaders. Coaching can occur at any of three levels:

- Top-down (such as when a supervisor or organizational superior coaches a subordinate; also known as classic coaching)
- Peer coaching (colleague to colleague)
- Bottom-up coaching (such as when a subordinate coaches a leader or superior)

Subordinates have opportunities to coach leaders, especially leaders who are new. For example, a team member could describe how certain behavior by the leader is having a different effect than intended (e.g., "I'm sure that you did not mean to threaten Stanley when you said that 'it was up or out on the project,' but that is how he interpreted your message"). Importantly, leaders implicitly signal when they are open to coaching.

NAVIGATING THE COACHING ROLE Coaching involves at least three distinct phases: initiating the coaching, active coaching, and then closure coaching.

Initiating the Coaching Coaching can be invited or uninvited. For example, a colleague may honestly not know what is wrong. Leaders often may be shielded from important, potentially upsetting information because subordinates are involved in an elaborate cover-up game. Some people are rabidly hungry to find their weak spots and they soak up advice and suggestions like sponges; many others are defensive and rejecting. They externalize the problem (e.g., "It's not my fault that the deadlines are missed, it's our lousy IT support that is to blame").

Active Coaching Coaching cannot occur unless the coachee accepts the role of being coached. Openness to coaching is a function of the person and the situation. Friday at 4:55 P.M. is not an ideal time to initiate a coaching session. The key to successful coaching is to encourage the colleague to play as active a role as possible.

Closure Coaching Like many organizational activities, coaching is part of the psychological contract. As such, it makes sense for people to openly discuss whether the coaching is a relationship, whether will be ongoing, or if it is terminal and one-shot in nature.

Management Education Choices

Your management education will never be complete. Much like the experience of flow described earlier, every experience will be a part of your education. However, we do not imply that you should not seek more formal, structured educational experiences. Companies in the U.S. spend billions of dollars developing their employees and the level of investment is growing.[50]

You have several choices when it comes to continuing education, as depicted by Exhibit 15.13. One choice is degree versus nondegree programs. Degree-granting programs require extensive entrance criteria (entrance tests, hefty tuition, and often, the financial support of your company), and they represent a significant time commitment (usually between two and five years, depending on whether you are full-time or part-time). One implication of degree programs is grading. Nearly all degree business classes have a letter grading system and 90 percent use a 4.0 grading scale.[51] However, there is some debate as to whether grading leads to an instrumental focus on grades as the ultimate outcome of education, distracting both students and professors from intrinsic aspects of teaching and learning.[52] Moreover, there is serious doubt as to whether grades have any predictive value. Pfeffer and Fong cite six empirical studies using business school samples that show no correlation between GPA and career success as measured by salary, promotions, or number of job offers.[53]

Another consideration involves the setting. In traditional programs, classes take place in real time in a classroom setting with the instructor and students all present. In the virtual classroom, instructors and students don't interact physically, but communicate via information technology (fax, e-mail, Internet, etc.). Hybrid models involve some amount of distance learning and real classroom learning. Another consideration is the degree of customization of the program. Fully customized programs are ones that are designed entirely around the wish-list needs of the customer. Usually several months of meetings with key executives and team members are conducted in a discovery process that yields a needs-analysis. Some programs may be partially customized, such as when companies might select different existing modules to put together in a full program. (An analogy would be a manager receiving a CD track of their favorite songs as compared to having new music written just for them.) Finally, noncustomized programs usually represent extremely popular, highly road-tested, and winning material.

EXHIBIT 15.13

Management Education Choices

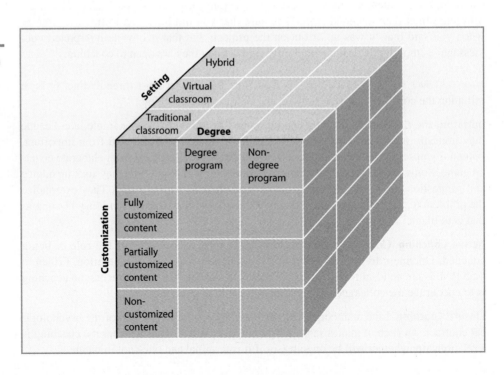

Here, we outline five key considerations that any person should weigh when choosing from among the vast array of management education choices.

- ◼ *Scientific basis:* Management is a science. As a scientific endeavor, it is incumbent upon the provider of management education to offer a theoretical and empirical basis for the practical advice and business strategy offered. The first and foremost consideration anyone should have before plunking down serious money, and even more precious time and energy, is to determine whether the course offered is based on scientific data. Even better is if the science is written up not only in the form of popular books, but has also passed muster at the highest pinnacles of academia—scientific journal publication. Most people would never want to read a journal article, as the golden-nugget-to-superfluous-detail ratio is shockingly low. The real advantage of journal publications is that the science has been reviewed by subject-matter experts.

- ◼ *Experiential learning:* If your job requirements involve real situations, such as negotiations, teamwork, and change management strategies, why on earth would you settle for purely academic bullet points decontextualized from real situations? We believe passionately in the power of experiential learning, whether it is in the form of business simulations, exercises, or interactive case studies. (See Exhibit 15.14 for a dramatic type of simulation involving dance.)

- ◼ *Feedback:* Our own research on learning and knowledge transfer indicates that it is the feedback element that is the critical ingredient in producing change in behavior. If every answer is a right answer, then we have not learned anything. Insist on objective standards for performance. The best courses are ones that walk through the right approaches as well as ones that are distinctly less effective. Benchmarks are great as well.

EXHIBIT 15.14   Dance of the MBAs

"Faster! Faster!" A wispy, gray-haired man in black sweats and a T-shirt shouts at 24 Wharton MBA students as they run barefoot around a theater. He's tearing around, too. "Lean! Move! Don't look at the floor!" he yells. The students obey, awkwardly, a few knocking into one another, one landing in a heap.

These future managers are learning about leadership and collaboration from Jonathan Wolken, cofounder of the modern-dance troupe Pilobolus. So far, though, the Wharton kids look as if they'd be content just to survive the daylong workshop unbruised. After half an hour, Wolken finally asks, "So how's this working for you?" Not so well, is the consensus. He points out spaces between students that open up as folks move and shift positions in the room. "Use your peripheral vision to see the hole before it's even there. Move in. Be purposeful, and people will fall in place around you," he says.

Suddenly, the metaphors for business and life dawn on the faces in the room. "Don't just smash into people. Make adjustments, and make them smoothly. It's only a mistake if you acknowledge it. Otherwise, it's just another way to learn." Wolken could just as easily be advising an entrepreneur to sharpen his radar for new business prospects and lead by example, or counseling an executive to see opportunity in failure.

The students split into small groups and are given a daunting task: Create and perform a dance. Wolken challenges them to ask, "What can you do with what you've got?" Three groups create exuberant performances, complete with lifts and full story lines. But the fourth, with no dance experience and saddled with one decidedly uncoordinated reporter, is at a loss.

Two hours later, we return to Wolken's original premise: Forget traditional ideas of dance. Just figure out what you can do that's interesting enough for people to look at. We choose to sit quietly, in a line, and just breathe. Occasionally, someone stretches or rolls her head. It is quiet, extremely uncomfortable to watch, and ultimately captivating. The simplest solution has turned out to be the best.

Source: Overholt, A. (2004, July 1). The dance of the MBAs. *Fast Company, 84,* 39. Reprinted by permission of Mansueto Ventures LLC via Copyright Clearance Center.

■ *Networking opportunities:* Your enjoyment of the program is a function of three key elements: you (the energy you bring and whether you show up for class and work with others), the quality of the institution (the timeliness of content and the availability of the instructors), and finally, the quality of the classmates or other participants. Most people find themselves enjoying the off-line conversations with co-participants more than the formal class sessions. A good class session is designed to stimulate the incidence of off-line conversations. For example, such experiences might occur when "friendly competitors," perhaps of two different pharmaceutical companies, find themselves in the same room during a three-day course on negotiations. It's worthwhile to find out how big the classes are and who is there. (Where do they come from?) If global business relationships are high on your list, you are going to be disappointed if you walk into a room and everyone is from the United States.

One question that companies might raise is whether investing in employees' skills increases or reduces turnover. Consider the arguments: If a company supports their high-potential employees continuing their education, this may endear the employee to the company (desired result). On the other hand, the employee who is exposed to new people may form relationships with others, start to question her allegiance to her own company, and join a new company. Benson, Finegold, and Mohrman tracked 9,439 salaried employees of a large company and found that participants in tuition reimbursement programs for education exhibited reduced turnover while the employees were in school.[54] Voluntary turnover increased when people earned graduate degrees (e.g., MBAs), but was significantly reduced when employees were promoted after earning their degree.

■ *Long-term institutional relationship:* Your choice of education is very important for you, your company, and the providing institution.

Conclusion

Some people who read this chapter believe it should have been the first one in the book. Perhaps it would have even helped students study better for this course and learn to start to use the self-sustaining tools we have talked about here. However, we think its proper place is at the beginning of the student's real journey into the organizational world. By the end of this book, you are probably thinking that organizational behavior is anything but intuitive and anything but highly circumscribed. Bluntly put, successful management is the hardest, least well-defined job on the planet. You owe it to yourself to take care of yourself from the inside out. Sure, it is nice to have the power suit and the accoutrements that are the mark of the business world, but this chapter has taken us on the journey inside.

Notes

1. Quote attributed to Mark Twain.
2. What your disaffected workers cost. (2001, March 15). *Gallup Management Journal, 1*(1), 1–2.
3. Watkins, M. (2003). *The first 90 days: Critical success strategies for new leaders at all levels* (p. 3). Boston: Harvard Business School Press.
4. Ibid.
5. Ibid.
6. Ibid., p. 241.
7. Hofman, M. (2003, October 1). The 90-day difference. *Inc. Magazine,* p. 38.
8. Weintraub, A. (2004, January 26). "I can't sleep:" Insomnia and other sleep disorders are wreaking havoc on our health and taxing the economy. Drug companies see an opportunity. *BusinessWeek.*
9. National Sleep Foundation (2002, April 2). 2002 "Sleep in America" poll. Retrieved May 2, 2006, from

http://www.sleepfoundation.org/_content/hottopics/2002 SleepInAmericaPoll.pdf.
10. Goldberg, R. *Sleep aids: All you ever wanted to know . . . but were too tired to ask.* National Sleep Foundation. Retrieved May 2, 2006, from www.sleepfoundation.org/sleeplibrary/index.php?secid=&id=65.
11. Twenge, J. M. (2000). The age of anxiety? Birth cohort change in anxiety and neuroticism, 1952–1993. *Journal of Personality and Social Psychology, 79*(6), 1007–1021.
12. Robins, L. N., Helzer, J. E., Weissman, M. M., Orvaschel, H., Gruenberg, E., & Burke Jr., J. D., et al. (1984). Lifetime prevalence of specific psychiatric disorders in three sites. *Archives of General Psychiatry, 41*(10), 949–958.
13. Murray, C. J. L., & Lopez, A. D. (1997). Alternative projections of mortality and disability by cause, 1990–2020: Global burden of disease study. *The Lancet, 349,* 1498–1504.

14. Groppel, J., & Andelman, B. (1999). *The corporate athlete: How to achieve maximal performance in business and life.* New York: John Wiley & Sons.

15. Loehr, J., & Schwartz, T. (2001). The making of a corporate athlete. *Harvard Business Review, 79*(1), 120–128.

16. Hochschild, A. R. (1997). *The time bind: When work becomes home and home becomes work.* New York: Henry Holt.

17. Salthouse, T. A. (2004). Localizing age-related individual differences in a hierarchical structure. *Intelligence, 32*(6), 541–561.

18. Loehr, J., & Schwartz, T. (2003). *The power of full engagement: Managing energy, not time, is the key to high performance and personal renewal.* New York: Simon & Schuster.

19. Bogacz, K., Dr. (2005). Evanston Northwestern Health Care.

20. Davidson, R. J. (2004). Well-being and affective style: Neural substrates and biobehavioural correlates. *Philosophical Transactions of the Royal Society (London), 359,* 1395–1411.

21. Csikszentmihalyi, M. (2003). *Good business: Leadership, flow and the making of meaning.* New York: Viking.

22. Peterson, C., & Seligman, M. (2004). *Character strengths and virtues: A handbook and classification.* Oxford: Oxford University Press.

23. Myers, D. (2004). Happiness. In *Psychology* (7th ed.). New York: Worth.

24. Diener, E., & Seligman, M. E. P. (2004). Beyond money: Toward an economy of well-being. *Psychological Science in the Public Interest, 5*(1), 1–31.

25. Frey, B. S., & Stutzer, A. (2002). What can economists learn from happiness research? *Journal of Economic Literature, 40*(2), 402–435.

26. Graham, C., & Pettinato, S. (2002). Frustrated achievers: Winners, losers and subjective well-being in new market economies. *Journal of Development Studies, 38*(4), 100–140.

27. Diener, E., & Oishi, S. (2006). Are Scandinavians happier than Asians? Issues in comparing nations on subjective well-being. In F. Columbus (Ed.), *Politics and economics of Asia.* Hauppauge, NY: Nova Science Publishers.

28. Diener, E., Nickerson, C., Lucas, R. E., & Sandvik, E. (2002). Dispositional affect and job outcomes. *Social Indicators Research, 59,* 229–259.

29. Staw, B., Sutton, R., & Pelled, L. (1994). Employee positive emotion and favorable outcomes in the workplace. *Organization Science, 5,* 51–71; Graham, C., Eggers, A., & Sukhatankar, S. (2004). Does happiness pay? An exploration based on panel data from Russia. *Journal of Economic Behavior & Organization, 55*(3), 319–342.

30. See note 24.

31. Pavot, W., Diener, E., & Fujita, F. (1990). Extraversion and happiness. *Personality and Individual Differences, 11,* 1299–1306.

32. Miner, A. G. (2001). *Experience sampling events, moods, behaviors and performance at work.* Unpublished doctoral dissertation, University of Illinois, Urbana; George, J. M. (1995). Leader positive mood and group performance: The case of customer service. *Journal of Applied Social Psychology, 25,* 778–794.

33. Harter, J. K., Schmidt, F. L., & Hayes, T. L. (2002). Business unit–level relationship between employee satisfaction, employee engagement, and business outcomes: A meta-analysis. *Journal of Applied Psychology, 87*(2), 268–279; Srinivasan, R., & Pugliese, A. (2000). Customer satisfaction, loyalty and behavior. *The Gallup Research Journal, 3*(1), 79–90; Swaroff, J. B. (2000). Validating "The Gallup Path": A study of the links between loyalty and financial outcomes in healthcare. *The Gallup Research Journal, 3*(1), 41–46.

34. Judge, T. A., Thoresen, C. J., Bono, J. E., & Patton, G. K. (2001). The job satisfaction–job performance relationship: A qualitative and quantitative review. *Psychological Bulletin, 127,* 376–407.

35. Cohen, S., Doyle, W. J., Turner, R. B., Alper, C. M., & Skoner, D. P. (2003). Emotional style and susceptibility to the common cold. *Psychosomatic Medicine, 65,* 652–657.

36. Danner, D., Snowdon, D., & Friesen, W. (2001). Positive emotions in early life and longevity: Findings from the Nun Study. *Journal of Personality and Social Psychology, 80*(5), 804–813.

37. Harker, L. A., & Keltner, D. (2001). Expressions of positive emotion in women's college yearbook pictures and their relationship to personality and life outcomes across adulthood. *Journal of Personality and Social Psychology, 80,* 112–124.

38. Schimmack, U., Oishi, S., Furr, R. M., & Funder, D. C. (2004). Personality and life satisfaction: A facet level analysis. *Personality and Social Psychology Bulletin, 30,* 1062–1075.

39. Vansteenkiste, M., Lens, W., & Deci, E. L. (2006). Intrinsic versus extrinsic goal contents in self-determination theory: Another look at the quality of academic motivation. *Educational Psychologist, 41,* 19–31.

40. Kasser, T., & Ryan, R. M. (1993). A dark side of the American dream: Correlates of financial success as a central life aspiration. *Journal of Personality and Social Psychology, 65,* 410–422; Kasser, T., & Ryan, R. M. (1996). Further examining the American dream: Differential correlates of intrinsic and extrinsic goals. *Personality and Social Psychology Bulletin, 22,* 280–287.

41. Seligman, M. (2002). *Authentic happiness: Using the new positive psychology to realize your potential for lasting fulfillment* (p. 9). New York: Free Press/Simon &Schuster.

42. Grant, H., & Higgins, E.T. (2003). Optimism, promotion pride, and prevention pride as predictors of well-being. *Personality and Social Psychology Bulletin, 29*(12), 1521–1532.

43. Brickman, P., Coates, D., & Janoff-Bulman, R. (1978). Lottery winners and accident victims: Is happiness relative? *Journal of Personality and Social Psychology, 36*(8), 917–927.

44. Thrash, T. M., & Elliot, A. J. (2003). Inspiration as a psychological construct. *Journal of Personality and Social Psychology, 84,* 871–889.

45. Pulley, M., & Gurvis, J. P. (2004, July 1). The ultimate learning experience. *Across the Board, 41*(4), 42.

46. Cohen, Doyle, Turner, Alper, & Skoner, "Emotional style and susceptibility," p. 281.

47. Witvliet, C. V. O., Ludwig, T. E., & Vander Laan, K. L. (2001). Granting forgiveness or harboring grudges: Implications for emotion, physiology, and health. *Psychological Science, 12,* 117–123.

48. Hackman, J. R. (2002). *Leading teams: Setting the stage for great performances.* Boston, MA: Harvard Business School Press.

49. Nigro, N. (2003). *The everything coaching and mentoring book.* Avon, MA: Adams Media.

50. Frazis, H., Herz, D. E., & Harrigan, M.W. (1995). Employer-provided training: Results from a new survey. *Monthly Labor Review, 118,* 3–17; Spitzer, D., & Malcolm, C. (2001). Link training to your bottom line. *American Society for Training and Development [ASTD].* Retrieved on 2 May 2006 from www.astd.org/NR/rdonlyres/65AA2A39-E40A-412D-A836-C849BAD51B27/5950/750201.pdf.

51. Riley, H. J., Checca, R. C., Singer, T. S., & Worthington, D. F. (1994). *Grades and grading practices: Results of the 1992 AACRAO survey.* Annapolis Junction, MD: AACRAO Distribution Center.

52. Beatty, I. (2004). Transforming student learning with classroom communication systems. Research Bulletin No. ERB0403: Educause Center for Applied Research.

53. Pfeffer, J., & Fong, C. T. (2002, September). The end of business schools? Less success than meets the eye. *Academy of Management Learning and Education,* 78–95.

54. Benson, G., Finegold, D., & Mohrman, S. A. (2004). You paid for the skills, now keep them: Tuition-reimbursement and voluntary turnover. *The Academy of Management Journal, 47*(3), 315.

Glossary

Abilene paradox. pluralistic ignorance; occurs when a desire to avoid conflict comes at the expense of making good decisions.

Active inquiry process. method of helping and coaching that includes pure inquiry, exploratory diagnostic inquiry, and confrontative inquiry.

Aggressive managers. one form of "toxic managers," aggressive managers are ruthless, volatile, bullying, homicidal, frantic, sexual harassers, chauvinistic.

Anchoring. when people attempt to extrapolate an estimate, based on some initial starting value.

Approach-approach conflict. choosing between two or more attractive options.

Approach-avoidance conflict. choosing options that have both desirable as well as undesirable aspects.

Arbitrators. third parties who have power to impose a settlement in a dispute.

Attention. the noticing, encoding, interpreting, and focusing of time and effort on issues and answers.

Authority ranking. relationships in which people have asymmetric positions in a linear hierarchy, within an organization in which subordinates defer to, respect, and follow the directives of superiors and superiors are responsible for subordinates.

Autonomy. the degree to which team members believe they have freedom to make decisions.

Avoidance-avoidance conflict. choosing from among two necessary evils.

Balanced contract. the hybrid form of relational and transactional contracts; shared values and commitments are present alongside the need to attain specific business goals.

Baserate fallacy. occurs when people choose to rely on a single, vivid data points, rather than much more reliable data.

BATNA. a negotiator's best alternative to a negotiated agreement.

Behavior sequence. consists of things that people say and do that are directed at some goal.

Behavioral theories. argue that leadership, like other management competencies, is a skill.

Big Five. set of core personality dimensions, also called the "five-factor model" of personality—openness to experience, conscientiousness, extraversion, agreeableness, and neuroticism.

Bodily mimicry. the tendency for people who are communicating to mirror one another's bodily movements and posture.

Breakeven point. the point at which new leaders have contributed as much value to their new organizations as they have consumed from it.

Bystander effect. the tendency for an individual not to intervene in an emergency as the number of perceived others increases.

Carnegie model. suggests that decision makers are highly desirous of making rational decisions, but because they lack time and energy, they cannot devote infinite resources to decision making.

Case studies. essentially write-ups of actual business situations, conducted following an organizational event, and published in OB journals.

Central persuasion route. when people process information or make decisions with great care and consideration, carefully weighing and reviewing each fact.

Centrality. refers to how much your work and contributions are part of the core values and activities of the organization.

Citation counts. scientific measurement of journal articles on a particular subject.

Classroom research. research conducted in classrooms, rather than a laboratory, that allows random assignment to conditions.

Cognitive dissonance theory. people desire their behaviors to be consistent, or congruent with their attitudes; if they sense an inconsistency or incongruence between their beliefs and behaviors, they feel dissonance, an aversive state, and they are driven to reduce this incongruence by either changing their behaviors or attitudes.

Cognitive mechanisms. the way in which most people reason about situations.

Cognitive rules (CR) model. assumes that people possess cognitive rules that they employ to match a given situation.

Collaborative model of communication. focuses on how both parties of the conversation work together to ensure that they have a common understanding of each utterance in a conversation before they move on to the next utterance.

Collective self. in terms of group membership, contains those aspects of the self-concept that differentiate the in-group members from members of relevant out-groups.

Common information effect. the tendency for group members to discuss what they already have in common, instead of discussing unique information that individual members may possess.

Communal relationships. relationships in which people feel a personal responsibility for the needs of others in the relationship.

Communal sharing. relationships in which people are highly responsive to the needs of the others involved.

Communication medium. refers to the mode or method of communication, such as telephone, fax, face-to-face, etc.

Communication. the dynamic process of transmitting and receiving meaningful information.

Comparison level (CL). refers to what a person believes he or she is entitled to in a given relationship.

Comparison level for alternatives (CLalt). refers to the alternatives to a person's current relationship.

Comparison with similar others. the tendency for people to choose someone of similar background, skill, and ability with whom to compare themselves.

Competence. encompasses our belief that a person possesses the technical and interpersonal skills to carry through with his or her promise.

Compliance. occurs when people do what they are asked to do, even though they might prefer not to do it.

Componential intelligence. the ability to think abstractly and process information effectively.

Compromise agreement. in negotiation, occurs when negotiators divide resources equally down the middle.

Compromise. occurs when people resolve their concerns about ethical standards and their own behavior by adopting a midpoint.

Confirmation bias. the strong tendency to seek information that confirms what we already know (or want to believe).

Conformity. occurs when people change their beliefs or behaviors in ways that are consistent with what they believe to be the group's standards.

Conformity pressure. occurs when a group persuades an individual to agree with them in belief and in behavior.

Consistency mechanisms. refer to the principles of cognitive dissonance.

Contact hypothesis. based on the principle that greater contact among members of different groups increases cooperation and trust between group members.

Contagion. the social process by which emotions, ideas are passed from one person to another.

Contextual intelligence. the ability to adapt to changing environmental conditions and to shape the environment.

Contingency theories. argue that leadership and leadership style depend on aspects of the people and the situation.

Contingent contracts. a method of resolving different beliefs in a negotiation situation in which negotiators agree to base final decisions upon some future state of affairs.

Co-optation. occurs when rewards are used to change attitudes regarding unethical behaviors.

Correspondent outcomes. in relationships, people try to coordinate their activities so as to maximize the benefits to both partners.

Counterarguing. refers to the natural tendency for targets of persuasive messages to argue against the persuasive message when they do not agree with it.

Creative team. develops new products, ideas, or services.

Creativity. the production of novel or useful ideas.

Crimes of obedience. immoral or illegal acts that are committed in response to orders from an authority.

Cross-cut role assignments. people who hold memberships in more than one team simultaneously.

Culture. the personality of a group; the unique character of a social group; the values and norms shared by its members that set it apart from other social groups.

Curse of knowledge. the tendency for informed, knowledgeable persons, such as experts, not to be able to communicate their knowledge to others.

Decision-making skills. judgment skills; the ability to identify and evaluate different courses of action to solve problems and challenges.

Descriptive model of decision making. describes or models what people actually do when making decisions (which may not be optimal).

Descriptive research. the study of people's actual (rather than idealized) behavior.

Desensitization. the fact that people's sensitivity to almost anything may decrease over time.

Deterrence-based trust. involves sanctions, predicated on fear of reprisal if trust is violated.

Distributive justice. the science of how people allocate resources.

Distributive negotiation. the study of how people allocate resources.

Double-loop learning. occurs when errors are corrected by changing the governing values and then the actions.

Downward comparison. occurs when people compare themselves to someone who is less fortunate, of lower rank, less able, or lower in status.

Dyadic interaction. occurring when two people emit behavior in each other's presence.

Egocentric bias. the tendency to give ourselves more credit than others give us and give ourselves more credit than we give others.

Elaboration likelihood model of persuasion. argues that people are motivated to engage in thoughtful consideration of the pros and cons of an argument under some circumstances, but under other conditions, they use peripheral cues that have nothing to do with the merits of an argument.

Emotional intelligence. the ability to perceive emotions in ourselves and others and to use those emotions to guide behavior.

Encoding and decoding. in communication, the terms, symbols, and language with which the sender (encoder) embodies the message and those that the receiver (decoder) uses to parse the message.

Equality matching. relationships in which people keep track of the balance or difference between the organizational actors; turn-taking, voting, equal distribution, and quid-pro-quo relationships.

Equality rule. blind justice; prescribes equal shares for everyone concerned.

Equity rule. proportionality of contributions principle; bases rewards and outcomes on what people have contributed.

Equity theory. states that people's judgments of fairness are based on the perceived ratio of their own inputs and outputs relative to the ratio of the inputs and outputs of others.

Ethical and moral skills. personal awareness of one's own ethical principles and morals.

Ethical thinking. the cognitive means by which people reason when they are faced with situations that involve values.

Evolutionary change. in terms of organizational change, also known as incremental change; carried out in a slow, methodical, step-by-step fashion and is very focused.

Exchange relationships. relationships in which people give and receive benefits with the expectation of receiving comparable benefits in return soon afterward.

Exit. in relationships, a destructive, active course of action; a person actively ends a relationship.

Expectancy theory. focuses on people's motivation to do work.

Expected utility theory (EU). prescribes a theory of rational behavior; a person acts in a way that maximizes his or her decision utility or the anticipated satisfaction from a particular outcome.

Expected value principle. the sum of the value of a particular object (or outcome) multiplied by the probability of its occurrence.

Experiential intelligence. the ability to formulate new ideas and to combine seemingly unrelated facts or information.

External aspects of personality. include geographic location, income, personal habits, recreational habits, religion, educational background, work experience, appearance, parental status, and marital status.

Extrinsically motivated. when a person does a job or activity because it will bring rewards such as money or fame.

Fairness heuristic theory. because ceding authority to another person provides an opportunity for exploitation and exclusion, people feel uncertain and uncomfortable about their relationships with an authority figure; people ask themselves whether the authority can be trusted not to exploit them and establish a fairness judgment, which serves as a fairness heuristic that guides the interpretation of subsequent events.

False uniqueness bias. the tendency to view oneself as different (in a positive direction) from others.

Faulty rules. with regard to ethics, company policies that are ambiguous, out-of-date, or simply wrong in the eyes of the manager and therefore subject to creative revision.

Field studies. research investigations conducted within actual organizations.

Final offer arbitration. a method of dispute resolution in which a third party selects only one of the two demands submitted by the involved parties.

Finke's model of creativity. evaluates the usefulness of creative ideas as a function of two factors: creativity and realism.

Fixed-action patterns. mindless shortcuts for enacting repetitive behaviors.

Fixed-pie perception. in negotiation (often faulty), belief that one's own interests are at complete odds with those of the other party.

Fixed-sum negotiation. in negotiation, a situation in which whatever one party gains, the other party loses in a direct fashion.

Forked tail effect. in person perception, once we have formed a negative impression about someone, we tend to view everything else about him or her in a negative fashion.

Fundamental attribution error. the tendency of people to ascribe dispositional reasons to explain the behavior of others and discount the impact of the situation.

Gain sharing. a form of remuneration in which employees are offered a share of any increases in total organizational productivity against a specified benchmark.

Garbage can model. model of organizational decision making; argues that instead of problems leading to solutions in organizations, organizations create solutions even before they have defined a problem.

G-factor intelligence. "general" intelligence.

Goal-compatibility. the extent to which the leader and his or her followers share the same goals.

GPA theory. goals–plans–action; speakers produce messages to accomplish goals, and thus develop and enact plans for pursuing goals.

Group value model. states that people identify with social and organizational groups; these relationships are a critical part of their self-concept, and they seek to build long-term bonds with valued organizational members.

Groupthink. in terms of decision making, involves a deterioration of cognitive vigilance, lack of reality testing, and failure of morality among group members as a result of group pressures toward conformity of opinion.

Guilford's three-factor model of creativity. assesses creativity in terms of three dimensions: fluency, flexibility, and originality.

Halo effect. in terms of person perception, the tendency to generalize that a person has a number of desirable traits on the basis of one positive trait (e.g., the tendency to believe that a physically attractive person is also intelligent).

Hidden self. with regard to the Johari window, aspects of the self that are known to us but are hidden from others.

Hierarchy of needs. Maslow's theory of basic human needs—physiological, safety, social, esteem, and self-actualization needs. In order to satisfy higher-order needs, lower-order needs need to be satisfied.

Hindsight bias. the tendency for people to believe that something was inevitable after it happened, though they could not predict it.

Homogeneity bias. refers to the tendency to view out-group members as "all alike," while seeing one's own group as much more diverse.

Human capital. a composite of a person's education, skills, and experience; a summation of talent and expertise.

Ideal performance state (IPS). according to Groppel and Andelman, a condition in which people can bring their talents and skills to full ignition and sustain high performance over time.

Identification trust. based on a person's ability to empathize with another person.

Illusion of control. refers to the tendency for people to believe that they exert more influence over situations than they actually do.

Impaired managers. one profile of "toxic managers," impaired managers have ADHD (attention deficit hyperactivity disorder), anxiety, depression, post-traumatic stress disorder, burnout, bipolar disorder, and/or alcohol/drug addiction.

Implicit leadership theories (ILTs). the theories and beliefs that subordinates hold about leaders.

Impression management. the means by which organizational actors try to convey particular impressions that others develop of them.

Incentive pay. a form of remuneration in which extra pay is tied to performance.

Incrementalism. with regard to unethical behavior, the gradual socialization, particularly of newcomers, of behavior.

Indirect speech acts. the indirect ways in which people ask others to do things.

Individual level of analysis. one level of analysis in organizational behavior; focuses on how the individual organizational member thinks, feels, and acts as a result of the actual or implied presence of others.

Influence. a persuasion tactic, of a more temporary nature than power, varying from situation to situation; also, the ability of a person to change the behavior of another person.

Informational influence. the tendency for people to be persuaded by rational arguments, facts, and data.

Innovation. also known as implementation; the realization of actual ideas in the form of products, services, or whatever might be productive for an organization.

Inoculation. in persuasion, refers to the ability of a target of a persuasion attempt to protect him- or herself against a persuasive argument by, for example, derogating the source.

Instrumentality. the belief that performance will be rewarded.

Integrative negotiation. involves creating value where it does not immediately or obviously exist; also, the art and science of leveraging interests so as to improve the outcomes of both parties.

Intellectual bandwidth. a function of a person's capacity to transform data into wisdom.

Interdependence theory. analyzes the pattern of interaction between people in terms of outcomes that people incur in the form of rewards and costs.

Interests. in negotiation, the underlying motivations that drive a person to make a particular demand.

Interpersonal ethics. how we treat others.

Interpersonal level of analysis. one level of analysis in organizational behavior; the focus on how people in organizations relate on a one-on-one level with others.

Interpersonal skills. one of several emotional intelligence skills; the ability to successfully interact with others.

Intrapersonal decisions. also known as individual decision making; decisions we make on our own.

Intrinsically motivated. when a person enjoys doing an activity or a job for the pleasure it brings, rather than material outcomes.

Knowledge-based trust. one of three types of trust; derives from a person's history of interaction with another person.

Knowledge-brokering process. in the innovation process, occurs when an idea is imported from one domain and moved into a new context.

Laboratory studies. one research methodology in organizational behavior; research conducted within universities and research institutions, allowing the researcher maximum possible control.

Leader–Member Exchange model (LMX). operates on the premise that leaders give different employees (subordinates) differential amounts of attention and treatment.

Leadership neutralizer. something that prevents a leader from having influence and negates the leader's efforts.

Leadership substitutes. anything that acts in place of a formal leader, including a variety of "situational" factors.

Leadership. a person's desire to take control and to set direction; also, the ability to influence people to achieve an organization's or group's goals.

Learning skills. one of several important managerial skills; the ability to objectively reflect upon one's strengths, weaknesses, and areas of improvement; not only to accept critical feedback but to consistently seek it out.

Lewin's theory of change. based on a force-field theory in which two sets of opposing forces within an organization (forces for change and forces for resistance) determine how and whether change will take place.

Loyalty. in relationships, one of four possible reactions to conflict; a constructive but passive course of action; a person passively waits for things to improve.

Management. a function that must be exercised in any business or team.

Manager-led team. one of four types of team as identified by Hackman; a team in which the manager acts as the team leader and is responsible for defining the goals, process, and functioning of the team.

Market pricing. in relationship theory, relationships in which people are highly sensitive to market worth of others and engage in cost-benefit analysis when interacting with others.

Mediators. in dispute resolution, a third party who suggests possible resolutions; mediators who have process control but no outcome control.

Message. in communication, the information that a sender wants to share with other people.

Message distortion. in communication, refers to how senders may distort information because they have a bias to present information that they believe will be favorably received by the intended recipient.

Message learning. in persuasion theory, refers to the degree to which the target comprehends the message.

Message tuning. in persuasion, involves the tendency for a message-sender to tailor messages to specific recipients.

Meta-analysis. a research methodology in organizational behavior that involves combining data from several original studies in one large data set to measure the size of an effect or to solve an enigma.

Meta-communication. in communication, the ability of a person to communicate about how they communicate.

Motive arousal. in persuasion, the extent to which a target is motivated to change her or his behavior.

Multiple intelligences. in intelligence theory, the belief that a person's intelligence is not measured by a single factor, but rather that there are eight intelligences—linguistic, musical, logical-mathematical, spatial, bodily-kinesthetic, interpersonal, intrapersonal, and naturalist.

Multiple offer strategy. in negotiation, the technique of presenting the other party with at least two (and preferably more) multi-issue proposals of equal value to oneself.

Narcissistic managers. one of several "toxic" management styles; narcissistic managers are preoccupied with themselves and concomitantly devalue others and have an inflated sense of entitlement.

Needs-based rule. in fairness theory, the belief and practice of allocating resources to those who most need them; welfare-based allocation; states that benefits should be proportional to need.

Negativity effect. in perception theory, the tendency for perceivers to be heavily influenced by one piece of negative information about someone, perceivers put a lot of weight on that negative information.

Neglect. in relationships, one of four possible reactions to conflict. Neglect is a destructive, passive course of action; a person passively allows the relationship to deteriorate.

Noise. in communication theory, refers to anything that blocks a signal or makes a signal difficult to detect, including both mechanical and linguistic barriers.

Nonverbal communication. in communication theory, anything that is not words.

Nonverbal leakage. in communication theory, the nonverbal signals that a person is not aware of sending.

Norm. a generally agreed on set of unwritten rules that guides the behavior of people in organizations.

Norm of self-interest. the pervasive belief that people are self-interested.

Normative model of decision making. in decision theory, a model that presents an ideal method by which people should make decisions.

Optimal distinctiveness theory. argues that a person's collective identity derives from the interplay of two opposing social motives, inclusion and differentiation.

Organizational behavior. also referred to as OB; the study of how the thoughts, feelings, and behaviors of individuals and groups in organizations are influenced by the actual, implied, or imagined presence of others.

Organizational culture. the values, norms, and outwardly visible signs of organizational members and their behaviors, including the shared beliefs of organizational members.

Organizational ethics. the norms that people are exposed to every day in their organization.

Organizational level of analysis. one level of analysis in organizational behavior; represents the broadest level of looking at the organization, its culture, and its norms.

Organizational-level decisions. decisions made at an organizational level.

Organizational life cycle. a predictable sequence of stages of growth and change of an organization.

Osborn's four rules for brainstorming. in creativity, a technique for enhancing creativity in groups and prescribes; expressiveness, nonevaluation, quantity, and combining several ideas.

Other-awareness. one of four emotional intelligence skills; empathy, the ability to perceive emotions in others and to take their perspective.

Outcome control. in dispute resolution, having the power to impose binding agreements on parties to a negotiation.

Overconfidence bias. the tendency for people to place unwarranted confidence in their judgment of their abilities.

Path-goal theory. a particular leadership theory that focuses on how leaders can best motivate their employees to achieve group and organizational goals.

People-focused leaders. a type of leadership style in which leaders are highly considerate of others.

Performance-based judgment calls. in ethical decision making, managerial decisions that bend the rules for the purpose of enhancing individual or organizational performance.

Peripheral route of persuasion. in persuasion theory, two routes of persuasion are identified: a direct route and a peripheral route. The peripheral route argues that message recipients do not always process information carefully; they engage in automatic processing, particularly when people are not involved, not concerned about being accurate, and do not recognize that others are attempting to change their attitudes.

Perspective taking. the ability to look at a situation from the point of view of another person.

Place-time model of social interaction. considers two key dimensions, of how people communicate virtually, whether organizational actors are located in the same physical space and communicating at the same time.

Pluralistic ignorance. in decision making, when people are unaware that others feel the same way that they do.

Postsettlement settlement. in negotiation, a technique whereby negotiators first reach a mutually agreeable settlement and commit to it, then attempt to mutually improve on it.

Potency. the collective belief of a team that it can be effective.

Power. the ability of a person to control the actions of another person in a relationship.

*p*Power. personal power; the degree to which a person desires to use and have power.

Prescriptive model of decision making. in decision making theory, models that help, improve, or otherwise coach people to improve their decision making.

Prescriptive norm. dictates what should be done in a situation.

Prevention focused. one of two chronic orientations that people may hold with respect to reaching goals; prevention-focused people are concerned with safety and responsibilities and generally avoiding negative outcomes.

Prevention pride. refers to the sense of achievement people feel when they use vigilance to achieve a goal.

Primacy effect. the first pieces of information we learn about people exert more influence on our overall impression of them than does subsequent information.

Private self. with regard to the Johari window, aspects of ourselves that we are aware of but others are not.

Problem-solving team. one of three types of work that a team can do according to Larson and LaFasto; problem-solving teams attempt to get answers to vexing questions, see patterns in myriad data, and resolve issues that remain open.

Procedural justice. in fairness theory, the science of how people enact justice.

Process conflict. centers on disagreements that people have on how to approach a task, specifically who should be doing what, and on how the group is achieving its goal.

Process consultation model. a model of coaching in which help-givers follow three techniques, including: diagnostic inquiry, exploratory inquiry and, finally, confrontative inquiry.

Process control. disputants or third parties who have control over procedures and processes, but not outcomes.

Production blocking. in creativity, the tendency for people to perform less creatively when they are simultaneously focused on another task; multi-tasking.

Profit sharing. a form of remuneration in an organization or a system in which a portion of a company's bottom-line economic profits are given to employees.

Promotion focused. one of two chronic orientations that people may hold with respect to reaching goals; promotion-focused people are concerned with achieving their aspirations and accomplishments.

Promotion pride. refers to the sense of achievement people feel when they use eagerness to attain a goal.

Proscriptive norm. dictates behaviors that should be avoided.

Prospect theory. a descriptive model of decision making that predicts that people are risk averse for gains and risk-seeking for losses.

Prototypes. in cross-cultural research, central tendencies which recognize that substantial variation is likely even within a given culture.

Proximity effect. the tendency for people to communicate with others who are physically close to them.

Pseudo-cues. in perception theory, cues that may not be very meaningful when forming judgments about someone or something; non-diagnostic cues.

Psychological contract. a contract that is not legally binding, but creates an interpersonal obligation; an individual's subjective belief in the exchange relationship between himself or herself and a third party, based on an exchange of promises to which both parties are bound.

Punctuated equilibrium model. a model of change that predicts that organizations (and teams) often do not follow a smooth, linear pattern of change; rather, change often emerges in the later stages of an organization or group's life.

Quality circles. groups of employees who meet regularly to discuss the way work is performed and to find new ways to increase performance.

Rao's PRESS model. a prescriptive model of organizational change that outlines five key steps in a leader's 100-day change plan, including persuading, recruiting, energizing, staffing the change team, and sequencing change.

Rationalization. in organizational ethics, mental strategies that allow people to view their corrupt acts as justified.

Receiver. in communication theory, the individual, group, or organizational unit for which information is intended.

Reciprocity effect. the tendency for people to reciprocate the behavior they receive from others.

Recognition. a form of organizational reward, usually nonmonetary or noncash, designed to increase employees' motivation to achieve organizational goals.

Reengineering. in terms of organizational change, the process by which managers redesign how tasks are bundled into roles and functions to improve organizational effectiveness.

Reference group. with regard to persuasion and influence, a group that is important and meaningful to a person.

Relational contract. a long-term or open-ended employment arrangement based on mutual trust and loyalty, in which rewards are loosely conditioned on performance and derive from membership and participation in the organization.

Relational model of authority. focuses on the conditions under which an authority is perceived to be a legitimate decision maker and is given discretionary power to make decisions for a committee.

Relational self. with regard to self-perception, the tendency for some people to define themselves in terms of their one-on-one relationships with specific others.

Relationship conflict. also known as personality conflict or affective (emotional) conflict.

Representativeness bias. in decision making, the nonrational tendency for people to make judgments on the basis of stereotypical cues or information rather than by using more deliberate processing or quantitative data.

Reservation price. the quantification of a negotiator's BATNA (best alternative to a negotiated agreement).

Restructuring. in terms of organizational change, also called reorganization; the process by which managers change task and authority relationships and redesign organizational structure and culture to improve organizational effectiveness.

Retributive justice. in fairness theory, the science of how people "get even" and "retaliate."

Revolutionary change. in terms of organizational change, also known as radical change, carried out in an explosive, all-or-nothing fashion and is organization-wide.

Rigid managers. one class of "toxic managers," rigid managers are compulsive, authoritarian, oppositional, controlling, dictatorial.

Risk technique. a structured discussion method that aims to reduce group members' fears about making decisions.

Scarcity. in persuasion theory, the tendency for people to desire things and people that are hard to get as more valuable than those that are within easy reach.

Self-awareness. one of four emotional intelligence skills; the ability to understand emotions in ourselves.

Self-directing team. one of four types of teams as identified by Hackman; also called self-designing team; members determine their own objectives and the methods by which to achieve them.

Self-efficacy. the belief in one's capabilities to organize and execute the sources of action required to manage prospective situations.

Self-fulfilling prophecy. also known as behavioral confirmation; when we make dispositional attributions for a person's behavior, we often treat the person in a way that engenders that very behavior.

Self-governing team. one of four types of teams as identified by Hackman; the team is responsible for execution of the project, managing their own performance, designing the group, and also for the organizational context itself.

Self-limiting behavior. a type of negative decision making that occurs when we suppress our concerns about a decision; self-censorship.

Self-managing team. one of four types of teams as identified by Hackman; also called self-regulating team; members monitor their own work and are responsible for creating their own performance conditions for achieving their goals.

Self-perception theory. states that people do not spend a lot of time attempting to align their behaviors and attitudes; they infer their attitudes by looking at their behaviors.

Self-regulation. one of four emotional intelligence skills; the ability to control emotions and impulses.

Self-serving bias. refers to the tendency for people to view themselves in a positive light.

Sender. the individual, group, or organizational unit that wants to share information with some other individual, group, or organization to accomplish a communication goal.

Servant leadership. a style of leadership in which the leader puts the needs and interests of the team ahead of his or her own.

Similarity-attraction principle. states that people are attracted to and prefer to spend time with others who hold attitudes that are similar to their own.

Single-loop learning. occurs when errors are corrected without questioning or examining our basis assumptions.

Situational approach. with regard to theories of leadership; the "great opportunity," not "great person," theory of leadership that holds that situations often "select" leaders.

Social capital. a person's web of personal and business networks of people, information, ideas, leads, business opportunities, and so on.

Social comparison. the act of comparing ourselves to others for informational purposes or self-aggrandizing purposes.

Social exchange theory. analyzes how people in relationships exchange rewards and costs.

Social impact theory. theory of group influence that examines the conditions under which a group is most likely to exert influence on a person as a function of the size of the group and the relevance of the situation.

Social influence. sometimes called normative influence; occurs when people change their beliefs to gain acceptance and approval by a valued group.

Social loafing. also known as free-riding; refers to the fact that people work less hard when they are part of a group than when they are working alone.

Social meanings model of communication. in communication theory, this model examines how nonverbal cues, such as gestures, touch, interpersonal distance, and eye gaze, are used along with verbal language in social interaction.

Social skills. one of four emotional intelligence skills; a large, complex set of abilities in terms of relating to other people, creating trust, and sustaining relationships.

Sociotechnical systems theory. a model of organizational change that focuses on how organizations can change roles, tasks, and technical relationships to increase organizational effectiveness.

sPower. socialized power; a person's need to express power in socially acceptable ways.

Stereotyping. the tendency to make judgments of others based on their membership in certain groups, not based on knowledge of the person him- or herself.

Tactical team. one of three types of work that a team focuses on according to Larson and LaFasto; its objective is to execute a well-defined plan.

Task conflict. also called cognitive conflict; conflict about the issues, not about the people behind the issues.

Task-focused leaders. are concerned with getting the work done, and are relatively less concerned about maintaining harmony among the team.

Team. a group of interdependent people working toward a shared goal.

Team context. refers to the broad set of organizational factors that affect teamwork.

Team culture. the personality of a team; the customs, culture, and spirit of the team.

Team level of analysis. one of four levels of analysis in organizational behavior; the team level of analysis focuses on how teams in organizations set goals, resolve conflict, and achieve results.

Team mental model. the degree of correspondence between team members' individual mental models.

Team performance. refers to all the different and important ways in which an organization might evaluate the performance of a team.

Technical skills. job-related skills that refer to depth and breadth of subject matter.

Theory E. in terms of organizational change, change based on economic value.

Theory O. in terms of organizational change, change based on organizational capability.

Thibaut and Walker's model of procedural justice. argues that people are motivated to maximize their personal gains in their interactions with others and seek to control procedures so that they can indirectly control outcomes.

Third party. in dispute resolution, an individual (or collective) who is external to a conflict and tries to help the parties reach agreement.

Total Quality Management (TQM). a model of organizational change that involves an ongoing and constant effort by all of an organization's functions to find new ways to improve the quality of the organization's products and services.

Traditional arbitration. a form of third party dispute resolution in which the arbiter hears both sides' positions and then imposes his or her own settlement.

Trait theory. an approach to leadership that seeks to identify personal characteristics possessed by effective leaders.

Transactional contract. characterizes employment arrangements with short-term or limited duration, primarily focused on economic exchange; specific, narrow duties; and limited worker involvement in the organization.

Transactional leadership. a style of leadership in which leaders motivate by exchanging rewards for high performance and noticing and reprimanding mistakes and substandard performance.

Transactive memory system. an implicit team-level information processing system that is an extension of the human information processing system.

Transfer of affect. in persuasion theory, refers to the fact that people often have strong emotional reactions to different things and sometimes persuasion occurs because people simply transfer the emotions they have for one thing to another thing.

Transformational leadership. a style of leadership in which leaders rely on intrinsic motivation to mobilize organizational actors.

Transition acceleration. refers to the ability of new hires to move quickly from the transition of being hired into their new job and being on top of their job, regardless of their level in the organization.

Transitional contract. usually present when elements of an organization change, such as during a merger or acquisition, often leading to uncertainty, distrust, instability, and high levels of turnover.

Transparent self. one of four quadrants in the Johari window that refers to aspects of ourselves that we are aware of and that others are aware of as well.

Trust. an expression of confidence in another person (or group of people) that you will not be put at risk, harmed, or injured by their actions.

Unaware self. one of four quadrants in the Johari window that refer to aspects that others see in us, but we fail to see in ourselves.

Unethical managers. one type of toxic management; unethical managers are antisocial or unethical opportunists.

Uneven communication problem. in most groups, a minority of people do the majority of the talking.

Upward comparison. the tendency for people to compare themselves to someone who is superior in terms of status or rank, or who is more accomplished.

Utility function. in decision theory, the quantification of a person's preferences with respect to certain objects.

Voice. one of four possible reactions to conflict in a relationship; voice is a constructive, active intervention; a person actively discusses problems, seeks help, tries to change some aspect of the situation, or is otherwise positively engaged; also, letting people speak their mind and be heard.

Whorfian hypothesis. the idea that the language people use determines (to some degree) the way in which they think and behave.

Photo Credits

Chapter 1, 3, Duncan Smith, Getty Images, Inc.–Photodisc; 5, David Young-Wolff, PhotoEdit Inc.; 7, Ryan McVay, Getty Images Inc.–Photodisc; 10, Greg Kuchik, Getty Images, Inc.–Photodisc

Chapter 2, 25, Jim Bourg, Getty Images, Inc.–Photodisc; 31, Steve Cole, Getty Images, Inc.–Photodisc

Chapter 3, 51 (top left), Art Resource/The New York Public Library; 51 (top right), The White House Photo Office; 51 (bottom left), Corbis/Bettman; 51 (bottom right) Archive, Photo Researchers, Inc.

Chapter 4, 68, Robert E. Daemmrich, Getty Images Inc.–Stone Allstock; 70, Photolibrary.com

Chapter 5, 82 (top), Eric Draper, The White House Photo Office; 82 (middle), D. B. Owen, Black Star; 82 (bottom), Getty Images Inc.–Hulton Archive Photos; 83 (top left), Corbis/Bettman; 83 (top right), Mike Stewart, Corbis/Sygma; 83 (bottom left), Delahaye, SIPA Press; 83 (bottom middle), David Tumley, CORBIS–NY; 83 (bottom right), Getty Images Inc.–Hulton Archive Photos; 84, Mikael Karlsson, Arresting Images

Chapter 6, 95, Reuters NewMedia Inc., Corbis/Bettman; 98, Photolibrary.com; 101, Peter Hvizdak, The Image Works

Chapter 7, 110 (left), Corbis/Bettman; 110 (right), The University of Louisville; 119, Tony Freeman, PhotoEdit Inc.; 120 (top), Chris Knapton, Getty Images–Digital Vision; 120 (bottom), Mario Beauregard, AGE Fotostock America, Inc.; 126, Dorling Kindersley, Dorling Kindersley Media Library

Chapter 8, 136, Marc Bove, Pearson Education/ PH College

Chapter 9, 157 (top), Markus Matzel/Das Fotoarchiv, Peter Arnold, Inc.; 157 (top middle), Klaus Andrews, Peter Arnold, Inc.; 157 (bottom middle), Photolibrary.com; 157 (bottom), Chris Alan Wilton, Getty Images Inc.–Image Bank

Chapter 10, 183, Stock Montage/Hulton Archive, Getty Images Inc.–Hulton Archive Photos

Chapter 13, 236, Spencer Grant, PhotoEdit Inc.

Chapter 14, 256 (top left), David Buffington, Getty Images, Inc.–Photodisc; 256 (top right), Getty Images, Inc.–Photodisc; 256 (bottom left), Getty Images, Inc.–Photodisc; 256 (bottom right), Jonnie Miles, Getty Images, Inc.–Photodisc; 260, Steve Cole, Getty Images, Inc.–Photodisc; 261 (far right), Duncan Smith, Getty Images, Inc.–Photodisc; 261 (middle right), Left Lane Productions, CORBIS–NY; 261 (middle left), Daisuke Morita, Getty Images, Inc.–Photodisc; 261 (far left), Keith Brofsky, Getty Images, Inc.–Photodisc; 264, Corbis/Reuters America LLC; 266, Doug Menuez, Getty Images, Inc.–Photodisc

Chapter 15, 274, Garo, Photo Researchers, Inc.; 276, Messiah College; 279, Martin E. P. Seligman; 283 (top), Anthony P. Bolante, Corbis/Bettman; 283 (bottom), AP Wide World Photos; 287, Dave King, Dorling Kindersley Media Library

Name/Author Index

Subject Index